A Sin Against the Future

Northeastern University   1898–1998

Advisor in Criminal Justice to Northeastern University Press
GILBERT GEIS

VIVIEN STERN

A Sin Against the Future

Imprisonment in the World

Northeastern University Press
BOSTON

Published in Great Britain by Penguin Books Ltd., London. Published in the United States of America by Northeastern University Press, Boston, by arrangement with Penguin Books.

Library of Congress Cataloging-in-Publication Data
Stern, Vivien.
    A sin against the future : imprisonment in the world / Vivien
Stern.
        p.   cm.
    Includes bibliographical references and index.
    ISBN 1-55553-362-0 (alk. paper). — ISBN 1-55553-361-2 (pbk. :
alk. paper)
    1. Prisons—Cross-cultural studies. 2. Imprisonment—Cross-
cultural studies. 3. Criminal justice, Administration of—Cross-
cultural studies. I. Title.
HV9443.S74   1998
365—dc21   98-18997

Composed in Sabon by Rowland Phototypesetting Ltd., Bury
St. Edmunds, Suffolk, England. Printed and bound by Edwards
Brothers, Inc., Ann Arbor, Michigan. The paper is Glatfelter
Offset, an acid-free sheet.

PRINTED IN THE UNITED STATES OF AMERICA
02 01 00 99 98   5 4 3 2 1

This book is dedicated to the memory of Frederick Stern, my father, who died on 1 September 1995 aged eighty-six.

Table of Contents

List of Tables

Acknowledgements

Many people have helped me to produce this book. Friends all over the world have supplied material, looked at drafts and made comments. I owe an enormous debt to Professor Nils Christie of Oslo University, who is an inspiration to penal reformers all over the world.

Julita Lemgruber from the Department of Justice in Rio de Janeiro, Brazil, Marc Mauer from the Sentencing Project in Washington and Al Bronstein and Jenni Gainsborough from the National Prison Project of the ACLU have all given a considerable amount of help. Yuichi Kaido from the Centre for Prisoners' Rights in Japan, and Valery Abramkin and Valery Sergeyev from the Moscow Prison Centre have made an invaluable contribution.

From Penal Reform International I must thank Ahmed Othmani, Wendy Singh, Rani Shankardass, Alexander Petrov, Fiona Hunter, Marie-Dominique Parent and Louise Mason. I could not have put so much material together without the help of many of the staff at NACRO and in particular Paul Cavadino, Mervyn Barrett, Linda McMorrow and Geraldine Buggy. I am also grateful to Andrew Barclay and to Raphael Mokades for their help with the research for the book.

My copy editor Donald Wilson from Penguin Books deserves especial thanks. He has been unfailingly understanding, utterly helpful and committed to maintaining the highest standards. I am also very grateful to Mark Handsley of Penguin Books for initiating the project and staying with it through many ups and downs.

I owe a great debt to Professor Norval Morris who concluded that the irresponsibility of US politicians had generated the enormous growth of imprisonment in his country. He described this irresponsibility as 'a sin against the future'. His thinking has inspired not only the title of this book, but also much of the content.

Finally I must thank Andrew Coyle for all his support and encouragement.

The author and publishers gratefully acknowledge permission to quote from the following copyright material:

John Braithwaite, *Crime, Shame and Reintegration*, Cambridge University Press, Cambridge, 1989.

Antonio Cassese, *Inhuman State: Imprisonment, Detention and Torture in Europe Today*, trs. Jennifer Greensleaves, Polity Press, Cambridge, 1996.

Roy D. King and Mike Maguire (eds.), *Prisons in Context*, Clarendon Press, Oxford, 1994, by permission of Oxford University Press.

Nelson Mandela, *Long Walk to Freedom*, Little, Brown and Co. (UK), London, 1994.

Jerome G. Miller, *Search and Destroy: African-American Males in the Criminal Justice System*, Cambridge University Press, Cambridge, 1996.

Wilbert Rideau and Ron Wikberg (eds.), *Life Sentences: Rage and Survival Behind Bars*, Random House, New York, 1992.

Raphael Samuel, *East End Underworld: Chapters in the Life of Arthur Harding*, Routledge and Kegan Paul, London, 1981.

Aleksandr Solzhenitsyn, *One Day in the Life of Ivan Denisovich*, trs. Ralph Parker, Victor Gollancz, London, 1962.

Americas Watch, *Brazil: Prison Massacre in São Paulo*, Human Rights Watch, New York, 1992.

Asia Watch, *Prison Conditions in India*, Human Rights Watch, New York, 1991.

Human Rights Watch, *Prison Conditions in the United States*, Human Rights Watch, New York, 1991.

Human Rights Watch/Asia, *Prison Conditions in Japan*, Human Rights Watch, New York, 1995.

Human Rights Watch Children's Rights Project, *Children in Confinement in Louisiana*, Human Rights Watch, New York, 1995.

Human Rights Watch Women's Rights Project, *All Too Familiar: Sexual Abuse of Women in US State Prisons*, Human Rights Watch, New York, 1996.

(To order a copy of these reports, please contact Human Rights Watch, 33 Islington High Street, London N1 9LH, UK.)

The extracts from 'The Contemporary Prison' by Norval Morris, from *The Oxford History of the Prison: The Practice of Punishment in Western Society*, edited by Norval Morris and David J. Rothman, copyright © 1995 by Oxford University Press, Inc., used by permission of Oxford University Press, Inc.

The extract printed on page 140 from *Memoirs from the Women's Prison* by Nawal el Sa'adawi, published in Great Britain by The Women's Press Ltd, 1986, 34 Great Sutton Street, London EC1V 0DX, is used by permission of The Women's Press Ltd.

The extract printed on page 335 from *No Full Stops in India*, Viking, © Mark Tully, 1991, is used by permission of Mark Tully, c/o Rogers, Coleridge and White, 20 Powis Mews, London W11 1JN.

The extract from *Bitter Winds* by Harry Wu © 1994 Harry Wu is reprinted by permission of John Wiley & Sons, Inc.

While every effort has been made to contact copyright holders the publishers would be pleased to hear from anyone not acknowledged.

Foreword

Reading this book has not been easy. I cannot say that I have enjoyed it, and yet it is one of the most worthwhile books that I have read.

Perhaps I need to explain a bit about my own background to make my response to this extraordinary book more understandable. Because of the incredible historical changes in my country, South Africa, I have found myself on both sides of the prison system.

At the age of twenty-three I was imprisoned for seven and a half years for opposing apartheid. Many of the descriptions in Part One of this book about the hurt and deprivation that prison inflicts on prisoners, I can identify with from experience. Although it is not easy to admit openly, I am still suffering the effects of those prison years every day. Dickens was right when he wrote that daily tampering with the mysteries of the brain is immeasurably worse than any torture of the body.

I hesitate to write this, my intention not being to solicit personal sympathy, but personal identification helps one understand what a terrible system imprisonment really is. One can only be horrified when one begins to understand the terrible suffering that is being inflicted on a daily basis on millions of prisoners – and the long-term effect this has on the general sanity of our world. It is also from this perspective that one can understand the words of Judith Ward, who served eighteen years before being cleared of the charges against her. Vivien Stern quotes her in Part Two: 'Never could I forget, put it all behind me. I will never forget – more importantly – I will never let you forget.'

It is interesting that Judith Ward first says that she *could* never forget, and then, that she *will* never forget. The question about how much good it does her to remember is thus really irrelevant. *She cannot forget.* In a very real sense, although she has finally been released, her prison sentence will continue for the rest of her life. The more critical challenge of her statement is that *we* should never forget.

Nor will those who read this book, and allow the personal and very disturbing descriptions of people imprisoned in various prison systems throughout the world to touch them, be able to forget. The strength of Vivien Stern's book is that she is not engaged in some cold academic analysis. This is a book written by a person who has travelled widely and visited various prisons but who has not allowed the incredible amount of suffering to harden her nor make her unresponsive to the deep personal and emotional suffering of each of the individuals who is incarcerated. This says much about the human being that Vivien Stern is, and has contributed greatly to the quality and impact of this book.

But who are *we*, that should not forget? We are all the readers of this book. We are the criminologists who write and theorize about the use of prisons, we are the public who – self-righteously and angry about crime – demand more and harsher prisons, we are the politicians who are being pressurized by the moralizing and angry majority into turning a system of justice into a system of crime control. *You and I are we.*

If you are someone either involved or interested in prison reform, or at least the running of prisons, I am writing to you as a colleague. Through the irony of history, which can sometimes be far stranger than fiction, I became a member of the South African parliament a few years after my release and chairperson of the parliamentary committee overseeing the Department of Correctional Services. More than half the members of my committee had themselves been political prisoners. The jailed had become part of the system of jailers, faced with a society under tremendous strain because of high levels of crime, demanding harsher action against criminals and longer prison sentences . . .

None of those on the parliamentary committee who had been prisoners themselves would disagree with one of the central messages of this book: that it is impossible to train people for freedom in conditions of captivity. I am proud that this committee tried its best to improve the conditions of imprisonment in South Africa and had some success, though limited, in exposing and changing some of the worst excesses in our prisons. However, I am sad to say that during the past three years of the committee's existence, the number of prisoners in South Africa's prisons increased sharply to more than 125,000, overcrowding worsened and South Africa's first democratic parliament passed legislation to lengthen prison sentences and to make it more difficult to obtain bail.

When reading Vivien Stern's book you can understand why this happened in the case of South Africa and why, in general throughout the world – and not only in the United States, which is probably the worst example – prison populations are growing. But understanding it does not mean that we dare accept this situation. If one comes to the conclusion, together with Vivien Stern, that prisons are actually fatally flawed, and if you continue to remember that you are one of the *we* addressed by Judith Ward, then each one of us has a duty to continue to search for *a better way*.

The last chapter of this book poses the question: *A better way?* Having been on both sides of the bars, I know that one should not be over-idealistic and romantic about this challenge. Vivien Stern is not unrealistic either about the many obstacles to this search. Nor does she deny that it will be a slow, arduous process we will have to be engaged in, a process which will often be characterized by the setbacks rather than its successes.

The contradictions of a flawed system that imprisons and destroys more and more people's lives, that places unbearable financial constraints even on the economies of the richer, developed nations, but still fails to rehabilitate criminals, demands from us that we continue searching for a better way. It will be extremely difficult to do so, but we must continue to support the efforts of Penal Reform International and similar organizations to ensure more humane conditions for prisoners. At the same time we should make every effort to shift gradually our resources out of imprisonment and into violence prevention, helping disturbed families, providing more educational opportunities, supporting the children who (without help) will become the next generation of prisoners, and generally creating new alternatives which involve members of the public and utilize the skills present in so many people for mediating and resolving conflict.

This is the critical challenge that Vivien Stern poses to all of us. We have no option but to face up to it if we want to be able to live in a society that is both safe and democratic.

Carl Niehaus
Ambassador of South Africa to the Netherlands

Introduction

This book has taken a long time to write. It has been written alongside a full-time job as Director of the National Association for the Care and Resettlement of Offenders (NACRO) until May 1996 and a voluntary role as Secretary-General of Penal Reform International. In that capacity I have visited prisons in many parts of the world, met and talked to many prisoners, sympathized with prison staff struggling with and feeling shame at the conditions in which they have to work and the prisoners have to live. I have been involved alongside many others in supporting penal reformers fighting for the cause of prisoners and trying to improve prisons. Some of these, particularly from the developing world, have barely enough to live on themselves. Sometimes they put their own lives in danger through their commitment to the fair treatment of people in detention.

Seminal in dictating the shape of the book was an astonishing event held in Oslo in May 1995. Following the publication of his book *Crime Control as Industry*, Professor Nils Christie of Oslo University brought together in his university prison administrators at the highest level from the United States, Canada, Russia and Western Europe along with academics, penal reformers, a journalist from the Canadian Broadcasting Corporation (CBC) and the distinguished philosopher Ivan Illich. The subject was the growth in the use of prison and the threat this posed to the security of the world. The journalist, David Cayley, produced a series of programmes for the CBC covering the ground discussed at the Oslo seminar. The seminar, those programmes and the work being done by dedicated reformers all around the world have inspired this book and given me the background to set out the case for a change in our system. I only hope it does them justice.

This book is entitled *A Sin Against the Future: Imprisonment in the World*. As we enter the next millennium we would do well to reflect on the institutions we bring with us from the present one. We should ask whether they still serve us well. Do they help or hinder progress towards a better, safer world? One of these institutions is the prison. We take prisons for granted. Everyone has them. It is as normal to have prisons as to have schools and hospitals.

But we need to understand them – to comprehend their manifestations all around the world and to see how what is done in Britain is but part of a great carceral machinery stretching from Iceland to New Zealand and from Russia to Ecuador. All parts of the world have their version of a place where the door is locked on the outside and the occupant does not have a key. When the colonizers went to Africa, the traditional ways of doing justice were swept away, to be replaced by prisons built on the colonizers' model. Of what benefit to these, mostly developing countries, has the prison been?

Other questions call for an answer. What is prison for? In whose interests does it operate? Does it achieve its stated objectives? What is the official international view of how it should work? Is this a reality, or a façade behind which appalling unlawful acts are carried out in the name of law and order? Which country is top of the league table for decent, humane, rehabilitative prisons? Have the people who have tried to make it work succeeded? Is there, somewhere, the good prison? Or is the idea of prison intrinsically flawed, a mechanism with a contradiction at its heart?

Prison as it is used today, as the mainstay of the system of punishment for offences against the criminal law, may be a Victorian relic, but it is not falling into disuse. On the contrary its use is expanding greatly in the Western world. There is a debate about why the number of prisoners is growing so rapidly. Some argue that it is because there is more crime. Others say the connection between crime rates and use of imprisonment is tenuous. In fact, they say, the increase in incarceration in the 1990s is due to a new and deeply punitive public mood, engendered by the shrinking of welfare spending and by economic and social insecurity.

The effects of this growth on democracy as we know it must be faced. Should we, as some American commentators argue, carrying some British politicians with them, accept that we have to imprison a lot more people than we do currently in order to keep the rest of society safe? Is the pre-eminent human right the right of law-abiding citizens to walk the streets in safety? How many other rights should be sacrificed to achieve this? Does prison 'work'? Will imprisoning many more people 'work'? And if it will, what percentage of the human beings in any society is disposable in this way, in order to allow prison's good effects to be felt? And if it will not, what then?

This book argues that it is indeed time to look again at the institution of prison. It was created in quite a different age, as an alternative to transportation to the colonies or to Australia or to replace physical punishment. An institution devised for the needs of the eighteenth and nineteenth centuries and carried on throughout the twentieth with only minor changes needs to be reviewed for the twenty-first century.

It urgently needs to be reviewed for three reasons. First, prison provides a setting in which profound abuses of human rights can be carried out under the reassuring justification that this is needed to protect the public. Second, imprisonment no longer fits modern societies and their needs. It is inefficient. In many cases it gives rise to more problems than it solves. Third, the use of imprisonment needs to be reviewed because it poses a threat to our future.

Locking up massive numbers of people as an answer to social problems is likely to be as big a danger to us in the future as polluting the environment and using up the natural resources of the globe. Processing many of the world's unemployed young men through universities of crime will not protect the rest of the population nor create a safe world. Once they have been processed, the large minority trained during imprisonment to see society as their enemy will present a greater threat than they did at the beginning of their criminal career.

We must ask a further question. How much imprisonment can a society afford? What shall we have to go without in order to have such a large percentage of people made dependent on state funding? Suppose the costs become unsustainable. Perhaps we shall move to find a cheaper way, putting prisoners in work camps where order is kept by armed guards and electrified fences. What sort of society would we have created then?

There must be better ways of making society safe and protecting people from those who want to assault them or take their belongings. Experiments are being tried in many parts of the world to find other, less harmful methods. Will they work? How can they be made acceptable to a frightened, insecure public?

This is a book about imprisonment around the world. It looks at how many countries and cultures deal with their violent predators, social deviants, misfits and at how people are consigned to prison simply through poverty. It looks at who ends up in the prisons of the world and who works in them. It tries to expose the waste, the horror and the heroism of the growing incarceration business.

It goes wider and links prison use to culture and society. The number of people in prison and the type of prisons we have are not perhaps determined by the amount of crime and the type of criminals in our society but by our culture, the value we place on liberty and the way we view our fellow citizens. Are they fellow citizens or are they enemies? In the end we get not the prisons we need but the prisons we deserve.

The book is divided into four parts. Part One sketches in briefly how imprisonment came to be the main punishment for criminal offences and describes the way that imprisonment is approached and the amount it is used in different regions of the world. Part Two looks at life in prison, the similarities across regions and across traditions, how prison is inevitably a deformed society and how minorities such as women and young people fare within it. Part Three considers the efforts being made around the world to improve prisons, to mitigate their inbuilt destructiveness and to snatch some rehabilitative value out of the jaws of negativity. Part Four looks at two possibilities for the future: one, the path of more and harsher crime control, much of it provided by the private sector, in an increasingly divided and dangerous society; the other a search for a better, more satisfying system that reconciles and heals the breaches caused by crime.

Prison is a generic term. In many countries other names are used to describe the places which are referred to as prisons in this book.

Names such as detention centres, correctional facilities, remand houses, reformatory schools and many others are in use. These are all basically prisons. Many people are also locked up, before they have been charged and processed and whilst investigations are being carried out, in police stations, lock-ups and compounds. Some of the worst conditions are to be found in these places. Some of the most serious torture is carried out there. They are worth inquiring into in their own right and are not the subject of this book.

PART ONE

Imprisonment Around the World

We were soon moved to the Johannesburg Prison, popularly known as the Fort, a bleak, castle-like structure located on a hill in the heart of the city. Upon admission, we were taken to an outdoor quadrangle and ordered to strip completely and line up against the wall. We were forced to stand there for more than an hour, shivering in the breeze and feeling awkward . . . A white doctor finally appeared and asked whether any of us was ill. No one complained of any ailment. We were ordered to dress, and then escorted to two large cells with cement floors and no furniture. The cells had recently been painted and reeked of paint fumes. We were each given three thin blankets plus a sisal mat. Each cell had only one floor-level latrine, which was completely exposed. It is said that no one truly knows a nation until one has been inside its jails. A nation should not be judged by how it treats its highest citizens, but its lowest ones – and South Africa treated its imprisoned African citizens like animals.

Nelson Mandela, upon arrival for the first time in prison[1]

1. *A Prison is a Prison*

[Prison officials] . . . are cardinals, . . . pontiffs . . . [they] preside over and
organize an extraordinary ceremony in society, a ceremony without which
society probably could not exist. This ceremony, ritual, what is its
purpose? Its purpose is not to do something but to say something . . .
prison is . . . a huge ritual organized in such a way that everybody says
'Thank God I am not there.'

Ivan Illich, speaking to David Cayley on the CBC series *Prison and Its Alternatives*[1]

Rio de Janeiro is much visited by tourists who go there to admire
the Sugar Loaf Mountain and the statue of Christ the Redeemer
and bask on Copacabana Beach. Few are likely even to know of the
existence of Presidio Ary Franco Prison, where 1000 prisoners live
in a crumbling, rat-infested building. The prison is surrounded by
an ancient-looking forty-foot-high wall. The wall is topped by wire
and within the wall is a second wall. On each corner of the inner
wall are watchtowers manned by armed guards. The entrance to
the prison is through a barred gate which is opened by a prison
official wearing jeans and a T-shirt. The prison governor also wears
jeans and a T-shirt. In his office he keeps trophies from unsuccessful
escapes: an imitation gun made of paper; a book of photographs of
a tunnel that some prisoners had dug for many metres underground
before they were found, deep under the prison wall, digging away.

The prison is laid out in a series of spurs. Running along the
centre of each spur is a corridor with a large room on either side.
Many of the prisoners live in these large rooms. Each holds about
twenty men with two-tiered bunk beds. The beds are a recent
innovation. Before the installation of the beds, prisoners had slept
on the floor. At the back of the rooms is an area containing the
lavatory and shower. All the natural light comes from a skylight
above the lavatory area. The rooms are high and criss-crossed with
washing lines where clothes hang to dry.

Most prisoners are in their cells for twenty-three hours a day. The twenty-fourth hour is spent exercising in a fairly spacious yard covered with scrubby grass. Once a week they are allowed a visit from their families. Trusted prisoners are allowed out of the dormitories and run around delivering orders to prisoners through the bars – a packet of cigarettes or a cheese sandwich – from the prison shop. These trusted prisoners also give out drinking water. Visitors are received with great interest. The prisoners crowd up to the bars of their cells to talk and, if the visitor seems official, to hand over little notes asking for help in pursuing some matter, either with the authorities or with a lawyer.[2]

In this prison, in 1993, an incident took place in one of the spurs. Someone threw a bottle containing inflammable chemicals and thirty-two prisoners burnt to death. Two prison guards were indicted for having thrown the bottle and were still awaiting their trial in early 1997.

Kyrgyzstan is a small country with a population of 4.4 million squeezed between China and the new republic of Kazakhstan. It was a Soviet republic but became independent in 1990. It is a country of snow-capped mountains and lakes, of horsemen whose favourite leisure-time pursuit is a game played on horseback which involves fighting for possession of the carcass of a dead goat. Away from the cities, the people, the Kirghiz, live in tents, called yurts, decorated with mosaic-patterned carpets. Yet, in spite of this traditional way of life, in the centre of the capital, Bishkek, is a familiar sight, an old building put up in the last century, with a high wall and watchtowers at the four corners with armed guards. It holds about 2000 prisoners, mostly awaiting trial. The prisoners live in crowded dormitories, every inch of floor space filled with the bunk beds, a screened-off lavatory and a washbasin. Sometimes they get out for an hour's exercise. Sometimes they spend the whole twenty-four hours in the dormitory. Not surprisingly, given the closeness of the living conditions, the spread of TB is a major problem.[3]

The central prison in Harare in Zimbabwe is also overcrowded, holding about 2000 prisoners. There is work for about 400 of them.

They tailor prison uniforms, make sandals out of old car tyres, bind books and a creative prison officer teaches the most talented to make the famous Zimbabwean stone carvings. The prisoners are not paid for their work. Some struggle to pursue their education, sitting in a barn-like room in small groups, clustered around a prisoner-teacher, making notes on the only paper available, the daily ration of toilet paper. Some live in cells so small there is room for just a laid-out blanket and a bucket. Others live in dormitories, furnished with nothing but forty folded-up blankets, twenty along each side of the room, each taking up about eighteen inches and with not enough room for anyone to stretch out without getting his legs tangled up with those of the man opposite.[4]

In South London, just four miles from the Houses of Parliament, is Brixton, a bustling cosmopolitan inner-city area. Near the heart of Brixton, with its shops and market, you turn into a narrow cul-de-sac and are confronted by high walls and barbed wire. This is the entrance to Brixton Prison. Inside the prison, which was built in 1819, live 800 men, some awaiting trial, some serving their sentences. They live not in large dormitories but in cells built in Victorian times to house one person and now normally holding two. They collect their food from trolleys and eat in their cells. All the cells have lavatories, recently installed. Brixton prison is in the classic galleried style, with large wings of several storeys reached by iron staircases and with netting stretched across between the galleries to prevent prisoners on the upper floors throwing objects or, in despair, hurling themselves over the railings to the ground. For a few hours each day the prisoners might have a chance to go to an education class, exercise in an enclosed tarmacadamed yard, do some arts and crafts, play pool and table tennis or watch television. For the rest of the day the majority of prisoners are locked up with another prisoner in a small cell with only a few books, newspapers and a personal radio for company. They have limited access to a telephone.[5]

Rio de Janeiro, Bishkek, Harare and Brixton are miles apart, separated by geographical distance, culture and history, yet prisoners and prison staff from any one of the four would instantly recognize the activity going on in the other three. They would recognize the buildings from the outside and at a distance as prisons. The walls, the gate, the security features such as barbed wire and watch towers are quite distinctive and unmistakable. If they were transplanted they would know at once what the basic rules of survival were, for staff and for prisoners. They would recognize the prison smell, of too many ill-washed people in a small place, inadequate sanitary facilities and overcooked food.

The problems caused by bodily functions, urination and defecation, would be readily understood. If there were lavatories they would appreciate them because they would understand the alternative, the slopping-out ritual where prisoners have to live for hours in the same room as buckets or pots holding their bodily wastes and then empty them in overflowing sewers. They would sympathize with those emptying the buckets and those whose job it was to supervise the procedure.

They would not be surprised to see the overcrowding; they would understand the pressures from outside, which prison staff cannot control, to cram more and more human beings into a small space, regardless of the impact on living and working conditions; they would know the high level of tension overcrowding creates and the diseases it helps to spread.

They would also recognize the prisoners, probably organized into groups or gangs for status, identity and protection. It would be easy for them to identify the leaders, the terrorizers; and the victims – those, often young, who are bullied, brutalized and used. They would realize when going into a room of forty prisoners which one was the 'baron', the boss-man of the room, the one who said nothing but watched and smiled in approval or glowered at what his fellow prisoners were saying to the foreign visitors. Both staff and prisoners would expect to live with the fear of violence.

Some things are not the same. Certainly the degree of deprivation imprisonment imposes will vary considerably. Some prisoners are living in single rooms with their own lavatory and washbasin, television and personal computer, perhaps following a university-level education course and seeing their partner once a week for a private visit. Others are living in spartan huts in a bleak prison camp, working in a prison factory to contribute to the national economy. Others have nothing to do but struggle to survive in an insanitary dormitory in a crumbling overcrowded building, depending on their families for the food and medicines that keep them alive.

The way one is received when visiting prisons can vary enormously. At some, the entrance is through a bleak guardhouse, decorated only with the rules about the punishments for bringing in illicit items displayed on the wall and there is a large unsmiling custodian who says, 'It is my duty to tell you that if you are taken hostage the authorities will make no concessions in trying to obtain your release. Do you still want to enter?' At others the entrance is a large barred gate where you push through crowds of people, mostly women, carrying large shopping bags full of provisions for their sons and husbands, and explain to the uniformed and harassed officer with the power to unlock the gate that you are an official visitor. At others the visit starts in a pleasant room, with pictures on the walls painted by prison artists and flowers in vases on low tables.

Yet, in spite of the differences, it is the sameness of imprisonment that stands out, the features that are common across countries and cultures, irrespective of level of economic development or form of government.

Everywhere, most of the people subjected to imprisonment, about nineteen out of every twenty, will be men, usually young men, usually from the poorer parts of society, often graduates of homes for unwanted children, reformatories for young delinquents, people who are now moving along the well-trodden path into the prison for grown-ups that their earlier experiences have prepared them for.

Women are also sent to prison, but in much smaller numbers. Nearly all women to be found in prisons around the world are poor, exploited and abused. Perhaps they have killed a husband or a lover. Sometimes they have transported drugs at the behest of someone else to get enough money to survive or educate their children. Often they are addicted to drugs themselves. Sometimes they are pregnant or have new babies when they are sent to prison. In some countries they can keep their babies with them. In others the babies are removed and given to family members or put in institutions.

Some of those in prison have committed terrible, violent and heinous crimes. Many are awaiting trial and have as yet not been convicted of anything. In some countries the majority of those in prison have not yet been tried. In Venezuela the proportion is three-quarters.[6] A large proportion of the world's prisoners are in prison for stealing and breaking into houses. Some have committed no crime but are locked up because of their ideas or who or what they are. In some countries people spend longer locked up before their trial than the length of the sentence they could be given if convicted.

In all the prisons of the world are to be found the poor, the dispossessed, the minorities that face discrimination in the society outside prison. In all prison systems there is always the potential for violence. Prisons are often dangerous places for those they hold. A London newspaper reported in 1994 that a prisoner intended to sue the Home Secretary for damages after he had been raped and assaulted in a twelve-hour ordeal by a violent cell-mate in Durham Prison. His solicitor described what had happened to his client. The cell-mate had:

> shaved our client's head with a razor-blade, removing all his hair and causing cuts to his scalp. He had also shaved off his pubic hair . . . He punched him about the face and upper body. There was then a violent act of buggery.[7]

Group violence is also endemic and riots are common. Many people around the world saw in 1990 the rioters of Strangeways Prison, Manchester, in the North of England, on the roof of their prison, which had been destroyed by riot, holding out for twenty-three days. Prisoners often try and attract attention by climbing on to the roof. Three months after the Strangeways riot, prisoners in Leipzig, in East Germany as it then was, climbed on to the prison roof to protest about their conditions. The Interior Minister negotiated with them and the disturbance ended peacefully.[8] In São Paulo, Brazil, on 2 October 1992, at least 111 prisoners were killed and thirty-five wounded by military police who were called to Block 9 in the House of Detention after a scuffle broke out between two gangs of prisoners, allegedly over payment for marijuana. Apparently 'the police fired randomly into cells and killed prisoners who were offering no resistance, including prisoners who had stripped naked'.[9]

As a result, in March 1993, 120 members of the São Paulo military police were charged with homicide, attempted homicide and causing injuries whilst on active duty. In 1996 the case was still in progress.

In May 1990 prisoners took control of the Ruzyne prison in Prague and held it for four days. The siege was ended by anti-terrorist troops with stun grenades and one prisoner was killed.[10] In 1993 at a hard-labour camp in Vladimir region east of Moscow, a protest for better conditions led to five prisoners being shot dead and another fourteen injured.[11]

When Pope John Paul II visited Venezuela in 1995, he stopped at the notorious Catia prison in Caracas and called on the government to reform the prisons. According to officials, about twelve prisoners were killed there every month, although the prisoners said the number was higher. The prison was demolished in February 1997 and the prisoners moved to other prisons. A woman who had regularly visited her son in the prison told a reporter from the *Financial Times* that she 'saw a young prisoner being stabbed to death. They then cut his body into parts and threw him out of the window.'[12]

In Sabaneta prison in Maracaibo, Venezuela, in 1994 more than one hundred prisoners died and many were injured in a battle between prisoners. In October 1996 in La Planta prison near Caracas, twenty-five prisoners burnt to death after tear gas and fire bombs were allegedly fired into their cells by guards.[13]

All prisons to some extent create bonds of solidarity amongst prisoners against those who lock them up. There are the unwritten rules and laws of the prison world, the prisoners' code. The penalties for breaking the code can be meted out without mercy.

Prisons for the young are much the same the world over. Children from unloving homes or no homes at all are classed as criminals needing punishment rather than as children needing care. They express their misery and anger by terrorizing others or mutilating themselves whilst learning how to survive in a world of violence and distorted values.

Everywhere people who work in prisons feel that, in the eyes of the public, the stigma attached to prisoners attaches to them too. It seems to them that their part in the law-and-order business is the least glamorous and the least appreciated. In television series about crime, prison officers are never the heroes. The activity of the criminal justice process, the police investigation, the court case, the verdict and the judge's sentence are the stuff of drama and great entertainment. Then the excitement is over. It is replaced by the unglamorous work of prison staff, locking and unlocking the same doors for years and years.

The world of prisons is a gloomy one, filled with the misery of individuals and the inhumanity of systems. Yet every now and then a light gleams. Someone, somewhere tries to run a prison in a different way. Reason and humanity rather than tradition and indifference dictate the treatment. The prisoners are treated as individuals. Their eventual return to society becomes the focus. The regimen of the prisons strives to mirror normal life outside. Human dignity and worth is recognized and respected. Such experiments emerge, shine for a while, then tend to die when there is a change of personnel or political direction.

Outside each prison will be the public, knowing little about what goes on, but fearful about rising crime and wishing to believe that locking people up in prison is the way to stop it. Public knowledge of prisons is scanty. Some people believe that prisoners are treated too well. They object when prisons seem to be too nice; but they also object when prisons are too nasty and a prisoner commits suicide or a riot breaks out. They are not sure what prisons are meant to do: is it to lock people up, make people better, stop them getting worse, teach them a trade, given them psychiatric treatment or make them suffer? In poor countries these dilemmas are sharper. Prisoners have to be fed and cared for, whilst outside on the street fellow citizens may be dying of hunger or lack of medical care.

So imprisonment is obviously not an easy answer. It brings problems in all directions. In democratic societies, where politicians are accountable, it brings problems. No ambitious politician jumps for joy when offered the position of minister responsible for prisons. It is a job that is hard to do well – how will your success be measured? – with the potential for scandal and crisis never far away.

Also, imprisonment is a prime focus for human rights abuses. One set of human beings is under the control of another, dependent on them for food, the opportunity to perform their bodily functions, access to the outside world, work, exercise. When someone dies behind the high prison walls cover-up is easy; asking questions is hard.

Is imprisonment effective at least in doing what it sets out to do, protecting society from crime? Unfortunately not. Locking up a dangerous violent person will prevent that person causing injury or doing harm to others in society whilst locked up. But many of those in prison are not dangerous or violent. Most will leave prison in due course and live once again in society. Their stay in prison will probably leave them more prone to crime and will have damaged those elements that bond people to society, such as relationships with family and friends, the chance of a place to live and a job, the chance of being respected and esteemed by others.

There is no doubt that the problems of imprisonment are many and its effectiveness is at best dubious. Yet there are prisons in almost every country of the world. Those countries without prisons send their prisoners elsewhere, finding another state prepared to incarcerate their citizens for cash. In many ex-colonial countries prisons were built by the colonizers to lock up opponents of colonial rule. Now they are often used in these same countries to silence opponents of the post-colonial regime. Developing countries all have imprisonment as the cornerstone of their penal systems, even though it makes even less sense than it does in the rich world. For poor countries there is no logic at all in a punishment system based on rendering people unproductive so that the state has to take on the responsibility for feeding them. Yet they all do it. In fact, the use of imprisonment is high and rising throughout the world. The next chapter looks in more detail at how imprisonment became entrenched in all the penal systems of the world and the great differences in its level of use.

2. The Western Tradition of Imprisonment

I believe that very few men are capable of estimating the immense amount of torture and agony which this dreadful punishment, prolonged for years, inflicts upon the sufferers; and in guessing at it myself and in reasoning from what I have seen written upon their faces, and what to my certain knowledge they feel within, I am only the more convinced that there is a depth of terrible endurance in it which none but the sufferers themselves can fathom, and which no man has a right to inflict upon his fellow-creature. I hold this slow and daily tampering with the mysteries of the brain, to be immeasurably worse than any torture of the body: and because its ghastly signs and tokens are not so palpable to the eye and sense of touch as scars upon the flesh; because its wounds are not upon the surface, and it extorts few cries that human ears can hear; therefore I the more denounce it, as a secret punishment which slumbering humanity is not roused up to stay.

Charles Dickens describing the new method of punishing people by locking them up in solitary confinement that he saw on his visit to America in 1842[1]

In the Caribbean Sea just off Venezuela lies the small island of Aruba with a population of 65,000. Aruba is a part of the Kingdom of the Netherlands. The main industry is tourism and the island is well covered with architecturally bizarre holiday complexes. At the far end of the island, on a rather bleak piece of land on the seashore, is another architecturally bizarre building, a brand new, state of the art, top-security prison. The prison was paid for by the Dutch government and become operational in 1990. It cost 22 million Dutch guilders (about £8.5 million). Its security is awesome. First there is an inner wall topped with razor wire, then a gap, then an outer wall also topped with razor wire, and finally a fence fortified with an alarm system.

The internal structure is also remarkable – a series of small living units built round a central area where the staff sit watching video cameras and pressing the buttons that activate the opening of all the doors. One of the units in this top-security construction is intended for minor offenders (for example, those who have not paid their parking fines). It consists of one large high room where all the prisoners live together. It has barred cage-like gates through which the prisoners can look into the living area. There are small slits in the back wall of the unit through which a mere glimpse of the outside world can be obtained.

This unit and all the others are under the permanent surveillance of video cameras. There is therefore no privacy at all in this area except for some slight screening of the lavatory and shower. The women's unit has a double row of cells with room for three women in each cell. The women's cells also have cage-like barred doors and are under video surveillance. The only privacy is behind the three-foot-high wall that screens the bathroom area. In this unit too the only sight of the bright tropical outside world is through small slits in the back cell wall.

The living units for male adult prisoners also consist of cells each containing three prisoners, but there is one difference. Some of the cells in these units do not face inwards. The cell doors face the outside world. However, the view of the outside world that the prisoners get is not an agreeable one. First they will see vertical green bars, then a white concrete wall with circular holes in it and then a white concrete wall beyond that with rectangular holes in it. The effect is such as to produce a very rapid feeling of nausea. The prison officers in this unit cannot see the prisoners personally at all but can see them on their bank of TV screens.[2]

This bizarre construction prompts a number of questions. Who decided to build a top-security prison in a country where most crime is non-violent and petty and where a long sentence is regarded as one of eight months or more?[3] Who decided to build a prison with so little access to light and air on a tropical island? Who felt that, in a place so small that personal relationships are all-important, the right prison was one controlled by electronic surveillance and high-tech gadgetry? How did such a completely Western construct end up on the beach of a South American island anyway? Nothing is appropriate to the climate, the culture or the crimes of Aruba.

Aruba prison is a very concrete symbol of how an idea, born out of eighteenth-century Europe, has found its way to many parts of the world, with deeply unfortunate consequences. Prison itself of course is not a modern idea. Putting people under lock and key, throwing them into the Tower of London, the Bastille in Paris, the Peter and Paul Fortress in St Petersburg, into dungeons underneath big castles or into small lock-ups or bridewells in towns and cities, is not new. It is very familiar from history, legend and literature. The Bible tells the story of Joseph, who became the trusted servant of Potiphar, one of Pharaoh's chief ministers. He was thrown into prison after having been falsely accused of impropriety by his master's wife.

The use of imprisonment as the main way of punishing crime, however, is different. It is a fairly recent development. In the eighteenth century in England, hanging was the most severe penalty and it was applied widely. You could be hanged for many offences, including murder, violence, theft of property over a certain value, housebreaking, arson and removing parts of Westminster Bridge. Flogging and branding were also available to the judges and sometimes people were placed in headstocks, called the pillory, and put on public show to be abused and reviled by the citizenry. Most punishments indeed took place in public, including executions, and the spectacle was an important part of the message. By seeing what could happen to those who transgressed, it was felt, other offenders would be deterred. Only minor offenders were sent to prison, as were debtors and people waiting to be executed.

As the century wore on, hanging became less acceptable. Juries would not convict those accused of petty crimes who would, if found guilty, face the gallows. Statistics show this process at work. Between 1749 and 1758, 527 people were convicted by the courts of an offence for which they could be hanged. Of these, nearly 70 per cent were actually executed. Between 1799 and 1808 the percentage actually hanged of those convicted of a capital offence was down to 16 per cent. Sometimes judges commuted the sentence because the offender seemed to be genuinely sorry. Sometimes the jury thwarted the death sentence by valuing the goods stolen at

39 shillings (the hanging level was 40 shillings stolen in a house or on the highway).[4]

But, if they were not to be executed, what was to become of the offenders found guilty of serious crimes? They could not be set free. They had to be kept somewhere and punished somehow. Many were transported to the American colonies. That came to an end in 1776. So they were crowded into the hulks, disused and rotting boats anchored on the River Thames and elsewhere. These hulks posed more and more of a problem for administrators. Disorder and disease threatened to break out. Then another idea took hold. Why not send criminals to the far side of the earth, to Australia? The terrible story of transportation to Australia has been well told by the Australian writer Robert Hughes in *The Fatal Shore*.

He describes how the convicts were taken to sea ports for the first voyage to Australia:

> The convicts came rumbling down to the Plymouth and Portsmouth Docks in heavy wagons, under guard, ironed together, shivering under the incessant rain. The pale, ragged, lousy prisoners, thin as wading birds from their jail diet, were herded on board, spent the next several months below; orders forbade them to exercise on deck until the flotilla was out of sight of land.[5]

Altogether more than 160,000 men, women and children, some as young as eleven, made the terrible journey. Many died on the way. Many more died in the penal colonies of Australia. Some went on to become prosperous citizens of the new country. But even in its heyday, transportation was seen as flawed. How could it in fact be a punishment when those transported went to a better life than they faced in the slums of England in the Industrial Revolution? The essayist Sydney Smith wrote ironically to Sir Robert Peel in 1826, saying that the real meaning of a sentence of transportation was to do a favour to a convicted offender. It was as if the authorities were saying:

> Because you have committed this offence, the sentence of the court is that you shall no longer be burdened with the support of your wife and family. You shall immediately be removed from a very bad climate and country over-burdened with people to one of the finest

regions of the earth, where the demand for human labour is every hour increasing, and where it is highly probable you may ultimately regain your character and improve your future.[6]

It is common for those not enduring them to view penal sanctions through rose-tinted spectacles. Sydney Smith's perception, as that of many others who have felt that prisons were holiday camps, agreeable hotels with free lodgings and food, bears little relation to reality. This vision of the benefits of being transported to Australia would not have been recognized by those undergoing the thirty-six-week voyage with a chance of death as high as one in four and the harshness of the chain gang for those who survived the voyage. However, a parliamentary committee set up in 1837 to look at transportation condemned it 'as being unequal, without terrors to the criminal class, both corrupting to convicts and very expensive'.[7] In 1868, transportation to Australia was finally abandoned.

Another set of ideas about how to punish criminals had been slowly developing and by the time transportation was losing its attractions these ideas had taken a firm hold. In earlier centuries punishments were based on the idea of inflicting pain on the body, removing the criminal elements by banishment or transportation or, at the most extreme, imposing death. Now the notion of another way was developing, a different approach entirely. It was aimed not at eliminating criminals from society or inflicting pain upon them. The new way aimed to work not on the criminal's body but on his or her mind. This approach had had its followers for many decades. The novelist Henry Fielding, author of the rollicking novel *Tom Jones*, was in the 1750s a magistrate in the county of Middlesex. He thought there was a need for 'an intermediate penalty combining "correction of the body" with "correction of the mind".' He suggested 'solitary confinement in new houses of correction built on a cellular plan'. 'Solitude and Fasting' would, he thought, be a very effective way of bringing 'the most Abandoned Profligates to Reason and Order'.[8]

These eighteenth-century thinkers saw crime rather as doctors saw illness. It was contagious, so those suffering from it had to be separated one from another. And it could be cured by treatment. If a sick body could be cured of its illness, surely a sick moral sense could be cured too?

Also influential was the great prison reformer John Howard, who had visited prisons in England and throughout Europe and returned disgusted with the squalor, disease and overcrowding that he had seen – and smelt. According to Professor Seán McConville:

> When Howard made his extensive visitations in the 1770s he was obliged to travel on horseback because the smell given off by his clothes, just from a few hours contact, did not permit of coach travel. Even his notebook had to be spread open before a fire and disinfected before he could use it.[9]

Howard reacted with proposals for a new, orderly, hygienic prison system. Jeremy Bentham, the philosopher, dreamt up his idea of a Panopticon, a circular prison where from one place, one guard could see every prisoner all the time, and an inspector would keep under surveillance both the guard and the prisoners. From the United States came the models that influenced the development of prisons in Britain and in those places colonized by Britain. Two different models of imprisonment had developed in the United States, the 'silent' system and the 'separate' system, and both models had their supporters and detractors.

In 1842 Charles Dickens visited the exemplar of the separate system, the enormous Eastern Penitentiary in Philadelphia. He describes how each cell had a double door, the inner of barred iron and the outer of thick oak. The door had a flap through which the food was passed. A prisoner had in his cell a Bible, sometimes other books, writing materials, razor, plate, can and basin and a weaving loom, workbench or wheel. From the cell the prisoner could enter a tiny walled exercise yard. Most striking, according to Dickens, was the silence. When a prisoner arrived at the prison, he entered with a black hood over his head. He was taken to his cell and he never left it until he had served the whole of his sentence.

> He never hears of wife or children; home or friends; the life or death of any single creature. He sees the prison-officers, but with that exception he never looks upon a human countenance, or hears a human voice. He is a man buried alive; to be dug out in the slow

> round of years; and in the mean time dead to everything but torturing anxieties and horrible despair . . . His name, and crime, and term of suffering, are unknown, even to the officer who delivers him his daily food . . . though he live to be in the same cell ten weary years, he has no means of knowing, down to the very last hour, in what part of the building it is situated; what kind of men there are about him; whether in the long winter nights there are living people near, or he is in some lonely corner of the great jail, with wall and passages and iron doors between him and the nearest sharer in its solitary horrors.[10]

Dickens was horrified by the inhumanity of this treatment. This was the separate system. The silent system, in place at Auburn in New York, allowed the prisoners to mix with each other during the day whilst they were working, but not to communicate. A characteristic of the regime at Auburn was liberal use of whipping for those prisoners who broke the silence rule.

In 1834 the British government sent William Crawford, soon to become one of the first ever government-appointed Inspectors of Prisons, to the United States to study these two systems and report back on which he thought was the best. He returned to England converted to the separate system so denounced by Charles Dickens eight years later. Dickens knew enough about human beings to see how futile and misguided were the aspirations of those who had set up the system of solitary confinement and how impossible it was that such a way of treating people could lead to any good. So did another writer on prison from quite another tradition. Dostoevsky in *The House of the Dead*, through his hero Aleksandr Petrovich Goryanchikov, says of the effects of 'the belauded system of solitary confinement' that it

> attains only false, deceptive, external results. It drains the man's vital sap, enervates his soul, cows and enfeebles it, and then holds up the morally withered mummy, half imbecile, as a model of penitence and reformation.[11]

Crawford clearly did not see its real effects. He accepted the whole idea. In solitary confinement, he said in his report, 'The mind becomes open to the best impressions and prepared for the reception of those truths and consolations which Christianity can alone impart.'[12]

However, if the system were to be adopted in Britain it would need to be modified. It would be impossible to find the money that would be needed to convert all the old prison buildings so that prisoners could be kept in solitary confinement. A single cell would be needed for each prisoner and a separate exercise cage. The costs would be enormous. So a compromise would be acceptable. Prisoners could be allowed to work in the same room as other prisoners providing strict silence was observed and work never took precedence over the requirements of religion.

Here can be seen two elements that often feature in prison developments. There is the seduction of ideas that claim to have the power to cure criminals of crime and which there is a deep wish to believe. Such ideas are unfortunately always based on delusions. There is also the interaction so often seen between lofty notions of how to run an effective prison system, crushed by the reality of lack of money. Always in such circumstances some compromise, make-do-and-mend system is installed instead.

Out of all this investigation, analysis, conflict between different philosophies and optimism sprang up in Britain those great monuments to the new penal philosophy: Pentonville, which was opened in 1842; Parkhurst, the equivalent for juveniles opened in 1838; and Perth in Scotland, opened also in 1842. This new punishment was a real punishment. It satisfied both the punishment seekers and the reformers. The separate system of total solitary confinement was adopted, although prisoners were only subjected to it for the first eighteen months of imprisonment. They were put in cells, with a workbench, a bed and a Bible. The door was locked and they were left to think, to work and to pray.

The main features of these nineteenth-century prisons are well known. Ingenious devices were employed so that prisoners were kept from having any contact with each other. When walking round the exercise yard, prisoners wore masks which allowed them to look down at their feet but not sideways or upwards. When prisoners went to the chapel they sat in little boxes so that they could see the chaplain straight ahead but could not make contact with the prisoners on either side. In some prisons the activity for the prisoners was working the treadwheel, a machine which required prisoners to turn a huge cylinder with their feet. They usually worked this machine for twenty minutes followed by a twenty-minute break, sometimes for ten hours a day. Some of the machines had a useful objective such as grinding corn but most did absolutely nothing but turn and turn. The pointlessness of this exhausting and humiliating activity was part of the punishment – much more of a deterrent than useful work.[13]

The new system was not a success. One problem was that prisoners succumbed to madness. In 1850, 32 prisoners per 10,000 had to be removed from Pentonville on grounds of insanity. The proportion for all other prisons not applying the separate system was 5.8 per 10,000.[14] As a result of the high rate of madness some changes were brought in. For example, the initial period of solitary confinement at Pentonville was reduced from eighteen months to nine months. The small exercise yards were replaced by a bigger yard where prisoners could exercise together. The masks were abandoned and the boxes in the chapel done away with.[15]

But prison continued to be an oppressive and cruel experience. In Arnold Bennett's *Clayhanger* trilogy, written at the beginning of the twentieth century, one of the central characters ends up in Dartmoor Prison. A small group of outsiders visits the prison. As the visitors walk along one of the wide prison corridors a group of prisoners comes towards them. Will they meet and confront each other? Will the convicts be able to look at the respectable ladies and gentlemen? Certainly not. As the visitors approach, the prison officer calls the prisoners to attention and shouts at them to turn and face the wall until the visitors have passed.

> The six captives turned, with their faces close against the wall of the corridor, obedient, humiliated, spiritless, limp, stooping. Their backs presented the most ridiculous aspect; all the calculated grotesquerie of the surpassingly ugly prison uniform was accentuated as they stood thus, a row of living scarecrows, who knew they had not the right even to look upon free men.[16]

Prince Peter Kropotkin, the Russian anarchist, who was imprisoned in both Russia and France in the latter half of the last century, showed a keen interest in English prisons too. Of Dartmoor he said,

> At Dartmoor, for instance, convicts will be considered as people who dare not have the slightest feeling of decency. They will be compelled to parade in gangs, quite naked, before the prison authorities, and to perform in this attire a kind of gymnastics before them. 'Turn round! Lift both arms! Lift the right leg! Hold up the sole of the left foot with the right hand!' And so on.[17]

It is another indication of the essential sameness of the prison idea across cultures and decades that eighty years later exactly the same practice of turning faces to the wall was to be seen in prisons in Romania and Hungary, and the searching dance is described as part of prison life in Japan.

Penal philosophy moved on and in the early decades of the twentieth century the hopes that had earlier been pinned on religion were transferred to other forms of treatment, including psychology. The prison system moved into the treatment era. Prisoners were seen somewhat as patients in need of cure. Prisons became places for a range of professionals to work at their craft. It was felt that if prisoners were classified correctly and the right medicine was applied then they would be cured of their criminal ways. For young people between the ages of sixteen and twenty-one was developed a new institution called Borstal, named after the village in Kent where the first one was situated. The length of time the young people spent there, within certain limits, would depend on how well they did. When they were retrained and ready to live a crime-free life, they would be released.[18] Alexander Paterson, the famous English prison commissioner appointed in 1922, felt confident in saying to a Committee of Inquiry, 'The problem of recidivism is small, diminishing, and not incapable of solution.'[19]

These systems were going to work, he felt sure. Criminals were going to be cured. Then times changed. Disillusionment with treatment set in. Many research studies established that generally it did not succeed. Sending people to prison did not cure crime. In fact, prisons almost seemed to make people worse.

But decisions about prisons are rarely made on the basis of

evidence or reason. The fact that something does not succeed is not usually a reason for stopping it. The movement away from treatment ideas had reasons other than the simple fact that they did not work. A deeper change in perceptions of people and human behaviour had taken place. The basis of the treatment idea was that there was something wrong with the personality of the individuals that could be altered by whatever was done to them in prison. The new view was different. It saw prisoners in relation to their families, communities, socio-economic background and life chances. What had happened outside, before they came in, and what would greet them on release were more important than anything the most talented psychologist could do in prison.

Thus developed the view of prison that is current in most West European countries today. Basically prison is damaging, to the individual, the family and the community. It has few positive results. Its costs are high. There are the direct costs of the prison buildings, the staff, the security. In 1998/9 the prison system in England and Wales is expected to cost £1.545 billion.[20] The cost per prisoner per week in England and Wales in 1995/6 was £466.[21] In France the budget for the prison system in 1996 was 6.9 billion francs.[22] In the United States the costs, estimated at $40 billion a year, are remarkable and escalating.[23]

Then there are the social security costs of a family when the breadwinner has been taken away. Arrangements have to be made to care for the children of an imprisoned mother and this has costs both short- and long-term. Further costs arise from the damage caused by imprisonment – the costs of the ex-prisoner who is homeless, who cannot find a job because of the stigma of a prison record, and the family break-up that can result.

Two implications follow for the modern view of the place of prisons in criminal policy and how prisons should be run. First, prisons policy is based on reducing the damage prisons inflict. So prisoners are helped to keep in touch with their families, to learn useful skills in prison and to relate to the values of the outside world rather than the values of the prison world.

Second, in most West European countries, government policy aims to keep the numbers going into prison as low as is acceptable to the public and to the judges. Governments use devices to reduce the numbers in prison. Parole systems allow prisoners to be released before the end of their sentences under supervision and with certain conditions. In some countries low-risk prisoners are released early under amnesties so that prison numbers go down. In others sentenced offenders have to wait in a queue until a place is available. Sometimes prison sentences on non-dangerous offenders are imposed in a symbolic way so that the shame and stigma is suffered but not the actual prison sentence. Such sentences are suspended so long as the offender is of good behaviour and does not offend again for a certain period of time.

In pursuance of this policy of minimal use of prison, governments also work to set up alternative ways of punishing people. Such alternative penalties need to satisfy the requirements of punishment by depriving an offender of some aspect of liberty but also need to incorporate some positive elements, for example reparation, and a commitment to self-improvement. In Western countries a range of such penalties can be found: community service, attendance at a day centre to learn useful skills, paying a fine or compensation to victims.

These ideas lie behind the approach to imprisonment accepted in Europe and put into practice in some degree in Western Europe, but particularly in the Nordic countries and the Netherlands. In some Swedish prisons, for example, when you ask to see the visiting room, perhaps expecting a large area with tables and chairs and a refreshment corner, you are shown instead a corridor off which are a number of small rooms with beds and chairs. These are the individual visiting rooms and visits are in private.[24] In the Netherlands until 1993 every prisoner was kept in a single cell. When there are too many prisoners and not enough accommodation they do not cram the prisoners in. They let some out. Also in the Netherlands, if you have a complaint about a decision made by those who are guarding you, you can complain to a committee made up of ordinary citizens. If they find your complaint justified they can overturn the prison authorities' decisions. Criminologist Gerard de Jonge has said, 'In the eyes of some people Holland looks like a prisoners' paradise.'[25]

In Sweden prisoners are warned in advance of the arrival of visitors and those who do not wish to be viewed may withdraw until the visitors have passed through.[26] In Finland some prisoners work rebuilding a fort on an island in the middle of Helsinki harbour. They live in eight-roomed huts with kitchenette and living area, earn the market rate for the job and get eighteen days' leave per year.[27] In Nyborg Prison in Denmark prisoners are not provided with their meals by the authorities. They buy their own groceries in the prison supermarket with their wages and cook their own meals in the prison's modern kitchens when they wish.[28] In the Netherlands prisoners in open prisons generally go home every weekend.[29] In Germany prisoners are entitled, unless there are good reasons against it, to twenty-one days' home leave every year.[30]

This style of imprisonment arouses shock and bewilderment amongst the visitors from poorer countries who come to Western Europe to learn how they can reform their systems. Delegations from Latvia, Estonia, Russia, react with disbelief on seeing prisoners living in conditions better than most free citizens of their countries could ever dream of.

Unfortunately governments in, for example, the Caribbean, India and many countries in Africa, have not had the economic, social or political opportunities to develop in the Western way. They are left with a system of prison buildings, many over 100 years old, designed on a model of imprisonment devised in Europe in the nineteenth century, unsuitable then to the needs of their climates and cultures and by now thoroughly discredited. Imprisonment is for them an imported idea that can bankrupt their exchequers by its high cost.

The prison in Aruba, described at the beginning of this chapter, is an example of an inappropriate development created in the 1980s. The world is dotted with similarly inappropriate developments that go back to earlier centuries and embody the legacy of British penal history. St Catherine's District Prison in Jamaica is a hideous example of this legacy. Over 1000 prisoners are crammed into a building that dates back many years and was built to hold 650. A large proportion of the prisoners lives in long, three-storey stone blocks. The blocks are so dark that someone standing in the entrance would not be able to see further into the block than the door of the third cell. The cells are very small with low ceilings. The little light there is comes from a small window in the outer wall. Each cell often holds three people and the floor area is covered by three sleeping mats spread out and one slop bucket. Activities are limited. Small tailoring and mechanics workshops occupy barely a couple of dozen prisoners. Education is available for a few more. Most prisoners are unlocked for some hours a day but pass their time wandering around the yard. Keeping contact with families is not helped by the visiting arrangements. Visits take place in a small room off the gatehouse which is the entrance to the prison. The prisoner stands one side of a grille covered with glass and shouts at the visitor who stands on the other side. In any case such visits usually last about five minutes.

The history of the development of British penal policy in the nineteenth century, the echoes of Pentonville in the 1850s, still linger in the office of St Catherine's District Prison, where the chalkboard on the wall lists the numbers and classes of prisoners in prison that day, where the single cells squash within their confines the three people that now have to live in them, where there are no facilities for sports or proper workshops because there is no room within the walled enclosure.[31]

In India, imprisonment as a form of punishment was introduced by the British in 1773. The prison rules date back to 1894.[32] A report on Tihar Central Jail in New Delhi was produced by the Delhi Human Rights Trust in 1993. Apparently the jail is still administered according to the rules of the 1894 Act with some amendments brought in in 1988 which actually reduce the rights originally given to prisoners. For example, in the tradition of British administration, the requirements of the 1894 Act were very specific. They laid down the entitlements of each prisoner to exact amounts of food: for example, 230 grams of vegetables and 70 grams of dal per day. The modifications remove this requirement and allow the superintendent to fix the rations. The original colonial rules required that every prisoner should have a 'masonry sleeping berth' which should be constructed 'with a slight slope down from the head'. The space between every two berths should not be less than two feet. This rule has also been changed to allow the authorities discretion to overcrowd, a necessary move since the prison, built for 2487, held in 1996 more than 8000.[33]

In Africa, where prisons as the mainstay of the penal system were brought with the colonizers, prison as an institution fits particularly badly with the culture and values of society. In 1995, when the present author visited Chichiri prison near Blantyre, Malawi, there were 957 prisoners, 523 remand and 434 convicted. Technically there was room for 600 although the figure for capacity is very unscientific since it seems not to be based on any assessment of floor space, or number of beds – there are no beds – or number of cells – they do not have many cells – or number of blankets to lie on – there is a shortage of blankets. This is a pseudo-military system, as in many ex-British colonies. So the staff, male and female, wear a militaristic uniform, carry a little stick under their arm and when a superior hoves into view they salute, say 'Sir' and then call out the number of prisoners they have got in their section.

The visiting party was led by the prison commissioner. After walking round the prison the commissioner summoned all the prisoners, remand and convicted, and they sat on the ground. The visitors stood on the steps leading from the upper to the lower yard. Before them sat the 900 or so prisoners (all those who were not out working on government buildings or too sick to get off their blankets). Some were wearing the prison uniform of cream cotton short-sleeved, V-necked overshirt and shorts. Some were wearing their own clothes (the remand prisoners). Some of the clothes were complete, others were strips of clothes and several ragged shirts, one on top of the other; some had no shirts at all. Somehow they all, in rags or not, managed to retain a great deal of dignity. One prisoner in a wheelchair, who seemed to have no legs, had another prisoner looking after him. Many were scratching themselves urgently.

The commissioner asked the prisoners if they had any questions or complaints. They clearly had already chosen a spokesman. They called him and he got up and picked his way through the seated mass to the front. He was a young man called Charles. He was wearing a complete prison uniform, calf-high wellington boots, very dark sunglasses with one lens missing and a piece of tartan rag tied round his waist. He explained that the food, blankets and clothing were not adequate. All the prisoners clapped. The food is the same every day. They get one bar of soap twice a month. If they complain they are moved to other prisons. They are short of medicines. They cannot play football. The commissioner queried this and asked what had happened to the footballs given by the International Committee of the Red Cross. The superintendent muttered that they were in his office.

Charles continued. The terrible congestion in the cells leads to sickness. He thinks he will be victimized as a result of making these complaints. He thinks he will be transferred to another prison. He then went on to say that the staff stole the blankets given to the prisoners and sold them. The staff sold the plates issued to the prisoners. The welfare officer (a prison officer appointed to see to prisoners' complaints) does not carry out that task at all. There was loud applause from the assembled prisoners at each of these points.

Other prisoners then got their say. One said that complaints never get past the staff to any higher authority. The remand prisoners complained that cases do not get to court, sometimes for years, and they are left to languish. A prisoner called Henry complained that they did not get reading materials such as newspapers. George complained that there were no books that could give technical education and no technical training. Ephraim protested about the lack of work and special diets for those who are sick. Everyone gets the same maize porridge and beans. One prisoner complained that prisoners ill-treat other prisoners and the staff just look on without intervening. The food is too soft so prisoners get diarrhoea. The dispensary does not give adequate treatment. A Mozambican said that he had been there on remand for two years. They are locked in at 3 p.m. and it gets very hot. Once they are locked in there is nothing more given to them. Two remand prisoners complained about the length of time they had been on remand. Some had been waiting five years. There were loud cheers and applause at this point.

The 900 prisoners were guarded by five unarmed staff standing around and joining in the debates and discussion. They seemed perfectly at ease so it was reasonable to assume that it was quite normal and safe to have all 900 prisoners together at one time at such a gathering. Walking around the prison there was no locking and unlocking of gates, no evidence of prison staff carrying keys, nothing to suggest that security was an issue at all. The perimeter was easily scalable and security did not feature once in any discussion.[34]

Much about this prison raises questions. In few countries of the world would a meeting of 900 prisoners take place in the presence of only five unarmed staff. In few prisons of the world would 900 prisoners be restrained by a low fence. Rarely would such a friendly and good-humoured meeting be conceivable. If all this is possible the question must be asked, why the need for the traditional model of the prison at all?

It is clear that in all countries of the world imprisonment is seen as the axiomatic underpinning of crime policy. Everywhere, there is a prison system, prison administrators and staff, a prison budget. In countries where normal institutions are being established after a long period of chaos and war, one of the tasks of the reconstructors is to re-create a prison system. In Cambodia, for instance, the prisons date back to the French colonization of the 1920s or were built during the Vietnamese occupation. Now that the institutions of this profoundly damaged country are being rebuilt, so are the crumbling, decrepit prisons. In 1994 the United Nations Centre for Human Rights sent experts to advise the Cambodian prison service on how to run decent, safe, secure prisons without keeping prisoners in chains, locked in dark unventilated rooms twenty-four hours a day.[35]

So what does all this incarceration add up to? What is the population of the prisons of the world? How many people are locked up on any one day, in any one year?

It is difficult to know the answer to this question because in some countries, such as China, the number of people in prison is secret. However, the United States group Human Rights Watch estimates that the daily worldwide prison population is 106 per 100,000 or at least 5.3 million people.[36] That figure does not include many millions held for a short time in police stations, detention centres and other lock-ups.

The next question is where are all these prisoners? Are they evenly distributed around the world? What pattern of the use of imprisonment should one expect? If it is different in different countries, would this difference relate to crime rates or culture? Would it measure whether a country was more or less punitive? Or would it relate to economic level (prison is after all very expensive) or culture? Are there nations that just do not feel comfortable with locking people up? Do some nations just value liberty more than others?

The first, perhaps very surprising, answer to these questions is that there are enormous differences in imprisonment rates between seemingly similar countries. While imprisonment plays a part in the crime policy of every country, some use it lavishly. Some use it with considerable parsimony. In some countries people will be in prison for very minor offences. In others most of those imprisoned have committed a crime involving violence.

One way of assessing what prison is used for in different countries is to look at the sentenced people in prison on any one day and set down the offence for which they have been sentenced. The other way is to look at all the sentenced prisoners entering the prison in any one year and record their offences. The first method gives an indication of the sort of people the prison authorities have to deal with as their daily work. The second gives a better idea of what a country uses its prisons for. The figures for England and Wales illustrate this distinction. In 1996 the prison gates clanged shut behind 83,000 convicted people. But for some of these their stay was short: 8500 of them were in prison for not paying a fine. Some 29,000 were imprisoned for burglary and other property offences. Violent and sexual offences accounted for 16,600 and drug offences for 6000. So just over a quarter of those entering prison each year had been convicted of violence or drug offences.[37]

When a count is done on any one day, a snapshot or census taken of the actual prison population, the picture is different. In England and Wales the snapshot is always taken at the end of June. On 30 June 1995 nearly 43,000 sentenced people were in prison. Of these, nearly half were in there for some sort of violent or sexual offence and 13 per cent for a drug offence. Fifteen per cent had been convicted of burglary and nearly one in ten for theft and handling stolen goods.[38]

Looking at prison populations in this way gives an indication of how punitive a country is in its use of prison. Countries where a high proportion of the prison population is incarcerated for violence could be a country where prison is reserved for serious offenders and others are given community-based punishments. In the Netherlands, for instance, nearly half of those in prison on 1 September 1994 had been convicted of an offence involving violence or illegal drugs.[39] In Turkey a quarter of those locked up in 1994 were there for theft without violence.[40] In New South Wales in Australia one-third of those sentenced to prison were there for offences involving violence and sexual offences, one-third for offences against property and 12 per cent for drug offences.[41] In Morocco figures published in 1994 show that theft accounted for 40 per cent of those in prison; violence, 10 per cent; murder, 6 per cent; using drugs, 17 per cent; and other offences, 27 per cent.[42] In Japan in 1993 more than a third of sentenced male prisoners were imprisoned for property offences and fraud, 6 per cent for any offence involving violence against the person and more than a quarter for offences against the 'Stimulant Drug Control Law'.[43]

Figures for the United States show a very different picture from Japan. In 1992, nearly half a million people were admitted to prison in 38 states to serve sentences of more than one year. Of these, three out of ten had committed a violent offence. Fifteen thousand were convicted of murder and over nine thousand of rape. Slightly more than three out of ten were there for stealing of some sort. Another three out of ten had committed some offence connected with drugs, either possessing them or trafficking in them.[44]

In order to compare the tendency of countries to lock people up, a measure has been devised to describe the relative amount of imprisonment imposed in any country. This imprisonment rate is expressed as how many out of each 100,000 of its population are in prison on any one day. It covers all those known to be in an establishment within a country's official prison system and includes those in prison pre-trial and those already convicted and sentenced.

Table 1   Imprisonment rates in selected countries for the latest available date (given in brackets)

Country	Prisoners per 100,000 population
Albania (1994)	30.0
Australia (1995)	89.1
Austria (1995)	85.0
Bangladesh (1992)	37.0
Belarus (1995)	505.0
Belgium (1995)	75.0
Brazil (1996)	95.5
Bulgaria (1996)	110.0
Canada (1994)	119.0
Colombia (1995)	87.0
Croatia (1994)	50.0
Cyprus (1995)	30.0
Czech Republic (1995)	190.0
Denmark (1995)	65.0
England and Wales (1997)	120.0
Estonia (1997)	300.0
Finland (1995)	60.0
France (1996)	91.4
Germany (1995)	85.0
Greece (1995)	55.0
Hungary (1995)	120.0
Iceland (1994)	40.0
India (1992)	23.0
Ireland (1995)	55.0
Italy (1995)	85.0
Japan (1992)	36.0

Kazakhstan (1995)	560.0
Latvia (1997)	406.0
Lithuania (1997)	325.0
Luxembourg (1994)	109.0
Malaysia (1992)	122.0
Moldova (1996)	375.0
Netherlands (1995)	65.0
New Zealand (1994)	128.0
Northern Ireland (1995)	106.0
Norway (1995)	55.0
Poland (1995)	170.0
Portugal (1995)	125.0
Romania (1995)	200.0
Russia (1996)	690.0
Scotland (1997)	127.0
Singapore (1992)	229.0
Slovak Republic (1995)	150.0
Slovenia (1994)	50.0
South Africa (1992)	368.0
Spain (1995)	105.0
Sweden (1995)	65.0
Switzerland (1995)	80.0
Thailand (1992)	159.0
Turkey (1995)	80.0
Ukraine (1995)	390.0
United States of America (1996)	615.0

Sources: Council of Europe, *Penological Information Bulletin*, nos 19 & 20, December 1994, Strasbourg; 'Prison Populations in Europe and North America', HEUNI, Helsinki, 1997; US Bureau of Justice Statistics; Australian Bureau of Statistics; information published or provided by Ministries of Justice or the Interior in various countries; Amnesty International, London, 1996

The lowest rates in the developed world are to be found in Western Europe. The latest figures show most countries in the European Union with rates under 100 per 100,000, although even here there are wide differences. Then there is a cluster of countries which had totalitarian governments and have now become democratic or are in transition to democracy. In most of these, imprisonment rates are higher than in Western Europe. Russia has the highest figure of those countries for which information is available. The United States has the next highest. A number of other democratic countries find their place between the West European and ex-Soviet bloc countries. The figures for Asian countries span a wide range. With 36 people incarcerated per 100,000, Japan has a very low rate in relation to most other industrialized countries. In fact, the use of imprisonment in Japan has resisted all the trends of the developed world. In 1950 Japan had 103,000 prisoners. In 1975 the figure had come down to 46,000 and in 1992 it reached its lowest since the Second World War at 45,000.[45]

Statisticians raise a number of questions about these figures.[46] It is sometimes suggested that they are inaccurate, that the figures published by governments do not include all their incarcerated people, or the figures give a false impression of a government's imprisonment policies. For example, some prison systems are also responsible for secure mental hospitals where mentally disordered offenders are detained. Others are not. In the Netherlands, for example, those convicted of serious crimes such as murder or rape are often made subject to an order to go to a special mental hospital run by the health authorities. In the United Kingdom also, such hospitals are the responsibility of the Department of Health. Some countries keep their incarcerated juveniles in the prison system. Others deal with delinquents under eighteen in a different way and lock them up in establishments run by the social welfare services. Such points are interesting but of no great significance in invalidating overall comparisons of imprisonment rates, since the differences between countries are so large.

A more important question is what conclusions does a comparison of imprisonment rates lead to? Why does the United States imprison 615 of its citizens out of every 100,000 and Finland 60? Is it simply because relatively there are more than ten times more criminals in the United States than in Finland? Or is it because each US convicted criminal gets a prison sentence ten times longer than a Finnish one? Or perhaps Finnish offenders are given a fine when in the same circumstances a US offender would get five years in prison? Is it to do with the culture and institutional arrangements of each country? Perhaps people in some countries feel more punitive towards their fellow citizens when they break the law than others. Indeed some countries, for example the United States, still impose the death penalty whereas countries in Western Europe have abolished it.

Perhaps a low rate in some circumstances is not an indication of a humane and progressive system at all but of a system where confidence in the legal processes is so weak that law-enforcement officials take the law into their own hands and shoot suspects out of hand. It is sometimes suggested that this is the position in some South American countries and in India. In its report for 1996 Amnesty International suggests that there were hundreds of such extra-judicial executions in India in 1995.[47] In Venezuela dozens of people may have been killed by the police during police operations.[48] In Brazil hundreds of people were similarly executed by police and death squads and there were reports of people 'disappearing'.[49]

All these factors play a part. Certainly, the amount of imprisonment imposed by countries for the same crime varies enormously. In the US the mandatory sentencing structure for drug offences leads to people convicted of possession of small amounts of illegal substances serving a prison sentence. In Britain, someone convicted of such an offence might be cautioned by the police and not prosecuted at all or, if taken to court, would probably be fined. In the Netherlands, such an offender would probably not even be taken to court.

Those researchers who are dissatisfied with the measurement done by relating prison population to overall population have suggested another method of comparison, that is relating the prison population in any country to the recorded crime rates. Problems of comparability still exist with this measure because crime is defined and crime rates are measured differently from one country to another. However, this method has been used by British researchers who have shown that in relation to recorded crime rates, England and Wales had a lower prison population per 100,000 recorded crimes in 1993 than Portugal, Belgium, France, Ireland, Norway, Greece, Germany or Italy.[50]

So there are very marked differences in the use of imprisonment in seemingly similar countries. Of all these, two stand out as having a use of imprisonment dramatically different from the rest of the world. These are the United States and Russia. Both are worthy of much more detailed analysis. In the next chapter we turn to the special case of the United States.

3. The Great Incarcerator: The United States

> It must be acknowledged that the penitentiary system in America is severe. While society in the United States gives the example of the most extended liberty, the prisons of the same country offer the spectacle of the most complete despotism.
>
> Gustave de Beaumont and Alexis de Tocqueville, *On the Penitentiary System in the United States and its Application in France*[1]

Imprisonment is a big enterprise in the United States. More than one and a half million people are locked up on any one day.[2] Over ten million Americans will see the inside of a prison or jail cell in any one year.[3] It is also a growing enterprise. In 1996 there were more than three times as many prisoners as there had been in 1980.[4] The prisons themselves are vast, sometimes holding as many as 5000 people. The expenditure is enormous, estimated at $40 billion a year.[5] The conditions in which some prisoners are kept are the most extreme in the developed world.

The US prison system is the stuff of legend and movie. Many people know of the Birdman of Alcatraz or the famous blues musician Leadbelly who sang his way out of prison in Louisiana.[6] Much has been written about George Jackson, the Soledad brother killed in San Quentin prison in California.[7] The 1971 revolt at Attica prison in upstate New York is still remembered. At Attica the prisoners took control, held hostages and demanded the presence of a group of outside observers including the chairman of the Black Panther Party, Bobby Seale. The revolt ended in the storming of the prison and the deaths of forty-three men.[8]

Many of the medieval attributes of imprisonment seem to linger on. US prisoners often wear leg chains whenever they are outside the prison walls. Uniforms, when they are worn, are sharply prison-like, distinctively carceral. More recently, old images of the chain gang were revived by the re-establishment of chain gangs in Florida and Alabama. Prisoners from the Limestone Correctional Facility (a state prison for convicted adult prisoners in Alabama) were taken to a work site wearing white work suits and caps with 'Alabama Chain Gang' emblazoned on the front. Chain-gang members were drawn from Alabama's medium-risk offenders and spent between one and three months on the chain gang. Whilst working on the gangs the 400 prisoners lived in one large dormitory built to house 200. They were forbidden to watch television or smoke and could drink coffee on Sundays only. According to Amnesty International, prisoners are

> woken in the early hours of the morning and taken to their work site ... They are then made to kneel down where they are linked together at the ankle in groups of five with a large 'handcuff' and a 2.5-metre steel chain which weighs 1.5 kilos ... Work on the gang lasts for 10–12 hours often in hot sun, with very brief breaks for water and an hour for lunch ... The only toilet facility available to chain gang inmates is a portable chamber pot behind a makeshift screen. Inmates remain chained together when using it. When the chamber pot is inaccessible, inmates are forced to squat down on the ground in public.[9]

In August 1995, rock-breaking chain gangs were introduced. Prisoners engaged in rock-breaking were chained together with leg irons and a 2.4-metre chain and worked for ten hours a day with a break every twenty minutes, for five days a week. In May 1996, a prison guard shot dead a prisoner on the chain gang, allegedly in response to the prisoner becoming involved in a fight. Following the incident and the barrage of international criticism the state governor banned chain gangs from Alabama's prisons in June 1996.[10]

However, medieval cruelties continued. Prisoners who refused to work were handcuffed to a 'hitching rail', which is a metal post usually used for tying up horses, and spent hours standing in the hot sun, unable to sit down or use a toilet. A lawsuit against the practice was brought by the Southern Poverty Law Center supported by the American Civil Liberties Union.[11]

A particularly notorious chain gang was the all-female group shackled together by Sheriff Joe Arpaio of Phoenix, Arizona. Sheriff Joe Arpaio made the headlines frequently in 1996 because of his extreme penal policies. When his local jail became too overcrowded he erected green canvas tents on some waste ground to hold 1600 of the local prisoners. When the women prisoners broke the rules they were put into small four-person cells for twenty-three hours a day. The only way to get out was to volunteer for the chain gang. The women on the gang cleared rubbish in the city centre in full view of the general public.[12]

The system is so large that almost any variant of imprisonment can be found somewhere in the US. There are small jails with half a dozen cells, often run personally by the local sheriff. There are enormous, overcrowded prisons holding thousands of prisoners where the individual can only assure protection by belonging to one of the prison gangs. For some prisoners life in prison means living in a low-security camp out in the wild countryside, working as a firefighter for the forestry department or removing graffiti from state parks. Well-heeled prisoners convicted of financial crimes may end up in a federal prison a bit like a health farm.

Because of its size the prison system is not only varied, but complex. A 'jail' is a specific and different institution from a 'prison'. Prison euphemisms are to be found at their most developed in the United States and the generic term for all prisons would be 'correctional facilities'. The 1.6 million prisoners in the United States are distributed between three different levels of prison, depending on a number of factors: whether or not they have yet been tried, the nature of their crime and the length of their sentence. The three different levels of prison are the local jails run by counties and municipalities, state prisons such as San Quentin in California or Attica in New York, and federal prisons run by an agency of the federal government, the Federal Bureau of Prisons.

LOCAL JAILS

The jails are, according to Kenneth Kerle of the American Jail Association, 'at the bottom of the criminal justice hierarchy in influence'. They serve 'as the dumping grounds for the arrested

Table 2   The structure of the US prison system

Type of prison	Function
Local jails run by local counties population on 28 June 1996: 518,500[13]	to hold pre-trial prisoners; short-sentence prisoners; rearrested violators of probation, parole and bail conditions; juveniles and mentally ill people pending transfer; state or federal prisoners when there are no places for them because of overcrowding
State prisons run by the states population on 31 December 1995: 1,027,000[14]	to hold prisoners generally sentenced for more than one year under state law
Federal prisons run by Federal Bureau of Prisons population on 31 December 1995: 100,250[15]	to hold prisoners convicted of or charged with federal offences such as those involving immigration, national defence, certain drug-related offences

criminal, the chronic drunk, the DWI [driving while intoxicated], the mentally ill, the homeless, and juveniles ranging from the runaway to the amoral killer'.[16]

They also seem to suffer from the whole range of prison problems. Many are overcrowded and the physical conditions are bad. The human rights group, Human Rights Watch, based in the United States, studied US prisons, including jails. They concluded that jails 'often have very limited recreation facilities, house inmates in windowless cells, and provide little or no privacy to the detainees'.[17]

Many prisoners in jails are housed in dormitories rather than in cells. For example, the Human Rights Watch investigators found that at the Sybil Brand Jail for women in Los Angeles the women slept in dormitories each holding between 130 and 156 people.[18] At the Otis Bantum Correctional Center on Rikers Island in New York City, 1200 prisoners lived in dormitories or on the deck of converted ferry boats. The bathrooms, which in some dormitories had no shower curtains, and the toilets, which had no doors, were located in full view of the guards, stationed behind a glass wall and able to oversee four dormitories at once from their posts.[19]

Violence is a widespread problem. In August 1990, according to Human Rights Watch, there was a disturbance at Rikers Island jail which led to 120 prisoners needing medical attention. The disturbance arose from industrial action by the prison staff. They had barricaded the only bridge leading to the island, making it impossible for supplies to be delivered or for the prisoners' visitors to cross over. The prisoners barricaded themselves into their dormitories as a protest. They were overpowered by the staff who then, according to the official report into the incident, beat the prisoners in retaliation. Eighty-one prisoners needed medical attention for head injuries and twenty-one members of staff were injured, although none required hospitalization.[20]

A prisoner who had spent some time on Rikers Island wrote about it for the magazine of Brixton Prison in London.

> Zoo. That's the nearest word I can use to describe Rikers Island, the prison colony that houses twenty thousand of New York's most violent men and women. It's on an island surrounded by a river and has about nine different jails . . . The jail I went to was the convicted facility, which was just like a squalid hole with three thousand of the city's junkies, crack heads, and pickpockets all under one roof.[21]

Even worse violence is reported in the jails and police cells of Mississippi. According to journalist Kate Muir, the city jail in Jackson, Mississippi, is 'unremittingly grim'. It has sixty or so cells, and is part of the police precinct. Much of it

> lacks natural light. It is dank. The air-conditioning – vital in 100°F summers – does not work properly . . . The drunk tank – the first stop for many inmates – smells of aged urine, vomit and bleach, has a hole in the stone floor which serves as a lavatory . . . It is sordid and depressing.

Between 1987 and 1993 more than fifty men and women died in police cells and jails in Mississippi. These deaths were described as suicides but there are doubts as to the real cause of death.[22] In March

1993 the US Commission on Civil Rights held hearings in Mississippi jails and heard allegations that a number of black prisoners who were found hanged had actually been lynched. In June 1993 the US Justice Department notified jail officials in Jones County, Mississippi, that the jail there violated prisoners' rights. Security, medical and mental health care and suicide prevention measures were all inadequate.[23]

Louisiana seems to be not much better. In 1996 the Justice Department took a legal case against a sheriff and the warden of a parish jail there because of allegations that they ill-treated prisoners. Apparently staff at the jail strapped prisoners into a device called 'the chair' and left them there for days in their own excrement.[24]

Visiting arrangements are often not conducive to maintaining family relationships. At the jail in Nashville, Tennessee, and the two jails in Los Angeles visited by Human Rights Watch, prisoners were separated from their visitors by a glass wall and had to communicate by a telephone. However, at the Sybil Brand Jail in Los Angeles and at Nashville an exception is made for women prisoners. They may have actual contact with their visiting children. In Los Angeles a woman prisoner has to complete a parenting course before she is allowed this contact with her children on visits.[25]

There are major problems with health care. At the Los Angeles County Jail there has been controversy about the use of physical restraints on mentally ill patients. In July 1991, when Human Rights Watch visited, ten out of the forty-five patients in the mental observation unit were in restraints. However, a nurse told the visiting delegation that guidelines were followed and at least once every two hours the restrained people were released and allowed to move their arms and legs.[26]

At the privatized Hernando County Jail in Florida run by the Corrections Corporation of America prisoners have had to pay for health care since July 1994. The money is taken from the prisoner's account. If the prisoner has no money he leaves prison with a debt and the county collects what is owed from the prisoner's property or assets. The doctor says that charging encourages prisoners 'to find the most appropriate way to treat their problems. They learn to treat minor medical conditions and to seek professional care

when necessary.'[27] A county jail in Pennsylvania also started charging
prisoners part of the costs of their medical care. The prisoners went
to court to challenge the legality of the charges and the federal
district court judge supported the policy of the jail.[28]

Many prisoners in United States jails are mentally disturbed. The
number of such prisoners has increased as the United States has
moved towards what is sometimes called 'care in the community'.
In the past, mentally ill prisoners could easily be transferred to
mental institutions but this is now much more difficult. It is estimated
that about one-third of the jail population requires some form of
mental health care.[29]

STATE PRISONS

The second level of imprisonment in the United States is the state
level. Most crimes are prosecuted under state law and offenders
sentenced to a prison term will normally serve their sentence in a
state prison. Many state prison systems are in themselves much larger
than those of most European countries. The largest is California's,
which had 147,700 prisoners in 1996. New York's, with nearly
70,000, and Texas's, with over 132,000, are also much bigger than
many European prison systems.[30] Imprisonment rates between states
also vary considerably.

Much of the accommodation is severely overcrowded. It is also
grim in other ways. In Tennessee State Penitentiary the cells have
no windows. At Florida State Prison at Starke prisoners are often
locked up for twenty-four hours a day in cells with no furniture. A
prisoner at Starke described his cell to Human Rights Watch:

> Peeling paint on walls, leaking plumbing, broken glass in windows,
> dim lighting, roaches, rats/mice, ants, mosquitoes, moldy pillows and
> mattress, covered with filth, which have no plastic covers, unbearable
> heat in the summer, intense cold in winter.[31]

Some US state prisons can be dangerous places. Prison gangs are
a prevailing feature. They are very evident in prisons in California,
where a prisoner would be in real danger without the protection of
a gang. Human Rights Watch report that in the maximum-security

Table 3(a)   Ten states with the highest rates of incarceration

State	Prisoners per 100,000 population
Texas	653
Louisiana	568
Oklahoma	552
South Carolina	515
Nevada	482
Arizona	473
Alabama	471
Georgia	470
Mississippi	464
Florida	447

Table 3(b)   Ten states with the lowest rates of incarceration

State	Prisoners per 100,000 population
North Dakota	85
Minnesota	105
Maine	111
West Virginia	136
Vermont	143
Utah	173
New Hampshire	174
Massachusetts	175
Nebraska	185
Rhode Island	186

NB: These figures relate to state prisons only and do not include either federal prisons or county jails.
Source: Bureau of Justice Statistics, *Prison and Jail Inmates, 1995*, US Department of Justice, 1996

prison in Stateville in Chicago, Illinois, gang membership in 1986 was running at 85 per cent.[32] A prisoner there, Sam Gutierrez, wrote a detailed diary for one day for Professor Norval Morris of Chicago University. He says,

> Gang activity is another addiction of our prison. Gang membership is known to the prison authorities but there is not much they can do about it. They try to move gang leaders about, from one prison to another, but this only briefly interrupts gang activity – new leaders promptly emerge. The gangs influence who moves safely in prison and who gets into trouble with the prison authorities . . . The influence of gangs in Stateville is much the same as it is on the streets, though mercifully they are not equipped with guns here, only with shanks [prison-made knives].[33]

In Puerto Rico, according to Human Rights Watch, 'Gangs regulate numerous aspects of prison life . . . through their own codes.'[34]

Rules governing visits to prisoners vary from state to state. Usually prisoners are allowed a visit once a month. Conjugal visits are not normally permitted but in California and also in Mississippi prisoners are allowed forty-eight-hour visits with their immediate family in special trailers.

Portrait of a Californian Prison

Folsom, a state prison in California, is a historic prison. In fact, it is two prisons. One is a modern high-security prison. The other is the old-fashioned traditional prison which would look familiar to many people who have seen American prison films. Outside the prison wall at Folsom is an art and craft shop where tourists can buy objects made by prisoners, such as two-inch-square pink-painted model cells containing a small pebble with 'Jailhouse Rock' painted in small letters above the cell bars. Near the shop is the 'picture point' where tourists can stand and be photographed against the backdrop of the grey granite walls and watchtowers of old Folsom.

In May 1993 there were 3400 prisoners held at Folsom.

It had originally been built for half that number and so was very overcrowded. About 30 per cent of the prisoners were black, 30 per cent Hispanic, 30 per cent white and 10 per cent of other backgrounds.

Three levels of security are available at the prison. The high-security prisoners are held right in the middle of the prison. They live in the inner section consisting of a large yard surrounded by cell blocks. The cell blocks constitute the outer wall for the high-security prisoners. They are not allowed beyond it. Medium-security prisoners are allowed to go outside the cell blocks where there are exercise yards and training centres. Minimum-security prisoners are allowed even further. They can go outside the outer wall to maintain the grounds.

The living quarters are very traditional. The prisoners live in cells rather than in dormitories. The cells are quite small, about half the size of a cell in a nineteenth-century British prison. All the cells have two bunks, a very small washbasin, a lavatory and a shelf on which many prisoners put their television sets. With two large men inside it the cell seems overpoweringly full, almost as if the men have had to be squeezed in. The doors are the characteristic American open-barred type so the occupants have absolutely no privacy. The whole cell, including the lavatory, is visible to any passer-by.

The cell blocks are five tiers high and on the level of the fourth tier are long walkways, high above the ground on the wall facing the cell block. Here stand the 'gunpeople', both men and women, heavily armed and patrolling up and down the 'gunwalk', as the walkway is called. One of the cell blocks is differently designed with cells both sides, so the gunpeople have to stand at the far end, from where it is apparently very difficult to shoot because of the long distance. California is one of only eight US states where prison staff carry arms inside the prison.

Meals are taken in a large dining-room. The dining-room is furnished with fixed steel furniture, each

table having four stools. The food is served through
hatches in a way which makes it impossible for the
prisoner serving the food to know which prisoner is going
to receive it. The prisoners get a substantial cooked
breakfast. Their lunch is a 'sack', or packed lunch, and
they eat a hot dinner, the last meal of the day, from
4 p.m. onwards.

The dining-room also has gunpeople high above the
room on walkways. The dining-room ceiling is riddled
with bullet holes. Apparently there had been a time when
every week saw seven or eight shootings in the
dining-room. The decision to shoot belongs to the
gunperson. It is based on an assessment as to whether
what is happening below in the dining-room is likely to
result in death or serious injury. If it looks, for example,
as if a prisoner is going to stab another, the gunperson
can shoot. Often gunpeople fire warning shots into the
ceiling to calm everyone down.

The arrangements for prisoners to have visits from
their families and friends are impressive at Folsom.
Visiting times are from 9 a.m. to 2 p.m. four days a week
and prisoners can have visits for the whole of that time
provided the visiting area is not too crowded. One
evening a week visits are allowed up to 7 p.m. for people
who cannot visit during the day. The visiting area is an
enormous converted assembly hall which retains the rows
of seats. Outside is an additional area, covered but with
the sides open to the sun and the sky. There is a cafeteria
providing refreshments.

There are also facilities for weekend visits. Top-security
prisoners can have family visits for up to seventy-two
hours as often as every six weeks in a three-room
apartment with kitchen and bathroom within the prison
itself. Lower-security prisoners can meet their families in
a three-roomed Portakabin which is equipped for family
living.

The old death row area where prisoners used to be held

before execution consists of cells with no water or electricity and which, in contrast to the rest of the prison, have very solid doors. In the same area as these cells was the equipment for the hangings. As prisoners got nearer their turn to be hanged they would be moved along the cells, gradually getting nearer to the gallows. The block has now been converted to a music practice room. Instead of a gallows it houses a large set of drums and the door has been insulated with an old mattress to deaden the noise of the drumming.

The warden (prison governor) at Folsom is a woman. By Western standards the level of staffing is not high. On a wing of 600 prisoners there would be about seven staff. Four of these would be working with the prisoners, locking, unlocking and organizing. The other three would be on walkways with guns.

Many of the changes brought about in Folsom have been instituted as a result of court action. All the arrangements for putting prisoners in segregation were declared illegal by the courts and new facilities for segregation had to be built at the new prison. In May 1993 there were apparently about 1300 lawsuits being brought by prisoners against the institution.

Notes made by the present author of a visit in May 1993

FEDERAL PRISONS

The federal prison system holds far fewer prisoners than either the jails or the state prisons. Those convicted of or charged with a federal crime are placed by the court in the custody of the Federal Bureau of Prisons. Also some prisoners are transferred from state prisons. The Bureau then decides where to place the prisoners. Once that decision has been made prisoners are transported to their designated prison either by bus or by contract carrier airlines. There is also a fleet of aircraft operated by the US Marshals service which can be used. Another method is the 'voluntary surrender' method. Every month about fifty-five sentenced prisoners make their own way to the designated prison. Apparently very few fail to turn up.[35]

In federal prisons all those fit to work are required to do so. All those who have a history of substance abuse have to participate in drug education programmes and all those without a high school diploma (45 per cent) are required to attend literacy classes. Prisoners are allowed radios in their cells or cubicles but not television sets, although an exception is made for handicapped prisoners.[36]

Conjugal visits are not allowed in federal prisons but prisoners are allowed several visits a month and these usually take place in large rooms equipped with tables and chairs and sometimes with vending machines and a microwave oven. Most prisoners can make reversed charge phone calls.[37]

The US Congress has approved legislation which will allow the Federal Bureau of Prisons to collect 'user fees' from federal prisoners equal to the cost of one year's imprisonment. It is estimated that one in ten of the 30,000 new prisoners who enter the federal system each year may have enough money to pay for at least their first year of imprisonment. The fees could bring in up to $48 million a year. The money will be used to pay for drug and alcohol abuse programmes.[38]

Prison service annual reports usually feature bright colours and photographs of smiling prisoners working at computers, chatting to prison staff, cultivating gardens, winning awards for the best pigs or for the highest amount of money raised for charity. The annual report of the Federal Bureau of Prisons for 1994 sets a very different tone. It is grainy black and white. The cover picture is of a row of people in riot gear, with just helmets and weapons visible. Inside are pictures of the Attorney-General, Janet Reno, and the head of the Bureau, Kathy Hawke. Then there are full-page pictures of an officer in full riot gear and of a helicopter spraying water on to a fire started by prisoners. A picture caption says, 'All staff participate in basic correctional training'. The picture is of a woman shooting with a high-powered weapon. Then there are two more pictures of staff in riot gear, charging with guns at the ready. Negotiations with hostage-takers are depicted. At the back is a piece in memory of an officer killed by a prisoner in Atlanta. The report for 1993 has a similar aura, with pictures of fortified fences, searchlights, grey windowless buildings, watchtowers. There is a picture of a corridor with some barred cages and human beings behind the bars. The caption says,

> In BOP Special Housing Units, every inmate moving out of a cell must be placed in handcuffs, searched, and escorted by from one to three staff. This makes the simplest activities more time-consuming. Not all moves go smoothly.[39]

A section of the report devoted to staff training is illustrated by a group of staff at shooting practice.

When the 1995 report appeared it had no pictures. Apparently the Bureau was short of money.

BOOT CAMPS

In response to prison overcrowding and in the hope of finding a more successful and less expensive remedy for crime than prison, some states set up in the mid eighties what are called 'shock incarceration programmes', also known as 'boot camps'. In 1993 these were running in twenty-nine state administrations[40] and in the federal system.[41] Boot camps are also being run by some jail administrations.[42]

An example is the programme in Louisiana set up in 1987. Prisoners on the programme start off by spending ninety to 180 days in a medium-security prison participating in a rigorous programme of work, physical exercise and drills as well as drug education and other rehabilitation activities. Those who succeed at this part of the programme are given parole and they undergo intensive supervision in the community. The supervision involves four contacts a week with the supervisor, staying at home between the hours of 8 p.m. and 6 a.m., carrying out community service and working. Drug and alcohol screening is part of the supervision.[43]

The Federal Bureau of Prisons opened its first boot camp for men in Pennsylvania in 1991 and its first camp for women in Texas in 1992. The programme consists of, according to the Bureau's 1992 report, 'physical labor and intensive self-improvement programming for 17 hours a day, 6 days a week'.

The women in the boot camp in Texas work in the forest,

> clearing brush, maintaining trails and recreational facilities for the public . . . The other three days of their regimen . . . include physical conditioning, drug abuse counselling, religious services and training in life coping skills, literacy and vocational skills.

Both prisoners and staff are forbidden to smoke. If prisoners finish their six-month stint successfully they are allowed to serve the rest of their sentence in what are called 'community correctional facilities', that is a type of hostel, day attendance centre, or confinement at home.[44]

Evaluations of the boot camps suggest that they cost about the same as regular prisons, are no more successful in keeping people out of further trouble unless they are combined with a variety of other services and activities and include a period of six to nine months follow-up in the community, and do not generally reduce the number of people in prison unless prisoners are selected from the existing prison population. As much as 60 per cent of boot-camp leavers are rearrested within a year.[45]

RACE AND IMPRISONMENT

A most striking feature of the US prison system is the racial mix of the prison population or, as one commentator describes it, 'the intolerable racial disproportion in America's prisons and jails'.[46]

Six per cent of the population of the United States is black (i.e. African-American) and male. Almost half of all the men in prison are African-American. African-American men are imprisoned at a rate nearly six times higher than white men. Out of every 100,000 white Americans, 306 are in prison. The figure for African-Americans is 1947 per 100,000.[47] When broken down by gender the figures are similarly disproportionate. Out of every 100,000 white women, 20 are in prison. The figure for African-American women is 143.[48]

According to the Washington, DC-based Sentencing Project, on an average day in America one out of every three African-American men aged twenty to twenty-nine is in prison or jail, on probation or on parole.[49] A study conducted of young African-American men in Washington, DC in 1992 showed that more than four out of every ten African-American men aged eighteen to thirty-five were in prison, on probation, on parole, on bail or being sought by the police with a warrant.[50] Official statistics suggest that nearly three out of ten black men face the prospect of going to prison during their lifetime, a figure that does not include the likelihood of going to jail.[51]

The chance of the young African-American man coming under the control of some part of the criminal justice system is higher than his chances of going to college for higher education. In 1992, 583,000 black men were in prison. Only 537,000 were in higher education.[52] Table 4 shows how, for New York and California, Hispanics are grossly over-represented, a fact often concealed by combining the rates for Hispanics with whites.

Table 4   Ethnic disparities in the US prison system

State	Incarceration rate				Ratio black/ white
	Black	*White*	*White non-Hispanic*	*Hispanic*	
California	1668	317			5.26
	1668		217	518	7.69
New York	1138	202			5.63
	1138		53	1158	21.47

Source: Marc Mauer, 'Intended and Unintended Consequences: State Racial Disparities in Imprisonment', Sentencing Project, Washington, DC, January 1997

RAPE IN PRISON

In US prisons most days pass for most prisoners not with violence and assault but with boredom, a grinding 'dull sameness'. Sam Gutierrez begins his diary of a day in Stateville with a warning:

> if you expect the usual prison tale of constant violence, brutal guards, gang rapes, daily escape efforts, turmoil and fearsome adventures, you will be deeply disappointed. Prison life is really nothing like what the press, television and movies suggest. It is not a daily round of threats, fights, plots . . . though . . . a sense of impending danger is always with you.[53]

But there is violence. In 1987 prisoners brought a case against the Glades Correctional Institution (GCI) in Florida, complaining that they had all been raped in similar circumstances. According to the evidence given in the case and reported by Human Rights Watch,

> a 25-year-old inmate was raped during his second night at GCI, as he was beginning to take a shower. He was grabbed and held at knife-point and told that if he hollered, he would die. He was penetrated anally by two or three inmates. He was so traumatized that, after being transferred to the Reception and Medical Center for dental surgery, he slashed his wrist with a razor blade to keep from being brought back to GCI.
>
> A 27-year-old was attacked by five inmates and dragged into the shower. The inmates raped him at knife-point 3 times over a period of 35–40 minutes.
>
> Another inmate was raped 5 times by 3 inmates while held at knife-point on the bunk below his.[54]

In 1973, Stephen Donaldson, then aged twenty-six, found himself in jail in Washington, DC after he had been arrested at a Quaker prayer demonstration at the White House against the bombings in Cambodia. He was subsequently acquitted. During his first night in jail he was repeatedly gang-raped. He then became the president of the organization Stop Prisoner Rape until his death in 1997. According to Stephen Donaldson, writing in *The New York Times*, in most prisons 'rape is an entrenched tradition, considered by prisoners a legitimate way to "prove their manhood" and to satisfy sexual needs and the brutal desire for power'.

Stop Prisoner Rape estimates that 'some 60,000 unwanted sexual acts take place behind bars in the United States every day'. In the course of a year 'some 130,000 adult males in prisons, 123,000 in jails and 40,000 boys held in juvenile and adult facilities' are victims.

Most of the victims are 'young, straight, and non-violent, unable to defend themselves'.

Very few of these rapes are reported to prison officials, it is claimed, because of the dangers in prison of becoming known as an informer, the humiliation of having to admit what has happened and the fear of being classified as homosexual. The consequences of being a rape victim can be grim:

> the combination of rape and HIV can turn a sentence for a non-violent offense, an inability to make bail, and even a status offense for a juvenile into a potential death penalty decreed by no legislature and no judge.[55]

Stop Prisoner Rape argues that

> Full of rage and without the opportunity to receive psychological treatment for Rape Trauma Syndrome, these men and boys will usually return to the community far more violent and antisocial than before they were raped. Some of them will become rapists themselves.[56]

From 1973 Stephen Donaldson fought to convince the courts that prison officials should be held liable if a prisoner is raped by other prisoners. Eventually he succeeded. A prisoner, supported by lawyers from the National Prison Project, filed a case seeking to determine under what circumstances prison officials are liable for preventing prisoner rapes because they constitute 'cruel and unusual punishment' under the Eighth Amendment to the US constitution. In 1994 the US Supreme Court ruled that prison officials are so liable if they fail to act when they know that prisoners are at substantial risk of being harmed by others.[57]

The problem of rape in prisons has also been recognized in a very practical way. Stephen Donaldson made a twenty-seven-minute audio tape specifically directed at men in jails and prisons called *An Ounce of Prevention*, emphasizing sexual assault avoidance tactics, and *Becoming a Survivor*, a ninety-minute tape for those who have already been victims of sexual assault in prisons.

In 1995 a senator in Illinois got some publicity for promoting new legislation about rape in prison. The legislation he proposed would place three additional duties on the Illinois Department of Corrections. The first would be to count the number of rapes committed in prison, the second to warn incoming prisoners of the danger of being raped, and the third to provide prison staff with two hours of training in how to prevent sexual assaults and respond more effectively when they occur. The senator was moved to do this by what had happened to one of his constituents. The twenty-five-year-old man had been imprisoned for theft. He had been repeatedly raped at a Correctional Center and had become infected with HIV as a result.[58]

SUPER-MAX PRISONS

Perhaps the feature of American prisons that has most disturbed those working to protect human rights is the growth of super-maximum-security prisons, 'super-max' or the 'maxi-maxis' as they are called. They can now be found in several states – Arizona, New York, Connecticut, Indiana, Maryland and Missouri – and in the federal system.

The super-maximum-security prison is an important part of the American prison tradition. It started with the infamous Alcatraz, now a tourist attraction in San Francisco Bay but once the ultimate symbol of harsh incarceration. Alcatraz was closed and replaced in 1963 by a prison called Marion, in Illinois. Within Marion is a special control unit. The treatment in the unit, which has become a model for other super-max prisons, was devised after events which took place one day in October 1983. Whenever prisoners left their cells, their hands were handcuffed in front and they were escorted by two guards. On 22 October a prisoner named Thomas Silverstein was being escorted to the shower by three guards. He was walking in front of them. He stopped at the bars of the cell of another prisoner. When he turned round he was holding a home-made knife and one hand was free of the handcuffs. He fatally stabbed one of the officers.

Later the same day another prisoner, Clayton Fountain, determined to outdo Thomas Silverstein, stabbed one officer and injured two others. The events of that day had a profound effect on the way the most violent prisoners were treated. From then on prisoners leaving their cells had their hands handcuffed behind their backs. The services they needed were brought as near to them as possible.

Chaplains and doctors came to the cells to deal with them. Prisoners exercised on their own. Apart from that they were in their cells for twenty-three hours a day.[59]

The conditions at Marion led to prisoners bringing court cases against their treatment. In 1988 a case was heard in which the prisoners claimed that the conditions were in breach of the Eighth Amendment to the constitution which prohibits 'cruel and unusual punishment'. The federal court heard how prisoners are treated at Marion:

> when an inmate is outside his cell he is handcuffed and a box is placed over the handcuffs to prevent the lock from being picked; his legs may also be shackled. Inmates are forbidden to socialize with each other or to participate in group religious services. Inmates who throw food or otherwise misbehave in their cells are sometimes tied spread-eagled on their beds, often for hours at a stretch, while inmates returning to their cells are often (inmates of the control unit, always) subjected to a rectal search; a paramedic inserts a gloved finger into the inmate's rectum and feels around for a knife or other weapon or contraband.[60]

Sunday Times journalist Russell Miller visited Marion in 1993. He describes the first sight a visitor gets of the prison: 'a squat, grey complex fuzzily obscured by a double wire fence topped with coils of stainless steel razor wire'. The complex is surrounded by eight observation towers. In each tower are guards armed with M12s, M16s, 12-gauge shotguns, .38 calibre handguns and guns designed to shoot steel cable into the air to disable helicopters. The function of the regime at the prison, according to Miller, is

> psychological emasculation, to crush the spirit, strip a man of the last vestige of defiance and force him to conform to the most punitive system the courts will allow and the public will tolerate.

Control Unit prisoners, he says, are

> treated like extremely dangerous and unpredictable wild animals. They are never moved from their cells without being in chains ... Before their cell doors are opened they are placed in leg irons and handcuffed behind their backs. Outside their cells they are always escorted by three officers carrying metal-tipped clubs known as 'ribspreaders'.[61]

The numbers in Marion are now being reduced – there were 157 prisoners in the top-security unit in 1995. But the Federal Bureau of Prisons has opened a new top-security prison in Florence, Colorado, built on an old radioactive dump.[62] There the prisoners have an average sentence of more than forty years. In the cells the furniture is immovable and there is no soap dish, toilet seat or toilet handle, as all these could be made into weapons. The cells have cement floors painted grey. The building is designed so that prisoners will not be able to see other cells or the Rocky Mountains through the small windows. The visiting room has a glass window that can withstand two hours of being beaten with a hammer. Visitors can communicate with the prisoners they are visiting by phone. When the 'worst' prisoners leave their cells their hands will be handcuffed behind their backs. They will be shackled in leg irons and accompanied by three guards. These prisoners have no television in their cells and they will be allowed one fifteen-minute phone call every three months.[63]

Florence is a federal prison. State prison systems are following the lead of the federal system and establishing their own 'Florences'. There is such a prison at Pelican Bay in California. Pictured from the air, the prison presents a bleak picture: 'All trees and greenery are shaved off the earth. Concrete, asphalt and gravel have replaced the redwoods. There is not a living thing within reach of . . . the prisoners.'[64]

The Pelican Bay State Prison is, according to a leaflet about it put out by the Communications Office of the Department of Corrections, 'geographically isolated' on California's northern border with Oregon. One side of the prison houses normal maximum-custody prisoners, that is, 'those who can hold jobs, go to school and mingle with other inmates'. The other constitutes the 'high-tech' Security Housing Unit. Those, the leaflet says, 'assigned to Pelican Bay's SHU [pronounced shoo] have none of these privileges' because 'they have proven by their behavior in prison that they cannot be housed safely with general population inmates'.

Under the heading 'Earning a Trip to SHU', the leaflet explains how prisoners are chosen: 'Most are sent there for committing violent acts while in prison such as murder, assault, initiating a riot, threatening staff or other inmates, or being caught with a weapon.' The procedure is described: 'An administrative review committee considers the evidence and listens to the inmate and witnesses. If the charges are verified, inmates can be given a SHU term ranging from a few months to five years.' Other prisoners sent to the SHU have a sentence without a fixed time limit. These are the 'known' gang members or gang affiliates. For them 'the department conducts a thorough investigation to document the inmate's gang activities and reviews his status every 120 days'.

No attempt is made in the leaflet to pretend that the conditions in the SHU are comfortable or humane. Most prisoners, it says, are housed in single cells. The cells have 'heavy, perforated doors', which 'limit an inmate's ability to assault others without obstructing visibility into or out of a cell'.

There is no cell furniture as such. The bunks 'are molded into the wall and toilets have no removable parts that could be used to make weapons'. Movable objects that are allowed – clothing, bedding and personal effects – are 'x-rayed before being placed in a cell'. The cells are grouped into 'pods' of eight, four on one level and another four on the level above. There is a shower on each floor. The cells have no windows but, according to the leaflet, 'several overhead skylights flood each pod with natural light'. Prisoners are allowed radios and televisions but they have to listen to them through earphones.

There are six pods in a block and at the centre of the six pods is a control room. From the control room the officer has a clear view of all the pods and from there operates the doors and controls entrances and exits. The exercise yards are concrete and are twenty-six feet by ten feet. The walls are eighteen feet high. The yards are half covered with a see-through Plexiglas roof so that prisoners can be protected from the rain and snow. The other half is covered with wire mesh. There are video cameras at each end so that the officer in the control room can see the exercising prisoner at all times. At least ten hours a week exercise is allowed. No exercise equipment is permitted 'for security reasons'.

The architecture of the SHU ensures that prisoners never have to leave it. The cells where they live and the rooms where other functions such as medical treatment or legal research are carried out are all within the same 'building envelope'.

> A secure system of corridors is monitored by control rooms. To aid in the secure operation of the complex, the upper level corridors are restricted to staff only. Heavy mesh grating on the floor of the upper corridor allows close scrutiny of activity below.

The leaflet asserts that most, but not all, prisoners are 'allowed a limited amount of unescorted movement within the pod'. They can walk alone within their four-celled part of the pod to the shower or to the exercise yard, but only one prisoner is allowed out at a time. Self-evidently this 'reduces the frequency of physical contact between staff and inmates and greatly diminishes the risk of assault'.

Leaving the pod is more complicated. When a prisoner leaves the pod to see the doctor, meet counselling or other staff, do legal research, attend hearings or receive visits from family and friends, he is 'placed in restraints', that is his hands are handcuffed behind his back and he is chained to other prisoners.

There are regular visiting days. For visits the prisoner is escorted into a 'small, secure cell'. The visitor sits opposite, on the other side of a glass screen. The prisoner and the visitor communicate through a telephone.

The law library is so constructed that prisoners using it can be locked in individual cells there. The leaflet comments, 'The court has ruled that inmates may share legal materials with each other.' However, the materials are searched by staff before they are passed from one prisoner to another. The court has also ruled that prisoners in the cells in the library should be allowed to talk to each other but there is no explanation of how this is done.

Prisoners are not allowed to go to religious services. The chaplains deal with each prisoner individually by going to see him either in the unit or talking through the slot in the cell door.

Staff deliver everything the prisoner needs: food trays, letters, supplies from the prison shop, medicines. The law library is run by staff. The only prisoners who have contact with other prisoners are those who share cells. Prisoners from the maximum-security side of the prison work in the SHU but they are kept strictly separate from the SHU prisoners and they wear special jumpsuits to distinguish them from the SHU prisoners.

The leaflet about the SHU is illustrated with photographs. One shows a windowless concrete bunker-like building without any trace of vegetation, not even a blade of grass. This is the outside of the SHU. Another shows a guard in uniform holding a machine-gun and looking through a network of bars. Another has the rather disingenuous caption, 'Holding their legal documents behind them, inmates are escorted one at a time to individual cells in the law library'. Since their hands are in cuffs behind their backs, it would be difficult to hold their documents anywhere else. Another photo is of prisoners being examined by a smiling health worker whilst two officers clutching weapons stand each side of the prisoner, glowering. There is also a picture of a bare concrete yard with two prisoners exercising.

The Department of Corrections maintains that the 'state-of-the-art' unit is 'designed to safely and securely manage the state's most violence-prone inmates'. The claim is that after about 1600 disruptive prisoners were transferred to Pelican Bay SHU in 1989, the rest of the state's prisons 'became safer and inmate violence dropped statewide'. In 1993 the prisoners' lawyers brought a case to the district court in San Francisco arguing that the conditions in the Security Housing Unit were illegal, inhumane and likely to cause psychological damage. They alleged that about 950 of the 1500 prisoners at the unit in fact shared cells. Putting people with histories of violence together for nearly twenty-four hours a day in such restrictive conditions had led to many assaults. In three years there had been more than a thousand. They also complained of the lack of due process in committing prisoners to the unit, alleging that the committee meeting of the review body which decided on cases lasted only a few minutes and was more or less a rubber stamp. Merely being suspected of gang membership was a reason to be sent to the unit.

To get out of the unit was very difficult. The prisoners alleged that they had to confess to gang involvement and name others. If they had no information and were not eligible for parole, there was no way out. A sentence to the unit was 'a sentence of unending terror, deprivation and isolation'.[65]

Cell extractions, as they are called, are another feature of such units. The prisoners at Pelican Bay alleged that when a prisoner refused to obey a direct order, even on a minor matter, a cell extraction team was summoned. Then, it is alleged, a supervisory member of staff fired

> one or all of the following weapons at a prisoner in his cell: electric lasers, gas guns and mace. Then a team of four to five correctional staff, dressed in riot gear with face visors, 'rush' the prisoner . . . The guards attack the prisoner using these weapons, and kick and punch him as well . . . When the prisoner is subdued guards frequently 'hog-tie' the prisoner.[66]

The prisoners won their case. In January 1995 San Francisco judge Thelton Henderson ruled that the prison was in breach of the law and had 120 days to reform itself. Judge Henderson, in his ruling, described eleven violent assaults on prisoners.

> One had four teeth knocked out, another's scalp was partly torn back and he received no medical treatment until the flesh started falling off. Another's jaw was fractured, and one guard bent back a man's arm, thrust through the slot where they deliver meals, until the bone broke. They heard the crack throughout the building.
>
> Visitors have been startled to see naked men confined outside in tiny metal cages for hours during bitter weather. Inmates were handcuffed in the 'hog-tied' position, ankles and wrists almost meeting, and left for up to ten hours.[67]

The conditions in the Security Housing Unit amount to 'almost total sensory deprivation'. A psychiatrist examined fifty men and found seventeen of them were psychotic or suicidal.

The California Department of Corrections responded to the court judgement by pointing out that the unit has stopped the worst practices. Isolation is reserved for the 'worst of the worst'.

Following the establishment of the extreme high-security conditions at Marion in 1983, thirty-six states have set up their own super-maximum-security units or prisons. In Florida there is the windowless Q wing at Starke prison. Prisoners in the wing never go outside and some have been there for seven years. In Oregon State Penitentiary there is a Disciplinary Segregation Unit where prisoners have everything – clothing, bedding and possessions – taken away from them, and have to earn them back item by item for good behaviour. In 1991, when the prison at Southport in New York State was turned into a super-maximum-security prison, all the teaching and counselling staff were removed.[68]

THE GROWTH IN THE US PRISON POPULATION

The growth in the US imprisoned population has been remarkable. The percentage increase has been 7.8 per cent annually since 1985.[69] At the end of 1985, one in every 320 US residents was incarcerated.[70] By mid 1996 it was one in every 163. Since 1990 the average growth in the total population in custody has been 1686 each week.[71]

Table 5   The growth in the US population in custody, 1980–95

1980	501,886
1985	744,208
1990	1,148,700
1995	1,585,401

Source: Bureau of Justice Statistics, *Prisoners in 1994* and *Prison and Jail Inmates, 1995*, US Department of Justice, 1995 and 1996

What is the explanation for this extraordinary level of growth in numbers incarcerated? One answer is the 'war on drugs'. The Californian criminologist Elliott Currie says,

> Twenty years of the 'war' on drugs have jammed our jails and prisons, immobilized the criminal justice system in many cities, swollen the ranks of the criminalized and unemployable minority poor, and diverted desperately needed resources from other social needs.[72]

This has led to mandatory minimum sentences for drug offenders, however minor the offence. When federally prosecuted, a sentence of at least five years is required for possession of more than five grams of crack cocaine with intent to distribute. One year in prison without parole is the sentence for anyone convicted of selling drugs within 1000 feet of a school. In Michigan the mandatory sentence for possession of less than a pound and a half of cocaine with intent to distribute, even for a non-violent first offender, is life without parole.

During the period 1985–95, the number of sentenced prisoners in state prisons more than doubled. The overall increase was 119 per cent. The increase attributable to offences against the drug laws was 478 per cent (see Table 6).

Table 6   Increase in sentenced state prisoners by most serious offence, 1985–95

Type of offence	1985	1995	% change
Violent	246,200	457,600	+86
Property	140,100	237,400	+69
Drug	38,900	224,900	+478
Public order	23,000	66,100	+187
Other/unspecified	3,200	3,000	−6
Total	451,812	989,000	+119

Note: numbers do not add up exactly because of rounding
Source: Bureau of Justice Statistics, *Prisoners in 1996*, US Department of Justice, 1997

In 1993 it was reported to the US Congress that judges of every federal circuit had adopted resolutions against the mandatory minimum sentences for drug offenders.[73] An organization has been set up, Families Against Mandatory Minimums, which campaigns for the abolition of such sentences. Julie Stewart, the president of the organization, writes in the newsletter:

> Most members of Congress aren't stupid. They know that these sentences have failed to reduce illegal drug use or the rate of crime in this country. Most of them understand that a non-violent first offender probably doesn't deserve ten years in prison. But none of these factors outweigh their concern that repealing mandatory minimum sentences might look bad in their home districts. Represen-

tatives, who must be reelected every two years, are particularly sensitive to doing anything that could be construed as being 'soft on crime'.[74]

Another cause of the great increase in the number of prisoners is a tougher approach to those who break the conditions of their court order. Thirty per cent of prison admissions in 1992 were due to violations of some order of the court, either parole, probation or conditional release. This compares with 17 per cent in 1980.[75]

Recent developments in United States penal policy suggest that the trend is not going to be reversed in the near future. The 'three strikes and you're out' policy means that anyone convicted of three serious or violent felonies will be sentenced to life imprisonment on the third. The expression comes from baseball. The law was first introduced in Washington state in 1993. In 1994 it became federal law and to date there are such laws in twenty-four states.

The 'three strikes' law has put numerous offenders in prison, including one man who stole a slice of pizza and another who stole two pairs of jeans from a shop. The pizza-stealer was twenty-nine-year-old Jerry Dewayne Williams. He had a history of petty property offences but no serious violence on his record. The crime that earned him his three-strikes fame was to snatch a piece of pizza from four children on a seaside pier. In January 1997 his life sentence was reduced.[76] Another was Duane Silva. He was one of the first to be sentenced under the three-strikes law and received his life sentence for burgling a house. His two previous convictions involved setting fire to two rubbish bins and setting fire to a parked van.[77] California's Supreme Court has considered the 'three strikes' law which requires judges to impose sentences of twenty-five years to life imprisonment on people committing a third offence who have already been convicted for two serious offences. It has decided unanimously that the law is unconstitutional and that judges still have the power to ignore convictions for previous offences if they wish.[78]

The United States is equalled in its relative use of imprisonment only by Russia. Russia has never been known as a 'land of the free' and perhaps it is less surprising there. It is to the Russian system of imprisonment that we turn in the next chapter.

4. The New Gulag: Russia

I have to confess that sometimes official reports on prisoners' deaths do not convey the real facts. In reality, prisoners die from overcrowding, lack of oxygen and poor prison conditions . . . Cases of death from lack of oxygen took place in almost all large pre-trial detention centres in Russia. The critical situation in SIZOs [pre-trial prisons] is deteriorating day by day: the prison population grows on average by 3500 to 4000 inmates a month.

General Yuri Ivanovich Kalinin, then head of the Penitentiary Department of the Russian Ministry of the Interior, speaking to a committee of the Russian parliament in 1994[1]

According to the available figures, Russia has a greater proportion of its citizens in prison than the United States. This may not cause much surprise. In many ways Russia and its history seem interwoven with exile, imprisonment, forced labour and suffering.

Russian literature tells us much about the place of prison in Russian life. From Tolstoy's *Resurrection* and Dostoevsky's *The House of the Dead* to Solzhenitsyn's *One Day in the Life of Ivan Denisovich*, imprisonment and the long journey to exile or hard labour in Siberia have formed a central theme in the Russian experience. Millions of Russians experienced prison during Stalin's purges. Millions perished. Such a legacy is not easy to come to terms with.

It might be thought that the end of communism and the fall of the Soviet empire would have meant the end of the Russian gulag. However, it has proved very difficult to bring about a revolution in this aspect of Russian life. In 1996 Russian prisoners were still dying, not in the salt mines or from shooting by prison guards but from lack of oxygen, TB and lack of food. TB is rampant in Russian prisons. The rate is forty times higher than in the general population and in July 1995 there were 45,300 prisoners in special tuberculosis units and many others with the illness in ordinary prisons and labour camps. The appalling conditions affect staff as well as prisoners.

In 1995, forty-one prison workers in Russia are known to have committed suicide. Prison numbers are high and growing. The prison population halved between 1986 and 1989 because of a relaxation of prison policies, a lower crime rate and an amnesty granted to certain prisoners in 1987, but since then the rate has been moving inexorably upwards.[2] Latest figures give the number of prisoners as over one million.[3]

Are the Russians going to be able to find a way to escape this aspect of their history? How did the 'gulag archipelago' develop into the monster it is today?

In his great penal reform novel, *Resurrection*, Tolstoy, through the story of a nobleman driven by guilt to follow to Siberia the woman he has ruined, describes every stage of the penal process. It begins in the filthy provincial remand prison in St Petersburg, where disease and misery flourished.

Once the trial processes have been completed and sentence confirmed, the convicts leave the remand prisons for the long journey to Siberia. In a section that the tsarist censors originally excised from the novel, Tolstoy describes vividly the great exodus. The prisoners were counted and then counted again. They stood for many hours in the boiling heat, their ankle chains clanking until at last they were ordered to start walking to the train that was to take them part of the three thousand mile journey. Only the very infirm, pregnant women and those with children were allowed to travel in a cart. Some, physically weakened by their imprisonment, collapsed during the walk and died on the road. The trains were overcrowded, filthy and verminous. The last section of the journey was completed on foot with the prisoners wearing leg chains and the men, handcuffed in pairs, covering fifteen to twenty miles a day. A prisoner who had been carrying his little girl wrapped in a shawl since his wife had died of typhus earlier on the journey was beaten by the guards. The child was wrenched from him so that he too could be handcuffed.[4]

Two other great Russian writers, Dostoevsky and Solzhenitsyn, have both devoted whole novels to describing life in the camps. Dostoevsky's main character in *The House of the Dead*, Aleksandr Petrovich, spent ten years in a prison camp in Siberia for murdering his wife, and the book consists entirely of his descriptions of life in the prison and relationships with the other prisoners. He describes his arrival at the prison fortress, a large enclosure containing several buildings. Some of these buildings are the barracks where the prisoners live. One is the kitchen; another is the storehouse and the stables. The middle of the courtyard is a big square where the prisoners line up to be counted, at least three times a day and sometimes much more often. At night they are locked into the barracks.

Throughout their imprisonment, at all times, the prisoners wear on their legs fetters weighing from eight to twelve pounds. Aleksandr Petrovich was particularly puzzled by one fact. The fetters were

> never removed from a convict, whatever illness he may be suffering from ... it never struck one of the doctors even to petition the authorities that a patient seriously ill, especially in consumption, might have his fetters removed.[5]

He describes a prisoner dying in the prison hospital:

> It was terrible to see that long, long body, the arms and legs wasted to the bone, the sunken belly, the strained chest, the ribs standing out like a skeleton's. Nothing remained on his body but a wooden cross and a little bag with a relic in it, and his fetters.[6]

Solzhenitsyn's hero, Ivan Denisovich, also served a sentence of ten years. He describes the minutiae of a day in the life of the Siberian prison camp, the layers of clothes and rags the prisoners put on, expertly trying to trap a little warmth as they march off to work in temperatures of $-27°C$, the clustering round the camp thermometer, kept in a sheltered place, to see if by any chance it has breached the low of $-41°C$ when work is stopped and the prisoners may stay in the barracks; he also describes the dominance of food in all thoughts, dealings and relationships, the eking out of a chunk of bread and the use of the crust as a spoon to wipe clean a bowl of porridge.[7] A century separated the experiences of Aleksandr Petrovich and Ivan Denisovich. There had been some changes, but the basic principles of the system of imprisonment remained the same.

It is a very different tradition of imprisonment from that described in Chapters 2 and 3 of this book, the tradition that emerged from Western Europe and America in the eighteenth century. The Russian system had its basis in banishment and labour. After they had been sentenced, prisoners would be sent to serve their sentence many thousands of miles from their homes. Sometimes they were never to return. Instead they settled as ex-convicts in Siberian villages.

The basis of the prison regime was straightforward. There were no philosophical subtleties about what method was most likely to touch the prisoner's soul and bring about reform. There were no disagreements about the rehabilitative merits of solitary confinement versus silence. Prisoners were expected to work. They were organized in divisions for the purpose of work. Certain prisoners acted as work and division leaders of groups of other prisoners. Meddling with the prisoner's psyche or personality had no part in the regime.

This tradition is so markedly different that visitors from Russia coming to see prisons in the West, whilst impressed by the physical conditions and the educational opportunities offered to prisoners, are not convinced that the system is humane. The single cells, with spyholes in the doors, or the staff watching prisoners' movements on video cameras, or the prison in Washington, D C where the prisoners' dormitory has one wall made of glass, seem like an invasion of privacy that could be more oppressive than the work regime of the Russian system. Ex-prisoner and human rights activist Valery Abramkin from the Moscow Center for Prison Reform visited prisons in Canada, the United States and England. He was struck by the twenty-four-hour surveillance of prisoners by guards. 'One feels there like a fish in an aquarium. I'd rather do time in one of our prison camps.'[8]

In the Western tradition the big prisons were in the towns so that the citizens would see the imposing, fearsome portals and be filled with such dread that any temptation to crime would be resisted. In the Eastern tradition prisoners were exiled far from the main centres of population. They were sent to the places where the minerals – uranium, gold and diamonds – needed to be dug out of the ground, to the frozen north where the dams and railways had to be built (the railway from Baikal in Siberia to Amur in the far east was built by prisoners). They worked in the factories with the dangerous chemicals.

The discussion about the costliness of imprisonment and the effects it has on public expenditure would until recently have been unintelligible to a Russian official or minister with responsibility for prisons. Prisons did not *cost* money. They *made* money. Forced labour in the prison camps produced every sort of industrial product: machine tools, pumps, clothes, airline seats for the airline Aeroflot, kitchen equipment, office furniture. In one of the Ministry of the Interior buildings in Moscow was an enormous exhibition hall, on several floors, where prospective buyers would come to see the goods made in the prison camps and Ministry of the Interior salespersons would show them round.

In the Russian tradition the attitudes of the public to prisoners were also different from those in the West. In *The House of the Dead* Aleksandr Petrovich comments on a feature also described by Tolstoy, the giving of alms. At religious festivals the local people would come to the prison gates and give food and money to the prisoners. Tolstoy describes in *Resurrection* how, as the prisoners *en route* to Siberia trudged on foot from the place where the railway line ended to their final destination, alms were brought to them at their stopping places.

This was the system that became Stalin's gulag. It was already there, easy to expand to cope with the millions swept up in the Stalinist terror. People were sent to places like Vorkuta, beyond the Arctic Circle, where coal was discovered in the 1920s and where hundreds of thousands of people died. Most of them died building the railway for the coal to be transported out. According to the Polish writer Ryszard Kapuściński, every now and then, along this railway line little wooden boards are to be found. The boards note the number of people buried in each place. The figure 81 indicates the burial place of a thousand people. The camp book-keepers kept careful accounts of the number of people who died so that they could reduce proportionately the amount of bread rations available.[9]

Even worse was Magadan, capital of the area in the north-east of Siberia called Kolyma. For twenty-five years prisoners were sent from all over Russia to this desolate place to work in the mines. Three million people died there. They arrived by ship from Vladivostok and those who had survived the voyage walked down the gangplanks to the shore. According to Kapuściński,

> The first impression, noted in dozens of memoirs: From here I will not return. They were ordered into columns. Then the counting of the prisoners began. Many of the guards were illiterates, and counting large numbers caused them great difficulties. The roll-call lasted for hours. The half-naked deportees stood motionless in a blizzard, lashed by the gales. Finally the escorts delivered their routine admonition: A step to the left or a step to the right is considered to be an escape attempt – we shoot without warning![10]

After Stalin's death the oppressive penal system stayed in place although the numbers sent to the camps declined. Yet even with the decline it is still the case that since the early sixties, according to the Moscow Center for Prison Reform, 25 million people have been through the prison camps and jails, what the Russians call 'the Zone'. Maybe altogether as many as 50 million people passed through the gulag. In a society where so many people have been affected, where few families have remained untouched by the experience, the suffering and the injustice, imprisonment has a different meaning. Everyone would recognize the songs that have come from the labour camps and encapsulate the common experiences of millions of people.

Song written by singer and songwriter Gennady Molchanov, who spent fifteen years in Soviet prisons

Camp 1970

The loudspeaker crackles 'Lights out',
But sleep will not come to the barracks till midnight:
Someone's reading love poems aloud
While another knits socks for the winter blight.
Whether guilty or blameless of sin –
We all serve our penalty equal.
And above the overall din,
Comes the sound of the guitar and soft singing.

In the corner a candle is smoking:
Here they gamble for money on fate;
And behind the stool – tea is boiling.
Tea helps us to build and to live.
A crash resounds from the mess-room:
Looks like a quarrel brewing in the kitchen . . .
And above the general din,
Comes the sound of guitar and singing.

Behind the latrines I hear voices;
They're kicking someone to death;
While behind the bath-house . . . I'll omit
What occurs nightly down there.
And the warders are to stay awake
Till dawnbreak do they drone.
And above the resonant hum
You hear the prison guitar's free tone.

Darkness covers the light-life discreet;
By day we build communism . . .
And I scrawl my letter with speed,
Holding trifles of life in derision.
Whether guilty or blameless of sin –
We'll all serve our penalty equal.
And above the overall din
Comes the faint sound of guitar and singing.

From Gulag Tango, *1992*[11]

Valery Abramkin has told of his experiences in prison in the early 80s where he was sent for being involved in publishing an unofficial magazine.

> During my six years in Soviet prisons, I lived through many horrors. I saw people suspended on iron hooks stuck under their ribs. I watched German shepherds eat living human flesh. I sat half-naked in a cell where the temperature never rose above freezing. In burning summer I rode with thirty prisoners in a railway car built for six.[12]

On one occasion he was put in the punishment cell.

> I got there for having 'a disorderly bedside-table', that is, for keeping
> more books than a convict is allowed to have. It is a cell of six
> square metres. The walls are covered with iron. You are in constant
> semi-darkness, the window is firmly 'curtained-off' with a row of
> railings and a steel sheet with holes. There is a dim electric lightbulb
> behind the railing. There are eight people in the cell.[13]

CENTRAL EUROPE

Although the Russian prison system is unique and many features of
it relate to the size of Russia and to Russian traditions, the Russian
concept of imprisonment was imposed on the Central European
countries in the Soviet bloc. In the 1970s and 80s Poland, for instance,
had the largest prison system in Europe, apart from the USSR, with
an average 100,000 prisoners held in 209 prisons. By the early 80s
one out of every eight adults had been in prison at some time.[14]

The Director-General of the prison service in the Czech Republic
until 1995, Zdeněk Karabec, appointed since the coming of democracy, describes the system through the eyes of someone from a
country with a different tradition:

> In every former communist and socialist country prisoners were used
> as cheap labour. The planned economy depended on their labour.
> They were given work which honest citizens refused because health
> and safety conditions were so bad. Prisons had the appearance of
> concentration camps.[15]

The ideology behind the Soviet system is described by Pavel
Moczydlowski, a former sociology professor who went on to become
Director-General of the Polish prison system. Crime was seen as the
product of inequality in capitalist systems. Under communism it
would wither away. At first, therefore, the continuation of crime
was regarded as a leftover from the previous systems that would
eventually dwindle and die. But, in fact, it seemed to increase. Thus
an awkward question needed an answer. Why was there still crime
when social inequality had in theory been abolished? The answer
was found. Offenders were not just thieves or burglars. They were

really trying to reintroduce the capitalist system. The act of stealing was 'illicit privatization' and so it was a political act.[16] The offender was a class enemy and an opponent of the system, a counter-revolutionary. So the punishments were very severe. For stealing a chicken the penalty could be a prison term of five or six years.

There was another reason why the prison terms needed to be long. Since offenders were class enemies, something had to be done about them. They had to change into proper communist citizens. The system required a process of re-education. From the prisoner's point of view the best way of showing that one had been re-educated was to become an informer. 'Prisons became the hotbed of agents of the criminal and political police,' says Pavel Moczydlowski.[17]

The way in which the prisoners were treated reflected the view of them as enemies. According to Pavel Moczydlowski, 'the perfect specimen was an individual who no longer defended himself, a broken and defeated person ready to obey any order'. So

> the staff were equipped with machine-guns, clubs, gas, dogs, hand-cuffs, etc. to make them more powerful. Barbed wire, walls, bars and other similar elements of architecture supplemented the staff's special equipment. The staff were militarized for the maximum efficiency of their work.[18]

THE PROBLEMS OF THE RUSSIAN SYSTEM

The Russian prison system faces gigantic problems. It has the legacy of its past, the brutality and terror, the corruption and destruction of all human values. Varlam Shalamov, who spent twenty years in Russian prison camps, wrote,

> No one on earth should know camps. In the camp experience everything is negative – every single minute of it. A human being can only become the worse for it . . . Seeing the bottom of life is not the most dreadful part of it. What is most dreadful is when a man appropriates this bottom as his own, when the measure of his morality is borrowed from the camp experience, when the morality of criminals finds application in life.[19]

It has this legacy. And it has a shortage of all the material resources that it needs, as well as gross overcrowding because of the paralysis of the legal system and the stringent sentencing laws. There has been one great change. In the past all information about the gulag was a state secret. Now the system is open to the outside world. At the end of the 1980s *glasnost* began to affect the prison system, and academics, journalists and human rights activists were allowed in, to write about the system or even to make films about it. It soon emerged that the worst problems were in the pre-trial prisons, called SIZOs. When the UN Special Rapporteur on Torture, Professor Nigel Rodley from Essex University, visited Russia in July 1994 to establish whether the conditions in the pre-trial prisons could be regarded as torture he said after a visit to two such prisons in Moscow, 'The Special Rapporteur would need the poetic skills of a Dante or the artistic skills of a Bosch adequately to describe the infernal conditions he found in these cells.'[20]

One of these two prisons was Butyrka. Since it is in central Moscow, Butyrka prison is much visited and written about. It has a long history. It was built in 1771. Tolstoy collected his material for the novel *Resurrection* at Butyrka. Krushchev announced that he was going to close the Butyrka prison. But he did not implement the announcement. Instead a block of flats was built in front of it, so that it could no longer be seen from the street. KGB employees lived in the block of flats. The prison carried on its work behind it.[21]

The block of flats is still there, now rather desirable and occupied mostly by foreigners. The prison is also still there. In November 1992 it was visited by a delegation, including the present author, of participants in an international conference on prison reform in former totalitarian countries. The delegation heard that on the day of the visit it held 5200 prisoners, although built for 3500.[22] Of these, 450 were women. Four thousand five hundred of the prisoners were there awaiting trial. The cells, which would have been tightly packed with the forty prisoners they were built to hold, regularly held seventy or more. The prisoners could not all lie down at the same time and there were not enough bunks to go around, so prisoners took it in turns to sleep. Between the bunks was barely enough space to move. The cells were high-ceilinged and personal washing was draped on improvised washing lines above the bunks. At the end of the cell was a screened-off lavatory. Some cells had televisions. Washing facilities were minimal and when a cell door opened a wave of stinking air came out. Apparently the governor of the prison depended heavily on prisoner informants. Based on the information from these 'agents', about 200 prisoners had been identified as possible trouble-makers or escapers. They received particular supervision. There seemed to be no activities at all apart from watching television for those with access to a set. There were caged exercise yards on the roof, but with all the pressures on the basic running of the prison it was likely that the staff rarely had time to organize groups of prisoners to get up to the roof and down again.

The staff were pleasant, chatty, in despair about their lack of resources and very interested in how much prison officers were paid in England.[23]

Since then Butyrka prison has not improved. The Moscow Center for Prison Reform wrote in July 1994 to the Russian president, Boris Yeltsin, to describe a visit made to Butyrka by deputies from the Duma, the Russian parliament.

> Cells that under the law can house 28 people (2.5 sq. metres per person), now hold 90–100–110 prisoners. In order to receive a complaint from a prisoner, the deputies had to push through the crowd same as that in the bus in rush hours. After five minutes of staying in such a cell visitors get faint, but people spend years there: 3–5 years of pre-trial detention is not so rare. Prisoners have to sleep in three shifts. In the daytime there is no space to sit – most of the time people have to stand. Everybody scratch himself: some do it because of mange, some – because of louses, some – because of psychiatric disturbances. Those who spend in these conditions 5–6 months get covered with bleeding sores. There is a lack of basic medicines, for example, for those for mange (the budget money is not allocated). Staff is insufficient because of low salaries that are given with the delay. It should be noted that in 1938, under Stalin's rule, the number of prisoners in these cells did not exceed 80 people, the situation with food and medicines was not comparable with the present one.[24]

In the press release announcing the visit to Butyrka, the governor, Colonel Gennadi Nikolayevich Oreshkin, was quoted as saying,

'Every day I plead with God for bad weather, because when it is too hot, epidemics and deaths are unavoidable.'

Keeping the prisoners fed from day to day was a pressing problem. According to the press release, Moscow pre-trial prisons owed 400 million roubles to the bakeries and food storehouses that supplied them. Colonel Oreshkin said, 'Every day I swear at the suppliers over the phone. And when all the excuses have been exhausted I tell them calmly that if they don't deliver us the bread . . . I will inform the Moscow thieves of their address.'

During a five-day period when there was no bread in Butyrka, the jail was supplied by 'thieves in law' – bosses of the criminal world; 'the women were given condensed milk and the men ate canned meat'.[25]

Colonel Oreshkin told the *Washington Post* that his prison was so overcrowded that prisoners routinely collapse from lack of oxygen or swollen legs. Prisoners look forward to interrogation sessions because they can catch a few minutes' sleep. Tuberculosis is rife.[26]

In 1995 Colonel Oreshkin was moved from his post as governor of Butyrka prison. Perhaps he was too outspoken.

Butyrka has not changed much. In 1918, according to Solzhenitsyn, it was so overcrowded that they set up a cell for seventy women in the laundry. In 1938, 140 prisoners were crammed into a Butyrka cell for twenty-five and those newly arrested waited for several days on the stairs until a space was available in a cell.[27] When Solzhenitsyn himself was in Butyrka in 1946, eighty people were in cells built for twenty-five.[28]

The other prison visited by the UN Special Rapporteur was Matrosskaya Tishina. In October 1995 there were 460 inmates in the TB block of the Matrosskaya Tishina. The block was designed for 110 prisoners.[29]

One remarkable feature of the ex-Soviet system is its monolithic character. The Soviet prison system was ruled from Moscow and uniformity was the outcome. When standing in the pre-trial prison in Moscow, the Butyrka, one could be standing in a similar prison in St Petersburg. In St Petersburg, in the infamous Kresty prison, the largest prison in Russia, holding about 8000 prisoners with room for 3500, conditions are described as even worse than in Butyrka.

In 1990 a *Sunday Times* journalist, Jack Chisholm, got permission to pose as a prisoner and spend some time in Kresty. He was shown to his cell, already holding nine men in a space fifteen foot long by nine foot wide, with two others resident but out at court. He describes the conditions:

> The cell was filthy, and the stench of men living like animals in a cage was overpowering. Some crowded on to the two three-tier wooden bunk beds that were pushed against the walls. The others had been issued with bedding . . . but there was no space to lie down to sleep . . . One prisoner said he slept with his head resting over the cell's toilet, a hole in the ground.[30]

The uniformity stretched right out to all parts of the Soviet empire. In Almaty (formerly called Alma Alta), in Kazakhstan, the pre-trial prison, when visited by the present author in 1993, was in very poor physical condition. The accommodation consisted of medium-sized rooms which held between fifteen and forty-nine prisoners. Prisoners left their cells only to go for exercise for one hour each day. Again, the exercise yards were on the roof. There were triple bunks, with virtually no space between them. Each room had a toilet. There was no indication of books or other activities in the room. The atmosphere when the room door was opened was quite overpowering and many of the prisoners were clothed only in underwear.[31]

It is the same if one goes in the other direction, west, to Estonia. In Tallinn the Prison Number One, according to journalist Roman Rollnick, who visited it in July 1993, is 'like a grim medieval fortress'. In cell no. 88, there were thirty-one men who had to share sixteen beds. It was so tiny that they 'could only stand in small groups at the end of the beds'. Those who broke the rules were locked into 'a stinking, freezing, dark concrete box too tiny to stand upright and too small to lie down in'.[32]

Pre-trial prisons hold about one-quarter of Russia's prisoners. The rest are not in prisons as they are known in the West, that is large buildings with cells and dormitories. They are in work camps. The camps, or labour colonies as they are called, also retain many of the features made familiar by the Russian prison writers. The economics of the labour camps are important. In the past the labour camps were hugely profitable. The central administration provided only the finance for the staff salaries. All the running costs were paid from the profits of the industrial activities. Now that the market for many of the products has disappeared the financial problems in many labour colonies are acute.

Labour camps are divided into five categories: general, for first offenders serving up to three years; reinforced, for first offenders serving longer than three years; strict, for those who have been in prison before; and special, for the particularly dangerous and those whose death sentences have been commuted to life imprisonment. The fifth category is colony settlements or open prisons where prisoners can be transferred after they have served at least one-third of their sentence.

Strict Regime Colony Number 2 near Ryazan, a provincial capital about 200 kilometres from Moscow, held, in October 1993, 1500 prisoners. They had all been to prison at least once before and their sentence lengths were from one to fifteen years. The prisoners were making agricultural machinery, and worked six days a week on two shifts of eight hours each. They were paid at the same rate as industrial labourers outside prison. The prisoners' living quarters consisted of a barracks made up of a number of dormitories with about 150 beds in each. Each dormitory had its own toilet facilities and a television room, which was open from 8 p.m. to 10 p.m. One member of the prison staff was on duty in each dormitory. Each barracks had its own yard surrounded by a fifteen-foot wire fence. This was the prisoners' area of movement. Prisoners refusing to work or breaking the rules were sent to the punishment block.

Prisoners were allowed four short visits a year from their families and friends lasting between two and four hours. The visits took place in cubicles and until recently the prisoner and the visitor were separated by glass but this has been removed. Prisoners were also eligible for two long visits of seventy-two hours each year. These took place in a suite of small flats within the prison. These private visits with families have long been a feature of the Russian prison system.[33]

Some efforts are certainly being made by the Russian authorities to change the prison system. A whole range of new measures has been brought in to try and humanize a very brutal regime. In 1988, dietary punishment, which meant prisoners in punishment cells were given a reduced normal diet one day and bread and water the next, was abolished.[34] In November 1991, a presidential decree abolished the requirement that prisoners had to pay half of the money they earned back to the prison as a contribution to the running costs of the prison system, although they are still required to work an eight-hour day, six days a week.

In June 1992 amendments and alterations to the regulations governing the treatment of convicted prisoners were brought in. Putting prisoners in strait-jackets was no longer allowed. Prisoners in special secure units and those awaiting sentence had to be given bedding and allowed daily exercise outside. Prisoners should not be kept in special units for longer than six months. Prisoners had the right to personal safety. This meant that if they feared they were under threat from other prisoners and were likely to be attacked and they asked to be put in a place of safety, the prison staff were required to take action and remove them from danger. Freedom of conscience and the right to participate in religious activities and have religious books were recognized. Adult women prisoners could wear their own clothes. Male prisoners were allowed to have beards and moustaches and no longer had to have their heads shaved. Prisoners were allowed to see a private doctor if they could pay. The restrictions on prisoners' correspondence were abolished. More family visits were allowed and some prisoners were allowed home. Prisoners could use telephones where these were available. They were given the right to receive parcels from the very beginning of their sentence and to receive more in the parcels. They were allowed to send letters to the prosecutor, the court and other supervisory agencies without them being stopped or read by the authorities. Neither visits, parcels nor the right to buy food from the prison shop could any longer be withheld as a punishment.

Moves were made to reduce the criticisms of the camp regime as forced labour. Minimum wages were guaranteed for prisoners who met the production quotas. Certain categories of prisoners – pregnant women, women with children under the age of three held with them in prison, certain disabled people, men over sixty and women over fifty-five – were not required to work. Prisoners became entitled to twelve working days' paid holiday and sometimes even were allowed to spend the holiday outside the camp. Time spent in prison could now count towards the calculation of pension rights.

And Russian prisoners also received their privatization vouchers like every other citizen.[35]

An attempt was being made to change the whole rationale of the system. No longer were prisoners to be seen as labour to be sent where labour was needed. Instead, according to General Yuri Ivanovich Kalinin, then head of the Russian penitentiary system,

> In future we plan to allocate prisoners according to their individual needs rather than by type and length of sentence. This will prevent the former practice of allocating prisoners across the entire country. This served largely to confirm them in their criminal ways, to make new contacts, to share criminal experiences and indeed to spread crime even more across the country. At the same time, it made it difficult for families and friends to visit and increased the likelihood that prisoners would attempt to escape.[36]

THE RUSSIAN INFLUENCE

The Russian Federation is but one of the countries of the former Soviet Union. But the gulag system was empire-wide. The remit of the Ministry of the Interior ran across all the republics and prisoners were sent where the labour camps were. Many were sent to Central Asian republics, which are now independent states. Kazakhstan had a particularly high proportion of labour colonies within its borders[37] and problems in the prisons of Kazakhstan are exceptionally grave. A 1996 report by Amnesty International alleged that 'a brutal regime prevails in the pre-trial and penitentiary systems in Kazakhstan including deliberate ill-treatment of prisoners and appalling conditions of detention which amount to ill-treatment'.[38]

There were about 94,000 people in prison in Kazakhstan and about 20,000 of these in pre-trial detention in 1996.[39] There are seventy-eight prisons and other penal establishments. A major problem was shortage of food. Prisoners died from malnutrition. The press reported a case of cannibalism where five starving prisoners had killed and eaten a cell-mate.[40] It was estimated that 10,000 prisoners were suffering from tuberculosis and alleged that infection spread rapidly because of overcrowding. Sometimes prisoners were put into a cell with prisoners seriously ill with tuberculosis in order to expose them to infection as a punishment.[41]

The numbers in prison rose from 363 per 100,000 in 1992 to 560 per 100,000 in 1995. In spite of an amnesty under which nearly 20,000 prisoners were released in June 1996, overcrowding was still serious.[42] Some prisoners were kept in cells eight metres by six metres with sixty other people, sleeping in three or four shifts. Prisoners had fleas and scabies and cells were infested with lice and cockroaches.[43]

Punishments were said to be very harsh. Prisoners at Arkalyk alleged they were kept in punishment cells in complete darkness.[44] A former prisoner described a punishment cell at a corrective labour colony that measured one metre by one metre where prisoners would be left in isolation, almost naked, for up to fifteen days.[45]

The Deputy Minister of Internal Affairs, Nikolay Vlasov, announced at a press conference in April 1996 a ten-year plan to raise the standards of Kazakhstan's prisons but noted that Kazakhstan faced the same problem as Russia – there was no money to put things right.[46]

In Uzbekistan the penitentiary system has remained basically unchanged since independence. Ex-prisoners reported that the prisons are very overcrowded.[47] Turkmenistan has similar problems. Amnesty International claimed that 'Overcrowded and unsanitary conditions are said to characterize the whole of the Turkmen prison system.'[48] Apparently the Turkmenistan government admitted in 1995 that prisoners suffocated in overcrowded cells without fresh air during the summer heat. It is also suggested that the conditions caused a riot at a prison in Ashgabat and a number of prisoners were killed. It has also been alleged that in early 1995 prisoners in the Lebap Region ate stray cats and dogs because of a lack of food.[49]

Similar problems beset the prisons in Mongolia. In 1996, 340 prisoners died in prison.[50] The problem of lack of food for Mongolian prisoners comes from the old Soviet-system law which required prisoners to work to earn the money needed for food, clothing, bedding and power and heating. However, in the new market economy work was not always available to prisoners. Apparently, 'Officials freely admitted to Amnesty International that the general standard of prison conditions is unacceptably low. There is over-crowding, a shortage of clothing and medical supplies and poor sanitation.' The head of the Corrective Labour Department told Amnesty officials that when prisoners arrived from pre-trial deten-tion they were already sick and malnourished. The First Deputy Minister of Justice confirmed that there had been cases of prisoners being deprived of food whilst under investigation to force them to confess. In the last nine months of 1994, 274 out of 700 remand prisoners detained at Gants Hudag prison were suffering from malnutrition and seven had died.[51]

In Belarus, too, the system has not changed very much. Prison population figures give a rate of 505 prisoners per 100,000 general population in 1995. The system is still run on military lines and closed to public scrutiny. However, prisoners are now allowed to write letters. They are not required to shave their heads and may have televisions, radios and watches in their cells.[52] The Ministry of the Interior press officer commented on the prison situation that 'The number of prisoners in the republic has reached the highest level dur-ing the last three decades . . . The situation in correctional labor insti-tutions can be described in one word, tense.'[53] According to the Belarus League for Human Rights, Belarussian prisoners have been sent to an area near Chernobyl, where the environment is so polluted with radiation that no free workers would agree to go there.[54]

Letters from Prisoners in Belarus

The Belarus League for Human Rights has published a collection of letters sent to the League by prisoners and their families. In the letters prisoners describe some of their experiences:

One cannot say that our living conditions are satisfactory, they are very poor. If a prisoner goes for a bath, he will get scabs there for sure. There are no appropriate drugs, no treatment is offered and one may say that people are really decomposing here.

Convicts with no money on their current account are forced to sell their blood to be processed for plasma, and this is a very important factor in our conditions. With this sum of money a convict would be able to buy two packs of Astra [a local brand of poor quality cigarettes].

There is a real mess and disorder in our canteen and there would be no wonder if infectious disease were to break out. Besides, the food stuffs which must be used to prepare food for the convicts are simply being stolen. It is common practice at our correctional institution and when during roll-call a convict falls down because of malnutrition, no one is surprised.

And again convicts must put their hands to the wall, standing with their legs apart, and correctional officers beat them over and over again. Sometimes the officers fail to give the 'right' blow, e.g. traces of the beating remain on the body. Just imagine how convicts suffer from direct blows to the kidneys, scrotum and other vital organs, standing with their legs apart. When you go through it even a baton would seem a prank, when jailers 'apply' batons to backs, legs and tendons swearing terribly.

Letters from Belarussian Prisons at the End of the XX Century, (1995), *published by the Belarus League for Human Rights, Minsk*

The obstacles in the way of prison reform in the former Soviet empire are formidable. Humanizing the prison law, allowing televisions, parcels, phone calls and unshaved heads is important but only a first step in changing the way prisons are run and prisoners are treated. The economic crisis, the low salaries of the prison staff, the small numbers of staff available to run the prisons, combined with the relaxation of the rules, can lead to a situation where the staff feel under threat and defenceless and resort to violence to keep order. The lack of resources for retraining many thousands of personnel used to a completely different way of thinking and working, the instability of the central government and the risk of right-wing nationalistic sentiment all bode ill for the valiant efforts of the penal reformers in the Russian penitentiary administration and outside.

Valery Abramkin has highlighted the dangers of the continued existence of such systems. He says,

> When I have an opportunity to deliver lectures in Western universities for students or experts, it is difficult to explain what the gulag is, because in the West there is a notion that the gulag is a great number of prison camps for political prisoners, for those who opposed the Bolshevik regime. In my opinion, it is a very naive notion about the gulag. Because in reality there were not many regime adversaries in Stalin's prison camps, you could count them with your fingers. But what is more important, is to speak about the gulag as symbol rather than the gulag as such, it is a terrible system of suppressing, manipulating people and transforming them into slaves. It is an ocean of deadly horror splashing out on ordinary people.

In Abramkin's view, reform of the gulags is not possible. The whole system must be abolished and imprisonment done another way.

> The success of democratic reform in Russia is impossible until the gulag system – which still preserves many features of the totalitarian state – is dismantled. If some new dictator comes to power in Russia, the present penal system is ready to work even more effectively than Stalin's did.[55]

5. Mind Reform? China and Japan

The first horror of the Huangpu detention centre was sleeping. Thirteen or fourteen prisoners were crowded into a cell about three square metres in area. In the daytime there was room to sit with our legs up, bodies touching. But at night we would be squeezed into two rows of straight bodies, with the rows head to head so as to fit more tightly together, like a row of frozen yellow fish. Even then there might not be room for everybody. In that case guards would beat the prisoners with bamboo truncheons and trample them with their boots to squeeze them into the line of sleepers.

In the winter, the prisoners could hardly breathe. In the summer it was worse. Each man wore only a pair of pants, but he was soaked with sweat. When we got up in the morning, the cement floor was covered with a pool of sweat half a centimetre deep and the prisoners' backsides were covered with swollen bedsores which hurt and formed scabs that bonded their pants to their bodies. As soon as you stood up to use the toilet the scabs would tear and your pants would be covered with blood.

A Hong Kong businessman imprisoned in Shanghai in 1986[1]

There is another gulag, less well known but equally threatening: the *laogai* of China. It is estimated that since 1949 more than 30 million people have disappeared in China's camps and prisons.[2] It could be said that the prison system in China is the ultimate in imprisonment, the worst of all prison worlds, a system where both the Eastern and the Western traditions merge. The cruelties of banishment to a forced labour camp are combined with the pressure on the personality and the mind to be remoulded and reformed. The purpose is clear. According to the Chinese authorities,

> People can be reformed. The great majority of criminals can also be reformed. Turning minuses into pluses and changing criminals into people who are useful to society are in conformity with the great Marxist ideal of liberating all of mankind.[3]

China too has its chroniclers of the prison experience, the writers who have managed to rise above their prison experience and turn it into great literature and a solemn warning. Zhang Xianliang was imprisoned in a labour reform camp in north-west China in 1958 for the crime of being a 'rightist', an 'enemy of the people'. He was twenty-one at the time. He spent the next twenty-two years of his life in prisons and labour camps. He began writing his diary in 1960 when he was in a labour reform farm. The farm had been established on land that every expert had said could not be cultivated since it consisted of white salt-flats. It had been turned into cultivable land but the work had cost innumerable lives.

The diary, *Grass Soup*, has echoes of *A Day in the Life of Ivan Denisovich*. It has an interesting history. Writing about the life in the camp was basically forbidden but Zhang Xianliang kept notes of the events of the day in a form that the authorities would not be able to object to if they were to discover them. They did discover them and in 1970 they were confiscated. When Zhang Xianliang was rehabilitated in 1980 the rule was that all the prison documents, such as records of performance, notes of self-criticism or statements by informers, should be destroyed. He managed to persuade the authorities that the diary should be kept and given to him. Using it as a basis he was able to delve into his memory and put the flesh on the bones of his cryptic notes.

The diary was written at the time of the great famine in China, when it is estimated that hunger killed about 30 million people. Life was at least as hard for the prisoners as for the rest of the population. For example, the entry for 14 July 1960 read, 'Morning dug up plants, afternoon picked through them.'[4]

The annotation for this entry describes how the troop leader took the group of convicts out to dig up grass. They were required to dig up enough grass to feed the entire camp. Therefore each prisoner had to dig up twenty-seven and a half pounds of grass. ' "If you don't make it, you're not going to eat!" The troop leader stood on a high point and yelled down at us. Then he found a dry, cool spot to lie down.'[5] The day ended well. Zhang Xianliang pulled up enough grass to get his bowl of grass soup. Also his diet was supplemented by some raw grass. As he says, 'A certain percentage of what I dug I ate.'[6]

The horrifying effects of the experience of the prison camps come over through the anecdotes. Zhang Xianliang tells of an incident that happened one afternoon when all the convicts were out cutting grass. On the top of the canal bank above where they were working appeared a young woman leading a small child. The two of them stopped to tidy themselves up. The woman rebraided her hair and shook the dust off the little girl's clothes. She had travelled hundreds of miles, by bus, train, road and rough country tracks, in some places carrying the little girl on her back. Eventually she had found the camp where her husband was imprisoned. She was carrying a small black and white bag. All the prisoners assumed it contained food. Who was the lucky one whose wife had brought him food? It was a very small bag and contained very little food, probably enough for one meal. To save that much the mother and daughter would have had to put aside grain from their own starvation rations 'kernel by kernel' for a year. Zhang Xianliang and the other convicts stopped work in anticipation of the moving scene that was to come of the lucky prisoner meeting his wife and child after a long separation. The prisoner's name was called and he walked towards his wife and child. However, instead of the moving scene, the loving embrace, he roughly snatched the bag from her hand and crawled up to the top of the canal bank clutching it.

> He threw himself down, in the full sun, and urgently ripped at the fabric. His two elbows were cocked outward, like a man pulling a bow, while his ten fingers violently pulled the bag apart. Then he began stuffing the things inside into his mouth.[7]

The woman did not follow him up the bank. She sat at the bottom, with her child in her arms, crying silently. The convicts went on with their work. Zhang Xianliang became absorbed in the difficult problem of how to carry some stolen sweet potatoes back to the barracks without being discovered when suddenly there was 'a piercing, gut-rending cry from above'.[8]

The wife had climbed the bank to talk to her husband once he had finished eating. She found that he had cut his wrists with his scythe and his blood was flowing and staining the water of the canal below bright red. She collapsed beside him. Eight convicts, four men and four women, were summoned to carry each of the bodies away.

Why did he do it? No one knew. Maybe it was out of shame for what he had done, maybe to free his wife from him so that she could disassociate herself from a 'bad element' and start a new life, maybe just because he wanted to die.

In one of Zhang Xianliang's earlier books, *Getting Used to Dying*, a particularly striking description is of the occasion when an important order came down from above. The relatives of those who had died in the camp between 1958 and 1960 were bringing a case before the Public Security Bureau in Beijing and, 'in order to meet their demands, the leadership decided to present each litigant with a bag of bones'. The prisoners who had survived were sent to the camp graveyard on bone-collecting expeditions. Never mind whose bones were dug up. ' "So long as they are human bones, they'll do fine," ' said the high official who had come to the camp to get the order carried out. ' "If you can't tell whose bones they are . . . how can they?" ' he asked.[9]

The work quota was ten complete skeletons. The troop leader shouted, ' "You're to get every bone in a skeleton. You're not to leave out as much as one toe. The whole thing gets dug up and put in the bag: whoever misses a bone pays with one of his own." '[10] The bones were to be put in plastic bags, a real luxury item that the prisoners rarely saw. The troop leader managed to steal two of these plastic bags and Zhang Xianliang stole one, which he secreted under his sleeping pad to keep out the damp and kept right up until his second release.

The task of digging up the bones turned out to be not too difficult.

> I gradually worked out a general procedure of bone packing: starting first with the skull, then the vertebrae, then the collarbone. I worked on through to the shoulder blade, the upper arm, the ribs, the breastbone, down to the toes, not missing a single crushed bone . . . Some of the corpses had been gnawed by wild animals and pecked by birds, so that the bones were scattered like a stack of rotten firewood that has tumbled down. We were too lazy to work on this kind of skeleton, and would use it only for spare parts when needed. If a relatively complete skeleton was lacking a toebone or a shinbone, we'd pick one up from somewhere else and toss it in.[11]

In 1993 Zhang Xianliang set up a trading company in Ningxia in the north-west of China, in the area where he had been imprisoned, to bring work to the local people and help them to take advantage of China's developing market economy.

Bao Ruo-Wang (Jean Pasqualini) was half Corsican and half Chinese. He was given twelve years' imprisonment for counter-revolutionary activity. He did not show enough signs of repentance so he was placed in solitary confinement. His hands were handcuffed behind his back and he was pushed into a room so small he could not stand or lie down, only sit or squat. The door had two holes, one for the guards to look through and one for the food spout at the bottom of the door. The cell contained a wooden bucket and an electric lightbulb – on permanently. He dozed through the first night. The next morning his handcuffs were moved to the front. Then a rusty can was thrown in his cell. He was told to hold the can under the spout. The food, a sort of cornmush, came through the hole in the door. It was so hot that he dropped the tin. The guard yelled at him, ' "That's wasting food: blood and sweat of the people. You can be severely punished for that." ' After eating, his hands were cuffed behind his back again. Then he had to urinate.

> But how? The only way to get it into the bucket . . . was to stick my foot in it and piss down my leg. There was no question of pulling my shorts down. And even if I managed that, how would I get them up again? I pissed down my leg.[12]

When the guard came for the handcuff-changing ritual, Bao Ruo-Wang said to him,

> 'I'm sorry . . . I wet my pants.'
> He looked at me as if I were a caterpillar or a toad.
> 'So what?'
> 'Can't I change them?'
> 'Change them! Do you know where you are?'[13]

Then there were the lice. 'I watched them grow fat. My skin teemed with them . . .'[14] After ten days he was dragged up, 'handcuffed, filthy and stinking',[15] for a public confession and soon afterwards his time in solitary ended.

A particularly courageous Chinese ex-prisoner who has written about his experiences is Hongda Harry Wu. Harry Wu got into trouble with the authorities whilst he was a student in Beijing and in 1960, without being formally charged or facing a court trial, he lost his liberty for an unspecified period. His imprisonment began in a detention centre where prisoners were held before allocation to labour camps. From the detention centre he was transferred to a steel factory in the windswept mountains in the far north. That prison needed no walls to keep the prisoners from escaping. The rocky mountain crags ensured that there was no way out.

From the steel factory Harry Wu was moved to the lowlands, to a prison farm. It was here, during the nationwide famine, that many prisoners died of starvation. After nine years at the farm he was transferred to a coal mine in Shanxi province. There his status changed. He became a 'resettlement prisoner'. Resettlement prisoners were allowed to sit together at meal times, talk amongst themselves and even mix socially with the women at the mine. They were allowed to visit the nearest village on their days off, write letters, ask for an annual trip home and for permission to marry. But they were not free to leave. In 1979, after nineteen years of imprisonment, Harry Wu was released. In *Bitter Winds* Harry Wu describes how he learnt to survive in the harsh world of the labour camps. When he arrived at the detention centre he was a young student from a comfortable background. One of his first experiences at the detention centre shocked him. All the prisoners were ordered to get into pairs, strip to their undershirts and search each other for lice. He had never seen a louse.

From a peasant imprisoned for stealing chickens, called Big Mouth Xing, he learnt the basic lessons of survival, which he describes in a way that echoes the thoughts of the Russian ex-prisoner Varlam Shalamov.

> I had learned how to steal, how to protect myself, and finally how to fight ... I had a new ethic of survival. In those surroundings I could not afford compassion or generosity or decency. No one would help me but myself.[16]

The struggle to find food was as important for Harry Wu as for Zhang Xianliang. He discovered how fruitful rats' nests can be, when the rat has stored them full of rice, corn and wheat. He learnt how to skin frogs and plunge them into thermos bottles full of boiling water to cook them. He saw good people unable to survive.

In 1985 he left China for the United States and gained US citizenship. Since then he has campaigned ceaselessly against the human rights abuses in the Chinese prison system. He pretended to be a businessman looking for goods to buy and went back to China to visit factories and production sites in order to establish that China was exporting products made by prisoner forced labour. Importing goods made by forced labour is illegal in both the United States and Britain, not because it is an abuse of human rights, but because it constitutes unfair competition. Speaking at a press conference in Geneva in 1995 he said,

> Last April I visited and filmed a forced labour camp in Sichuan province known as the Xinkang Asbestos Mine ... In that camp more than five thousand prisoners are forced to mine and process asbestos, many using their bare hands, all without protection ... No matter what their sentence, these prisoners have effectively been sentenced to death, a slow, lingering and painful death.[17]

He was arrested by the Chinese authorities during a visit to China in June 1995 and held for offences that could lead to the death penalty, before being released just before the wife of the US president, Hillary Clinton, was due to visit China to attend the Beijing Women's conference.

Confirmation of Harry Wu's position on forced labour comes from other sources. A report in the *Sunday Times* of 1 January 1995 begins:

> A gang of prisoners trundles handcarts across a winter landscape in northeast China. It is Christmas Day and inmates at the Beishu graphite mine are working to keep the wheels of British industry turning.

According to the *Sunday Times*, evidence has been obtained that the Beishu graphite mine has been selling graphite to British and German companies for years. Although the Chinese authorities deny that products are exported from its prison camps, the *Sunday Times* reporter who went there posing as a graphite buyer saw 'abundant' evidence of forced labour. Prisoners were marching in double file. Trucks with 'Beishu Prison' stencilled on the sides were parked inside the factory gates. Behind the plant was a walled compound with watchtowers and guards.[18]

NUMBERS IN THE *LAOGAI*

The facts about the numbers deprived of their liberty in China are difficult to come by and complicated by definitions. There are three forms of deprivation of liberty. People who have been convicted of a crime by a court are sentenced to reform through labour, called *laogai* in Chinese. They can be sent to prison but most convicted prisoners serve their sentence in a camp. According to Harry Wu only 13 per cent of convicted prisoners are in prisons.[19]

Opportunities to visit places of detention in China are not generally available but a number of foreign delegations have been able to visit the municipal prison in Shanghai. This prison was visited by a British human rights delegation led by Sir Geoffrey Howe, a former Foreign Secretary, in 1992. The delegation was given an escorted tour of the prison and there were no possibilities of private talks with prisoners, apart from a meeting with two British prisoners serving sentences for drug offences. The delegation asked about the destination of the clothes and shoes made in the prison and whether they were destined for export to foreign countries. They were told that 'there was a Ministry of Justice regulation that no prison-made goods could be exported. The prison governor said that he checked each order to confirm this.' But, as the Howe report notes, 'We were not, of course, able to confirm the accuracy of any of these statements.'[20]

In 1994 a British delegation on juvenile delinquency, of which the present author was a member, visited China. That delegation too visited Shanghai prison. Shanghai prison was built by the British and echoes classic British prisons in its architecture. The outer gate is very large and imposing and has a small wicket gate in it. The prison is right in the city of Shanghai and one part of it looks out on a busy street. The cells that face on to the street have their windows covered with wooden shutters so that some air can still circulate but no one can see in and the prisoners cannot see out.

The tour started in what was described as a training workshop. The machines were packed closely together and prisoners, with shaved heads, were grinding metal. They were greeted by the visitors but smiles did not come readily in reply.

After the workshop the visitors went upstairs to a living area, where, it was stated, the 'intellectuals' lived. These were prisoners who had completed their education before coming to prison and therefore were doing technological tasks, such as designing things and working with computers. One cell had been turned into a drawing office.

The design of the living area was one often seen in prisons in the United States. The cells have no access to direct natural light. They have barred cage-like doors and these lead on to a corridor. At the other side of the corridor the natural light comes in from the outside world. The corridor was wide and was not, as it would be in England, filled with pool and table-tennis tables but with large desks where prisoners sat working at books and designs. The cells, shared by two prisoners, were about five feet wide, eight feet deep and about ten feet high. The two prisoners slept on a wooden floor on matting with a blanket as covering. In China, south of the Yangtze River, there is traditionally no heating, so in Shanghai in winter it can be quite cold. The delegation was told that the prisoners are locked in from 8.30 p.m. until 5.30 a.m. Since they have no access to lavatories they are given a slop bucket for the night. They wear blue cotton uniform suits with a distinctive convict-type stripe down each trouser leg and across the chest and the back. In the presence of the delegation they did not speak to each other and stood to attention unless they were working.

The delegation also visited what is known in British prisons as the centre, the circular area in the middle of a prison from which all the wings radiate. The wings were several storeys high. As in Britain, netting was stretched across the centre on each landing, presumably to stop prisoners either committing suicide by throwing themselves off the landings or throwing objects down from their landings. On the ground floor one of the wings had been turned into an art gallery which the delegation visited. The loud whirr of machinery could be heard and it turned out that the other floors were a factory. However, the delegation was assured that none of the products made there were for export.

Following the tour the delegation was led into a concert hall for a performance by a prison band that is accustomed to performing for foreign visitors. The compère who introduced the acts spoke good English. The prisoners in the band had longer hair than those in the workshops and were wearing smarter versions of the prison uniforms than the other prisoners. The performers consisted of a brass band, which played Western and traditional Chinese music, a tenor who sang 'Sole Mio', and a flute soloist. The final turn was a mixed choir of men and women singing 'Gaudeamus Igitur'.

The prison governor explained the rules. Prisoners could write one letter a month. They could receive as many as they liked. All incoming and outgoing mail was read. The reason for reading the mail was to see if prisoners were getting any bad news from home and to prepare them for it, the governor said. They were allowed one visit per month and three to five direct family members could visit. The minimum length of the visit was thirty minutes.

Prisoners were graded into three grades, A, B and C. They all start at Grade C when they enter and every day they get a mark. The marks accumulate. On average it takes six months of reasonably good behaviour to get from grade C to grade A. The basis of getting the marks is laid down. They are not just awarded on the whim or personal likings of the prison staff. Of the 3000 prisoners currently detained in Shanghai prison 1200 were in Grade A.

The type of family visit they get depends on their grade. Grade A prisoners can have lunch with their family after the visit and can get weekend leave for important festivals, which means about four times a year. Grade B and C prisoners can go home on compassionate leave for reasons such as funerals but a prison officer goes with them.

As in Russia, informers were an integral part of the system. The governor informed the delegation that there were the 'public informers', that is the prisoners who wear red bands to show they are trusted by the prison administration and have various roles in supervising other prisoners. Everyone knew they were informers.

However, since it was impossible, said the governor, for the prison guards to see everything, there were also secret informers. Their identity really was secret, so not one of them had ever been knifed in the back by the other prisoners. They were, the governor felt, very necessary to keep order.

Should it be necessary to subdue prisoners, tear gas and electric probes (batons that carry an electric shock) are used. The punishments the governor can give are confinement and bad marks. The marks count towards the grading and are therefore very important. Confinement can be imposed for up to fifteen days. Prisoners in confinement get the same food as the other prisoners but they cannot watch television and they cannot have visits from their families. According to the governor there was no homosexual activity in prison because the prisoners are supervised at night every ten minutes by staff and by trusted prisoners.[21]

Shanghai prison seemed to be the favoured venue for foreign visitors to China interested in penal matters. Sue Howell, the American woman who accompanied Harry Wu on his ill-fated trip to China in 1995, had studied in Shanghai in 1994. She too had been taken on a tour of Shanghai prison. 'They showed us paintings of happy prisoners and essays by happy prisoners . . . They even had prisoners singing and dancing,' she said.[22]

Another form of deprivation of liberty in the Chinese penal system is re-education through labour. This is imposed by the authorities without any formal legal process and is called *laojiao* in Chinese. It is imposed on people committing offences not deemed serious enough to be brought to court and also those who refuse to work, behave disruptively or 'obstruct public officials from performing their duties'.[23] The length of time people spend in the camps undergoing re-education through labour is usually from one to three years but can be extended to four. Those undergoing the penalty are often placed in the same camp as sentenced prisoners but sometimes in different work teams and under different rules. The figures given to the human rights delegation led by Sir Geoffrey Howe were that in 1992, 160,000 people were undergoing re-education through labour at that time. Exactly the same figure was given to the delegation on juvenile delinquency visiting China in 1994.

The third form of deprivation of liberty is forced job placement. After leaving the labour camp, prisoners are not necessarily free to return to their former lives or to outside society. They may be required to stay and work in a prison factory or farm.

Also there are many millions in pre-trial detention and police lock-ups. Local authorities can hold anyone thought to be a nuisance in some way in a detention centre under the 'shelter and investigation' regulations.

The exact number of people in China undergoing some form of deprivation of liberty is therefore hard to determine. Many different estimates are made. According to Harry Wu, there are between four and six million in reform through labour,[24] three to five million undergoing re-education through labour[25] and between eight and ten million undergoing forced job placement.[26] The Chinese authorities, in a submission to the United Nations Committee Against Torture made in January 1992, state that

> China currently has 684 prisons, including the reform-through-labour camps and the 37 re-education centres for juvenile offenders. The number of prisoners is 1,206,795, i.e. 1 prisoner per 1000 inhabitants.[27]

Later figures are quoted in *The Times* in January 1995. According to a leading prison official in the Ministry of Justice, 1,285,000 people were imprisoned in China's 690 prisons, including 27,000 women and 10,000 people under eighteen. Of these just under 3000 were what China calls 'counter-revolutionaries' and others call political prisoners.[28]

It is difficult to reconcile these very different pieces of information and reach an informed conclusion. Certainly with the opening-up of the Russian system and the efforts to reform it, the Chinese *laogai* is the last great secretive gulag.

IMPRISONMENT IN JAPAN

The Chinese system is the extreme end of a tradition of imprisonment that seems to have its roots not just in communism and oppression but in an Eastern tradition. Prisons in Japan have many of the same features. In March 1994 there were 45,000 prisoners in the fifty-nine

Japanese prisons, of whom 37,000 were sentenced and 1512 were women. With space for 64,000, Japanese prisons are not, therefore, overcrowded.[29]

Fuchu is an attractive town of 200,000 inhabitants on the outskirts of Tokyo. The prison at Fuchu is the largest in the country, with a capacity for 2598 prisoners. On the day the present author visited in February 1996 it held 2206. They were classified as recidivists serving less than eight years. The prison was surrounded by a high grey wall and the side of the wall facing an area of private housing had been painted with a pale blue sky and green trees, in a not very successful attempt to disguise its function. The prison held 488 foreign prisoners from forty-five countries and speaking twenty-eight languages. The cell block holding the foreign prisoners, as with every other part of the prison, was spotlessly clean. The cell blocks were three storeys high with the cells opening off both sides of a long corridor. Each cell held one prisoner. The foreign prisoners had Western-style beds. Each cell had a toilet which faced the door and was unscreened. There was a small table and a television set. The windows were large and gave excellent light to the cells. There was no heating in the accommodation block. The light switch was controlled from outside as were the radio and TV. The television programmes are controlled by the prison. Apparently the prisoners are allowed to watch sport and entertainment programmes but not the news. Newspapers can be provided but they are checked beforehand for matters 'detrimental to security', which are cut out before the prisoners see them.

The Japanese prisoners lived in group rooms holding up to six people. The rooms were large and set out with *tatami* mats. Kit was laid out with mathematical precision. Each prisoner had a small storage area above his bed. There was a separate toilet area. The large windows gave generous light. All the living areas were intensely cold. There was no heating.

There was one large yard about the size of a football pitch where prisoners apparently exercised each day. There was also a large auditorium where the prisoners were entertained from time to time by well-known artists.

There were five small visiting boxes for the 2200 prisoners, which indicated that very few received visits from their friends and families. The room was divided into two by a large double skin of plastic glass. A small circle was pierced with holes to allow the prisoners to talk with their visitors. Up to three visitors could sit on one side of the glass. On the prison side there were two chairs set closely together, one for the prisoner and one for the guard. Children were allowed to visit.

The prison has an extensive industrial complex with a series of large workshops on two levels. They included facilities for shoemaking, woodwork, bookbinding, printing and textiles. Each workshop had upwards of fifty prisoners with an average of two instructors and two guards. The prisoners were deep in concentration on what they were doing. Each stood or sat at his work place with his head bowed over his work. No eye was raised as the visitors passed, neither did the prisoners look at each other. There was a deathly hush throughout the whole place except for noise from the machines. Apparently the prisoners were allowed to talk, but only during the morning and afternoon breaks and at lunch time.[30]

Pre-trial prisoners are held in detention centres. The Tokyo Detention House is the largest pre-trial prison in Japan and holds 2050 prisoners, looked after by 538 staff. It has room for 2452 prisoners so, like other Japanese prisons, it has spare capacity. During the tour, whenever the group of visitors passed any prisoners, they immediately turned their faces to the wall until the party had passed.

Many prisoners lived in single cells each with a large window giving plenty of open light. There was an unscreened toilet in each cell and as the visitors walked by and peered in without warning the prisoners could easily have been using them at the time. The cell floor was covered in *tatami* mats and there was a small table. Prisoners were in each cell, usually sitting on the floor at the small table, reading or writing. All their bedding was folded up in exactly the same way. There was no heating in the unit and, given the time of year, it was bitterly cold. Some prisoners, all of whom wore their own clothes, were clearly shivering. They spent at least twenty-three and a half hours each day in the cell. There were a number of single exercise pens where prisoners walked on their own for at most thirty minutes each day. Prisoners were not allowed to talk to each other and, although side by side in cells, were in effect in isolation.[31]

The Japan Federation of Bar Associations and the Centre for Prisoners' Rights in Tokyo have campaigned tirelessly against prison conditions in Japan. In 1992 the Federation produced a booklet on the human rights situation in Japanese prisons which aimed to 'contribute to greater attention by the world to the many affronts to human rights and human decency contained in our country's system of penal detention'.[32]

According to their pamphlet, prisons in Japan are governed by a law of 1908 which sets out the basis for the authority of prison staff but contains no provisions for the protection of the rights of prisoners. Attempts to introduce a new and updated prison law have so far been unsuccessful.[33] Much is therefore left to the discretion of prison directors. However, typical convicted prisoners in Japan could undergo any of the following experiences. They could have a strip-search on arriving at the prison which includes inserting a glass rod into the anus. Every morning they can expect a cell search and whilst it is going on they must stay motionless in the cell in the *seiza* position, a formal position where they have to sit on their heels. After a while it causes numbness. They can expect to be searched on the way to and back from work and this involves a strip-search that Japanese prisoners apparently call the 'can-can' because they have to stand completely naked, raise their arms above their head and alternately raise each leg for the guard's inspection.

They might be forbidden to wipe away the sweat from their faces except at specified times. They must all wear grey cotton clothing issued by the prison and often the clothes are old, or torn or do not fit.

Every day before work begins they might have to shout the 'Five Principles' in unison. These are: always be honest, sincerely repent, always be polite, keep a helpful attitude, be thankful. Every prison has its own set of rules which can prohibit anything from suicide, running, writing on walls or watching others play the game *go*. All prisons specify precisely where one's toothbrush, soap and cup must be placed.

As in China, a system of gradings operates. Newly sentenced

prisoners start at Grade 4 and are promoted according to staff views on their behaviour and attitude. As they progress up the grades their entitlement to buying items, visits and sending and receiving letters increases. Grade 4 prisoners can write one letter a month and Grade 1 prisoners one letter a day. New Year greeting cards may only be sent to approved people and prisoners cannot receive cards from unauthorized people. All male prisoners, except those in Grade 1 and those shortly to be released, have their heads shaved.

All letters are censored.[34] In 1985 officials at Tokyo detention centre censored a letter from a woman prisoner to her lawyer about her life there because 'it might disturb the order of the detention centre and interfere greatly with its operations'.[35] In 1991 the Tokyo district court ruled that the censorship was illegal and she was awarded compensation. Prisoners are allowed three books at a time as well as up to seven books needed for studying.[36]

Much of the attention focused on abuses in Japan's prisons has related to the punishments given for offences against discipline. The number of prisoners punished each year is high. The most common penalty is disciplinary confinement. According to the Bar Federation this means that the prisoner 'is required to sit all day long in a designated place within his cell. All reading material is removed from the cell.'[37] Protective cells intended for prisoners needing to be restrained are also used as punishment. Prisoners in the protective cell are often bound with metal or leather restraints. They then have to eat and carry out their natural functions without the use of their arms.[38]

The system of pre-trial detention has been widely criticized. After being arrested, Japanese suspects are usually kept in police detention for up to twenty-three days where they are interrogated to obtain a confession. They have access to a lawyer only after indictment, when they have been transferred from the police station to a detention centre. They stay in the detention centre until they are sentenced, and then they are transferred to a prison.[39]

Human Rights Watch visited Japan in July 1994. The most striking aspect of Japanese prison life, they found, is the restrictive and repressive style of the prison regime. The prison rules regulate almost every aspect of a prisoner's daily life. They cover where to put every object in the cell and how to put it in its place. They require any writing to be done in a special notebook with numbered pages that is regularly inspected. During the cell inspection, which happens every day, the rules require of the prisoners that they should arrange their clothing and sit quietly in a kneeling position facing the door. Until all the cells have been inspected and the order to relax is given, prisoners must not converse, leave their seat or read. They must continue to sit in the kneeling position and wait.[40] Once the lights are out they must not read, talk or stand up and walk about the room. They must not cover their face with a blanket or futon whilst sleeping even though there is a dim light on in the cell day and night. They must not use the blanket as a sheet or wrap the blanket or sheet around their waists.[41]

Contact with the outside world is severely restricted.[42] In detention centres prisoners can have at least one and sometimes three visits a day but all visits are through a partition with no physical contact and there is always a prison officer present, taking notes of the conversation. Sentenced prisoners can only be visited by close relatives. At the beginning of the sentence, prisoners are allowed one fifteen-to-twenty-minute visit a month. As they work up the grade system more visits are allowed. Nearly all visits are through partitions and monitored by a prison officer who takes notes.[43] All letters in and out are read by staff and may be censored.[44] There is no access to telephones.[45]

Human Rights Watch was particularly concerned about the use of solitary confinement. It is the most frequently used punishment and is imposed for two months at a time. It involves no contacts with the outside world, no reading and no exercise.[46] According to the report, 'using the toilet is allowed only at specified times and throughout the day the prisoner is required to sit motionless in a prescribed position'.[47]

In 1996 an American prisoner, Kevin Neal Mara, who was serving four and a half years in Fuchu prison for marijuana possession, sued the Japanese government for compensation for ill-treatment he alleged he suffered in prison. Apparently he was severely punished for offences such as opening his eyes when his name was called before a meal in violation of the rule requiring prisoners to keep their eyes shut until everyone is seated in the dining hall. He was given ten days in segregation. He was given five days in segregation for wetting his hair to straighten it, which was interpreted as a violation of the prison rule barring hair washing. He was put in a protective cell for two days and had to wear a leather belt with handcuffs that held his left arm in front of him and his right hand behind him. He had to wear trousers with a slit in the crotch to use the toilet without using his hands.[48]

The attitude towards prisoners is summed up by the Bar Federation.

> The officials guarantee a certain standard of living for those who are obedient, but this is only viewed as a matter of grace on their part, not a matter of rights. Anyone who rebels against the order of the prison has all privileges removed and receives inhumane treatment. Japanese prison officials force upon the inmates the feudal ethos of shame and munificence.[49]

So approaches to imprisonment around the world are rather different. But not so the experiences of the people subjected to it. Prisoners all around the world have much in common. We now move on to consider who is in prison and what happens to them there.

PART TWO

A Deformed Society:
The Prison World

'When you get out, you'll put prison behind you like a bad dream,' someone once said to me.

How can I forget? Every nuance of this place is known to me. Every echo of a closing door. Every sliding, shuffling, footstep. Every voice unseen I recognize. I know what is happening before it happens, every minute of every day and what will happen in future days.

Even in the silence of the night, footsteps tiptoe in my mind, spyholes squeak, a soft sobbing disturbs my sleep, a faint humming of some lonely soul's radio . . .

All of these things, and more of which I am unconsciously aware, invade my dreams, become part of me – my nightmare, I can never put them behind me . . .

If, once free, through some aberration of the mind, I chance to forget. I look around, at my parents aged and withered, at the children grown without me – at the world turning – at the wasted life that is me.

Never could I forget, put it all behind me. I will never forget – more importantly – I will never let you forget.

Judith Ward, writing in Durham Prison, where she served many years before being cleared of the charges against her and was released, having served eighteen years[1]

6. People and Imprisonment

> The French prison itself, organized as it is according to ancient regulations, is nothing but an absurd machine for breaking those men who are thrown into it. Life there is a kind of mechanized madness; everything in it seems to have been conceived in a spirit of mean calculation how best to enfeeble, stupefy and numb the prisoner and poison him with inexpressible bitterness.
>
> Victor Serge, *Memoirs of a Revolutionary*[1]

A universal feature of imprisonment is the way it snatches its participants from everyday life and places them in an abnormal environment, divorced from their routines, and exposed to quite different pressures and imperatives. Prison is an upside-down world, a single-sex environment with an inverted class structure. Its population reflects the inequities and injustices of the wider society, and relationships with the outside world are mediated through censors and eavesdroppers. Constructive human reactions and behaviour become more difficult. Confinement and security impose a range of indignities and absurdities on those who are confined and those who confine them.

BEING IN PRISON

Many have felt impelled to record the strange experience of imprisonment, perhaps to make it more bearable, to record what happens in order to make sense of it for themselves or to communicate it to others so that they too might understand. Some of these were writers who became prisoners, others were prisoners who learnt to write.

Two famous ex-prisoners went on to become presidents of their respective countries. Václav Havel from the Czech Republic and Nelson Mandela of South Africa both wrote about life in prison. In their writings they throw light on how various aspects of the prison experience affect those living through it.

Havel highlights two aspects of prison life often commented on by prison writers. The first is the way that in prison all the customary coverings of polite life are stripped away by the environment.

> Everything here is more elemental, somehow: social relationships and mechanisms that are hidden and masked in complex ways outside appear in all their nakedness; everything is bare, as it were, unmediated, transparent; everything can be seen with greater clarity . . . It is a kind of convex mirror.[2]

The second is an unexpected discovery. One might imagine that life in prison is endlessly boring with nothing to do except count the minutes passing by and with no worries, as everything is provided by the authorities. According to Havel it is not like that at all.

> You have plenty of worries here all the time . . . you're always having to chase after something, arrange something, hunt for something, keep an eye on something, fear for something, hold your ground against something. It's a constant strain on the nerves . . . exacerbated by the fact that in many important instances you cannot behave authentically and must keep your real thoughts to yourself.[3]

Nelson Mandela also reflected on how time passes in prison.

> Prison life is about routine: each day like the one before it, so that the months and years blend into each other . . . Time slows down in prison; the days seem endless. The cliché of time passing slowly usually has to do with idleness and inactivity. But this was not the case on Robben Island. You were busy almost all the time with work, study, resolving disputes. Yet time nevertheless moved glacially.[4]

Visits from family are the cause both of joy and of despair. Visits make you realize suddenly, according to Havel, that the other world from which you came is not a dream. It actually exists. However, as time goes on and the separation becomes longer, it becomes more difficult to communicate with visitors, however close the relationship, because the distorted world of the prison claims more and more of the attention and energy of the imprisoned one.

Nelson Mandela occasionally had visits from his wife Winnie and tiny daughter Zenani.

The light moments in prison could not make up for the low ones. Winnie was allowed to visit on a number of occasions when I was in Pretoria and each time she brought Zenani, who was then beginning to walk and talk. I would hold her and kiss her if the guards permitted, and towards the end of the interview, hand her back to Winnie. As Winnie was saying goodbye, and the guards were ushering them out, Zeni would often motion for me to come with them, and I could see from her small puzzled face that she did not understand why I could not.[5]

What is the real meaning of imprisonment? According to Nelson Mandela,

Prison not only robs you of your freedom, it attempts to take away your identity. Everyone wears a uniform, eats the same food, follows the same schedule. It is by definition a purely authoritarian state that tolerates no independence and individuality. As a freedom fighter and as a man, one must fight against the prison's attempt to rob one of these qualities.[6]

Relationships become distorted. You are thrown into the most intimate contact with other people, perhaps sharing cramped living quarters with them day and night and then they are just as suddenly whisked away. Nelson Mandela describes the process:

One can be in extraordinarily intimate circumstances with someone for months, and then never see the person again. It is dehumanizing, for it forces one to adapt by becoming more self-contained and insulated.[7]

Both Nelson Mandela and Václav Havel reflect on the meaning of freedom and its loss. For the first it is 'being able to take a walk whenever one wants, going into a shop and buying a newspaper, speaking or choosing to remain silent, the simple act of being able to control one's person'.[8] For Havel, in prison, 'one lacks the very opportunity to choose'.[9]

From the perspective of these highly educated prisoners, prison is a new world, a world with the skin peeled off, where time has a different meaning and it is a struggle for the prisoner to retain a sense of identity and a connection with the world outside.

In *The True Confessions of an Albino Terrorist*, Breyten
Breytenbach writes of his feelings when he was sentenced
to prison

*It is 25 November 1975 when I am sentenced. I shall not
be seeing the stars again for many years. In the beginning
I don't realize this; I don't miss them; and then suddenly
it becomes very important, like chafing sores in the mind
– something you've taken for granted for so long you now
miss the way you'd miss a burial site if you died in space.
It is not natural never to see stars, or the moon for that
matter – it is as cruel as depriving people of sound. I see
the moon again for the first time on 18 April 1976 when,
at about twenty-three minutes to four in the afternoon, I
am in the largest of the three exercise yards, which has
towering walls, making it rather like a well. I looked up
and to my astonishment saw, in a patch of sky above, a
shrivelled white shape. Could it be a pearl in my eye? Was
it the afterbirth of a spaceship? No, it could only be the
moon. And they told me that she'd been hanged, that she
was dead.*

*The sun and its absence become the pivot of your daily
existence. You wait. You build your day around the half
an hour when you'll be allowed out into the courtyard to
say good morning to the sun. You follow its course in the
universe behind your eyelids. You become its disciple.
The sun knows not of the justice of man. You know
exactly where it touches at what time – winter, autumn or
summer – and if you are lucky, as I was for some time, to
be kept in a cell just off the main corridor with windows
giving on to the catwalk which was not closed to the
outside, you would have a glimmer, a suspicion, a
hair-crack of sunshine coming in during certain seasons,
but never reaching far enough down for you to feel it. I
used to climb on my bed, stand on my toes on the
bedstead, and then, sometimes, for something like two*

> *minutes a day, a yellow wand would brush on top of my hair. Of course, you develop an intense awareness, like a hitherto unexplored sense in yourself, for knowing exactly when the sun rises and when it sets without ever seeing it. With the first shivers of the very early morning, even before the call for waking up sounded, I used to get out of bed and try to position myself in that one spot of the cell where the warder could not see me directly and then for half an hour sit in* zazen, *and I could always feel in me a very profound source of light inexorably unnighting the outside; with eyes half closed I could feel it first tipping rose the roof made of glassfibre, giving shapes to the trees one knew must be growing not far off because the birds talked about these trees, and then jumping over the walls which were made of red brick, and generally investing the day.*[10]

For others it is more immediately totally brutal and horrifying. Alhaji Baba Nagaji arrived at Kano prison in Nigeria. His handcuffs were removed and he was pushed into a cell crowded with prisoners.

> They asked me what my name was. Before I could answer someone gave me a blinding slap in the face. I was blinded temporarily and the pain made me put my hands to my eyes. I heard someone say something like 'How can Presido ask you your name and you refuse to answer?' I was trying to tell them I did not refuse when I was kicked in the stomach and I fell to the floor. They beat me until someone asked them to stop. He was the Presido. By that time I was tasting blood in my mouth.[11]

Mohammed Bakut arrived at Sokoto prison in Nigeria and was also put into a cell crowded with others.

> They slapped me and when I asked what I had done to deserve that they gave me another slap. They said I should remove my trousers. I was reluctant to do that and they beat me some more. The O.C. Executioner told me to lie on the floor and to do like when I am making love with a woman. They asked whether I had a wife, and I said, 'Yes.' One of them – he was the adviser to the Field Marshal –

> he said that now I was in prison other men would be making love
> to her. Then they said I should lie on the floor and show them how
> I did it with my wife. I did it – I was afraid they would beat me
> again.[12]

According to the authors of *Behind the Wall*, a study of prison
conditions in Nigeria, whether a prisoner is greeted by these initiation
rites depends on a number of factors: the mood of the cell leader,
the age of the prisoner, the perceived social status of the prisoner.
New prisoners from the higher social classes are the most likely to
be put through these softening-up rituals. A new prisoner will often
have everything of value stolen from him. He will be allocated the
sleeping place nearest the lavatory bucket and the job of emptying
and washing it. When the next new prisoner arrives the process
repeats itself and the worst sleeping position and worst job go to
the new arrival.[13]

Wilbert Rideau has been a life-sentence prisoner at Angola, the
Louisiana State Penitentiary, for thirty-six years and edits the
prison's uncensored news magazine, *The Angolite*. In one of his
articles, 'The Sexual Jungle', he tells the story of James Dunn. He
was first admitted to Angola in March 1960 when he was just
nineteen to serve a three-year sentence for burglary.

> A month after his arrival he received a call to go to the library when
> an inmate 'shoved me into a dark room where his partner was waiting.
> They beat me up and raped me. That was to claim me,' Dunn
> explains. 'When they finished they told me that I was for them, then
> went out and told everyone else that they had claimed me.'

James decided to submit. After all, he only had a relatively short
sentence to serve and he had seen what happened to those who did
not. During his first week at Angola he had seen fourteen men rape
one young prisoner because he refused to submit. 'When they finished
with him, he had to be taken to the hospital where they had to sew
him back up; and then they had to take him to the nuthouse at
Jackson 'cause he cracked up.'[14]

So James Dunn accepted his position and became his rapist's 'old
lady'. He did whatever he was asked to do: wash the man's clothes,
make his bed, prepare meals, give him massages and take care of

his sexual needs. His man was a heroin addict and once he sold James for two bags of heroin and the settlement of a $100 debt. Then James Dunn got his parole.[15]

He was back soon afterwards with a five-year sentence for burglary and violating his parole. He was expected to go back to his former role. He did so but he was now determined to free himself as soon as he could. When his 'owner' was released he did not sell or transfer James to a friend but left him to manage on his own. Others moved in but he fought them off. Eventually, in fighting them off, he killed one of them. That brought him a life sentence.[16] As the years went by he devoted himself to protecting young prisoners who arrived at Angola, showing them how to avoid being enslaved by other prisoners.[17] In 1987 his life sentence was commuted to forty years and he was released after serving twenty-two years.

Has the advent of AIDS affected behaviour in the 'sexual jungle' of Louisiana State Penitentiary? According to Rideau, not much. Since the 'overwhelming majority' of the 5200 prisoners there are serving sentences that will require them to stay in prison until they die, the terrors of AIDS are not so great.[18]

The outside is replicated but amplified on the inside. There is both an official and an unofficial sorting-out of prisoners into classes or groups. Some prisoners come from the higher levels of society outside and manage to ensure that once inside their treatment is better and different. In England, for instance, imprisoned professionals, police officers, solicitors, financiers, usually spend only a short while in a closed prison before being sent to an open prison where conditions are more congenial for them and activities take place that reflect their interests. In Phnom Penh prison in Cambodia prisoners generally live together in large rooms with an open latrine and a water trough. But a general involved in a coup attempt lives with his family in a suite of rooms at the end of a corridor.[19] In some South American countries there is a special building, called a *pension*, where prisoners who can pay can be given a room separate from the violence and overcrowding of the main jail. In some countries of the former Soviet Union, prison directors are faced with the problem of mafia prisoners offering to buy satellite television for the benefit of everyone in the prison, but with some pay-off in return of improved prison conditions for the benefactor. Buying a bed in the hospital is one route out of the common cell for wealthy prisoners in some countries.

In India prisoners are divided into three categories: A, B and C. In other systems these categories would denote security level, but in India they mean something different. They define social status. Categories A and B are people who 'by social status, education and habit of life have been accustomed to a superior mode of living'. Category C are 'prisoners who are not classified in class A or B'.[20] The category makes a real difference to the conditions of life. In the Indian state of Tamil Nadu, the amount spent on feeding a class A or B prisoner per day in 1990 ranged from 14 to 17 rupees. For a class C prisoner it was 7 to 8 rupees. Class A and B prisoners could buy extra food and fruit. Cs could not. The As and Bs could write and receive one letter a week, Cs one every two weeks. Category As could get any newspaper they wanted. Cs could only get newspapers from a prescribed list.[21]

Many prison systems have 'arrival' rituals like those that take place in some prisons in Nigeria. Those arriving for the first time in their hut in prison in Russia and meeting the other prisoners are subjected to the process called 'registration'. Apparently,

> Those subjected to registration are made to guess different enigmas. To dive down from the plank bed, to beat the head against the wall while running in full speed and so on. These are called 'tricks'. Such tricks number several hundred, they are impossible to remember all of them. Every generation thinks out something new. For example, you are thrown a brush and told: 'Play balalaika a little.' You must throw it back . . . Here is the test not for your smartness but for your knowledge. If you know the tricks you are the person of their circle. However, you can be tested in a more serious way: to blindfold, put you on the upper plank bed, tie up for the scrotum: 'Jump down.' If you do not jump, being scared, you will sign your sentence by yourself. If you do jump down, nothing terrible will happen, that was only a thread he was tied with.[22]

In the world of Russian prisoners there are four distinct castes of prisoners. The highest caste is the *blatnyie*. These are professional criminals, the so-called 'theives of law'.[23] They are the élite of the prison world and control the behaviour of the rest of the prisoners, the supplies of tobacco, vodka and clothes. They employ henchmen called 'athletes' or 'gladiators'.[24] The next caste is the 'men', the *muzhiki*. These are the ordinary, non-professional criminals, who end up in prison because of some petty crime. They got into a fight or stole something from work. Unlike the *blatnyie* they are going to return to normal life after their release.[25] The third group are the *goats*. These collaborate openly with the camp administration. They are the ones with the red armbands who fill the jobs of librarians, stewards, club managers, and are seen by the authorities to be 'on the self-correction way'. The fourth caste are the *cocks*. These are the outcasts, maybe those who have not paid their card debts, stolen from other prisoners, broken the norms of the group, people who sell themselves for cigarettes or protection.[26]

In other cultures there are also prison outcasts. In many Western countries these are the ones who have committed sexual crimes, people who have molested children, ex-policemen or prison officers, or those who inform to the prison authorities on other prisoners. In some countries these prisoners are called 'special protection prisoners' and are kept separate from the others in case their lives are threatened. In England, Rule 43 of the prison rules allows them to be segregated from the other prisoners and protected from attack. The writer Tony Parker wrote several books based on frank and detailed interviews with prisoners. He interviewed a fifty-eight-year-old man convicted of sexual assaults on small boys, whom he called Wilfred Johnson. Wilfred Johnson told him,

> All your time in prison you're scared to death that someone's going to find out. You know from how you hear them talk when there's some sort of similar case reported in the papers, and they all start discussing it among themselves. 'Make a note of his name,' they say, 'so that if he ever turns up in here we'll know who he is, we'll see he gets what he deserves.' . . . They mean it all right . . . someone like that's been set on by the others; and the screws won't lift a finger to help them either, you know; they feel the same way about it themselves.[27]

PRISON AND SOCIAL INJUSTICE

There is a great deal of prison literature. One way of making the experience more bearable is to write about it. But most people in prison do not write books. They are not the writing sort. Many of them cannot even write. Nelson Mandela, Zhang Xianliang, Aleksandr Solzhenitsyn are the exceptional prisoners. For many prisoners prison is not unexpected. Their parents went there. Their brothers, friends, maybe sisters go there. They are not surprised to find themselves there. They do not write reflections on the meaning of the loss of freedom. Most prisoners come from the poor, the minority groups, the uneducated, the unemployed, the mentally ill. The prison is the magnifying mirror which reflects and enlarges the unresolved social problems of the society which it serves.

Prisons are often to be found in the centre of large towns. Yet the population of the prison will not be a cross-section of the population of the town where it stands. The people in the prison will not be representative of all social groups. There will not be a gender balance, a racial balance or a wide age range. Some groups will very rarely be found there. Others will be grossly over-represented.

One very obvious, striking and universal difference between the people in prison and the population outside it is that most people inside will be men. Although women make up more or less half the population of the world, they make up on average about one-twentieth of the people in the world's prisons. Another under-represented group are the middle-aged and elderly. Most prisoners are young.

In 1992 the British government published an unusual study, a systematic account of prison life, based on detailed interviews with 4000 prisoners from every prison in England and Wales. The results showed how untypical English and Welsh prisoners are of the rest of society. More of them are under twenty-five. Only one in a hundred prisoners is aged sixty or over compared with over a quarter of the population in general.[28] Prisoners do not usually come from the managerial and professional classes. Of those who ever had a job, twice as many as in the population as a whole have done unskilled or low-skilled work.[29]

It is often said that disturbed backgrounds and traumatic childhoods lead to people ending up in prison. The 1992 survey of English and Welsh prisoners showed that although more than two-thirds had spent most of their childhood living with both their parents, more than one in four comes from a disrupted family background. Nearly four out of ten of the young prisoners, those under twenty-one, reported that they had been taken from home at some time during their childhood and put into the care of the local authority. These are very different figures from those for the population as a whole. The proportion having been taken into care is two out of every hundred.[30]

Prisoners are less likely to be married and more likely to be living with a partner to whom they are not married. Not surprisingly, prison breaks up marriages. The marriages of half of those serving between five and ten years in prison had broken up.[31] Educational levels are lower.[32] One-third had mostly played truant from school.[33] Employment backgrounds are worse. Many of those ending up in prison are unemployed.[34] One-third had a family member, sometimes a parent but more often a brother or sister, in prison already.[35] For many, violence is a part of life. More than a quarter of all men prisoners in England and Wales had at some time in their lives been injured badly enough in a fight to go to hospital for treatment. The figure for men generally is one in ten.[36]

This pattern is repeated all over the world. In the United States the majority of prisoners come from one-parent families.[37] Nearly half were high-school drop-outs.[38] Four out of ten prisoners in US prisons had a family member in prison.[39]

In Québec more than three-quarters of the prison population are repeat offenders. More than half of them have no high-school diploma. One in five suffered family violence or was sexually abused. Nearly a third have attempted suicide. Four out of ten are habitual drug users.[40]

In the developing world the connections between imprisonment and poverty are even sharper. Poor people cannot afford a lawyer. With no one to guide them through the labyrinth of the law or press their case, they will stay in prison before their trial, sometimes for years, and their eventual sentence will normally be a harsher one.

Table 7   Social characteristics of people in prison in England and Wales in 1991 compared with the general population

Characteristic	% Prisoners	% General population
Age		
17–20	18	7
21–24	22	9
25–29	22	9
30–39	22	17
40–49	11	18
50–59	4	14
60+	1	26
Gender		
male	96	50
female	4	50
Social class		
I, II, III non-manual	18	45
III manual	41	37
IV, V partly skilled, unskilled	41	19
Education		
no qualifications	43	34
university education	2	7
played truant more than went to school	30	3
Whether taken in care as a child	26	2
Marital status		
married	15	61
cohabiting	20	4
single	50	21
widowed	1	9
divorced	9	4
Employment prior to imprisonment		
employed	51	
unemployed	33	
living off crime	7	

Source: The National Prison Survey 1991, OPCS

In many countries the rich never go to prison. The lawyers see to that. In Brazil, 93 per cent of prisoners do not have their own lawyer to help them with their case. Nearly all prisoners are unemployed when they come to prison. Ninety-five per cent are poor according to the definition used in the official poverty statistics. Three-quarters are illiterate or near illiterate.[41]

The Commissioner of Corrections for Canada has summed up the concentration of poverty and disadvantage to be found in prisons all over the world: 'Most of our offender population is drawn from the underbelly of society.'[42]

OVER-REPRESENTATION OF MINORITIES

Prisons mirror the defects of their societies in other ways too. All round the world the same pattern can be seen. Prisons contain higher proportions than would be expected of people from groups that suffer from racism and discrimination. How does this disproportion happen? There are many reasons, often related to blatant discrimination in the wider society, and crude racism by the law enforcement agencies. Sometimes the disproportion arises from policies which concentrate minorities in poor areas and restrict their opportunities. Often the criminal justice processes tend to discriminate against minorities, sometimes in very subtle ways. At every stage of the process discrimination can enter. The police make decisions about which areas to police most actively, and which people to stop in the street and search for forbidden articles, weapons or drugs. The court officials may have the power to decide on the charges to lay in court. The court may decide whether or not to grant bail and be more prepared to grant bail to someone with a stable home and a good address. Discrimination can enter into sentencing and parole decisions. A study of sentencing carried out in the West Midlands in England in 1989 by Roger Hood, Director of the Centre of Criminological Research at Oxford University, found that when all factors were taken into account, black offenders were 5 to 8 per cent more likely to be sent to prison than comparable white offenders.[43] The cumulative effect of all this discrimination is the disproportionate number of minorities in the prisons of the world.

Both England and Wales and the United States show in their prison populations a gross disproportion of racial minorities. It has already been shown in Chapter 3 how unrepresentative of the US population as a whole the racial composition of their prison population is. In the United States 51 per cent of all state and federal prisoners are African-Americans. Nationally African-Americans are now imprisoned at a rate 7.66 times the rate for whites.[44] However, the overall rate conceals great geographical differences.

This is not a new phenomenon. According to Professor Coramae Richey Mann from Indiana University, 'such disproportionate rates have existed throughout a major portion of United States history and not only for blacks but also for other racial minorities'.[45]

When the state of North Carolina opened its first prison in 1870, more than three-quarters of those imprisoned there were black. In San Quentin prison in the 1850s the largest minority group were Hispanics, greatly over-represented compared to their numbers in California at the time.[46]

The drug laws have pressed particularly heavily on African-Americans. The sale and use of crack cocaine is punished much more severely than the sale and use of any other drug, including powder cocaine. Possession of crack cocaine by a first-time offender leads to a mandatory minimum sentence of five years. Possession of powder cocaine or any other illegal drug by a first offender can lead to a maximum of one year in prison. Human Rights Watch told the United Nations Commission on Human Rights, 'It takes 100 times more powder cocaine than crack cocaine to trigger the same mandatory minimum penalty.'[47]

The 'war on drugs' has led directly to more black people being imprisoned. For property crime the increase for black people was slightly higher, whereas for drug offences the white increase was 110 per cent and the black increase was 465.5 per cent.[48]

According to Marc Mauer of the Sentencing Project, African-Americans comprise '34 per cent of the arrests for drug possession, 55 per cent of the convictions for drug possession and fully 74 per cent of the people sentenced to prison'.[49] Yet research by the National Institute for Drug Abuse shows that in 1994 nearly two-thirds of

Table 8   State incarceration rates by race per 100,000 in 1994

State	Incarceration rate for blacks	Incarceration rate for whites	Ratio black/white
Georgia	1141	219	5.21
California	1668	317	5.26
Alabama	1183	218	5.43
New York	1138	202	5.63
Louisiana	1358	190	7.15
Oklahoma	2411	329	7.33
Michigan	1678	210	7.99
Florida	1635	195	8.38
Washington	1392	161	8.65
Massachusetts	819	86	9.52
Kansas	1626	159	10.23
Texas	1943	178	10.92
Utah	1771	142	12.47
New Jersey	1417	109	13.00
Illinois	1338	93	14.39
Wisconsin	1741	106	16.42
Connecticut	2250	130	17.31
Pennsylvania	1611	89	18.10
Minnesota	1275	56	22.77
District of Columbia	2966	84	35.31
National average	1433	187	7.66

Source: Marc Mauer, 'Intended and Unintended Consequences: State Racial Disparities in Imprisonment', January 1997

current cocaine users were white, 22 per cent were black and 16 per cent were Hispanic.[50]

In England and Wales controversy has dogged the method of calculation of the figures. However, government figures published in 1996 show that in 1995 black people were grossly over-represented in prison. One per cent of British men aged fifteen to sixty-four was black. The categories used here to define 'black' exclude those from South Asia and China. Ten per cent of British men in prison were black. One per cent of British women aged fifteen to sixty-four was black. Eleven per cent of British women prisoners were black. Another 5 per cent of the male prisoners were foreign nationals from ethnic minorities, as was one in eight of the women prisoners.[51]

This disproportion is not exceptional. In many other prison systems the over-representation of racial minorities is striking. For example, in New Zealand just over half of all the men sent to prison in 1995 were Maori and nearly two-thirds of the women. Yet only twelve out of every hundred New Zealanders are Maori.[52] In Australia the disproportion is even more striking. At the end of 1995 Aboriginals accounted for 1.7 per cent of Australia's population and 19 per cent of those in prison.[53]

Figures for the whole of Canada are difficult to come by but they are available for the province of Ontario. In 1992 the provincial government there set up a commission to investigate racial disparities in the criminal justice system. There was concern about the over-representation of black people in prison. The report of the commission showed that in 1993 black adults were admitted to prison at more than five times the rate of white adults. The rate was 706 per 100,000 for white adults and 3686 for black adults. Research showed that black people were more likely to be kept in pre-trial detention, and were more likely to be sent to prison when convicted for a drug offence. Two-thirds of black people convicted of a drug offence were imprisoned compared to just over one-third of white people.[54]

Native Canadians make up 2 per cent of the population of Canada. Yet in federal prisons, where all those serving sentences of two years or more are sent, 12 per cent of the men prisoners and 15 per cent of the women are native Canadians. In the prisons of the different provinces they make up between 19 and 30 per cent of prisoners.[55]

In the state of Rio in Brazil, 31 per cent of those in prison are white. The proportion of white people in the population of Rio state is 61 per cent.[56] In Eastern Europe the same pattern is found with gypsies or Roma. It is estimated that in Hungary half of all the prisoners are gypsies.[57] They are about 5 per cent of the Hungarian population.

Countries such as the United States, New Zealand and Australia lock up their minorities disproportionately. This feature is replicated in Western Europe but there the group affected is not indigenous minority citizens but foreigners. The proportions of foreigners in prison are at least double and often treble or more times the proportions in the country as a whole. In the Netherlands the proportion of foreigners in prison is five times the general population. In Sweden it is three times.[58] For Western Europe as a whole the average percentage of foreigners in prison is 19 per cent whilst foreigners make up an average of 7 per cent of the population.[59]

Who are these foreigners? They are often asylum seekers or poor immigrants. Talking of the situation in Italy, where in the early 1990s there was much publicity about politicians being sent to prison, Professor Massimo Pavarini of Bologna University says that 'for every corrupt politician lawfully detained, a hundred black immigrants are interned'.[60]

Prisons, then, are mainly occupied by the casualties of social policies: those, and the children of those, who have not managed to get for themselves a position with income, employment, family security and social acceptance.

DRUGS IN PRISON

Once they are imprisoned they face a world where the problems of society outside are magnified and the effects of society's problems send ripples through the whole system. Of no subject is this more true than when one considers the use of illegal drugs. It is impossible to talk about crime, prisons and prisoners without coming to the question of drugs. If there were no illegal drugs the face of crime and punishment would be very different from what it is today in many prisons of the world. First of all, as the United States situation shows clearly, illegal drugs are the reason many people are put there in the first place. Either they have used these substances, dealing in them is their business, they have committed a property or violent crime to get money to buy them, or they have committed a crime whilst under the influence of them.

Secondly, because of this connection, many of those who get sent to prison are addicted to drugs and while in there face all the medical problems of their addiction.

Thirdly, demand for drugs in prison is very high because of the large market amongst existing addicts and because prison is an environment where there is a captive, bored, largely depressed population eager for some release from the grim everyday reality.

The battle between prison administrations, trying to keep drugs out, and prisoners, trying to get drugs in, consumes a considerable part of the time and attention of those charged with the day-to-day running of prisons and highlights the fundamentally unsolvable problems of this institution that is at the junction of so many of society's contradictions. Enormous energy goes into stopping some prisoners getting some drugs. The prisoners expend enormous energy beating the latest system. More drug addicts are created by the prison environment. The drug addiction problem that got so many of them into prison in the first place is untouched by all this activity.

This battle has posed a particular challenge for those countries anxious to run humane prisons in a relaxed environment. Norway is a good example. Apparently about 35 per cent of prisoners in Norway are in prison for drug offences. The authorities estimate that around half of all prisoners take drugs in prison. To deal with this the Norwegian prison service has drug detection teams who carry out search operations backed up by urine tests and other restrictions.[61] A Norwegian academic, Lill Scherdin from the University of Oslo, describes the impact of drugs on prison life in Norway: 'prison management revolves around controlling the taking of drugs ... Urine tests are taken by all prisoners.'[62] Only those who test negative can mix with other prisoners. The rest are kept in isolation. One prisoner said, 'I am not taking a urine test. This is a conscious choice ... I have never used drugs but to give urine to be able to talk with people, no thank you! Because I refuse to give urine I am isolated twenty-three hours a day.'

Prisoners are similarly unhappy with the random strip searches after visits. One prisoner said, 'It's unbelievably humiliating to have to strip after the visit. It is difficult for me to stand naked in front of adults. It influences the whole atmosphere of the visit. I cannot relax because I know I have to undress.'[63] Some prisoners had decided they would rather not have their visits than go through the attendant humiliations.

Prisoners in England feel the same. Women prisoners claim they are required to strip and urinate in front of a prison officer in order to provide an uncontaminated sample. If they refuse they are placed on a disciplinary charge. Women prisoners told interviewers that they found the process humiliating.[64]

In Canada it has been estimated that about perhaps one half or even two-thirds of prisoners use drugs in prison.[65] In 1992, legislation was passed in Canada to allow random urine analysis of prisoners but in 1995 it was still not implemented because it was being challenged in the courts as unconstitutional.[66]

How do drugs get into prison? There are many ways, some obvious, others requiring a bit of ingenuity. Sometimes packages are thrown over the wall. Sometimes they are brought in after a prisoner returns from home leave or day release from the prison. Sometimes they are swallowed outside and then recovered once the prisoner is back inside the prison. Prisoners leaving the prison to go out on home leave can be put under considerable pressure from others to bring back drugs on pain of violent treatment if they do not comply. Sometimes they decide that the punishment they will get from the prison authorities for not coming back on time is better than the rough justice of the prison drug barons.

A prime route of entry is through the prisoners' visitors. In the United States, figures are collected for what they call 'drug interdiction activities' for people visiting prisons. In 1990 nearly all visitors were questioned about what they were bringing in, nearly all had their belongings searched, over half were subjected to a 'pat-down search', that is the sort of search given to passengers at airports, and one in four was subjected to a 'body cavity search'.[67]

In the United States, another method used to prevent the entry of drugs is to require prisoners to change their clothes when they arrive in prison or when they return from temporary release. This is the rule in more than two-thirds of US prisons. Drugs can also be supplied by corrupt staff. In some US prisons, staff are given a pat-down search on arrival at work.[68]

Prisons are always a source of myth and fantasy with so many different interests jostling for possession of the truth. So, with the level of drug use as with many other activities, it is difficult to know how far the general concern about drugs in prison is based on fact and how far it is a myth which serves the interests of prison staff or the imagination of the public.

In Sweden they have tried to find out. About 8000 people serving sentences of more than two months go to prison in Sweden every year. Of these, more than 3000 are known to have taken drugs before they came to prison. About a thousand of these go on to treatment programmes in prison. The rest refuse programmes and it is assumed they want to continue to take drugs. To control it the Swedish prison administration has developed a number of measures of which urine testing is one. About 80,000 urine tests are carried out every year in Swedish prisons. Everyone had assumed that in spite of these measures, drug misuse in Swedish prisons was extensive. So a study was commissioned to find out if this was true. The study was based on urine tests. A random sample of prisoners was urine-tested on Monday 18 April 1994. Monday was chosen because it was most likely to reveal the presence of the drugs smuggled into prison after weekend visits or weekend leave.

The results caused some surprises. Altogether, more than eight out of ten proved negative. The open prisons had the fewest drug takers. Nine out of ten were negative. The closed neighbourhood (local) prisons had the most. Eight out of ten were negative. The research study concludes, 'These findings scarcely support the view . . . that Swedish prisons are flooded with illicit drugs.'[69]

Figures from the US bear out this finding. Tests conducted on prisoners in state prisons in 1990 show that only one out of sixteen prisoners tested positive for marijuana, one in twenty-eight for cocaine, and one in seventy-five for heroin.[70]

After a series of high profile media reports about the high level of drug taking and a pilot scheme in eight prisons, mandatory drug testing was introduced into British prisons in 1996. A new prison rule was brought in making it an offence to refuse to give a urine sample. The prisons are required to test 10 per cent of their prisoners each month. Those who test positive are punished. The usual punishment is lengthening the prison sentence by adding some days: perhaps eighteen, maybe the maximum, that is forty-two.

Between April 1996 and March 1997, 57,700 samples were taken from prisoners in England and Wales under the random drug-testing programme. Twenty-four per cent were positive.[71] Drug testing takes up a considerable amount of prison staff time and it costs a lot of money. It has been estimated that the cost is around £8,500 a month for a prison holding 500 people.[72] It has been argued that random drug testing will have the opposite effect to that intended. Because cannabis shows up in the test for fourteen to twenty-eight days after taking it, but heroin only shows up for two or three days, prisoners will switch from soft to hard drugs.[73] Others say in defence of the tests that prisoners find them helpful because they take the pressure off them to conform and use drugs because everyone else does.

But in reality the whole process of testing is an irrelevance to drug addiction as a problem. The Advisory Council on the Misuse of Drugs in its report published in June 1996 said that early results of mandatory drug testing suggest that its 'capacity to influence the overall prevalence of drug misuse within a prison is likely to be limited'. Until something is done about providing treatment when drug abusers leave prison, 'no strategy to tackle drug misuse in prison has any chance of success'.[74]

SICKNESS AND DEATH

Prisons face the problem of having to look after a large number of people suffering from drug addiction. In addition, daily life in prison is dominated and distorted by the need to prevent prisoners getting access to illegal drugs. There is a third potentially lethal problem: prisoners injecting themselves with shared and dirty needles – and contracting HIV. Shared needles are one of the main factors in spreading AIDS in prison. A German prisoner described how it happens.

> As far as drugs are concerned there are shortages, but there is always someone who has something . . . So you ask someone, about whom you know that he shoots, to lend you his pump. Most of the time, these are rotten things with a blunt needle and used maybe fifty times over. But if you have got heroin, then you want to get your shot. You are not interested at that moment whether the needle is clean or not . . . When I served time in 1984, we didn't yet know about AIDS. But the situation was such that some months we only had one syringe, and all the junkies in the house used it. That must have been the time when I got my HIV infection. Probably all the others too, about a dozen. Some of them have already died . . .[75]

In some countries many prisoners are HIV-infected or have AIDS. In England and Wales eighty prisoners were known to be HIV-positive or to have AIDS in May 1996.[76] In state and federal prisons in the US in 1995, 2.3 per cent of the total population was HIV-infected or had AIDS, altogether about 24,200 people.[77] In 1995, over 1000 people died of AIDS in US state prisons.[78] More than one-third of the HIV-positive prisoners were in New York state, where the prisons housed 9500 people who were infected or ill with AIDS, 14 per cent of all New York state's prisoners in 1994.[79] The New York state legislature approved a system of allowing prisoners near death to be released to die at home. 'Near death' was interpreted by officials of the system as not being able to walk. So a twenty-nine-year-old prisoner with thrush, an AIDS-related cancer, hepatitis B and a tumour on his neck who could nevertheless still walk was denied medical parole and died in prison.[80]

When information about the possibility of prisoners being HIV-infected first reached the prisons, both staff and prisoners panicked. They were no better informed or humane in their approach than those in society outside. In many countries prisoners were kept in isolation or subject to restrictions. In Germany, in some states they were prevented from working in the prison kitchen or taking the job of prison barber, although these restrictions are now being lifted. Normally in Germany, HIV-infected prisoners are given a cell to themselves. If they share with another prisoner, the other occupant has to be told of their health status. They are less often awarded home leave but do get special food, including more milk and fruit.[81] In Poland, according to criminologist Monika Platek, 'infected prisoners are kept in separate cells, use separate bathrooms and washing machines and have their dishes washed separately. They are not employed in the kitchen or laundry.'[82] In the United States, 'there has been a clear trend in housing policy away from blanket segregation of HIV-infected prisoners'.[83]

Most consideration of the problem of HIV-infected people in prison ends up with a discussion about stopping the spread. And this leads to a clash between illusion and reality, between those who deny drug abuse and homosexuality in prison and those who accept that these activities go on and want to limit the health consequences. So there is a long-running discussion in prison circles about the desirability of providing clean needles in prison, providing bleach so that needles can be cleaned and whether to supply condoms. These measures have proved very controversial everywhere. Even where condoms are provided prisoners often will not ask for them because it affects their image with the other prisoners. In Norway condoms are available but in some prisons prisoners have to ask for them from the officer on duty outside the visiting room. Bleach for cleaning needles is available in some prisons in Norway.[84] In Germany condoms are available in some prisons but clean needles and syringes are definitely not.[85] In Rio state in Brazil condoms are available. At first they were freely available on request from the staff but this was not successful, as prisoners did not want to ask for them and thus identify themselves as being involved in homosexual activity. Then a new method of distribution was tried. A non-governmental organization that came into the prisons to provide education about AIDS took on the distribution and this was more successful.[86]

In India the situation is particularly delicate. According to a law of 1869 still in force, sodomy between consenting adults is an offence. In 1994 the then Inspector General of Delhi prison, Kiran Bedi, rejected a proposal by the Indian Medical Association that condoms be distributed in Delhi Central Jail where 8000 men are incarcerated.

Her reason was that they would not be needed. Overcrowding in the jail prevented any homosexual activity taking place there. The president of the Indian Medical Association disagreed. He claimed that he had carried out a survey which showed that overcrowding did not prevent sexual acts taking place.[87]

In England and Wales prison doctors can prescribe condoms but they are not often requested. This breakthrough came after years of opposition to making condoms available. A convoluted explanation was always given for the decision not to make condoms available. It was maintained that homosexual activity in a public place is unlawful and therefore it may be that under the law a prison cell would be regarded as a public place. The authorities could not condone such illegality by distributing condoms.

One of the saddest groups of prisoners is those suffering from mental illness. Ideally people who are sick do not go to a place of punishment but to a place of care and treatment. Unfortunately the prisons of the world contain many whose problems call for care in a hospital but are instead locked up in a prison, sometimes in isolation, perhaps smearing the cell with their own excrement, with the staff being able to do no more than observe them every fifteen minutes through a spy hole in their door to make sure they do not kill themselves. Sometimes they are to be found in a padded cell or tied up in canvas restraints. Some are hovering at the back of a dark cell wrapped in a prison blanket and staring wildly back at those peering in through the cell door. Many people who commit crimes do so because of their mental condition. Often they end up in prison, to the despair of the prison staff, who think they should be in hospital but cannot persuade a hospital to take them. Sometimes their guilt at the horror of what they have done leads to mental disturbance or a determination to commit suicide. In some countries the conditions of confinement induce mental ill-health.

If they show signs of violence to themselves or to others they are placed in protection cells, or strip cells. Andrew Coyle, then governor of Brixton Prison in London, described the treatment of mentally ill prisoners in Brixton at the beginning of the 1990s and the wing in which they were held.

I shall never forget the first day I walked into this wing. The walls were painted bottle green. Permanent semi-darkness meant that artificial lighting had to be kept on all day. The all-pervading smell was overpowering, a combination of urine, faeces and stale food. And the noise. An unrelenting cacophony of keening, wailing, shouting and banging, which went on even during the night. Each cell had a large flap in its door. These were usually open. A face, usually a black face, peered out from most of them, hungry for human contact. This was the reality of imprisonment for mentally disturbed offenders in London in 1991.[88]

In the Caribbean, mentally ill prisoners are often left to manage as best they can in prison. When the Caribbean Dependent Territories were inspected by the Chief Inspector of Prisons of England and Wales in 1989, he found in the prison in the British Virgin Islands a mentally ill prisoner who was

given an injection by the visiting male psychiatric nurse once a month. He is held down by officers for this purpose. Thereafter he joins in association for a week or so and he helps to clean the yard. For the remaining three weeks he is kept alone in his cell for twenty-three hours daily. Two officers take him out for a bath and exercise. He is violent from time to time . . . He receives no other treatment.[89]

There is much sickness in prison, mental and physical. And there is death. Prison is a gloomy place in which to die. According to life-sentence prisoner Rideau,

It's dying away from home, alone, with strangers, in the callous atmosphere of prison, being treated and cared for, more often than not, by an indifferent hand. It's grossly different from dying in the warmth of home, in the bosom of friends and relatives, which eases the sting of death somewhat. There is nothing in the prisoner's world that can soften the finality of death. A longing look out of a window reveals a world of guns, curses, and noise as callous as the concrete it's made of. There is no warmth, beauty or meaning – no last pleasures, touches, joys, words. In prison, there is nothing – you suffer alone and you die alone, feeding the fear and misery of those who must watch you die.[90]

Prisoners sometimes die in prison by their own hand. In some countries suicide in prison is not uncommon and the suicide rates are always higher than the rates in the general population. Figures for the late 1980s show that the rate was 4 times higher in English and Welsh and Scottish prisons, 10 times higher in Italian and between 11 and 16 times higher in US prisons.[91] In the period 1985−95, 482 prisoners killed themselves in prisons in England and Wales.[92]

PRISON STAFF

It is not only the prisoners who are not representative of the population of the world at large. It is also the staff. Antonio Cassese, first chairman of the European Committee for the Prevention of Torture, has called them 'shipwrecked men supervising other castaways'.[93]

In many countries the status of prison staff is low. Because of the stigma of their work and the suspicion and hostility of people outside the prison world they tend to stick together socially, mixing only with each other at work and outside work. In many countries their work is dangerous and fear must be ever-present. Often they handle this fear in a way which makes violence more likely and the danger even greater.

A woman prison officer in a women's prison in Nigeria explained why the prisoners are not allowed newspapers, magazines and radios.

> When they listen to radio, they may hear things which will trouble their mind and may cause a riot . . . Newspapers are even worse than radio . . . And they will make the prisoners strong-headed, they won't want to obey any more. People, you human rights people, talk all kinds of things in the papers, some are true, some are lies. When the prisoners read this kind of story or article, they will be deceived and they will become confused and they will be encouraged to challenge prison authority.[94]

In many countries staff are organized along military lines. In Russian prisons all staff − guards, teachers, doctors − will have a military rank and wear a military uniform. In ex-British colonies the sub-military ethos is very strong.

Often the staff endure to a certain extent the same hardships as the prisoners. As Ivan Denisovich said, 'it's not all milk and honey for them either, lounging on the watchtowers in such cold'.[95]

At a meeting with all the staff of a prison in Malawi held in 1995 where they had an opportunity to air their complaints, the matters that concerned them were day-to-day ones. There was a shortage of prison houses so the staff had to live far away from the prison. Walking to and from work on foot was dangerous because an ex-prisoner might attack them. A promise had been made to one officer that he would be able to train as a prison driver but there was no prison transport for him to train on. The prison welfare officer was expected to care for the welfare of prisoners but had no resources with which to meet their needs.[96]

Prison staff in most countries are male and traditionally the only role for women staff has been as workers in the prison office or as guards in the women's section. However, equal opportunities legislation has meant that in some countries women are taking up more jobs in men's prisons. In Denmark, about one-fifth of prison staff are women and the proportion is rising.[97] In the Federal Bureau of Prisons of the United States, more than a quarter of the staff are women.[98]

Manifestations of staff discontent are an important element in the combustible mix of elements that make up the prison environment. Many countries have a history of long-running disputes with prison staff. France in particular is noted for regular and turbulent outbursts of staff discontent. In August 1992 a prison officer working in Rouen prison was attacked by a prisoner and died two days later. Although technically prison officers are not permitted to take industrial action, the prison officers' trade unions called on the officers to blockade their prisons and let nothing in or out. The strike affected most French prisons and made conditions for prisoners much worse. They reacted by rioting. One prisoner protesting on a roof at a prison in Mulhouse fell off and was killed. One escaped from prison by helicopter. The following day another was shot while trying to escape by helicopter from a top-security prison.

Negotiations with the Minister of Justice were successfully concluded and the staff went back to work. Then, on 11 September, a serious incident took place at Clairvaux, the most secure prison in

France. Clairvaux, a twelfth-century Cistercian abbey converted into the French Alcatraz in 1808, has a fearsome reputation. Guns were smuggled in and two armed prisoners tried to escape whilst they were taking exercise. Gunfire was exchanged and one prisoner and one prison officer were seriously wounded. Both subsequently died. Whilst this was happening another prisoner got hold of a lorry and used it as a battering ram to break down the main gate and get away. After the incident at Clairvaux, 130 out of France's 182 prisons were blockaded by staff and the action lasted for two weeks. Police were called in to run the prisons. Prison officers and police fought each other outside Baumettes prison near Marseille.[99]

French prison staff may have some justification on their side when they take industrial action against the penitentiary administration and ask for more staff. The number of staff in relation to prisoners is one of the lowest in Western Europe.[100]

Prison staff, because of the nature of the job, become very closed and inward looking. They develop a strong sense of grievance about those who in their eyes do the easy part of the job with prisoners – the social work, the education. They, on the other hand, have to do the searching of prisoners' persons and property, the locking and unlocking, the administering of punishments. In many prison systems the clash of culture between the uniformed staff and the others is palpable. There is a hostile reaction when prisoners are called Mr or their hand is shaken. In an Australian prison, the nurses who worked for the health service wanted to call the prisoners in the prison hospital 'patients'. The prison officers found this unacceptable. A compromise was reached. The prisoners in the hospital were called 'the clientele'.

Because of their feelings of being undervalued and taken for granted, prison staff often resent and resist improvements for prisoners. The comments of a prison officer in Australia showing some visitors round could have been heard in many prisons of the world: 'I won't bother to show you the officers' mess. It's only got a couple of fridges. They never do anything for us here. It's all for the prisoners.'[101]

Status is often related to remuneration. In poorer countries, prison staff are very badly paid. In Cambodia, for instance, in 1995 staff were paid the equivalent of $15 a month and prison governors $30. A living wage for a family with two children would have been about $200 a month.[102] This situation provides the basis for a range of corrupt practices: stealing prisoners' food, taking medicines meant for prisoners, removing supplies such as bedding or educational materials for use or resale, receiving money for favours such as more visits or a better cell location, taking money to allow wealthy prisoners to escape, selling drugs to prisoners. In prisons in Brazil corruption is widespread, according to Elói Pietá, a member of the state parliament of São Paulo. Because of the secrecy surrounding prisons, the low wages of the prison staff and the scarcity of resources, everything in a prison can be sold: a vacancy in a better cell or pavilion, access to a doctor, a phone call, a transfer to another prison. A prisoner reported that the rate for a transfer from a closed prison to a semi-open one was around $10,000. The price of things that are banned such as drugs and alcohol, is higher still. It is suggested that assistance with an escape is the most expensive of all.[103]

THE INSOLUBLE PROBLEMS

Lady Constance Lytton was a suffragette, one of those English women who fought for the vote for women at the beginning of the century. She was sent to prison many times for her activities, chaining herself to railings and throwing stones at prime ministers. She spent many weeks in Holloway, the main women's prison in London. She noted that the balconies and the gap between the galleries were covered with wire netting to prevent the women committing suicide, 'a precaution,' she said, 'in every way most characteristic of the prison system . . . nothing is done to prevent or counteract the desire for suicide in prisoners . . . The evil is only met by artificial prevention of its consequences.'[104]

Until recently, many prisons in England did not have sanitation in the cells. Prisoners sharing cells sometimes with two or three others had to use buckets. For obvious reasons, prisoners locked up all night with this bucket used to throw packets of excrement out of the windows. The response of the authorities was to put wire netting over the windows so that the parcels could not be thrown out.

There were a number of suicides of young people in England in prisons for those aged under twenty-one. These young people killed themselves by turning their beds on their ends and hanging themselves from the iron bedrails. Beds in prisons for young people were then nailed to the floor. 'The evil is only met by artificial prevention of its consequences.'

When one problem is solved another is created. Prison disrupts family relationships and places people in a single-sex environment. Different countries solve this problem in different ways. In Brazil prisoners are entitled to conjugal visits with someone known to them for six months prior to imprisonment, if medical tests are satisfactory. Conjugal visits take place in the cell blocks where all the prisoners live and the staff only enter when there is trouble and then they go in in large numbers. If prisoners meet someone after they are imprisoned they have to be in contact for six months before the conjugal visits start.[105]

This is a solution but it brings with it many possibilities of coercion and abuse.

Giving prisoners access to telephones is another way of keeping family ties. Since cash is not normally allowed in prison, prisoners can buy phone cards. Phone cards then become the new currency and they are stolen and traded.

Drug testing could encourage prisoners to change their habits and move from cannabis to heroin. So a new testing technique is being developed, a test of prisoners' hair, which it is claimed will get round this problem.

Prisoners in some prison systems have nothing left but their bodies. So the body becomes a tool to use in the struggle. Breyten Breytenbach explains. 'The most popular carrying bag, or hidy-hole, is of course the anus . . . it is absolutely eye-popping when you see what objects can be hidden there: blades, knives, letters, money . . . always wrapped in plastic . . .'[106]

To get out of a prison where the situation has become desperate, prisoners also use their bodies. Breytenbach tells how they would 'procure a needle and thread, impregnate the thread with one's own excreta and then insert this under the skin by means of the needle. Left there for some time it was guaranteed to rot the flesh.'[107]

The Tokyo Detention House is the largest pre-trial prison in Japan and holds 2050 prisoners. It has a well-equipped hospital and eleven doctors on the staff. The Chief Medical Officer shows visitors a gruesome exhibition in a museum-type glass case of items called 'foreign bodies', which prisoners have swallowed 'in order to get out of prison' and a series of x-ray plates confirming the fact. His main work seems to be performing surgery to recover these items.[108]

In Romania in 1994, prisoners went through a phase of hammering nails into their skulls to get out of prison and into hospital. The doctor described the seventeenth case. The prisoner was twenty-three years old and had in his skull a rusty nail, completely embedded and covered with excrement. The doctor commented,

> All of them are young. The average age is under twenty-five. When one of them decides to do it, all the others from the cell block go to the prison hospital and say they can't sleep and each gets half a sleeping pill. The prisoners give their pills to the one who is going to hammer nails in his head . . . so he is under total anaesthesia when he starts introducing the nail.[109]

One group of people in prison highlights very starkly all the points made in this chapter about disadvantage and discrimination. That group is women. It is to the special situation of women in prison that we now turn.

7. Women in Prison

Who were the women who, day by day, trod the very stones on which my feet now stood? . . . How and why had they broken the law, in what way were they enemies of Society? . . . Child-burdened women who were left without money, without the means or opportunity or physical power to earn it, who had stolen in order to save their lives and that of their children, – thieves! Women who from their childhood had been trained to physical shame, women who at their first adolescence had borne children by their own fathers under circumstances when resistance was inconceivable. Women who had been seduced by their employers. Women deceived and deserted by their friends and lovers. Women employed by their own parents for wage-earning prostitution . . . Women who had been stolen in their bloom and imprisoned for purposes of immoral gain. If amongst such women, such criminals, there are many who are professionally thieves, prostitutes 'by choice', immoral 'past redemption' as it is called, sodden with drink, undermined by drug taking, their maternity transformed into cruelty, their brains worn to madness, what cause is there for surprise or reproach, and what hope is there of cure by imprisonment?

Lady Constance Lytton, suffragette, writing on the occasion of her first committal to prison, 1914[1]

In the small Caribbean island of St Vincent, women prisoners are kept in a crumbling, eighteenth-century fort. The fort is actually a tourist attraction visited for its historical associations and its excellent view of the capital, Kingstown. Few tourists would realize that behind the locked gate with a sign above it in large white letters saying 'Restricted Area' a dozen or so women are locked in, only ever leaving the five rooms of their prison for an occasional trip on to the roof to breathe the fresh air. The death penalty is in force in St Vincent and the gallows is up at the fort where the women live. From the roof of their prison the women prisoners have a good view of the gallows. They are looked after by a matron and an assistant. Their accommodation consists of three shared dormitories, a large communal bathroom, a sitting-room with a sewing machine and a large verandah. The prison for the women is so much of an after-thought, a makeshift arrangement on the fringes of the prison world, that it has no proper kitchen. The women's food is cooked in the men's prison and brought up the hill to the fort by van. There is no exercise area, no education, no real work and no vocational training.[2]

In Lilongwe, capital of Malawi, in southern Africa, women are imprisoned not in a separate prison of their own but in a women's section attached to a much bigger prison for men. In March 1995, twenty-three women were being looked after by six female staff. They lived in a hut built thirty years earlier as temporary accom-modation. It was made of corrugated iron. The windows were gaps in the corrugated iron covered with barbed wire. In one corner shielded by a door was a lavatory. Five children lived there with their mothers. One was four years old and had lived in the prison since she was one year old. The children were dirty and unhealthy-looking. Nine women attended a literacy class on weekdays. Otherwise there were no activities except cleaning and washing.[3]

Mo Lihua was imprisoned in China in 1989 after participating in a student demonstration. She was accused of incitement and making counter-revolutionary propaganda. She was sent first for investi-gation to the Women's Section of the Custody and Investigation Centre. The Women's Section was actually a large cell in the middle of a courtyard. It was a dark room containing only a large communal bed and hole in the ground for a toilet. There was no water so a terrible smell came from the toilet hole all the time. Rats nearly twenty centimetres long would crawl out of the toilet hole and run all over the women as they lay in bed. There was no glass in the barred windows and when it rained the bed and the bedcovers were soaked through. The prisoners got clean clothes or toilet paper only when they could be provided by their families.[4]

Many of the women in the world's prisons live in such conditions, either in a makeshift building, originally designed for some other purpose or in a small and neglected adjunct to a larger men's prison. In either case the arrangements are an afterthought, a response to a situation that no one quite knows how to handle. For the most remarkable fact about women in prison is how few of them there are. All over the world women make up a tiny minority of those locked up. The proportions are truly startling. On average only one out of every twenty prisoners is a woman. Women constitute roughly 50 per cent of the population of any country, yet provide only 5 per cent of its prisoners. This is not specific to any one country or region, but is reflected all over the world. There are variations. In Spain, the proportion of women in prison is 10 per cent,[5] in the United States over 6 per cent,[6] in France 4 per cent,[7] in Russia 3 per cent[8] and in Morocco it is 2 per cent.[9] But nowhere in the world do women make up more than one in ten of the whole prison population.

Who are the women in prison? The answer to this too is similar in every country. Women in prison are overwhelmingly poor. Many have themselves been victims of abuse, sexual or physical, sometimes from early childhood.

A comprehensive survey of women in state prisons in the US was carried out in 1991. It showed that they were likely to be unemployed at the time of their arrest.[10] More than half came from a home without two parents present. Nearly half had had a family member in prison. More than four out of every ten had been physically or sexually abused.[11] Two out of three had children.[12] Over 3 per cent were HIV-positive.[13] One in three was imprisoned for a drug offence and three in ten for offences involving violence. In nearly two-thirds of these violent offences, the victim was a relative or someone they knew. One in three of those imprisoned for murder had killed a husband, ex-husband or boyfriend.[14]

A similar study of women in federal prisons in Canada in 1989 showed that two-thirds had suffered physical abuse, and over half sexual abuse. The figures were much higher for women of aboriginal origin, namely 90 per cent physical and 61 per cent sexual abuse.[15]

Whilst studying the problems of women remand prisoners in Holloway Prison in London, researcher Silvia Casale observed an exchange during the reception procedure. A woman prisoner was being fingerprinted. 'You can't do that one,' she said. 'My husband cut it off.' There was silence for a moment in the reception department. Then the fingerprinting officer said, 'I'll lend you mine, love, shall I?' This prompted the woman to tell the officer about the fight with her husband when she had lost her finger. The prisoner and the officer then went off together, with the officer carrying the woman's paper bags full of her possessions.[16]

Insiders by Una Padel and Prue Stevenson is an English study of a small number of women prisoners. Martia left home for good when she was fifteen because 'things didn't go right in the house' and when she was sixteen she was put into a home for bad children.[17] Janet was in prison for supplying drugs. She 'had a horrific adolescence and childhood' and two nervous breakdowns whilst still a teenager.[18] Margy was taken into care at the age of three because of physical violence by her father.[19] Jean had a long history of severe depression and alcoholism.[20] Sharon came from a home where her stepfather sexually assaulted her as a child and beat her mother so severely that he blinded her.[21] Mary was put into a children's home when she was nine.[22] Lee's mother died when she was nine and she and her five brothers and sisters were moved from one foster home to another.[23] Joanne, aged forty-seven, had a nervous breakdown when her mother died and she spent years in and out of prisons and psychiatric hospitals.[24]

These women were interviewed in England. But their stories could be replicated in any other part of the world. A twenty-year-old woman in prison in Cambodia in 1995 was in the third year of an eight-year prison sentence for murder. She was pregnant when she was arrested. She was taken from prison to hospital to have the baby. The child would stay with her until her release. Her parents were poor wood-cutters and could not afford to look after the child. But they came to see her in prison once a year. She filled her time in prison doing the cooking for the staff.[25]

What crimes have these women committed that cause them to lose their liberty? Many of them have as yet been convicted of no crime. They are pre-trial prisoners. In Nigeria, between 70 and 80 per cent of women prisoners are awaiting trial.[26] Sometimes women will spend time in prison before conviction but not afterwards. In England, the figures are exceptionally high. Two-thirds of women locked up in prison before their trial do not get sent to prison when their case comes to court.[27]

For those who are convicted, their crimes are either petty, often arising from economic necessity, or are crimes of violence within the family, usually against a husband or partner, often a violent one. The Egyptian writer Nawal el Sa'adawi spent time in prison in 1981 as a political prisoner. There she met, amongst others, Fathiyya-the-Murderess. She

> was a poor miserable woman, planting and harvesting with her own hands, while her husband lounged about the house, a lazy bum. Eating, burping, smoking his waterpipe. One day, she came back from the field and found him on top of her daughter, her nine-year-old daughter. She struck him on the head with her hoe and got a life sentence.[28]

Many women are in prison for prostitution or crimes connected with prostitution. If they are in prison for a crime connected with drugs, it is often because they have carried drugs into another country for a paltry sum of money, persuaded by some drug dealer that they would not get caught and that it was easy money. Such women are often called 'mules', with the implication that they are nothing but beasts of burden.

The profile of crimes committed by women that lead them into prison is very different from the profile of crimes committed by men. Women's crimes are less often violent. Many are imprisoned for the 'crimes of poverty', stealing or defrauding social security.

Imprisoned women in England and Wales have shorter criminal histories than imprisoned men. In 1994, nearly two-thirds of women prisoners had two or fewer previous convictions compared with one-third of men. This figure includes one-fifth of women with no previous convictions at all compared with 16 per cent of men.[29] In

Table 9   Offences committed by imprisoned women compared with imprisoned men in England and Wales in 1996

Nature of offence	Women	Men
Violence	28.3%	45.4%
Theft and handling	18.1%	8.7%
Drugs	28.6%	12.8%

Source: Home Office, *Prison Statistics, England and Wales, 1996*

1996, 89 women in England and Wales were sent to prison because they did not have a television licence; when they were fined for not having one, they could not pay the fine.[30] In Blantyre prison in Malawi in 1995, one woman was serving ten months for theft. One was doing one year and four months for possession of Indian hemp. Another was serving eleven months for stealing cash. A fifteen-year-old was serving one year for theft of clothes. A young woman had been sent to prison for four years when she was sixteen for stealing a large amount of money. Another was doing three years for fighting at a beer party and one was in for three years for theft of a radio cassette player. One was serving five years for murder.[31]

With these substantial differences between imprisoned men and imprisoned women, in numbers, seriousness of crime and level of threat posed to society, one might suppose that some form of detention had by now been devised appropriate to the special circumstances of this very small number of highly disadvantaged women. In fact, this is not so. In every country there is a prison system for men, and women are everywhere tacked on as an awkward afterthought; in the same sort of buildings as men, only often worse; with the same sort of rules and regulations, though often more strictly applied; with the same sort of prison activities, though frequently more poverty-stricken. The punishment of women by the deprivation of liberty has never been seen as an opportunity to imprison in a different way. Women are always put in places modelled, regulated and programmed like the prisons for the twenty-times-more-numerous male prisoners.

In following the male model of imprisonment, prison administrations immediately face a difficulty. There really are not enough women prisoners to support an economically viable prison system. Even a large town or city will not produce enough women prisoners to justify a fully equipped women's prison. The obvious managerial answer is to put them all together in one, or a few places, where the numbers make the running of a whole prison worthwhile. But then of course they will have to be sent very far from their homes and families, which is bad enough for men but even worse perhaps for women, who tend to have dependent children with whom they want to keep in touch. The numbers are so small that separating types of prisoners from each other, convicted from unconvicted, young prisoners from adults, is quite impractical.

Putting them all together is one solution. Alternatively, large men's prisons can have small units attached to them where the women are kept, surrounded by high walls to ensure that the rules about keeping women separate from men are adhered to.

This approach is the main one used in Sweden, where some women prisoners are held in two women-only prisons and the rest are distributed around eighteen neighbourhood prisons which hold both men and women. Which solution would women prisoners prefer? Research carried out in Sweden found that more than half of the women would choose to be held in a mixed prison, with a further one in five saying either would do. However, the women who were questioned noted that when their numbers were very small their opportunities for vocational training were limited.[32]

In Slovenia the first approach is followed. There is one women's prison holding the country's women prisoners, thirty in all.[33] In Spain there are four women's prisons and other imprisoned women are housed in women's sections in male prisons.[34] In Nigeria there is one all-female prison. Otherwise women live in female wings attached to most of the country's 130 prisons.[35] In Portugal there is one women's prison.[36]

In Russia women are held in special prison camps for women. This means they are held very far, sometimes thousands of kilometres, from their homes. Women in Russian prison camps are also worse off than men because, whilst there are five different levels of security for men prisoners, for women there are only two: general regimes for first offenders and strict regimes for 'particularly dangerous recidivists'.[37] All too often, these particularly dangerous women recidivists, held in the two severe colonies for women with about a thousand prisoners in each, turn out to be persistent shoplifters and petty thieves.[38]

So there is already a serious problem in applying to this small group of women the ideas and structures of a system designed for a much larger group of people with quite different characteristics. Putting women in one prison for a country or a region so that it is large enough to provide reasonable facilities is one solution.

Spreading them in small groups around the men's prisons is another. Both are flawed. The first solution condemns women to be located many miles from what matters most to them, that is their families. The second means that women prisoners and the staff looking after them are seen as an untidy adjunct to a system not designed for them, so they receive inferior facilities.

The second dilemma facing those responsible for imprisoning women is similarly not soluble within the framework of imprisonment as it is currently conceived. What is to be done about the fact that some women are mothers? Some women come into prison pregnant and give birth during their sentence. Should they have their babies delivered in prison or in an outside hospital? What is to be done with their children? To take them away at birth or soon afterwards is cruel and may damage the child. To keep them means a young child is brought up in the abnormal atmosphere of a prison and at some point, should the mother's sentence be long, the child will in any case have to be separated from its mother.

Various solutions to this dilemma are in place. Most countries send imprisoned pregnant women to an outside hospital to have their babies. It was not always so. The suffragette Emmeline Pankhurst, imprisoned before the First World War for her activities in the campaign to win votes for women, said in one of her speeches in 1908,

> I was in the hospital at Holloway, and when I was there I heard from one of the beds near me the moans of a woman who was in the pangs of childbirth. I should like you to realize how women feel at helpless little infants breathing their first breath in the atmosphere of prison. We believe that if we get the vote we will find more humane ways of dealing with women than that.[39]

Sending women to outside hospitals as is done now in most countries is undoubtedly more humane, but even so Emmeline Pankhurst would probably still find plenty to shock her. When the European Committee for the Prevention of Torture visited France they found that when women prisoners went to civilian hospitals to have babies they were sometimes tied to their beds, both during labour and after giving birth. The Committee described this practice as 'a flagrant example of inhuman and degrading treatment'.[40] In a similar case in England the prison authorities apologized to a woman who was kept handcuffed whilst she was giving birth, so she could not even grip the bed rails in pain. She also had to feed her baby with the handcuffs on.[41]

This blanket application of rigid security rules, devised because of the need to keep male prisoners from escaping, is a feature of women's imprisonment that is particularly disproportionate. Electronic devices, guard dogs, handcuffs and closet chains (chains long enough to enable a prisoner to use the lavatory whilst still attached to a prison officer) are often excessive in relation to the risk posed by men prisoners. When applied to women, most of whom are imprisoned for non-violent offences and whose escape would pose no threat whatsoever to anyone, they are absurd. When there is one of the frequent about-turns in penal policy and rules are tightened up, the new rules apply to all prisoners without any assessment being made of the relevance or propriety of applying them equally to men and women. In 1996 the non-governmental organization NACRO published the result of discussions held in four women's prisons in England with 200 prisoners and staff. One of the women explained the effect of new security regulations that had been brought in following escapes and crimes committed by men on temporary absence from prison. The report tells of one woman whose daughter had been murdered while her mother was in prison.

> She had been escorted to the funeral and handcuffed. She was in tears when she told how she had thrown soil on the grave with her hand cuffed to an officer . . . She stressed the kindness of the officer but said she could never go out of the prison again if she was not on licence.

Other women complained about the new regulations that meant their children had to be searched before visits. Some had stopped their children visiting as it had upset them too much.[42]

In Nigeria women are subject to internal searches when they arrive in prison. A woman lawyer, Mrs Ojong-Ishie, imprisoned for participating in a religious demonstration, described the process:

the wardresses . . . begin to even kind of examine you . . . they touch
your breasts, they take you in and even want to finger you to find
out whether you have things inside . . . to find out whether you have
stuffed things in your womanhood. I think that's humiliating.[43]

Once the babies are born, what is to become of them then? And
what happens to women sentenced to prison who have just had a
baby? Practices in dealing with babies in prison vary considerably
from one country to another. In Bulgaria the law allows imprisoned
mothers to keep their babies until they are one year old.[44] In Sweden
mothers with babies can keep them up to the age of two,[45] in Poland
up to three,[46] in Germany up to six.[47] In Spain the law says six.[48] In
Russia children can stay until aged three or four and then women
are given two weeks' leave to take them home to be cared for by
relatives.

Babies in prison are often kept in special nurseries where the
mother can spend some time with them but the care is done by
professional care workers. This is the case in the countries of the
former Soviet Union; in Russia nearly half the women in prison
have children with them. In Portugal at the beginning of 1994, fifty
babies and infants were in prison with their mothers.[49] In Bulgaria
there are between three and five babies in prison every year.[50]

The European Committee on the Prevention of Torture had warm
commendation for the mother-and-baby unit at the women's prison
at Rebibbia, Italy. The fifteen-place unit held twelve mothers with
their babies under three years old. They lived in very good conditions
and a psychiatric nurse and a doctor visited frequently. The atmosphere of the unit was co-operative and sociotherapeutic and the
mothers were helped to develop their maternal skills.[51]

But women do not only have babies. Another major element of
difference between imprisoning men and imprisoning women is
what they leave outside. Women usually play the main part in caring
for the children in a family and frequently they are the sole carer.
The British National Prison Survey found that nearly half of the
women coming into prison had children living with them. When
they went into prison, half of them left their children with relatives,
fewer than a quarter with the father or partner and for more than
one in ten the child went to foster parents or into care.[52] Separation

from their children can be bad for them and bad for the upbringing of the children. For imprisoned women, leaving their children behind is often the worst aspect of going to prison. Often they fear that the children will be taken away from them and put permanently in the care of the authorities.

Because of the small numbers of women prisoners and the geographical distances, visiting becomes a major difficulty for grandmothers or aunts looking after the children of imprisoned mothers.

Children visiting prisons is in any case a delicate subject. Some countries allow no visits to prisoners from children under sixteen. In others attempts have been made to humanize visiting arrangements for children with their imprisoned mothers. At Bedford Hills Prison in New York three-quarters of the prisoners are mothers. According to Human Rights Watch this prison has made extensive arrangements for prisoners to keep contact with their children.

> In the summer, the facility runs week-long programs for inmates' children who are housed with local families and spend the day with their mothers on the premises. They play with their mothers in a large, toy-filled visiting room, and may also participate in a number of organized activities. In addition, they can also use a playground outside. Year-round, according to the warden, there are bus rides once a month from New York City and Albany, arranged so that children can visit their mothers without having to be accompanied by other relatives.[53]

On the other hand, the Tennessee Institution for Women and the Broward prison in Miami, Florida, when visited by Human Rights Watch in 1991, had no arrangements for visiting children and did not allow children to stay with their mothers. At Broward Institution, according to Human Rights Watch, 'Inmates are not allowed to hold visiting children on their lap during the visit and are allowed to give them a brief hug only at the beginning and at the end of the visit.'[54]

In addition to the problems of geographical distance, childbearing and separation from children, women prisoners are also the poor relations when it comes to the quality and choice of programmes they are offered. The activity for the majority of women prisoners in the world is probably sewing, as it has been since women's imprisonment became widespread. In the first purpose-built prison for women in Brixton in London, opened in 1853, women started off picking old ropes to pieces. If they were good and did this diligently and in complete silence for two months, they could progress to the next stage, doing needlework locked in their cells.[55]

All over Russia and the former Soviet Union women are sitting in enormous workshops at sewing machines. Sometimes they are making the little dresses that women prisoners in many countries of the world are required to wear (often with a headscarf to hide their hair). Frequently they are making uniforms for government employees or the military. Sometimes they are making clothes for sale on the open market or for a private company. Making teddy bears and other soft toys is a women's prison activity. Many women prisoners work in laundries, doing the washing for themselves and for neighbouring men's prisons and perhaps other government institutions. Rarely are they to be found learning computer skills, working in electronics, training for any skill wider than sewing, washing, cleaning or childcare. In 1981 the Canadian Human Rights Commission upheld a complaint of discrimination against women prisoners on the grounds that they were getting unequal access to prison programmes, poorer facilities, 'geographic dislocation' and higher security classification.[56] In 1990 a Canadian court found that the treatment of a woman prisoner, Ms Daniels, a native Canadian, violated the Canadian Charter of Rights and Freedoms because she would have to go to the one federal prison for women in Kingston, Ontario, many miles from her home area.[57]

What is it like to live in a women's prison? Judith Ward was twenty-five years old when she was imprisoned for planting bombs that killed twelve people. She was given twelve life sentences and spent eighteen years in prison. In 1992 her conviction was overturned and she was released, a victim of a gross miscarriage of justice. She wrote about her eighteen years in prison. Fifteen of those years she had spent in the top-security women's wing in Durham Prison. She describes an evening in 1975 in the special wing, called H wing, a unit for women in a prison for 1000 men, a place surrounded by a twenty-foot-high fence with razor-wire observed all the time by cameras.

The evening started off normally, with women watching TV or doing their washing, chatting to each other. Then Judith Ward went to the shower room.

> It looked as if someone had been murdered: there was blood on the walls, on the shower curtain, mingling with the water as it trickled down the plughole, past the unconscious, naked body of a woman.[58]

Monica, a drug addict serving four years, had slashed her arm through to the artery. Another prisoner, Janet, had been feeling depressed anyway and when she heard the commotion she smashed a mug and used it to do the same to herself. 'Cutting up,' says Judith Ward,

> is common in women's prisons. Male inmates tend to fight and be aggressive; women can also be aggressive, although the majority tend to withdraw into themselves and often relieve their depression, anger or guilt by inflicting pain on themselves.[59]

Leaving the prisoners to care for Monica the staff ran to the aid of Janet. Mary, in the room next to the shower, had saved up a week's supply of medicine, which she had just taken and at that point she went berserk and tried to climb out of her cell window, even though it was covered by three sets of bars and a grille. Six people were needed to restrain her until she became calm. Eventually it was all dealt with and the prisoners were locked up. Judith Ward lay in bed thinking,

> What kind of idiot was I, thinking that things would change, that some day I would be free of this life, this locking in, this depressing, claustrophobic box, filled with sad, frustrated despairing people? . . . Wouldn't it be better to end it all? . . . The idea was attractive. I searched around for something sharp, anything. I stared around the room and my eyes lit upon the records. I plucked one out of its sleeve, broke it and began to cut.[60]

She awoke to find her arms being bandaged and heard the governor's voice in the background, asking whether she would need her wounds to be stitched.[61]

The governor of Durham Prison at that time was a man and many men work in women's prisons. Controversy surrounds this question. The international rules make it clear that women should be guarded by other women. Abuse of women prisoners has long been a feature of the treatment of women who have lost their liberty. The women convicts transported to Australia often ended up in prostitution there.[62] In 1807 the son of the governor of the prison at Cold Bath Fields, London, is reported to have 'debauched' a woman prisoner.[63]

In developing countries the rule that only women should guard women is widely followed. Male staff only enter the women's compound in the presence of a female member of staff and male staff are not assigned to the women's section or to direct duties with women prisoners. In Nigeria, for instance, according to the Civil Liberties Organisation, the female wings of prisons are normally out of bounds to warders and male visitors. When men come in, for example to provide health care to the women, they are well guarded.[64]

In developed countries the rule is seen as conflicting with equal opportunities legislation and it is not followed. The deployment of male staff to women's prisons is widespread.

It brings problems. At the end of 1996 the Women's Rights Project of Human Rights Watch published a report on the sexual abuse of women in state prisons in the US. It was based on research carried out over two and a half years in four states and the District of Columbia. The research found that male prison staff had 'vaginally, anally and orally raped women prisoners and sexually assaulted and abused them'.[65] They had used their power over the prisoners to barter access to goods and privileges for sexual favours. They had used the opportunity given to them when pat-searching or searching rooms to 'grope women's breasts, buttocks and vaginal areas'. They had taken advantage of their position to spy on them whilst they were undressed in their living areas or in the bathrooms. They had subjected women to 'verbal degradation and harassment'.[66]

In California more than half the staff of the women's prisons are men.[67] According to the report, women in administrative segregation in Valley State Prison for Women who need extra sanitary napkins must ask for them one at a time, from guards who are usually men.

> One woman reported that she had to wait until she had menstrual
> blood running down her leg before she could get a sanitary napkin.
> In another reported case, male guards threw a packet of sanitary
> napkins on to the floor ... and the prisoner had to 'fish' for the
> packet by using a string, with which she was supposed to catch the
> packet and drag it along the floor into her cell. While she tried to get
> the napkins, the guards shouted encouragement and bet on whether
> she would be successful.[68]

In Michigan staff are apparently trained to use the back of their
hand rather than the palm when pat-searching women prisoners.
Nevertheless women prisoners reported that male staff frequently
used 'their open hands and fingers to grope or grip a woman's
breasts and nipples, vagina, buttocks, anus and thighs'.[69]

Women who pull away or object are given 'misconduct tickets'
and can be placed in segregation or lose some of the time off their
sentence. Normally in Michigan, strip searches should be performed
by officers of the same sex. But it is allowed for a male officer to
strip search a woman prisoner when she is to be transported outside
the prison or when there is an emergency. A male supervisor can also
be present during a strip search.[70] Women held in the Florence Crane
Women's Facility sleep in open dormitories. They have no privacy
when dressing or undressing and male staff can walk in at any time
with no warning. Prisoners reported that male officers patrol the
showers and toilets when the women are using them. The checks are
supposed to be to prevent sexual activity between the women, but
since the shower curtains and toilet doors reveal legs and feet the
pulling back of the shower curtains hardly seems to be justifiable.[71]

Also in Michigan, male staff have accompanied women to gynaecological examinations and remained in the room. One woman
complained to the prison warden that she felt uncomfortable
undressing and talking about her gynaecological problems to the
doctor in front of the male officer. According to the warden, the
officer had to keep the prisoner in his sight and she had a choice:
accept the male officer in the room, or no medical visit. Another
woman prisoner alleged that male staff handcuffed her to the bed
when she was in labour and positioned themselves so that they could
view her genital area whilst she was giving birth.[72]

Such situations could not occur everywhere. In England and Wales female staff are allowed to conduct pat-searches of men prisoners but men are not allowed to carry out such searches of women. The Supreme Court of Canada ruled in 1993 that female staff may frisk male prisoners and look into their cells without warning but did not allow male staff to frisk women prisoners.[73] In Canada in 1994 a scandal arose over the treatment of women prisoners by male guards that led to the resignation of John Edwards, the Commissioner of the Correctional Service of Canada, saying that 'a change in leadership would be the best course of action'.[74]

The incident occurred four days after a major serious outbreak of violence at the women's prison. According to the report into the matter by the Correctional Service of Canada, the outbreak of violence on 22 April 1994 was stopped by firing bursts of the chemical agent mace at the faces of the prisoners and then removing them in restraints to the segregation unit.[75] On 24 April one of the women in the segregation unit slashed herself and then went on to take another prisoner hostage. The hostage was released after mace was fired at the prisoner holding the hostage.[76] Shortly afterwards another prisoner tried to hang herself but she was immediately cut down.[77] On 26 April the prisoners in the segregation unit began throwing coffee and other liquids at the staff and tried to take a staff member hostage.[78] They did not succeed and then began to set fire to bedding. At this point the decision was taken to bring in an emergency response team (ERT) from the nearby men's prison.[79] Three hours later the all-male team entered the segregation unit.[80]

According to the report of the Correctional Investigator, who watched a video recording of the action, the task of the team 'was to remove one woman at a time from her cell, strip the cell of all effects, and return that woman to her cell'. The procedure for each of the eight women was roughly the same. The team entered the cell and if the woman was not already naked, ordered her to remove her clothes. One that did not comply immediately had her clothes cut off her.

> Each woman was then told to kneel, naked, on the floor of her cell, surrounded by ERT members while restraint equipment was applied. After the restraint equipment was applied, each woman was helped

back to her feet, backed out of the cell naked, then given a flimsy paper gown, and marched backwards by the ERT from her cell to the shower area.

The cell was then stripped of everything, including the bed; the woman was brought back, and left in the cell, in restraint equipment, with no blanket or mattress to lie on.

The Correctional Investigator found that 'The video tape of the deployment of the ERT shows a massive display of force being exercised in the face of virtually no resistance.'[81] The exercise was 'degrading and dehumanizing for those women involved'. It was initiated 'for the purpose of appeasing fragile staff psyches and boosting management's diminishing credibility in the eyes of its employees'.[82] According to the report, after the incident the women were held, some for up to eight months, in segregation cells

> initially stripped of all amenities, subject to twenty-four-hour-a-day camera surveillance and the wearing of restraint equipment whenever they left their cells. They were denied for extended periods of time bedding, clothing including underwear, basic hygiene items, personal address books, writing material, contact with family and daily exercise.[83]

He concludes,

> The Correctional Service of Canada, in responding to these concerns, has taken no action which can be seen as timely, adequate or appropriate. The Service's responses to this entire matter can be characterized as 'admit no wrong, give as little as possible and time will eventually resolve the matter'.[84]

A judicial investigation was then carried out by the Toronto appeal court judge, Louise Arbour. Her inquiry found that the Correctional Service of Canada had breached many of the regulations governing the treatment of prisoners. Prisoners who had been subdued with gas had not been decontaminated according to the procedures by being allowed to shower, wash and bathe their eyes.[85] The use of force was not properly documented.[86] The police should have been called in to investigate the assault on the prison personnel.[87] Prisoners in the segregation unit had been denied their one hour's exercise a day, access to lawyers and other officials such as the

Correctional Investigator, to books and activities, showers and cleaning. The strip search of women by men was against regulations and policy.[88] Furthermore, 'the inevitable brutality of this type of intervention, combined with the necessary physical handling of individual women by [men], while each woman is completely naked for a period of time, and then very improperly covered by a paper gown or bib' was, in the opinion of Judge Arbour, 'cruel, inhumane and degrading'.[89] Also keeping the prisoners in segregation for many months in punitive conditions was 'a profound failure of the custodial mandate of the Correctional Service'.[90]

Have women been excluded from the worldwide trend on increased use of imprisonment? They have not. In fact the number of women in prison is increasing, in some countries much faster than the rate of increase for men. In the US the prison population overall has tripled since 1980. The female prison population has increased sixfold.[91] In England and Wales the number of women in prison rose by 57 per cent between 1992 and 1995. The rise in the number of men prisoners was 29 per cent.[92] In June 1997 there were 2664 women prisoners.[93]

Even so the numbers are small and always have been. The history of the imprisonment of women is a history of dealing with ambiguity. There is a fascination with 'bad' women and many assumptions about women prisoners. The official rationale of women's imprisonment has through the ages concentrated on trying to turn these 'bad' women into good housewives and mothers. The prisons where they have been held have aped men's prisons, and the rules they have been subjected to have been men's prison rules with slight concessions such as being allowed to wear private clothes rather than a prison uniform. They have been kept in buildings and under a regime designed to deal with quite different problems. In most reports about prisons and penal reform they are an afterthought. Sometimes, as with the report by Lord Justice Woolf into prison disturbances in England and Wales in 1990, they are not mentioned at all.[94] They are, as the Nigerian Civil Liberties Organisation described them, 'the prisoners in the shadows'.

8. *The Young*

H[er] M[ajesty] was really interested in all you said about the youthful criminals. She would like to whip them, but it seems that that cannot be done.

Sir Henry Ponsonby, Private Secretary to Queen Victoria, writing to Home Secretary Sir William Harcourt in 1880[1]

Visiting prisons is a sad business. But the saddest aspect of it is seeing the young people, the fifteen-, sixteen-, seventeen-year-old boys. They have a cheeky bravado which often cloaks terror or despair. Many have a hollow-eyed, haunted look. In some countries it is not difficult to work out where this haunted look comes from. The prisons are large and mainly unsupervised. What nearly always happens to the fifteen- or sixteen-year-olds thrown into a dormitory with large numbers of older and bigger prisoners is easy to imagine. Their faces show the effects of their experiences. Even in the youth prisons of countries where the avowed objective is to protect the young prisoners and the official ethos is of care and protection, they still exude misery and hopelessness. They come with sorrows of their own, from their family background and previous experiences of rejection. Then in prison they are tormented and preyed upon by the older ones.

The poignancy of their current situation is made worse as one looks at them and is able to predict their future – now they are pathetic and tormented. Soon they will become the tormentors and abusers of the next batch of younger prisoners. After that most of them are destined to be regular inhabitants of the adult prisons. Amongst them will be the next generation of violent criminals who will end up serving long or life sentences. Their future seems mapped out for them. The process is inexorable. The work of the system, whether designed to punish, reform, rehabilitate or care, seems doomed to fail.

Simon Willerton was seventeen when he was sent in May 1990 to an adult prison in Leeds, in the north of England. Simon was pretty ordinary. He came from Bradford, the fourth in a family of five children. He went to school in Bradford. He was very small for his age. His head teacher said of him, 'He got picked on because of his size but he was the most harmless and affectionate boy we've ever had in school.'[2]

He was the sort of boy who was the last in the class to make a date with a girl and then she wouldn't turn up. His glasses fell apart and he held them together with Sellotape. He made friends with the school caretaker and spent hours with him, helping him in his work. He left school at sixteen and went on a government work-training scheme. Then he left home. He was given a council flat on a big public housing estate. His training scheme came to an end. In March he stole some lead and burgled the house of a ninety-one-year-old woman. He stole a purse. He was arrested and then released on bail. He stole a kettle from an unoccupied house. He was caught and released again, but with the condition that he lived at his flat. He moved out and sold the hot-water cylinder from the flat. This time he was remanded in custody, and locked up in Leeds Prison. There, he was moved from cell to cell to protect him from the constant bullying by other prisoners. He slashed his hands twice with a razor and ended up in the prison hospital. Once he was seen sobbing as he walked around the prison exercise yard. Once he tried to hang himself but his cell-mates cut him down. On 6 August he was beaten up again by other prisoners. That night he was found hanging in his cell.[3] Purely by chance the prison was visited the following day by the European Committee on the Prevention of Torture.[4] The Committee later declared that conditions in Leeds amounted to inhuman and degrading treatment or punishment.[5]

Jeffrey Horler came from Great Yarmouth on the east coast of England, where he lived with his mother and four brothers and sisters. When he was fourteen, he left home and was placed with foster parents for a while. He returned but was taken away from home again and placed with foster parents in the spring of 1991 after he was arrested for trying to steal a car. He got into further trouble and in August he appeared in court for setting fire to an old barn. This time, although he was only fifteen, he was sent to prison. He got a sentence of 118 days. There is no prison near his home so he was sent 200 miles away, to Feltham Young Offenders Institution, near London, the largest youth prison in Western Europe.

Three weeks after his arrival at Feltham his grandmother died. He was told about it a few days later and was very upset. He wanted to buy some flowers and go to the funeral. The prison staff were sympathetic and contacted the local social services department. The social services department would have needed to provide the transport to get him there because the prison was short-staffed. Without speaking to Jeffrey the social services decided not to take him. The social worker said,

> We considered the effect on Jeffrey. We knew him well and we believed that although he might well be upset about his grandmother's death, missing the funeral would not have a very great effect on him. We also considered the obvious practical difficulties – it is nearly 200 miles from Yarmouth to Feltham. That would involve someone in an 800 mile journey in two days. There was also the cost that had to be considered.[6]

He did not get over it very quickly. A fellow prisoner reported three weeks later that Jeffrey 'started talking about his gran who died about two weeks ago, I think. He told me that he was upset because he wasn't allowed to the funeral of his gran. He also said he didn't get many visits.'[7]

The next day a prisoner in a nearby cell heard him threaten to hang himself. They shouted to each other from cell to cell but after a while there was silence. Eventually the other prisoners called an officer. He found Jeffrey hanging by his shirt from the window. He was taken to hospital where he was certified dead. That day he had written a letter home.

> To Mum + Dad kids
> Hi all how are you Mum and Dad
> hop you are well
> . . . I have 19 days to go and then i will Be home
> i Will Be home a bat 2 .o.cock on 11 October
> i will see you at home.[8]

Between 1990 and 1996, twenty-six young prisoners in England and Wales succeeded in killing themselves and a further 650 made unsuccessful attempts. In 1996 there were three suicides, 108 attempted suicides and 879 assaults on young prisoners.[9]

Prisons for children and young people are given a variety of names: young offender institutions (as in England and Wales), reformatories (as in China), schools for reeducation (as in Romania). The names are intended to show that these are not prisons, but places of good intent, where the previous bad influences in the young people's lives will be corrected by caring people. They will be turned from their bad ways towards being good and useful citizens. In many countries in Africa children are thrown into prison with everyone else, although sometimes they are kept in separate parts. In Lilongwe prison, Malawi, in 1995, four of the young people in the juveniles hut were fifteen and three were sixteen. Thomas, aged fifteen, was imprisoned for possessing Indian hemp. Another fifteen-year-old was accused of stealing blankets and clothing; Justin was serving one year for theft of fertilizer.[10]

In Porto Alegre, in the far south of Brazil, is a young people's prison. In 1996 when visited by the present author it was newly built. The former building had recently been burnt down by the prisoners in a riot. The visiting group asked the staff what lessons about running the institution had been learnt from the riot. The staff replied that formerly 240 prisoners had been housed in a building meant for eighty. Now it held only 120. Also they had appointed two psychologists. The prison was run on the progression system. All the prisoners started in dormitory 1 and moved up as they did well, or stayed if they did not. Dormitory 1 for the new arrivals had about twelve raised concrete platforms, about eighteen inches between each, on which were a mattress and some blankets. Most of the boys were in bed because it was cold. They had nothing to do all day. They were smoking and playing cards. They are able to play football in shifts two hours a day. The group visited the art room and was invited to choose one of a number of colourful paintings on display. Then there was an opportunity to meet the artist, a fourteen-year-old called Nelson. He was tracked down cleaning his teeth in the shower in the segregation block. He was a small white boy. Since he was so small, the group presumed he got himself placed in segregation for his own protection. He was doing three years for taking part in an affray where someone was killed. His sentence would be reviewed after six months. All the boys in the institution were convicted of or charged with very serious offences. Next to Nelson in the segregation block was a juvenile serial rapist. The staff at the prison were very committed, impressive and depressed. When asked to make three wishes to improve the situation, they wanted cell accommodation rather than dormitories so the boys could be separated and the level of violence reduced, better-trained staff and training for the boys in skills so they might be able to get a job on leaving the institution.[11]

In Louisiana, young people's prisons are called Training Institutes. Louisiana has a very high rate of locking up children. Each year about 1500 children are held in secure institutions.[12] One of these children told some researchers from Human Rights Watch about the treatment of the children by those required to guard them:

> . . . all my ribs were purple. A new boy came in and I tried to help him so he wouldn't get beaten up, and then a guard pulled us both up and he slapped both of us and then he told me to raise my arms and he beat my ribs until they were purple and blue and I didn't tell my mom 'cause I knew she would start something.[13]

Grey walls, high chain-link fences, lavatories with no doors – this is the environment where some of Louisiana's most disadvantaged and damaged children are kept. The children are kept in isolation for long periods of time. There are four institutions for delinquent children in Louisiana. One is Tallulah. In the Tallulah institution, according to Human Rights Watch,

> All the buildings look alike, with gray siding and concrete floors; they are placed close together. The buildings are connected by concrete walkways, and the dormitories are enclosed by high chain-link fences. There is no grass on the property and no playing field. The gymnasium consists of a concrete floor and a roof held up by posts. This is also the visiting area.[14]

At East Baton Rouge the children sleep in dormitories holding between forty and fifty children. The bathroom area has three showers and four toilets. These facilities are not enclosed so there is no privacy for the people using them. Children cannot wear their own clothes. They are provided with clothes to wear, including jeans which have LTI, standing for Louisiana Training Institute, printed down the side of one leg.[15] At Bridge City institution the children have their heads shaved and have to keep their hair very short.[16]

They are controlled by being placed in isolation cells. These are 'small and bare except for a bed, a toilet and a sink. There are generally no windows . . . the doors have small windows for observation and slots through which food is passed at mealtimes.'[17] Children in isolation are let out each day for a shower. Otherwise they have nothing to do, and are not allowed books or writing materials.[18]

There is a visiting day once a month, but because of the long distances involved in travelling to the institutions, many of the children never have visitors. Telephones are available but many families are too poor to accept the cost of the phone calls.[19]

When they were asked the question 'What thing would you most like to change at the institution you are in?', nearly all the children said that 'they would like the guards to stop hitting them and they would like more food'.[20]

Conditions in juvenile detention in the former Soviet republic of Kazakhstan are also alleged to be very bad. Information emerged in 1996 about a penitentiary for boys in Almaty known as LA-155/6. It holds about 600 boys aged from fourteen to eighteen, some serving sentences of up to four years for petty theft. A video film taken in the institution with the title *The Experiment with the Cross* shows staff beating boys. It records the smaller boys describing how they have been raped by the older ones and films a boy describing how he prostituted himself for extra food and cigarettes. It shows how boys mutilated themselves in order to get into the hospital for a few days. A senior boy describes graphically how he climbed the ladder to become a 'boss'.[21]

The juvenile reformatory in China's capital Beijing is one of the Chinese penal institutions shown to foreign delegations. In December 1994 a delegation including the present author visited the reformatory. At that time it held 332 fourteen-to-eighteen-year-olds. A third were there for offences of theft, nearly a third for robbery, a tenth for violence and 17 per cent for sexual crimes. According to the head of the reformatory, it uses a policy of education to reform the young people. They spend half the day studying and half the day working. They are taught morality and self-discipline. The staff try to correct the bad habits of the youngsters by combining education with control. Every day the young people are examined in ideology, work, discipline, hygiene and cultural activities. They get marks out of twenty for these five things every day. These marks are put together into a weekly report and a monthly report. The results are used as a basis for rewards and punishments. The prisoners' date of release will depend on how they behave. Their families can visit them once a month for one hour and can bring food.

The delegation was shown a classroom containing about fifty young people with shaved heads wearing Mao suits and identification badges. They were sitting absolutely rigid with their hands on their knees, staring straight ahead and learning about Chinese history from a pleasant-looking teacher in uniform. There was a guard standing at the back. In another room prisoners were sitting at work benches making kitchen scales, apparently for sale on the domestic market. In a dormitory for the new arrivals were twelve boys with shaven heads sitting on stools that brought them about four inches off the ground, packed close together with not an inch of space between them. They sat like statues reading to themselves the rules of good behaviour of the institution and not even looking up or moving when half a dozen Western visitors walked into the room.

The high level of control in Chinese reformatories prevents, so those in charge say, the usual problems of juvenile institutions. The young people do not harm themselves, commit suicide or torment each other.[22]

In most reformatories they do all these things. Violence is part of the dynamic of these institutions. Many of the prisoners come from backgrounds where violence is part of their growing-up experience. Once in the institution violence is the determining factor in the relationships between prisoners. In some places the staff are also violent to the prisoners. A film *The Protégé* was made by Hungarian film maker Pal Schiffer about life in Tököl, the Hungarian prison for young men. It consisted of long interviews with prisoners serving sentences there who described their fear of the stronger prisoners and the violence they would inflict on themselves, cutting and damaging themselves, so that they would be sent to the prison hospital rather than have to stay in the dormitory. The film ended with the ritual rape of a new arrival.[23]

In the long prison tradition of trying to cloak an unpleasant reality by not calling things what they really are, the prison service in England and Wales calls violence between prisoners 'bullying'. Bullying is 'conduct motivated by a desire to hurt, threaten or frighten someone'.

Five examples of bullying are given in the prison service document about the prevention of bullying. The first is 'assault', including sexual assault. Then there is verbal abuse, including using threats and racist language. Prisoners can be forced to hand over their possessions. Money or the prison currency of tobacco, alcohol or drugs can be lent and then payment demanded with interest. Finally it can mean threatening prisoners going out on home leave to bring drugs back with them, with threats of what will happen to them or their loved ones outside if they do not comply.[24] A study of 'bullying' carried out in Britain between April and December 1994 found that nearly half of all young prisoners had been attacked or threatened in the previous month.[25]

A fifteen-year-old in a young offender institution in Yorkshire told a member of a Howard League for Penal Reform Commission looking into violence in young people's prisons,

> When I first went in there were those lads who called themselves the T and B's, meaning 'taxers and bulliers'. I was in a group whose ages ranged from fifteen to eighteen and I was one of the youngest there, so they all tried it on with me. Every time I came out for my meals I would get smacked or every time we cleaned our pads [cells] out on a Friday or Saturday, the lads came in and took anything they wanted . . . they were big lads . . . this seemed part of being inside. At my age I should have attended education but because I was being used as a walking punch bag, the officers kept me on the unit instead so they could keep an eye on me.[26]

Telling the staff what has happened and asking for the perpetrator to be dealt with would seem an obvious answer. But it is not so easy. A young man in Gloucester Prison said,

> I got threatened last night on association. They said, 'You're going to get it.' . . . I came in last Friday and someone tried it on straight away . . . I went to an officer and the guy got put straight on the ones [segregation] . . . and now we're getting it . . . we've had stuff shoved under our doors . . piss out of a bucket, bathroom cleaner, all sorts of stuff.[27]

Prisoners charged with offences that the other prisoners do not approve of are always at risk. A young prisoner had asked to be placed in a bare segregation cell and go without facilities and activities. He was questioned by the Howard League Commissioners:

> Q. Why do you think you were singled out?
> A. They found out why I was in here. I was beaten up badly with broken ribs. I didn't want to report it but an officer came into my cell and saw me. It . . . took several officers to move me to the hospital because I didn't want to go . . . because I knew they would make me tell who did this to me . . . When I came out of my cell, the group who did this to me were out in the corridor. I said . . . there's no way I'm walking past them, so the screws then knew who'd done . . . it to me.
> Q. Why did you request to move to the segregation block?
> A. I couldn't go back on the wing afterwards because they knew I'd told on . . . them. It's terrible in here, you have to run everywhere.[28]

This culture of violence cannot be put down to a few disturbed individuals. It is an intrinsic element of the life in a place where young men are locked up together. A victim of prison violence, who had gone on to inflict violence on others, said, 'Everyone does it. If I don't, someone else will. You've got to learn to stand up for yourself . . . I'm doing them a favour really. I don't hurt anyone . . . I usually only have to look at them.'[29]

Yet, in spite of their record of violence and abuse and their high failure rate, prisons for young people have been popular for more than a hundred years. Before that young people over the age of fourteen were treated in the same way as adults and those between seven and fourteen were treated as adults if it was clear that they knew what they were doing was wrong. They appeared before the same courts as adults, even if they were so small that it meant they had to stand on a box to be seen by the judge.[30] Hanging was no respecter of ages. Nor was transportation. In 1840 nearly half of those transported were under twenty-one.[31] In *The Fatal Shore*, Robert Hughes tells of James Grace, who was only eleven when he was transported to Australia for stealing ten yards of ribbon and a pair of silk stockings. John Wisehammer was fifteen years old when he was transported for stealing a packet of snuff from an apothecary's shop in Gloucester.[32] One transported youngster did not survive long in Australia. Thomas Barrett was hanged, aged seventeen, in Sydney, for stealing some 'butter, dried peas and salt pork'. At the foot of the scaffold, 'stammering and trembling and seeming "very much shocked", he announced that . . . he "had led a very wicked life." '[33] In 1833 Nicholas White, aged nine, was sentenced to death for stealing items worth two pence. But the death sentence was commuted to a whipping and then transportation for seven years.[34]

By the early decades of the nineteenth century the treatment of juvenile delinquents was being reconsidered in the light of wider social reform movements. Children convicted of crime began to be separated from adults. It was argued that putting them together contaminated the young and drove them towards a life of crime. Those who went to prison for a small misdemeanour came out ready to commit a serious crime. In 1847 a Select Committee of the House of Lords, the Brougham Committee, pointed out that for juveniles 'the contamination of a gaol or gaols as usually managed may often prove fatal, and must always be very hurtful to boys committed for a first offence'.[35]

A new idea was growing in influence. Children who committed crime did so because their upbringing had been deficient. They needed help to repair the damage of their upbringing, not punishment for something which not they but their parents were in fact responsible. The influential reformer, Mary Carpenter, said, 'the neglected child is the material out of which paupers and criminals are made'.[36]

If they were subjected to good influences rather than bad, they could be reclaimed for law-abiding society. In Mary Carpenter's view, 'These children have been hitherto so despised, that they hardly know whether there is in them anything to be respected. They therefore feel no respect to others. Yet let them be treated with respect, with true Christian politeness, and they will give a ready response.'[37] It was also argued from the practical standpoint that the young were more reformable. If they were given special care and treatment, they could be saved from a life of wickedness.

In the United States in the 1820s institutions for the delinquent young sprang up. Charles Dickens visited the House of Reformation for Juvenile Offenders in Boston, where he saw 'many boys of colour'. He saw them working, making baskets and hats, receiving schooling and singing a song 'in praise of Liberty . . . an odd and, one would think, rather aggravating theme for prisoners'. The boys were divided into four classes and they wore arm badges, showing the class they were in. New boys entered in the lowest class and had to work their way up by good behaviour. The objective was, so Dickens was told, 'to reclaim the youthful criminal by firm but kind and judicious treatment; to make his prison a place of purification and improvement, not of demoralization and corruption'.[38]

In England in 1838, a separate prison for criminal boys was opened at Parkhurst on the Isle of Wight where they were to be held before being transported.[39] The Home Secretary of the time wrote to the Committee of Visitors at Parkhurst to remind them that

> Every boy who enters Parkhurst is doomed to be transported; and this part of the sentence passed on him is immutable. He must bid a long farewell to the hopes of revisiting his native home, of seeing his parents.[40]

In 1857 nearly 2000 children under twelve and another 10,000 or so between twelve and sixteen were committed to adult prisons.[41] By then the Youthful Offenders Act had been passed. Under the influence of Mary Carpenter, reformatories for criminal children and industrial schools for neglected children began to be established to replace prisons.[42] The number of young boys in adult prisons fell.[43]

The next stage was to separate the whole process of dealing with juvenile offenders from the adult system, not just the prison but the court as well. At the end of the last century, special courts to hear cases against children were set up in Illinois and Colorado in the United States.[44] In Britain juvenile courts were established by the Children Act of 1908.[45] In these courts the proceedings were to be more appropriate to children and reformation the main aim.

In Britain in 1902 a new institution for young criminals was set up, which eventually came to be called a 'Borstal'. The first one was established in the village of Borstal, near Rochester in southern England, hence the name. The social historian Raphael Samuel wrote a biography of Arthur Harding, one of the first young people to go to Borstal. Arthur graduated into petty crime after a childhood of extreme poverty and deprivation in the 'Jago', a notorious criminal slum in London's East End. Any money that any of the family made was spent on drink by their mother, who was in continual pain after becoming disabled from being knocked over by a cart.[46] Arthur was sent to do hard labour at Wormwood Scrubs when he was first convicted, aged sixteen. His crime was helping a well-known thief called One-eyed Charlie to carry a bale of rags worth 18 shillings that Charlie had pulled off the back of a horse-drawn cart. As Arthur was a first offender he was given only one year. Charlie got three years' penal servitude.[47]

Eleven weeks after release from Wormwood Scrubs, Arthur was in trouble again for taking a watch from another boy. This time he got twenty months, but after three months at Wormwood Scrubs, according to Arthur,

> I was transferred to a place near Rochester ... We were the first Borstal Boys and the governor ... was keen to make the new system a success. He would visit the lads in their cells and urge them to do well in a trade ... We were also permitted more library books and the more backward lads were taught to read and write. I read *Oliver Twist* – that was the first time I came into contact with Dickens. You weren't kept in a cell. Every day there were physical exercises out of doors and these had a beneficial effect on my health.

Unfortunately Borstal, with all its kindnesses and good literature, could not compensate for the social conditions and pressures of London's East End in 1904. After his stay in the Kent countryside Arthur was fitter and taller and when he went back to his friends he was 'something of a hero'. He was 'the only one in the younger age-group to have done time' so they began to look up to him as a leader.[48] He set up a pickpocketing team and his criminal career was well on its way.

Arthur and the other young men in the institution at Borstal may have continued on their criminal path when they left but officialdom was convinced that Borstal was a good idea and in 1908 an Act of Parliament extended the concept. By the end of 1961 there were twenty-six Borstals in Britain and they became famous throughout the world. As Borstal was based on the idea that young criminals could be reformed, the length of stay was not fixed but depended on how well the young people behaved whilst there. Under the guidance of Sir Alexander Paterson, who took charge of Borstals in the 1920s, the regime was modelled on public schools.[49] Certainly much of what was done in Borstals was humane and caring, and there is much nostalgia for them in prison circles. But there is no evidence that they were more successful than any other carceral regime for young people. Borstals were abolished in 1983 but the name lives on and people often refer to young people's prisons, now called Young Offender Institutions, as Borstals.

After the heyday of the Borstal era the fact began to be accepted that any form of institution for young people is likely to be counter-productive and locking up children can only be justified when the young person is very violent, has committed a heinous crime, or is likely to harm him- or herself. The numbers of young people who were locked up dropped in Britain, the US and Western Europe.

It seemed as if the treatment of young people was entering a more constructive phase. But another unquenchable strand in the debate about punishing young delinquents is the long-running enthusiasm for some sort of harsh military-type sentence. If there cannot be whipping there should be some response which is clearly very unpleasant, where the young people are shouted at and made to run and jump and do everything very quickly. It is usually felt that this will be unpleasant, and so will deter and make the offender suffer, thus fulfilling the demand for punishment, and at the same time will help young people with sloppy and disorganized lives buck up their ideas. Andrew Rutherford in his *Growing Out of Crime* traces the way this idea persisted. In the 1930s the Magistrates Association was very keen on it. In 1942 a progressive magistrate, John Watson, set out the vision.

> What is needed is a small local establishment in which the discipline is of the sternest, the food of the plainest, where everything is done 'at the double', and where there is the maximum of hard work and the minimum of amusement: the kind of establishment a young offender would not wish to visit twice, and of which he would paint a vivid picture on his return home.[50]

This search continues for an illusory medicine that could easily and quickly, by a bit of marching and misery, cure the social problems caused by generations of poverty and dislocation. Its proponents never learn that the medicine does not work because it contains no ingredients that address the illness. It helps with the physical health and well-being, but does not touch the emotional, psychological or social.

The story of the short sharp shock punishments in England is an example of this obsession with the military model. In 1979 the Conservatives were hoping to be elected and as part of the election platform the very sensible and liberal-minded Home Affairs spokesman, William Whitelaw, promised that there would be glasshouse-style centres for young 'thugs and hooligans' that would 'wipe the smiles off their faces'.[51] Experiments in these square-bashing regimes were initiated and seriously evaluated by government psychologists. Unsurprisingly the results showed that the young people in the centres were not very different from Simon and Jeffrey, described at the beginning of this chapter – deprived, semi-literate, unemployed, unhappy. The new tough prison regime had no effect on the numbers of these young men who were reconvicted.[52] The response to these highly respectable research results was predictable. With the upside-down approach to rationality that discussion of harsh punishment for the young engenders, the politicians of the day took the decision to extend the harsh regime to a number of other young people's prisons. The experiment came to an end in 1988, when all the institutions for the young were subsumed under the new and deliberately vague title, Young Offender Institutions.[53]

Reformers thought that at last this most long-lived of the dragons was slain. Sub-military treatment for disturbed young men from the inner cities was over. They were wrong. In 1996 the British Conservatives had another try. This time they were after the real thing. Using a redundant actual glasshouse from the army, they proposed to set up a thirty-five-place military prison for young offenders. But they had considerable trouble filling it. Most of the young offenders in the care of the prison service were not eligible because they had too many physical, mental and psychological problems.

Not everyone with a military background thought they were a good idea. The English Chief Inspector of Prisons, General Sir David Ramsbotham, wrote in the *Reader's Digest* of January 1997:

> Recently, various overheated voices have been heard championing the merits of the boot camp – in which youngsters would be treated to 'glasshouse' military discipline. But for the life of me, I can see little point in forming young civilian offenders up in threes and marching them around ... What I would favour is a challenging regime including work, education, the opportunity to build self-esteem.[54]

Shortly after it came to power in 1997, the Labour government decided to continue the boot-camp experiment.

In Western Australia a work camp modelled on US boot camps had to close after eighteen months. It was devised, as was the short sharp shock in Britain, in an election period, when politicians tend to compete on law and order. It closed when it proved impossible to find enough suitable offenders to fill it.[55]

In the United States the latest doses of the medicine are the boot camps. Not surprisingly, boot camps are no more effective than other earlier versions of the marching medicine have been. An evaluation was done of three boot camps for juveniles set up as demonstration projects in Cleveland, Denver and Mobile. The camps provided a ninety-day programme with military discipline and physical conditioning in austere facilities. Participants were required to wear military-style uniforms. Some of the staff were from a military background. The evaluation concludes that the camps affected the behaviour of the participants whilst they were there but the improvement did not continue when they left. 'What appeared to be a promising prognosis at the conclusion of boot camp disintegrated during aftercare,' they say.[56]

And now the pendulum is swinging once again towards incarceration of young people. In the United States juvenile courts are regarded as not tough enough and many more young people are being reclassified and sent to the adult court for their trial, where adult penalties apply. In 1995 new legislation was passed in Texas which radically changed the treatment of juvenile offenders. The new law reduced from fifteen to fourteen the age at which a juvenile could be tried as an adult for capital murder and other crimes. It widened the list of crimes for which juveniles could be given prison sentences of ten, twenty and forty years. Most juvenile court cases would be opened to the public. Law enforcement agencies would be given access to data banks of juveniles' fingerprints and photographs.[57] A bill being discussed in the US Congress in 1997, the Violent and Repeat Offender Act, was intended to overhaul the juvenile justice system. One of its authors, Republican Senator John Ashcroft, said,

> We are living with a juvenile system that reprimands the crime victim for being at the wrong place at the wrong time, and then turns around and hugs the juvenile terrorist, whispering ever so softly into his ear, 'Don't worry, the state will cure you.'[58]

The British Conservative government, in power from 1979 to 1997, decided to set up a number of new prisons for children aged twelve to fourteen, to be called secure training centres and to be run by private contractors. The incoming Labour administration, after initial hesitation, adopted the idea. A new intolerance and brutality in attitudes is widespread. The language in which young people are described carries none of Mary Carpenter's 'Christian politeness'.

They are described in terms reserved for hated enemies. The *Daily Express* wrote in its opinion column in 1996:

> At one time our image of youthful callousness and cruelty was of children amusing themselves by pulling wings off hapless flies. Not any more. Who are these monsters, bereft of thought or conscience, who now prowl our streets? Simple. They are our children.[59]

9. *If Not Death, Then Life*

Do you understand what will happen to you?
Do you have any questions?
What do you want for a last meal?
Do you plan to make a last statement?
What do you want us to do with your body?
What do you want to do with your property?
Who do you want to have your money?
Who will witness your execution?
Do you know what we expect you to do?
Are you comfortable?
If not, what can we do?
If your stay is denied, who do you want to call?
What color clothes do you want to die in?

These are the questions all death-row prisoners have to answer in the final hours[1]

Earlier chapters have shown that most prisoners are poor. Many are from minorities and end up in prison because of discrimination. Some are women who have responded to the violence imposed on them by committing acts of violence themselves. Large numbers are the neglected children of the urban wastelands. Some have committed violent crimes, even murder, but the violent act was an isolated event prompted by extreme circumstances in a personal relationship. These circumstances will not occur again and they are not dangerous or a threat to anyone except perhaps themselves. They spend the rest of their lives consumed with guilt and a wish to atone. Their long prison sentence reflects the appalling nature of their crime rather than the need to protect people from them.

Most of the people in prison in most parts of the world will come into the above categories. But not all. A minority will be those for whom, it could be said, prison has been designed. Some of them will be cruel and conscienceless. Some will have committed crimes that are beyond imagination in their heinousness. A few are so dangerous that they are likely to be a threat to others, including those who guard them, for most of their natural lives.

How such people become capable of extreme violence and murder is a difficult and unresolved question with metaphysical overtones. Some would argue that they are just born evil. Maybe this is so, but it is also true that the backgrounds of people who commit appalling crimes have frequently been filled with violence and abuse.[2] But then not everyone who comes from such a background will end up re-enacting those experiences against others.

Whatever the background and the causes the question is still there. What is society to do with people who have committed the worst crimes? In many countries the answer is the one that has been in place for centuries: put them to death. Execution, by hanging, shooting, gassing, lethal injection, is in force for murder and other serious crimes in nearly half the countries of the world.

In countries where the death penalty has been abolished or fallen into disuse such people are given very long prison sentences. Sometimes these are called life sentences. Sometimes they actually mean imprisonment for life, staying in prison until death. The way such long-term prisoners are treated is at the heart of the implementation of human rights – they are the ultimate undeserving, the most extreme test of humanity, the touchstone for any prison system, and every society.

But first, let us look at death. This is a book about prison. So, it may be asked, why think about those whose stay in prison is but an episode on their way to the execution chamber? It is indeed a book about prison, but also about the appropriateness of prison as the mainstay of punishment. The death penalty is the ultimate statement in the debate about punishment. It highlights and defines it. What is more, the existence of the death penalty has an effect on prisons and prison life. Prisoners awaiting death are imprisoned in parts of the prison usually called death row. Their presence is felt by everyone. Death row in any prison is a strange place – with an aura of unreality, the antechamber to the gallows, inhabited by people seemingly perfectly healthy and full of life, yet waiting to die. It is very difficult at first for the visitor to talk naturally to people on death row. 'How are you today?' seems somehow inappropriate. Yet they are eager to talk, starved as many of them are of human contact or activity. They are not usually permitted to get involved in the prison's rehabilitation programmes – why should they be? They are often subject to the most stringent security precautions, so that they do not kill themselves and cheat the executioners of their rightful task.

When Breyten Breytenbach was imprisoned in South Africa in the 1970s, he discovered that many prisoners awaiting execution would try to commit suicide by diving head first from their bunks on to the cement floor. They never succeeded.[3]

Before the coming of democracy, South Africa was one of the world's greatest executioners. In 1987 there were more than three executions a week.[4] In his function as a prison cleaner Breytenbach used to clean the corridor from where there was a gate leading to the steps to the execution area.

> The steps lead to a room called the 'preparation room', where the final touches are put to those being prepared for departure – pulling a shirt straight, making sure that a hood fits snugly . . . from here, this antechamber, this terminus, the door opens into the execution place itself. Back of that again, but at ground level, is the area with big washbasins and tables with little furrows allowing blood to run off them. This is the place where the bodies are sluiced down and dissected if necessary. In any event, the doctor assisting has to make a little cut in the neck to verify the cause of death. Here too are the big ice boxes in which the bodies can eventually be kept.[5]

In South African prisons at that time, black or coloured prisoners only qualified for the white diet once they had been condemned to death. But for their last meal on earth, whites were given a whole chicken and blacks only a half.[6]

Death-row conditions are very harsh in some of those ex-colonies that follow old British prison rules and regulations. In the beautiful Caribbean islands with the warm white sands, palm trees and steel bands of the travel posters are to be found some of the most oppressive death cells. On the idyllic little island of St Vincent, in the prison in the capital Kingstown, death row is a special row of cells with barred front gates facing a corridor, so natural light is minimal and privacy is non-existent. The prisoners are clothed in undignified baby-like one-piece shorts-and-shirt suits in a dirty cream colour. They are guarded day and night by a special prison officer.

In 1988 in St Vincent two people, a father and a son, were hanged. The son tried to commit suicide three days before and had to have thirty stitches in his throat. The father took a dressing off his leg and stuffed it down his throat hoping that it would prevent the hanging being successful. The dressing was only discovered at the post mortem.[7]

In Glendairy Prison in Barbados in 1994, when a delegation including the present author visited, there were fourteen men on death row. Prisoners held in the death-row section of the prison had no natural light in their cells. All were in single cells. Cells were grille-fronted. They were dank and dark. There was no bedding to be seen, other than a mattress on the floor. It was not obvious at first that there was a human being in any of the cells. When one became accustomed to the half-dark one saw a palm of a hand against the grille. On closer inspection one saw a light pair of underpants and realized that a man was standing up against the grille. The prisoners were keen to talk to us. One man asked if we were visitors to the country. On being told that we were, he said, 'Welcome to Barbados.' Each prisoner was allowed thirty minutes' exercise daily in a small caged area. Eight prisoners at a time were placed in this cage.[8]

In the small unspoilt island of Dominica, prisoners who were facing the death penalty were held in a special security section. This special section was entered through a security compound. The block itself consisted of two rows of six cells facing each other across an open area. The back of the area was a solid wall. There was a concrete roof. The front was grilled and opened on to the entrance compound. The front of each cell was a grilled gate. A large metal sheet covered the section around the lock in the gate. There were no windows in the cells. Any natural light came through the front grilles. This meant that the cells were very dark; one had to peer to see the prisoners inside.

In September 1994 there were sixteen prisoners in this section. They were dressed only in underpants. Several had blankets around their shoulders. There were no beds, only thin mattresses on the floor. In one cell was a man who had been under sentence of death for six years. These prisoners spent all day and night in these cells, with the exception of thirty minutes for exercise and washing in the open yard.[9]

In Jamaica, death row is at St Catherine's District Prison where, in 1995, sixty-one prisoners were held. Executions have not taken place in Jamaica since 1988. But the story of death row at St Catherine's is a story of disturbance and death, although not legally sanctioned. In June 1990 three prisoners on death row were killed during a riot.[10] In October 1993 four death-row prisoners were shot dead by prison staff after they had allegedly tried to take prison staff hostage.[11] Two of the prisoners killed in October were due to have their death sentences commuted to life imprisonment following a decision of the Privy Council in London that to keep prisoners on death row for more than five years was cruel, inhuman and degrading treatment. Death sentences, the Privy Council ruled, should not be carried out on people held for more than five years. As a result, sixty-two death sentences were commuted to life imprisonment.[12] Another death-row prisoner was shot dead by prison staff during disturbances in February 1995. There are reports that in March 1995 many prisoners were beaten by prison staff. In April the well-known prisoner Ivan Morgan died in prison. He had been receiving medical treatment for stomach pains but the authorities had refused to let him go to hospital.[13] He was well-known because he had been on death row in Jamaica since 1974 and three times had been reprieved after being taken to the death cell for execution.[14] On one occasion, in 1987, he was told of his reprieve only forty-five minutes before the execution was due to take place.[15]

But, as with most punishment matters, the United States leads the Western world in enthusiasm. More states join the executioners every year. The number of executions has grown steadily since capital punishment was resumed in 1977.

Of the 56 executed in 1995, 33 were white, 22 black and 1 Asian; 49 were killed by lethal injection and 7 were electrocuted; 19 of them were executed in Texas. The average time spent on death row by the 56 was 11 years. The number of prisoners on death row has risen from 856 in 1981 to 2482 in 1991 to 3046 in 1995.[16]

Table 10   Executions in the US

1983	5
1984	21
1993	38
1995	56

Source: Annual Reports of Amnesty International

Who are they? Not surprisingly, they are disproportionately black – 40 per cent[17] – and disproportionately poor. They could not afford a good lawyer. Many of them are mentally disturbed.[18] The withdrawal of federal government funding in October 1995 for the legal aid centres that help prisoners on death row made it more likely that death sentences would be carried out, whether or not the trial was fair.

At the end of 1996 there was a flurry of executions in Virginia, bringing the total for the year to nine. The sixth person to be executed was Larry Stout. According to the *Washington Post* he grew up half white and half black in an otherwise all-white family. His stepfather, on parole for murder, would not let him be seen in public with the rest of the family. His mother tried to give him away 'but no one would have him'. One of his lawyers said, 'I think that Larry was given a very strong message when he was young that his life was worthless. The execution is just another step along that way.'[19]

The last words of the seventh person to be executed, Len Tuggle, were 'Merry Christmas.' The spokesman for the Virginia Department of Corrections told the *Washington Post* that with four executions in the past three weeks and two more for the week before Christmas the department's twelve-person executive team had suffered periods of 'high stress'. 'Obviously, this is the time of year for celebration and pleasant thoughts. Certainly, making the transition from putting someone to death and going home to look at the Christmas tree could be rather jolting.'[20]

The fair and impartial trial

A rich man stood before a Court of Law
found guilty of murder for his gain
His lawyers and doctors all gathered around
to describe why his victim has been slain

As the judge and the jury all listened on
the police told their obvious tale
And the decision was made that the person he slayed
was the one who should be in jail

The next case was called and a poor man walked in
his lawyers all paid by the state
The witnesses he called were not in the room
but the judge said the case could not wait

The jury all napped as the state made its case
its witnesses all called in a row
The poor man looked around the room with a frown
at the things his lawyer didn't show

He knew his was weary of public defense
and his caseload was way overrun
He didn't have time to check the whole crime
he just wanted to get the case done

The papers all said his client was dead
so he didn't really see any use
The jury said guilty so why drag it out
by a showing of constitutional abuse

The judge rose from his bench and looked round the court
and said we're all tired of this crime
I know that you're broke and probably don't vote
so it's useless to give you just time

The state's spending money to give you a trial
and your lawyer is just wasting his breath
I don't really know if it's right or it's wrong
but this court now orders your death

You have a right to appeal and I guess that you will
so I'll let those others decide
but from what I can see as for our society
it will be better off when you've died.

Danny L. King, writing from death row, Mecklenburg,
Virginia[21]

Death row in the United States is a harsh place. In 1988 Dr Jan Arriens from Cambridge started an organization called Lifelines. The members of Lifelines befriend and exchange letters with prisoners on death row in the United States who have asked for a penfriend. When the present author visited death row in San Quentin Prison, California, in 1993 there was a warm reception from the prisoners. 'Anyone from Britain is welcome here. British people write to us prisoners here on death row.'

From the letters of the death-row prisoners a picture can be built up of what it is like to spend many years on death row in places like Florida, Texas or Georgia. Toby Williams, a black man convicted in 1985 at the age of twenty-one and on death row in Texas, wrote,

> Imagine spending twenty-one hours a day and twenty-four hours on weekends in a tiny cell . . . To recreate, shower, visit, etc., you are stripped of your clothing in front of either males or females who open your mouth as you maneuver your tongue, run their fingers through your hair, raise your arms, lift your testicles, or run their fingers through your pubic hair, turn around to lift your feet, and bend over to spread your cheeks, while the guards search your clothing.[22]

Raymond Clark wrote to a Lifelines member, Mary Grayson, in Berkshire about his life.

> Except for four hours of outside exercise per week . . . I am locked in this six foot by nine foot steel and concrete box twenty-four hours

of every day. In two more days it will be exactly thirteen years I have lived/existed under these conditions.[23]

Raymond Clark was executed in 1990.

A man on death row in Virginia describes what he expects to happen to him:

> For at least fifteen days prior to the execution you sit in a cell some thirty feet from the [electric] chair . . . You can have coffee or juice whenever you want, just ask the officer. You are fed three times a day. You can make as many phone calls as you like. On the last day at 8 a.m. the death squad comes in and sits facing you, watching every move you make the rest of the day. At noon you get your last meal. At 10.30 p.m. you are shaved, head and left leg, given a shower and the execution clothes, then moved to the end cell which is completely empty except for a toilet. At 10.55 p.m. the entire death crew comes in and one way or another you are escorted to the chair. Two officers are responsible for getting you strapped in. The stomach and chest straps go first, then the arms and the wrists, then the legs. The wire to the left leg is connected and then the head piece is fitted in place. The warden asks you if you have any last words and then the leather mask is placed over your face. Then you sit there until the warden gives the signal. If it all works out right you get to the chair at 10.59 and are dead by 11.03. If there's a delay you could sit there till midnight.[24]

A new development in the administration of the death penalty in the US is the move in ten states to allow victims' families to watch the execution of the people who have killed their loved ones. The first such family in Texas were the Kelleys. The story of the Kelley family was the subject of a film on British television in 1996. The Kelleys had three children. Two, Mark and Kara, were murdered in 1988, shot dead when a robber, Leo Jenkins, broke into the family's pawn shop. The parents, and the third child, a daughter, Robin, won the right to watch Leo Jenkins being executed by lethal injection in February 1996. They were issued with guidelines on what to wear and how to behave and eventually took their places behind the glass wall separating the observers from the death chamber.

The question that absorbed the commentators was 'Did it work for them. Did it make them feel better?' The family told the British reporters that it did. 'Its like they took the cancer out of me,' Mrs Kelley said. Six months after the execution though, talking to Rod Williams who produced the TV documentary, she said, 'It has helped a bit – but the bottom line is I don't have Mark and Kara.'[25] Another question worth asking is whether the full weight of the law and authority of the state should also sanction people to feel cathartic and therapeutic release at the deliberate death of another human being. The implications of legitimizing that process of dehumanization, of giving it official approval, are worth reflection.

The death penalty was firmly in place in the Soviet Union before its break-up and its use seems deeply embedded. In Belarus it is still in force. When a delegation from Penal Reform International visited Prison Number 1 in Minsk in 1997, forty-one people were on death row. They were living in the dungeon-like basement of the prison in cells with arched ceilings. The walls were brown and the ceiling was white. One lightbulb gave a yellowish light and there was a window the size of a computer screen. When the door of one of the death cells was unlocked for the visitors, three men inside leapt up and stood with their faces to the wall and hands behind their heads. They were wearing uniforms with horizontal stripes. They were told to turn round, and did so, but kept their eyes closed. They were told to open their eyes and a conversation took place through the prison director. One prisoner was apparently twenty-three years old and had been sentenced ten months earlier. The prisoners never left the cell for exercise. What fresh air they got came through the tiny window.[26]

In Russia the facts about the death penalty are hard to come by. Only men are executed. According to official figures, sixteen people were executed in 1995. However, unofficial sources give the figure as ninety. More than 500 people were held on death row in 1996.[27] The system in Russia is that a date for execution is set, no one is informed, the prisoner is shot in the back of the head and the relatives are not allowed to retrieve the body.[28] Since it joined the Council of Europe in February 1996, Russia has been under pressure to introduce a moratorium on the death penalty.

In Japan the system is somewhat similar to that in Russia. In

December 1994 a man convicted of murder called Ajima Yukio was executed. He had been held for sixteen years on death row in Tokyo Detention Centre. He was executed in secret and his family and lawyers were not informed.[29] He himself was probably only informed a few hours before he was hanged that his sixteen-year-long wait was at an end.

China is regarded as the world's leading executioner. Amnesty International records 3500 executions in 1996 but it is assumed that the true figure is much higher.[30] In 1996, 1000 people were executed in just three months. At least sixty-eight criminal offences, many of them non-violent, are punishable by death. These include killing a tiger, reselling V A T receipts, pimping, habitual theft or stealing cultural artefacts.

But in China a death row is not needed. Prisoners are executed in public often within minutes of the end of the trial after a humiliating parade with billboards round their necks.[31]

In Western Europe the death penalty is hardly ever applied. Belgium abolished it in 1996. Turkey retains the death penalty but since 1984 has not carried it out. In San Marino, one of Europe's smallest states, no one has been executed since 1468.

Human rights supporters hope that it stays that way. The death penalty is a barbarous and dangerous punishment which diminishes the humanity of those who carry it out and those who approve of it. It does not deter. It merely brutalizes, cheapens human life and legitimates violence as a response. Its effect on prison and on the debate about punishment is to distort, dehumanize, and postpone the finding of solutions that could more easily heal the pain of victims' relatives and prevent more people becoming victims in future.

LIFE IMPRISONMENT

If not death, then life. In countries which have abolished the death penalty, life imprisonment is usually the ultimate punishment, the heaviest price the state can exact. When the death penalty was abolished in the UK in 1965, there was a search for a punishment that embodied the feeling that murder was a unique crime, requiring a unique protective but also symbolically severe punishment. The life sentence was deemed to meet this need and was brought in as the mandatory, that is the only possible, sentence that a judge can give someone convicted of murder.

Since then there has been much discussion about whether it is right that the judge should have no discretion in these cases. Many distinguished British jurists see the mandatory life sentence as a fetter on the discretion of the judiciary. It fails, so it is argued, to allow the judges to make very proper distinctions between very different sorts of crimes. A mercy killing of a terminally ill loved one should not attract the same sentence as shooting a bank clerk in a carefully prepared robbery. Also, the mandatory sentence leads to the use of devices that are less than honest, such as reducing a charge of murder to one of manslaughter to avoid the mandatory sentence.[32]

Another recent trend that has an effect on prisons and the way they are run is the widening of the life-sentence net. Once it was the only possible punishment for the uniquely heinous crime of murder. Now in the UK it is available for a range of offences in addition to murder. Manslaughter, other homicide and attempted homicide, other violence against the person, rape and other sexual offences, and robbery and arson can all attract a life sentence. The number of prisoners serving life sentences is increasing, both in the UK and elsewhere. On 30 April 1996 there were 3436 life-sentence prisoners in England and Wales.[33]

The life sentence has many implications for those concerned with human rights and with protecting prisoners from abuses. It is an indeterminate sentence, which means that prisoners sentenced to life either stay in prison for ever or someone has to decide when they will be released. Often once released they are subject to supervision by a probation or parole officer, usually for many years or until they die.

In some jurisdictions, such as the UK, the life sentence moves the decision on how long someone should serve from the court and the judges to the politicians. It also imposes heavy burdens on those administering the system and bearing the responsibility for making recommendations for release. Their recommendations could be

Table 11   Increase in number of life-sentence prisoners in England and Wales

1957	140
1970	730
1975	1129
1980	1584
1985	2051
1990	2795
1991	2896
1992	3000
1993	3095
1994	3192
1995	3289
1996	3489

Source: NACRO briefing *Life-Sentence Prisoners*, January 1995, and Home Office statistics

perfectly right. Or they could end in another murder or serious crime. From the perspective of the prisoner, freedom is taken away, perhaps for ever. Release will depend on reports, written by many different officials, which the prisoners may never see. Perhaps it will not be for ever but to regain freedom requires the prisoner to submit to the plans of the authorities, the treatment enthusiasms of the authorities, the latest psychological fad.

The process of deciding whether a life-sentence prisoner should be released or is safe to be released has been controversial and some British prisoners successfully complained to the European Court on Human Rights that the procedures were in violation of the European Convention. In England and Wales there are two sorts of life sentences: discretionary and mandatory. For offences such as rape, manslaughter or arson, a life sentence is available as one option when it seems to the judge that the person being sentenced has committed a serious crime, and is in 'a mental state which makes them dangerous to the life or limb of the public'.[34] The purpose is to observe how the prisoner's mental state develops and whether and when it becomes safe to grant release. For murder, the life sentence is mandatory. Yet once the sentence has been passed the two groups of prisoners are subject to the same release procedures even though these procedures were originally designed for those found guilty of murder.

Following a ruling by the European Court the procedures for release for discretionary life-sentence prisoners were changed so that the Parole Board follows a semi-judicial procedure in reaching a decision.[35] For the other type of life-sentence prisoners the decision about release is made by a politician, the Home Secretary. The Home Secretary may order the release of a life-sentence prisoner only when recommended by the Parole Board and after consultation with the judiciary. But the Home Secretary does not have to accept the recommendations made by the Parole Board. In 1992 the Home Secretary turned down nineteen of the Parole Board's recommendations. In 1993 he rejected seven.[36]

The basis on which the Home Secretary makes the decisions to turn down recommendations from the Parole Board is very controversial. There are three considerations: the length of time necessary for retribution and deterrence; whether it is safe to release the prisoner; and 'the public acceptability of early release'.[37] A committee chaired by a former Lord Chief Justice, Lord Lane, commented,

> The system confers on a politician decisions that are by their very nature sentencing decisions. This means that consideration of politics rather than justice may determine the length of offenders' detention. Politics often means vote catching.[38]

Those are the procedures for release. What about the time such prisoners spend when release is a distant dream and all that faces them is years and years of the same people, the same walls, the same exercise yard? Locking away such people, for so many years, shows imprisonment at its most extreme. How does the prison administrative machine cope with prisoners who are not going to come out? One problem to be dealt with is old age. Some prisons will become old people's homes, dealing with geriatric problems like loss of mobility and senile dementia. In Kingston Prison, in southern England, there is an 'elderly prisoner unit'. The weekly bulletin of the Prison Service brought the unit to the attention of those eligible to refer prisoners to it.

> All Lifer Liaison Managers are asked to note that HMP Kingston's elderly prisoner unit is now accepting life-sentence prisoners fitting the following criteria: sixty years of age and over, not requiring full-time medical cover, Category C and able to negotiate stairs.[39]

What about before they are old, when they still have all their strength and many years before them? What is it like to have to guard such prisoners facing very long sentences? How can prison staff look after people who will be there perhaps till they die? What can such prisoners look forward to? How can they be encouraged, kept cheerful? Do they become institutionalized? Certainly Václav Havel noticed such a tendency. He told his wife Olga,

> I've noticed that many prisoners who've been here . . . for years – have something hedgehog-like about them: their lives are a habitual, daily repetition of precise and polished routines; they go about in a kind of mild somnolence, following well-worn ruts, and are extremely irritated, even outraged, by any disturbance.[40]

Some of them will settle down into a kind of numbness, dwelling on what they have done. Tony Parker interviewed twelve life-sentence prisoners for his book *Life After Life*. One, whom he called Philip Derbyshire, had murdered his small son. He beat him, threw him on the fire, poured boiling water over him, hit him again and swung him against the wall. Philip told Tony Parker,

> More than once I've thought if we still had the death penalty and that's what the judge had passed on me as a sentence and I'd been hanged, that would've been the end of it. Sometimes I've thought that could never have been as bad as sentencing me to go on living with all this remorse. They don't let you out, you know, it's one of the things they take into account before they do, until they're sure you show contrition for what you've done . . . I've had treatment of all sorts . . . but none of them has ever cured me . . . There is no cure, not for me. The end of my life, that'll be the cure.[41]

He went on, 'Prison's where I belong. I'm outside humanity, both in humanity's eyes and mine.'[42]

Others fight against all of it, their crime, their imprisonment, the system. John McGrath was a prisoner in Scotland for many years. He spent five years in solitary confinement and wrote about his experiences. When the staff or governor tried to engage him in discussion about changing his way of dealing with imprisonment his thought was

> You do not touch me. There is nothing you can do to me that you have not already done. I am me and I am stronger and more powerful than you . . . Move me from cell to cell twice every day. Put another gate in front of my steel door. Surround me with cameras. Be as you are – weak, frightened, powerless. Now there is nothing left you can do to me. You cannot make me any harder, any more dangerous, nor any more loathing.[43]

Another of Tony Parker's interviewees was Alan Robinson, who killed a policeman when he was nineteen. When he started his prison sentence his answer to dealing with life imprisonment was to act tough. 'You let them see they're not going to break you, you'll keep your integrity of personality, you'll never bend the knee. That's what I did and I kept it up for . . . nearly six years.'[44]

Then one day an Assistant Governor came to see him in the punishment block. He sat down and asked Alan Robinson what he was doing. The response was: 'I told him to eff off out of it or I'd put one on him, or two if there was time before the screw outside came to his rescue. He said, "There isn't a screw outside. Go and have a look." '

Alan Robinson looked and it was true. There was no one outside to come to the Assistant Governor's rescue if he was attacked.

He said, 'You're taking a risk, mate, aren't you, down here on your own with a known animal like me? What're you trying to do, win the Queen's Award for bravery?'

The Assistant Governor, according to Alan Robinson a 'funny little bloke, bald head, middle-aged', asked him if he intended to carry on as he was, being a known animal, because if he intended to, 'that's all right, we can contain you, make no mistake about that'.

Then he left. Alan Robinson's reaction was to laugh. He thought,

> That little bastard's just threatened me. And what've I done? Have I picked him up and broken his back like I'd have tried to if he'd been a screw? No, I haven't. Have I thrown my table against the wall and dragged my bed up against the door and barricaded like I'd normally have done? No, I've not done that either. All I've done is stood here and seen the funny side of it.[45]

For a couple of months after the incident he was worse. Then he gradually began to quieten down.

What do most prison systems do with prisoners like Alan Robinson? Usually they go to special places, the lower depths of the prison systems, special units in the US like the special adjustment unit in San Quentin prison with the large notice on the gate, 'No warning shots fired in this unit'. If shots are fired here they are for real. Or they are in prisons like Pelican Bay, or Florence, in Colorado, which replaced the notorious Marion. In the UK there are special units at prisons like Whitemoor and Belmarsh. In France there are the notorious *centrales*. In Russia special isolation prisons are used.

Sometimes such prisoners are shared out. Every prison has to do its bit in taking the worst prisoners. So they are circulated around the system. In France the system is called *tourisme pénitentiaire*.[46] The euphemism used in England and Wales is less graphic. There the process is called 'continuous assessment'.

Sometimes a better solution is found. The special unit set up in the former women's block in Barlinnie Prison in Glasgow in 1973 took up to eight of Scotland's most dangerous prisoners. Life there was very relaxed. There were many visitors and day-to-day decisions on life in the unit were made at a weekly meeting. Prisoners were encouraged to spend their time in creative and artistic activities and several went on to become successful writers or artists. After about twenty years of operation, the special unit closed.

Dealing with high-security long-term prisoners who do not settle down into a hedgehog-like existence challenges all prison systems. After all, would not most people take desperate measures to escape even if they had nowhere to go and no one to go to, just to keep alive their sense of life having a purpose, just to see the world again and breathe free air? Because this is the normal reaction, the prison authorities often decide they have to subject long-term prisoners to stringent security measures. What then have such prisoners got to lose? Not much. So they fight the system. The system fights back. Their conditions worsen until they and their custodians are locked into a downward spiral of violence and extreme deprivation. When they have nothing else left they smear their own excrement on their cells and themselves.

Then, sometimes, a way out of the vicious spiral is found. The system makes an accommodation with them. They agree to stop fighting the system and the system gives them some rewards, decent living conditions, permission to keep budgies, cook their own food or attend art classes. Then there is a change in political control or the public finds out and there is an uproar. Why should these monsters be treated like this? It is an insult to the victims. Can the victims attend art classes or keep budgies? Of course not. Pressure is put on politicians to stop all the featherbedding, as it is described. Conditions for the long-term prisoners worsen. The authorities introduce measures like 'volumetric control'. What is 'volumetric control'? It means that a prisoner can have only as many possessions as will fit in two boxes with a prescribed volume. Once they are full up, every new possession means an old one has to go.[47] They introduce 'closed visits', which means that prisoners and their families and friends are separated at visits by a glass screen. They search babies and take off their nappies, supplying fresh ones after the search. Women's bras with underwires set off the metal detectors and they are asked to remove them. The Dutch, so famous for penal enlightenment, are not so enlightened when it comes to long-term prisoners. Some prisoners in the special security unit at Vucht prison are reported to be handcuffed whenever they leave their cells.[48] Eventually prisoners in such circumstances see no further point in co-operating. They begin to fight back. There may be destruction, serious injury, even death.

And so the cycle starts again.

These are the most extreme manifestations of state-imposed suffering. Are there any limits? Should there be? The next chapter looks at the growth of limitations, the rules.

PART THREE

Making Prisons Better

Extract from a 1991 interview between Clive Stafford Smith and Sam Jones, Louisiana's executioner. He is paid $400 per death.
SMITH: *Let me ask you this then. Say someone stabs somebody seventy-one times, would you be prepared to go in there and stab the person seventy-one times?*
SAM: *If it were required, I could do it, yes.*
SMITH: *You could? For four hundred bucks?*
SAM: *Well, the money don't have nothin' to do with it.*
SMITH: *What is the most gruesome thing you would be prepared to do for the four hundred dollars?*
SAM: *Whatever.*
SMITH: *You'd take a candle and sort of drop hot wax on them, pull their nails out and then kill them, or something like that?*
SAM: *If that's what they wanted. If that's what the state tells me to do.*

From Wilbert Rideau and Ron Wikberg, *Life Sentences: Rage and Survival Behind Bars*[1]

10. *The Rules*

Considered as a complex purposeful operation, the Holocaust may serve as a paradigm of modern bureaucratic rationality. Almost everything was done to achieve maximum results with minimum costs and efforts. Almost everything (within the realm of the possible) was done to deploy the skills and resources of everybody involved, including those who were to become the victims of the successful operation. Almost all pressures irrelevant or adversary to the purpose of the operation were neutralized or put out of action altogether. Indeed the story of the organization of the Holocaust could be made into a textbook of scientific management.

From Zygmunt Bauman, *Modernity and the Holocaust*[1]

Most people are familiar with the idea of human rights. They know about Amnesty International and its campaigns against torture. They know that women have rights. Children have rights. Minorities have rights. There is the right to a fair trial, to be presumed innocent until found guilty, to freedom of speech and assembly. Everyone has rights that should be protected. But prisoners . . . why on earth should prisoners have rights? Are they not the least deserving? Have they not forfeited their right to have rights? If prisoners are to have rights does it not diminish the whole idea of rights?

It does not. In fact there is a whole corpus of covenants, conventions, instruments, declarations and commentaries on the rights of detained people and many seminars and conferences explaining and promoting them take place every year. The starting point for them all is the United Nations International Covenant on Civil and Political Rights Article 10, which says, 'All persons deprived of their liberty shall be treated with humanity and with respect for the inherent dignity of the human person.'

This basic message is repeated in the European Convention on Human Rights, the African Charter on Human and People's Rights and the Inter-American Convention on Human Rights.

How did it happen that the world established and signed up to a set of rights for prisoners that are part of international law? The acceptance of the idea came after the Second World War. It emerged from the setting up of the United Nations and a determination never to let such things as had happened in the Second World War happen again.

The Charter of the United Nations, adopted in June 1945, reaffirmed faith in 'fundamental human rights, in the dignity and worth of the human person'. Three years later came the Universal Declaration of Human Rights, which was followed by all the covenants and conventions on human rights that make up the framework for the world on how states should treat their citizens. Article 5 of the Universal Declaration says, 'No one shall be subjected to torture or cruel, inhuman or degrading treatment or punishment.'

Why is this included? Why is there a specific article on detained people in all the major human rights conventions? The arguments are straightforward. Detained people are included because human rights extend to all human beings. It is a basic tenet of international human rights law that nothing can put a human being beyond the reach of certain human rights protections. Some people may be less deserving than others. Some may lose many of their rights through having been imprisoned through proper and legal procedures. But the basic rights to life, health, fairness and justice, humane treatment, dignity and protection from ill-treatment or torture remain. There is a minimum standard for the way a state treats people, whoever they are. No one should fall below it.

Those who drew up the Universal Declaration in 1948 had a clear picture in their minds of what a state can do to people it decides are its enemies. They had seen in reality or on film the concentration camps. They had heard and read of the mass deportations, using people as slave labour until they dropped dead from starvation or disease, putting to immediate death by gassing those who did not look strong enough to work well and be worth feeding, using some as guinea pigs for medical experiments and others to work in officers' brothels. The nations of the world resolved that in future states which had signed up to the Universal Declaration would know that their treatment of all people had to fall within the bounds of the values enshrined in it.

The rules that they drew up and all the guidance documents that accompany the rules are based on the thinking and analysis of scholars who have tried to understand how the horror of the concentration camps emerged from the seemingly civilized, advanced country that was Germany in the 1930s. Many of them have concluded that the concentration camps were not an aberration, the product of acts of madness by specially selected psychopaths. The Holocaust emerged from certain conditions which eroded the normal revulsion people have from committing violent atrocities. The sociologist, Zygmunt Bauman, in particular, in *Modernity and the Holocaust*, identified three preconditions for institutionalized abuse of human rights. The first is that the ill-treatment and torture should be authorized from above. When those in charge sanction the abuse, when it is seen as legitimate, when someone in authority has said that it is all right, many people will feel able to do it. Obeying orders is seen as a good thing to do. Questioning orders is not.

The second condition is that the behaviour is part of the routine, is laid down in the regulations, provided for in the rule book, is part of doing the job. This makes it seem normal and acceptable.

The third condition is when the victims of the cruelty are dehumanized. When it has been explained many times by what has been written and spoken that the people who are being tortured or systematically murdered are somehow different, wicked, are enemies, less than human, then it is easier to torture them. When they have been degraded and humiliated by having their heads shaved, not being allowed to wash, wearing ill-fitting or absurd clothes, or convict suits with large stripes, when their sanitary arrangements are undignified and they have to live in dirt and fight each other for food, then it is easier to say, 'These people are truly not like us. They are less than us. They do the human race no credit. They are like weeds or vermin. We owe them no right to good treatment or respect.' Then it can happen.[2]

Stanley Milgram was a psychologist from Yale University. In 1974 he published the results of some experiments he had carried out to see how far people were prepared to go in torturing others. The college students who were the subjects of the experiment were told they were participating in a scientific study aimed at making learning more effective. Other college students were to undertake learning tasks and when they made a mistake, the subjects were told to administer a very mild electric shock to them. Gradually the shocks the subjects were administering became stronger. Two-thirds of the students had no difficulty in carrying out the instructions to administer the shocks, even when the victims, hidden behind a wall, were screaming with pain.[3] When they asked whether they should continue, the organizer of the experiment reassured them, 'No permanent damage to the tissue will be caused.' So they carried on.[4]

If this analysis is right, then prison is a very high-risk environment for ill-treatment. The people that work in prisons belong to a hierarchy. The disciplines that enshroud the prison staff are usually strict and in many countries prison staff belong to the military and have military ranks. Prisons are usually governed by one person whose orders are expected to be obeyed. Individual initiative is not normally encouraged or highly valued.

Also, prisons are of necessity rule-bound. The routines, systems, ways of dealing with prisoners, what is allowed and what is not, when and how and where, are all set out in regulations, standing orders, decrees and instruments. Whatever is set down in the rules is presumably authorized and sanctioned by the legitimate authority. The Jamaican prison rules, handed down from the British and only recently revised, specified that flogging can only be inflicted with a rope whip

> consisting of a round wooden handle twenty inches long and one to one and a half inches in diameter with nine thongs of cotton cord attached to one end of the handle, each thong being thirty inches long and not more than three-sixteenths of an inch in diameter and knotted at the end or whipped at the end with cotton twine.[5]

Here we have cruelty, measured in numbers of thongs and six-teenths of an inch, sanitized and made respectable by the language of the law and the historic traditions of the British civil service.

Finally prison is a prime place for dehumanization. All the rituals lead in that direction. The prisoner arrives at the prison in a prison van with no lavatories. Clothes are removed and bodily orifices searched. The prisoner is bathed and reclothed in an ill-fitting, humiliating prison uniform. A number is allocated. Personal belongings are put in bags. The prisoner becomes dependent on staff for access to lavatories, washing facilities, hot food, letters from home, a chance to be out of the cell, help from the welfare services, everything.

If people are going to be ill-treated and abused, prison therefore seems to provide fertile soil. The potential for ill-treatment is increased because prisons are such closed places, often situated in the most remote areas. Families of prisoners are often too poor and vulnerable themselves to highlight the abuses their family members are subjected to. Many families wish to hide the fact they have a relative in prison, because of the social shame that imprisonment brings.

To provide safeguards against the possibility of ill-treatment, what goes on in the prison environment is governed by rules.[6] The basic principles of the Universal Declaration and the International Covenant have been elaborated into a range of other sets of rules. The most well-known are the United Nations Standard Minimum Rules for the Treatment of Prisoners. Then there is a host of more specific UN documents, including rules governing the detention of juveniles (under-eighteens) and prisoners under sentence of death and rules for people who work in prisons, such as doctors and law enforcement officials.

The United Nations Rules are sometimes criticized for being out of date, Eurocentric and woolly. There is some justice in this view. They certainly reflect a European view of imprisonment, and make assumptions about the amount of money that will be available for prisons that are unrealizable in developing countries. They also fail to deal adequately with the specific questions about women in prison and emphasize a treatment model that is now seen as untenable. On one or two matters, their stance is highly questionable. For example, Rule 9 (1) of the UN Standard Minimum Rules requires that when prisoners have to share accommodation 'it is not desirable to have two prisoners in a cell or room'. At least three is regarded as better. The object of this rule is apparently to reduce the possibility of homosexual activity. Rule 37 restricts prisoners' contact with people outside prison to the family and friends who are 'reputable'. Who decides who is 'reputable'? Information from the radio and newspapers should be available to prisoners, say the Rules, but only as 'authorized and controlled by the administration'.

These limitations have led to some people arguing that the Rules need to be revised, updated, made more relevant to developing countries and modern concepts of penology. In reply it is said that the time is far from appropriate. The mood that led to their adoption is no longer with us. The most powerful country in the world, with the strongest voice in international forums, the United States, sees fit to ignore them. Japan's prison system is frequently judged in the light of them and found seriously wanting, so Japan would probably therefore be keen to see them eliminated. In China a very different view of the purpose and conduct of imprisonment prevails. In the face of these considerations, most reformers have concluded that it is wiser to leave well alone and continue to promote the UN Rules in spite of the limitations.

Countries in Europe belong to the Council of Europe. The Council of Europe, often wrongly confused with the European Union, was founded in May 1949. One of its objectives was to work for the 'maintenance and further realization of human rights and fundamental freedoms'.[7] One of its first acts was to draft a new convention on human rights for Europe. This convention, the European Convention on Human Rights, came into force on 3 September 1953, the anniversary of the outbreak of the Second World War, and by December 1996 had been signed by (although not yet ratified by all) forty countries in Europe. The Council of Europe has also produced its own set of rules on imprisonment, the European Prison Rules, very like the United Nations version but more detailed. These rules, when drafted and subsequently revised in 1987, accorded well with the culture and living standards in Europe and did not give rise to the objections levelled against the United Nations version. However, with the expansion of the Council of Europe to include most of the East and Central European countries of the former Soviet bloc, similar questions are being raised about appropriateness and relevance. Can rules based on an idea of prisoners living in cells and receiving 'rehabilitative' regimes fit the model of the labour camps with dormitories and militarized staffing that is the basis of the system in the East?

In addition to the international framework, nearly all prison systems work within the legal framework of their own country. Prison systems are normally governed by prison acts, laws and regulations made in the country's legislature. The hope of the United Nations is that these rules will be based as far as possible on the United Nations' own rules.

A SET OF CLEAR PRINCIPLES

When all these rules are added together and the essence extracted from them, certain clear principles emerge about the nature of imprisonment that the international law-makers envisage.

First is the often-quoted if infrequently understood aphorism, 'Men come to prison *as* a punishment, not *for* punishment.' Sir Alexander Paterson, a famous English Prison Commissioner and reformer, used this phrase in the 1920s. 'It is,' he said, 'the sentence of imprisonment, and not the treatment accorded in prison, that constitutes the punishment.'[8] The fact of imprisonment, with the loss of liberty and freedom of choice and separation from friends and family that it brings, is the punishment. The loss is the punishment. The punishment is not another element to be added on and meted out once the person is in prison, through beatings, torture, deprivation of light, heat, bedding, food and water or medical care. Prison is a severe punishment, but prisons should not be punishing places. The punishment inheres in the idea of prison. The suffering that comes from loss of freedom and incarceration is enough suffering. Prisons should not be imposing any suffering other than that.

The second ideal shaping the post-1945 concept of imprisonment is an extension of the first. Prison should not be punishing. But there is a positive objective too. It should aim to be rehabilitative, although this in itself is not a justification for sending people there. People should never be sent to prison in the expectation that they will 'learn a trade', be 'cured of their addiction' or be 'taken care of'. Prisons should not be punishing, but even the most humane prisons are places for punishment.

So the idea that prison should aim to be rehabilitative is problematic. It is also difficult because belief in rehabilitation has been much tarnished by research findings showing that most programmes of seemingly rehabilitative value have very little effect on whether or not a prisoner gets into further trouble outside. In any case, it is argued – rightly – no one can force another human being to be rehabilitated. Change has to come from within the individual and to be willed. How can it make sense then for prisons to be expected to be rehabilitative? In fact, it can make sense, but only when we look more closely at the concept. It is not saying that people will *be* rehabilitated. It is saying that prisons should *aim* at rehabilitation. It is a description of the ethos, style of organization and management, the type of activities available and wider objectives. It means that the policy of the prison should begin from the fact that it is an institution guarding human beings, and that each one has the potential to do something good or become something good. Prisons should help prisoners to rehabilitate themselves. The treatment of the prisoners should reflect that ideal. So cruelty is forbidden, because that will not bring out the good in people. So are violence and brutality. Humiliation is not acceptable. Pointless labour such as dismantling old electricity cables that no one will use is out. Prisoners cannot be paraded in front of the public. Chain gangs are contrary to the rehabilitative ideal.

This requirement is the one above all others that distinguishes a prison in a modern democratic society where rights are respected from a labour camp or a concentration camp where the individuals are there purely to be got out of the way and used as cheap labour. A prison in a democratic society continues to regard the incarcerated as fellow citizens and treats them as such. A prison in a totalitarian country does not.

The third requirement is that everyday life in prison should be carried on within a framework of justice and fairness. Perhaps the finest exponent of this philosophy is Lord Woolf, the British judge brought in after the serious riots in Strangeways Prison, Manchester, in 1990 to carry out a judicial inquiry. He said,

> There must . . . be justice in our prisons. The system of justice which
> has put a person in prison cannot end at the prison doors. It must
> accompany the prisoner into the prison, his cell, and to all aspects
> of his life in prison.[9]

Judge Louise Arbour, appointed by the Canadian government to
carry out an investigation into the incident at the federal women's
prison where an emergency response team composed entirely of men
stripped a group of women prisoners naked, placed them in restraints
and removed them from their cells (see Chapter 7), adopts a similar
approach. She says,

> . . . the legal order must serve as both the justification and the code
> of conduct for correctional authorities since the confinement of
> persons against their will has no other foundation; it is not justifiable
> on medical, humanitarian, charitable or any other basis. The coercive
> actions of the state must find their justification in a legal grant of
> authority and persons who enforce criminal sanctions on behalf of
> the state must act with scrupulous concern not to exceed their
> authority.[10]

The way prisoners are treated has to be governed by a set of rules
and prisoners have to have access to these rules and be able to refer
to them when they need to. If the rules are broken some machinery
for redress has to be in place. Prisoners cannot do whatever they
like, but neither can prison staff. What prisoners are entitled to,
what constitutes an offence against the rules of the prison, how
offences are punished and how prisoners can appeal against any
decision made about them, all needs to be set out clearly in a way
that even illiterate prisoners or those speaking a foreign language
can understand.

LAWFUL DETENTION

The international rules about how prisoners should be treated can
be divided into a number of sections relating to all aspects of prison
life. But first it must be established that keeping the person in
detention at all is a lawful thing to do. So the rules make clear that
the first duty of prison officials is to ensure that any person who
is committed into their custody should rightfully be there. The

paperwork must be in order and properly authorized. The prison authorities must know and record the identity of the individuals concerned, the reasons for their imprisonment and the length of period of detention authorized by the court.

Rules of arrest and lawful detention

Article 9 of the Universal Declaration of Human Rights provides:

No one shall be subjected to arbitrary arrest, detention or exile.

This provision is confirmed in the International Covenant on Civil and Political Rights. Article 9 of this Covenant states:

9.1   *Everyone has the right to liberty and security of person. No one shall be subjected to arbitrary arrest or detention. No one shall be deprived of his liberty except on such grounds and in accordance with such procedures as are established by law.*

9.2   *Anyone who is arrested shall be informed, at the time of arrest, of the reasons for his arrest and shall be promptly informed of any charges against him.*

9.3   *Anyone arrested or detained on a criminal charge shall be brought promptly before a judge or other officer authorized to exercise judicial power and shall be entitled to trial within a reasonable time or to release. It shall not be the general rule that persons awaiting trial shall be detained in custody, but release may be subject to guarantees to appear for trial, at any other stage of the judicial proceedings, and, should occasion arise, for execution of the judgement.*

9.4   *Anyone who is deprived of his liberty by arrest or detention shall be entitled to take proceedings before a court, in order that a court may decide without delay on the lawfulness of his detention and order his release if the detention is not lawful.*

Principle 12 of the United Nations Body of Principles for the Protection of All Persons under Any Form of Detention or Imprisonment provides:

1 *There shall be duly recorded:*
   a) *the reasons for the arrest;*
   b) *the time of the arrest and the taking of the arrested person to a place of custody as well as that of his first appearance before a judicial or other authority;*
   c) *the identity of the law enforcement officials concerned;*
   d) *precise information concerning the place of custody.*
2 *Such records shall be communicated to the detained person, or his counsel, if any, in the form prescribed by law.*

Rule 7 of the United Nations Standard Minimum Rules for the Treatment of Prisoners requires that:

1 *In every place where prisoners are imprisoned there shall be kept a bound registration book with numbered pages in which shall be entered in respect of each prisoner received:*
   a) *information concerning his identity;*
   b) *the reasons for his commitment and the authority therefor;*
   c) *the day and hour of his admission and release.*
2 *No person shall be received in an institution without a valid commitment order of which the details shall have been previously entered in the register.*

PROVIDING THE MINIMUM

Having established that detaining the prisoner at all is lawful the rules go on to set out how that detention should be conducted. The matters covered by the rules can be divided into two broad areas. The first contains those things that a prisoner *should have* for a minimum level of humane existence. The second sets out what the authorities *should not do* to prisoners.

Looking at the first area, that is the minimum conditions that prisoners should be given, space is the starting point. One of the basics of humane imprisonment is the amount of space allocated to each prisoner to live in. If prisons are so crowded that prisoners have to take it in turns to lie down or they tie themselves to the cell bars so that they can sleep standing up, then the rules are not being kept. There is no universal norm for the amount of space that should be allocated to each prisoner, but it is certainly expected to be enough for a person to lie down, move about, and store a few belongings.

The accommodation also has to be habitable enough not to damage health or cause undue misery and suffering. If the accommodation consists of dark, dilapidated cells alive with cockroaches, if prisoners have to lie on a damp concrete floor with one blanket to cover them, if prisoners freeze in winter or suffer extreme heat in summer, the rules are being broken.

One of the basic problems that plagues most prison systems is sanitation. Unfortunately when people come to prison and have to spend much of their time locked up in a tiny unplumbed room they must, as the Rules describe it, 'comply with the needs of nature' somehow. And to do so they need toilet facilities of some sort. In outside society, people normally 'comply with the needs of nature' in private. Usually they are free to find and use toilet facilities when they need them. None of this applies in prison. Many of the world's prisoners live in rooms with no toilet facilities. Those who do have such facilities are normally sharing the room with at least one and usually many more people. The toilet facilities may be curtained off, or in a room with a full-length door at the end of the cell. They may also be simply in a corner of the cell so there is no privacy from the cell-mates or the official eye that can look through the peephole in the door at any time. In some prisons, prisoners who want to use the facilities have to call for a prison officer to unlock them electronically, that is by remote control. Only one prisoner may be 'electronically unlocked' at a time, so there may be a long wait.

That is not the end of the problems. In the end the sewage has to be removed from the prison. The toilets have to flush. The contents of the buckets have to go somewhere.

In Linhó prison in Portugal in 1992, a Council of Europe committee witnessed the disposal of the contents of the buckets.

> The cell doors were opened in sequence and the prisoners brought their buckets to the cesspit . . . by the time thirty or forty prisoners had used the cesspit, newly arriving prisoners were confronted with a mound of excrement and assorted rubbish piled up on the grille covering the cesspit, to which they added their own contribution. By this stage the stench in the slopping-out area was overpowering. The occasional prisoner would use one of the lavatories located alongside the cesspit – in full view of the newly arriving prisoners. Having emptied their buckets, prisoners would rinse them out; however, no detergent or disinfectant was provided. The mound of excrement was later cleared with a hose.[11]

Clearly some work needed to be done in Portugal before UN Standard Minimum Rule number 12 which requires that 'the sanitary installations shall be adequate to enable every prisoner to comply with the needs of nature when necessary and in a clean and decent manner' is implemented.

The rules also call for prisoners to have the chance to keep themselves clean. The prison authorities should be providing them with the toilet articles they need: soap, toothpaste, toilet paper, toothbrushes. The authorities have the responsibility of keeping prisoners clothed, with clothes that are warm enough in cold weather. Underwear must be changed frequently. The clothes that are provided should not be 'degrading or humiliating' – no striped pyjama suits or uniforms with arrows. Each prisoner should have a separate bed and bedding should be provided.

Food is very important in prison. The rules specify that sufficient and nutritious food should be provided and served at the normal hours in the country concerned. Prisoners should have access to drinking water. Exercise is also very important and evokes images of the famous engraving by Doré of grey-clad prisoners walking round and round in a grim walled exercise yard. One hour per day is the minimum called for in the rules. The right to exercise is taken seriously in most prison systems and incorporated into prison designs so that even the most secure dungeon-like cell block has access to a cage open to the sky – if it can be seen through the helicopter-proof wire netting – where prisoners can breathe fresh air and walk.

Article 18 of the Universal Declaration of Human Rights provides that:

> Everyone has the right to freedom of thought, conscience and religion; this right includes freedom to change his religion or belief, and freedom, either alone or in community with others and in public or private, to manifest his religion or belief in teaching, practice, worship and observance.

This freedom applies to 'everyone', including those in captivity. Prisoners must be able to practise their religion. If there are enough of a given denomination a representative should be appointed to the prison to visit regularly. The person appointed must be allowed by the prison authorities to hold regular services and visit the adherents. Prisoners must never be prevented from seeing a qualified representative of their religion. Prisoners should normally be allowed to attend religious services and have religious books.

Obviously most prisoners come to prison with belongings. Often prison becomes their only home and their possessions, scant as they may be, come with them. Prisons always restrict the number, kind and volume of private possessions a prisoner may have. The rest have to go somewhere else. But the prison authorities do not have the right to confiscate them. Arrangements have to be made to store them safely, account for them and return them to the prisoner on release. The rules, however, give the prison the right to dispose of any clothes that are flea-ridden or lousy.

The rules about prisoners start from the premise that their dignity must be respected. They must not be subjected to public ridicule or comment. From time to time it will be necessary to take prisoners out of prison, to go to court, to hospital or to another prison. At such times prison authorities must ensure that they enjoy as much privacy as possible. They must be protected from 'insult, curiosity and publicity in any form'. The transport they are moved about in should have enough ventilation and light and not subject them to unnecessary physical hardship.

This does not mean, however, that they should be locked away from the outside world and unable to communicate with or meet other people. On the contrary, the openness of prisons to the outside world is a basic protection against abuses and an opportunity for prisoners to prepare for their release. So there are rules about relationships with outside people and bodies and many battles have been fought to assert the right of prisoners to communicate.

Rules on contact with the outside world

Article 12 of the Universal Declaration of Human Rights provides:
no one shall be subjected to arbitrary interference with his privacy, family, home or correspondence.

Article 23 of the International Covenant on Civil and Political Rights states:
The family is the natural and fundamental group unit of society and is entitled to protection by society and the state.

The Standard Minimum Rules say (Rule 37):
prisoners shall be allowed under necessary supervision to communicate with their family and reputable friends at regular intervals, both by correspondence and by receiving visits.

Rule 79 applies to sentenced prisoners and requires that:
special attention be paid to the maintenance and improvement of such relations between a prisoner and his family as are desirable in the best interests of both.

Rule 44 (1) deals with notification of death, illness or transfer and requires that:
if a prisoner dies, becomes seriously ill or injured or is removed to a mental institution the prison director should inform the spouse, nearest relative or designated person at once.

Rule 44 (2) concerns prisoners and requires that:
they shall be informed at once of the death or serious illness of a near relative and if the illness of a near relative is critical the

> *prisoners should be able to go, escorted or unescorted, to the bedside.*
>
> *Rule 44 (3) gives the prisoner the right to inform his or her family at once of imprisonment or transfer.*
>
> *The Body of Principles states that:*
>
> *A detained or imprisoned person shall have the right to be visited by and to correspond with, in particular, members of his family and shall be given adequate opportunity to communicate with the outside world, subject to reasonable conditions and restrictions as specified by law or lawful regulations (Principle 19).*
>
> *Principle 20 gives further importance to the right to contact with family and friends by requiring that:*
>
> *if a detained or imprisoned person so requests, he shall if possible be kept in a place of detention or imprisonment reasonably near his usual place of residence.*

There are special rules for foreign prisoners. They must be allowed to communicate with the diplomats from their own country if they wish to.

The prison should aim to be rehabilitative or, as Article 10 (3) of the International Covenant on Civil and Political Rights says, 'the penitentiary system shall comprise treatment of prisoners the essential aim of which shall be their reformation and social rehabilitation'.

Both the UN and the European versions of the rules contain much about sending prisoners out better than when they came in, wanting to lead law-abiding lives, able to earn their own living and with a sense of responsibility.

These descriptions of the basis of prison treatment have implications for the activities that prisoners engage in. The first implication is that prisoners should have something to do. They should not spend all day locked in a dormitory or cell or sitting idly in a yard. Secondly, the activities they engage in should be purposeful and have some relevance to life outside prison and the skills needed to earn a living outside prison.

The rehabilitative goal has implications for the way in which prisoners are seen by staff. It requires that staff see prisoners as people with potential for change, growth and improvement.

All around the world the traditional rehabilitative basis for prison regimes is work. People expect prisoners to be working, and probably at something fairly unpleasant. We have seen that in the Russian and Eastern traditions prisons are labour camps. In the Western tradition most prison rules require prisoners to work, if work is available. The image of the prisoners sitting in a bleak workroom, bent with their needles over the mailbags, so many stitches to the inch or the prisoner is in trouble, is enduring.

What do the rules say about forcing prisoners to work? Article 8 of the International Covenant on Civil and Political Rights prohibits slavery. Paragraph 3 (a) provides 'no one shall be required to perform forced or compulsory labour'.

But this does not apply to prisoners. Paragraph 3 (b) goes on to state:

> Paragraph 3 (a) shall not be held to preclude, in countries where imprisonment with hard labour may be imposed as a punishment for a crime, the performance of hard labour in the pursuance of a sentence to such punishment by a competent court.

This may seem rather harsh and out of harmony with the spirit of the rest of the Covenant but the UN rules contain much about work and put forward a view which mitigates the hard-labour image of Article 8. They say of prison work that the work shall not be 'afflictive', i.e. it shall not be chosen because of its unpleasant and punishing qualities. No stone-crushing or oakum-picking allowed. As far as possible it should be a preparation for life in the outside world and be paid so prisoners can send money to their families and save for their release. The working conditions and hours should reflect society outside. Prisoners should have one day a week off. Prison work should be subject to the same laws on health, safety, industrial injury and occupational disease as apply in free society.

The rule-makers may have had a crystal ball to see the trend in the 80s and 90s to involve private industry in prison work. Or more likely they could still remember what prisons were like in the United States in the 20s and 30s, when prisoners were hired out to private contractors as slave labourers. In any case, they were alive to the dangers. The rules say that prisoners should be protected from any attempt to use them as forced or slave labour and their interests must not be subordinated to making a profit. Industries and farms should preferably not be run by private contractors and prisoners should always be under the supervision of the institution's personnel, even when engaged in work not controlled by the prison's administration.

But 'rehabilitation' is more than work. All the rules show a great faith in education and its power to change attitudes and behaviour. They suggest that those who could benefit should have access to further education. Young prisoners and those who are illiterate should be required to receive education. Prison education should be integrated into the education of the country so that reintegration on release is made easier and recreational and cultural activities should be provided in all institutions. There is even a special UN Resolution on Prison Education which asks the authorities to develop education for the whole person, taking the prisoner's cultural context into account, to ensure that education is an integral part of the prison regime, supported by the entire administration and to allow prisoners to take part in education outside prisons and to involve the community in education within prisons.[12]

The impact of the prison sentence should not be for ever. Once the prisoner has served the sentence the punishment is complete. Efforts should be made during the prison sentence to reduce the damaging effects of imprisonment on a prisoner's prospects. After release efforts should be made to reduce the social stigma and persuade the institutions of society to accept ex-prisoners back into society. It is understood that a prisoner leaving prison with no money, no home, no work and no acceptable clothes in which to go and seek a home or a job is going to find it harder not to return to crime. Prison administrations are therefore expected to make arrangements themselves or co-operate with other social agencies to make such arrangements for the aftercare of released prisoners.

Preparing prisoners for their return to the community is a constant theme running through the rules on work and education. The specific rules on preparation for release say that steps should be taken to ensure a gradual return to society for a prisoner, including a pre-release regime in the same or a different prison, or by 'release on trial' under some kind of non-police supervision coupled with social help. Those organizations that assist released prisoners should ensure wherever possible that released prisoners have appropriate documents and identification papers, suitable homes to go to, work, appropriate clothes, a means to reach their destination and to maintain themselves in the period immediately following release.

To make this happen, the agencies that help released prisoners should have access to the prisons and the prisoners and be involved with the planning for prisoners' release from the beginning of their sentences.

The spirit of these requirements is summarized in Principle 10 of the Basic Principles as follows:

> with the participation and help of the community and social institutions, and with due regard to the interests of victims, favourable conditions shall be created for the reintegration of the ex-prisoner into society under the best possible conditions.

THE RIGHT TO COMPLAIN

Contact with the outside world provides prisoners with one device for ensuring that ill-treatment is brought to light and abuses checked. Other methods are also allowed for. The human rights instruments require that everyone whose rights have been violated is entitled to a remedy. This right also applies to prisoners. For example, Article 13 of the European Convention says,

> Everyone whose rights and freedoms as set forth in this Convention are violated shall have an effective remedy before a national authority notwithstanding that the violation has been committed by persons acting in an official capacity.

Prisoners should have the right to challenge the conditions of their imprisonment or treatment while in detention. If the prisoner cannot bring a challenge it can be brought by a member of the family or anyone else. It should be responded to quickly, and the prisoner should not be victimized for complaining.

So that they know whether the rules of their imprisonment have been broken prisoners need to have access to the procedures which govern their daily lives. It is laid down that when they arrive prisoners should get information in writing about the rules of the prison, the disciplinary procedures and the systems for making complaints. If the prisoner cannot read, the information should be given orally.

Prisoners must be able to complain to someone in the prison about their treatment and there has to be a system for dealing with such complaints. The UN Rules are very specific. Prisoners must have the opportunity 'every day' to complain to the head of the prison or someone delegated by the head of the prison to hear complaints. Prisoners should also be able to take the complaint further if they are not satisfied. It is not good enough just to allow complaints to be dealt with by the people who are being complained about. They may be objective and fair but no one will believe it. So prisoners should be able to complain to visiting inspectors in confidence and send uncensored complaints to the central prison authorities or judges or any other officials who hear complaints. Complaints should be answered quickly.

Prisoners must be able to complain about the whole range of daily prison life. Something has not been given that should, in the prisoner's view, have been given: a job working in the kitchen, a move to a different cell, an extra phone call to a sick relative. Something has been taken away, such as having family visits across a table in an open room: visits are now to take place with a glass screen between the prisoner and the family. Something is wrong: the food is uneatable again; the food is stone cold; the food is being tampered with; people in authority have abused their power; the prisoner has been assaulted, beaten up, had possessions smashed during the search of a cell.

In Lord Justice Woolf's report, he underlined the need for an independent avenue of complaints:

... the presence of an independent element within the grievance system procedure is more than just an 'optional extra'. The case for some form of independent person or body to consider grievances is incontrovertible . . . A system without an independent element is not a system which accords with proper standards of justice.[13]

Provision for an independent investigation of prisoners' complaints is made in several countries. This provision frequently takes the form of an ombudsman dedicated to investigating complaints from all members of the public, including prisoners, by scrutinizing the working of public administration. In other countries there is the equivalent of an ombudsman who deals exclusively with complaints from prisoners.

So prisoners must have opportunities to make complaints without fear and have them attended to seriously and speedily. Making complaints, having enough food and water, space to live in, activities, education, preparation for release activities, a copy of the rules: the authorities must provide all these if they are to conform to the international standards.

THE PROHIBITIONS

Other rules specify what it is that the authorities must *not* do to prisoners. For example, they must not discriminate on racial grounds. Discrimination on the grounds of race, colour, language and religion is prohibited by all the global and regional instruments on human rights. Equality of treatment for individuals is a principle reasserted many times and in all conventions and instruments. Within this blanket prohibition, however, there is a further principle, which is that there should be specific protections for the rights of minorities as groups so as to preserve their identity and culture. These requirements apply equally to prisoners.

UN Rule 6 contains both these requirements. First, there must be no discrimination in the application of the Rules. Secondly the religious beliefs and moral precepts of the group to which the prisoner belongs should be respected. The UN Basic Principles have the same double requirement – no discrimination, but respect for religious and cultural differences.

A prison is a place where people are kept who do not want to be there. Some of them will make determined and well-thought-out efforts to get out. The easy answer would be to chain them up in some way: attach chains round their legs and fasten them to a ring cemented into the wall; handcuff them at all times; make them wear heavy chains, called fetters, so they cannot move fast. All these devices have been used in history and are still to be found in use somewhere in the world. The rules, however, forbid their use except in exceptional circumstances: 'Instruments of restraint, such as handcuffs, chains, irons and straitjackets, shall never be applied as a punishment. Furthermore, chains or irons shall not be used as restraints.'

Other instruments of restraint can be used, but only 'as a precaution against escape during a transfer, provided that they shall be removed when the prisoner appears before a judicial or administrative authority'. They must not be used longer than necessary. They can be used only on medical grounds if the medical officer agrees. They can be ordered by the prison governor to prevent the prisoners injuring themselves or property. The central authorities should make rules about the use of any restraints and see that the rules are applied.

Obviously torture is completely forbidden, in prisons as everywhere else. How far, then, can prisons go in punishing prisoners who break the rules without moving into the area of torture? They are already in prison. They have lost most things already. What else can be done to them? The rules set strict limits on the punishments that can be inflicted on prisoners and prescribe the sort of processes that have to be followed to discipline a prisoner.

The rules say that there must be a formal disciplinary procedure. It must be laid down clearly in the laws of the country or in regulations what is against the rules and what is not, what punishments may be given and who has the authority to impose these punishments. When prisoners are accused of breaking the prison rules and are likely to be punished they must have a procedure with many of the elements of a proper trial. They must know what they are accused of and be able to defend themselves, if necessary through an interpreter.

Definition of torture

The UN Convention against Torture and Other Cruel, Inhuman or Degrading Treatment or Punishment defines torture:

For the purposes of this Convention, the term 'torture' means any act by which severe pain or suffering, whether physical or mental, is intentionally inflicted on a person for such purposes as obtaining from him or a third person information or a confession, punishing him for an act he or a third person has committed or is suspected of having committed, or intimidating or coercing him or a third person, or for any reason based on discrimination of any kind, when such pain or suffering is inflicted by or at the instigation of or with the consent or acquiescence of a public official or other person acting in an official capacity. It does not include pain or suffering arising from, inherent in or incidental to lawful sanctions (1.1).

The UN Convention goes on to confirm the absolute nature of the prohibition on torture:

No exceptional circumstances whatsoever, whether a state of war or a threat of war, internal political instability or any other public emergency, may be invoked as a justification of torture. An order from a superior officer or a public authority may not be invoked as a justification for torture (2.2, 2.3).

It is in the punishments available that the prisons come nearest to crossing the borderline that separates legitimate prison treatment from torture. Since people are already in prison and have lost almost everything, inflicting further punishment on them requires some exercise of the imagination. The rules restrict that imagination.

> Corporal punishment, punishment by placing in a dark cell, and all cruel, inhuman or degrading punishments shall be completely prohibited as punishments for disciplinary offences.

So is using 'instruments of restraint, such as handcuffs, chains, irons and straitjackets'.

Common punishments in use around the world are putting prisoners in solitary confinement or putting them on a diet of bread and water. These are allowed in the rules but only when the medical officer has examined a prisoner and certified in writing that the prisoner is fit enough to undergo either. If it is agreed that the prisoner may undergo such punishments the medical officer has to visit the prisoner every day and tell the prison director to stop the punishment if it is damaging the prisoner's mental or physical health.

Another in the list of things the authorities are not supposed to do to prisoners is to give another prisoner authority over them. The rules say that no prisoner shall be used in any disciplinary capacity. Prisoners should not be chosen as head of a section or a dormitory and then allowed to decide who gets the best bed and who has to sleep next to the overflowing lavatory or clean up after the others.

MEDICAL CARE

So there are things a prisoner must have and things that must not be done to a prisoner. In addition there is the difficult question of medical care, which combines both. Prisoners should have access to good medical care. Also there are certain things that doctors should never do to them.

Health and medical care are particularly sensitive areas for the human rights of prisoners and are the source of much contention and possible abuse. The role of doctors in dealing with people who are confined against their will is delicate. Beneath the surface lurk potential evils such as using people in captivity as guinea pigs to try out new drugs or new treatments. Even when the prisoner agrees to the treatment, how free is the decision? The prisoner may think agreement will bring rewards for being co-operative or even an earlier release date.

The role of doctors in the management of the prison is also very contentious. How far are they working for the prison? How far do they owe a duty to the patients, however disruptive and violent they may be? Do they administer drugs only in the interests of the health of the patient or also in order to produce a quiet and ordered institution when asked to do so by the prison officials? What do they do when they examine an injured prisoner and it is clear that the prisoner has been beaten up by an official, either in the police station before arrival or in the prison? Could refusing access to the doctor be used as a punishment by prison staff against prisoners they do not like or wish to get into line, and what should a doctor do about it?

Doctors will see illnesses that are produced directly by the inhumanity of the prison regime: malnutrition perhaps, or diseases spread because of poor sanitation. Doctors will be required to carry out operations on prisoners to repair self-inflicted and sometimes terrible injuries. They will have to remove from prisoners' stomachs and throats objects that have been swallowed or inserted deliberately and in sheer desperation by the prisoner to get moved from the main prison into the hospital. They will have to sew up lacerated limbs. How long can they continue to do this before questioning the environment that produces people able to do such desperate damage to themselves?

Doctors also have official functions in the prison administration which can lead to conflicts. Often they have to certify that accommodation is fit for prisoners to live in, prisoners are fit for punishment, prisoners can continue to be kept in solitary confinement or hunger strikers should be force fed. In some countries they have a role in carrying out corporal and capital punishment.

In recognition of these difficulties and the potential for abuse there are a number of international sets of rules about the role of medical personnel in prison. In total the rules suggest that the following requirements should govern what doctors do in prison. They should not under any circumstances take part in administering cruel, inhuman or degrading punishments. They should not use prisoners for experiments. Prisoners should be receiving the same standard of health care as the general public outside prison and the care should be free of charge. Doctors should serve their patients, not the prison authorities. Every prisoner on admission shall have a medical examination. Prisoners should have the right to get a second medical opinion.

In dealing with HIV and AIDS in prisons, documents from the World Health Organization and the Council of Europe recommend no compulsory testing, confidentiality, measures to reduce the spread of infection and no segregation of infected prisoners. Whenever possible dying prisoners should be released from prison.

Some prison doctors have another function besides looking after prison patients. They have to be the 'prison medical officer'. The duty of prison medical officers, according to the rules, is to supervise the health of the prison. They should inspect the prison regularly and advise the person in charge on whether the food is good, the building and the prisoners are clean, the ventilation, light, heat and bedding are adequate and whether the rules on physical education and sport are being observed. As we have seen, they should certify prisoners fit for various sorts of punishment and visit them every day when they are being punished.

UNTRIED PRISONERS

All the rules discussed so far apply to all prisoners, whether they are in prison or detained in a police station or a temporary prison. But not all prisoners have the same status. The rules all make a major distinction between people who have been found guilty, convicted by a court, and sentenced to prison and those who have not. Prisoners who are waiting for their trial, imprisoned on remand, are regarded differently because the law sees them as innocent until found guilty. Therefore their rights should be especially protected.

The rules lay down that untried prisoners should normally sleep singly in separate rooms (Rule 86). Unless it causes a great deal of difficulty, untried prisoners should be able to get food brought in from outside (Rule 87). They should be able to wear their own clothes if they are suitable. If they have to wear prison clothes they should be given clothes that are different from the clothes given to the convicted prisoners. They cannot be made to work, although they can work if they want to. They must be able to use their own money to get things they want such as books and other items so long as they do not cause trouble with them. They must be allowed to be visited by their own doctor or dentist if the grounds are reasonable.

These rules show the underlying thinking about pre-trial prisoners. They must be kept separate from convicted prisoners, because

Rules on untried people who are detained

The Universal Declaration of Human Rights sets out clearly the presumption of innocence:

Everyone charged with a penal offence has the right to be presumed innocent until proved guilty according to law in a public trial at which he has had all the guarantees necessary for his defence (Article 11).

Article 14 (2) of the International Covenant on Civil and Political Rights sets out the same principle along with a series of other safeguards for ensuring a fair trial and the right of appeal. This principle also appears in the African Charter (Article 7 (1b)), the European Convention (Article 6 (2)) and the American Convention (Article 8 (2)).

Pre-trial prisoners are entitled to all the protections which apply to all prisoners. In addition, it is made clear that normal practice requires that accused but unconvicted persons shall:

be segregated from convicted persons and shall be subject to separate treatment appropriate to their status as unconvicted persons (International Covenant on Civil and Political Rights, Article 10 (2a)).

The Standard Minimum Rules for the Treatment of Prisoners emphasize the need for separation without any reservations. Rule 85 (1) states:

Untried prisoners shall be kept separate from convicted prisoners.

The Body of Principles calls for unconvicted prisoners to be kept separate from imprisoned persons 'wherever possible' (Principle 8).

it would not be right to expect innocent people to have to live with convicted prisoners. They are not convicted persons and should not be kept in a place where the ethos is that of containing people who have been given a prison sentence.

The list of what cannot be taken away from or done to them shows how far, although they are detained, they are expected to retain some of the liberties of free people: a choice of food, doctor, books, clothes. Being convicted means losing those choices.

Pre-trial prisoners are, by definition, waiting to be tried. So, for them, contact with their lawyer is essential and will loom large in their minds. In order to get a fair trial it is particularly important that pre-trial prisoners are able to keep in contact with family, friends and legal advisers so as to prepare their defence properly. The rules require that untried prisoners must be able to inform their families of where they are being kept and be able to communicate with them and receive visits from them subject only to necessary security restrictions. They must be allowed to apply for free legal aid where it is available. They must not be stopped from receiving visits from their legal advisers to discuss their defence. They must be supplied with writing material if they want it. Their legal advisers must be able to interview them 'within sight but not within hearing' of officials (Rules 92 and 93).

WOMEN AND THE RULES

The situation of women in prison does not receive a great deal of attention in the rules. However, the general requirement of non-discrimination and equal treatment is set out clearly in the Convention on the Elimination of All Forms of Discrimination Against Women of 1979. The Convention prevents any discrimination which denies to women the same protections and fundamental freedoms in all fields – political, economic, social, cultural and civil – as are accorded to men (Article 1). The Convention also calls for women to have equal access to the same opportunities as men in education and vocational training and for the elimination of stereotyped concepts of 'the roles of men and women at all levels in all forms of education' (Article 10 (c)).

The UN Rules apply to all prisoners whatever their gender.

However, there are also special requirements regarding women. The Rules require that men and women should be kept separate.

> Men and women shall so far as possible be detained in separate institutions; in an institution which receives both men and women, the whole of the premises allocated to women shall be entirely separate (Rule 8 (a)).

The UN Standard Minimum Rules have special requirements for women prisoners covering pregnancy, childbirth and child care. They call for pregnant prisoners to get all necessary pre- and post-natal care. Prisoners' babies should be born in an outside hospital if possible and if the baby is born in prison this should not be mentioned on the birth certificate. When mothers have new-born babies with them in prison there should be a proper nursery in the prison.

The Rules clearly require that imprisoned women must be protected from sexual harassment and exploitation by men.

JUVENILES AND THE RULES

In most countries it is an accepted principle that children and young people who are suspected or convicted of breaking the law should be treated differently from adults in a similar position. There are several reasons for this. Children are regarded as having less responsibility for their actions and the level of responsibility attributed to them increases as they grow older.

Children who have committed crimes are regarded as being more amenable to change and to learning different ways of behaving than are adults. Children and young people locked up in prison or pre-trial detention institutions are likely to be vulnerable to abuse and ill-treatment and unlikely to be able to protect themselves from it.

Because of this, most jurisdictions have a minimum age of criminal responsibility. Children below that age found committing crime are not subject to the criminal law but are deemed to need social help.

The Convention on the Rights of the Child was adopted by the United Nations General Assembly in November 1989. It contains a range of safeguards related to children and juveniles being dealt with under penal law. The definition of children in the Convention is those under eighteen years of age, except in states where the age of majority is attained earlier.

The Convention broadly repeats all the protections accorded to adults under the Universal Declaration of Human Rights and the International Covenant on Civil and Political Rights and states that these apply to children. It also prohibits capital punishment or life imprisonment without possibility of release (Article 37). It recommends the establishment of a minimum age below which children shall be regarded as not having the capacity to infringe the criminal law. It advocates measures for dealing with children without bringing them into court. It requires a child accused or convicted of infringing the penal law to be treated in a manner which takes into account 'the child's age and the desirability of promoting the child's reintegration and the child's assuming a constructive role in society'.

A detailed set of rules was adopted by the United Nations in 1985. These are called the Standard Minimum Rules for the Administration of Juvenile Justice (known as the Beijing Rules). They give special protection to juveniles remanded in custody. In 1990 another set of rules was adopted: the United Nations Rules for the Protection of Juveniles Deprived of Their Liberty.

Rules on the treatment of juveniles

Rule 19, on records, requires that:
- *all records on juveniles shall be kept in a confidential individual file;*
- *the file should be accessible only to authorized persons;*
- *where possible juveniles should have the right to contest what is on the file and inaccurate or unfair statements should be rectified;*
- *when the juvenile is released, the records should be sealed and eventually expunged.*

Rule 21 requires that records should be kept of details of notifications to parents and guardians of every admission, transfer or release of a juvenile. Rule 22 requires that such notifications should take place without delay.

Rule 27 calls for a written individualized treatment plan for juveniles staying long enough in an institution.

Rule 30 requires that detention facilities be decentralized and small enough to facilitate contact between juveniles and their families.

The design of detention facilities should be in keeping with the rehabilitative aim (Rule 32).

The clothing issued to juveniles, where they cannot wear their own clothing, should not be 'degrading or humiliating' (Rule 36).

Rule 38 states that 'every juvenile of compulsory school age has the right to education'; Rule 42 that there is a right to vocational training. Diplomas and educational certificates should not show in any way that they were gained in an institution (Rule 43).

Juveniles should have exercise opportunities for sport and recreation and time for leisure activities (Rule 47).

Contact with the wider community is important. Visits from family and friends should be allowed 'in principle once a week and not less than once a month' in 'circumstances that respect the need of the juvenile for privacy, contact and unrestricted communications with the family and the defence counsel' (Rule 59).

Physical restraint and force should only be used in the most exceptional cases and, following their use, the director of the institution should report the matter to the higher administrative authority (Rule 64).

The carrying and use of weapons should be prohibited anywhere where juveniles are detained (Rule 65).

Reduction of diet or restrictions on contact with family should never be imposed as a disciplinary or other measure (Rule 67).

Outside independent inspectors should be given regular and unrestricted access to juvenile facilities (Rule 72).

Both sets of rules stress that young untried should be kept separate from adults and should in principle be kept in separate institutions altogether (Rule 85 (2)). The Rules for the Protection of Juveniles Deprived of Their Liberty put a great emphasis on treatment, education, rehabilitation, within the context of protecting rights, as well as safeguards against stigmatization.

The Beijing Rules and the Rules for the Protection of Juveniles Deprived of Their Liberty make it clear that the punitive element in the imprisonment of juveniles should be minimized as much as possible. Locking up juveniles should be regarded as an opportunity to give them the tools they need to succeed in life outside and to make good the defects in their education and training. The negative aspects of prison life should be minimized. However, the rules try to avoid the trap of letting the authorities do whatever they like to a young person in the name of treatment. The treatment philosophy enshrined in them must accompany a respect for the individual rights of each young person. The treatment plans and programmes cannot override the juveniles' entitlements to be treated fairly. Contact with the family is regarded as very important and as a key element in rehabilitation. Efforts must be made to avoid stigmatizing a juvenile as someone with a criminal background, as this can seriously hinder the chances of making a success of life after prison.

THE MEANING OF THE RULES

So there are rules for almost everything and everyone. The rules lay down what can be done to prisoners, what cannot be done to prisoners, what prisoners must have, how women prisoners must be treated, what is acceptable in dealing with juveniles. Detailed requirements are set out about sleeping arrangements, food, water, lavatories, clothes, lawyers, letters, visits, exercise. Can all this possibly be legitimate?

A consideration of the rules is likely to provoke two different reactions, both sceptical. One reaction will be: surely prisoners should not be getting all this? Another will be: certainly they should be getting all this but can you imagine prison officers taking any notice and giving them all this?

The first group will say, 'It is quite ridiculous. They are prisoners after all. All these rules about prisoners. How on earth can they be justified? What do people outside get? Nothing like it. It makes people want to go to prison. What about their victims? Is it not ridiculous that people who are supposed to be being punished should be able to take every little complaint about cold coffee or lack of budgie food through an elaborate procedure and have a right of appeal?'

They will ask how prison officers can keep order when prisoners have all the rights. How can young and inexperienced prison staff exert authority when prisoners can undermine the staff by making complaints against them? These places are prisons. They are meant to be secure. Surely keeping prisoners inside must come above rights. If prisoners are out and about all the time working and being educated and attending cultural activities, it is easier for them to escape. So they have the right to attend religious services. This sounds fine. But if they are all together it can be dangerous. The Strangeways riot in Manchester in 1990 started at a service in the chapel.[14] If prison officers stop them going to church because they suspect a plan is afoot, they will be abusing the prisoners' rights.

People from poor countries will have even more reason to question the rules. Why should prisoners get enough to eat and be given medical care when those who have not broken the law often do not have enough to eat and cannot afford any medical care for themselves or their children?

The other group will say, 'It is quite ridiculous. These are prisons after all. People are there because no one wants them and everyone hates them. Who is going to bother to keep these rules or protest if they are not kept?' They cannot imagine prison guards taking any notice of that sort of thing. It is fine in theory, but in practice it will not work. Suppose a prison governor is dealing with a situation where a prison guard accuses a prisoner of attacking him. It is the prisoner that has the bruises. The officer sticks to his story. He says he acted in self-defence. The prisoner says the officer assaulted him. The governor knows that there are two sides in the prison, prison guards and prisoners, and all are watching and waiting to see who will win. It is obvious that the governor will find the prisoner guilty, never mind the prisoner's rights.

So racial discrimination is prohibited. What a joke. With all those black prisoners and white prison staff, what do they expect to happen? So many areas of prison life give scope for racist decision-making. Many facilities in prison are scarce and prisoners are competing to get them: the good jobs, good cell location. The prison staff can exercise enormous discretion in allocating all these desirable things. In some prison systems prison staff are required to write reports about individual prisoners which can affect their chances of early or conditional release or parole. How can racism be eliminated from these?

Whatever the rules say about preparation for release and training activities and other worthy ideas, everyone knows what the real priority of the prison governor is. No one in a position of authority in a prison ever got sacked for not providing education or rehabilitative or reformative activities. Many prison governors and even senior administrators have been sacked because prisoners have escaped from the prisons under their control.

So pre-trial prisoners are supposed to have so many rights. Why then do they often endure the worst, most overcrowded prison conditions? All this regulation of the punishments is fine but everyone knows that prisoners get a good beating if the staff decide they deserve it. What is the use of all the work preparation, the training and education? When prisoners get out, no one wants to know them anyway.

So there are many questions about the rules. Some people question whether the rules should exist at all. Others welcome their existence but think it is a cloud-cuckoo-land to expect them to be kept. The next chapter considers how far they apply to the reality of imprisonment, how they are enforced and by whom.

11. *Keeping the Rules: The Supervisors and the Inspectors*

Let me relate what we saw in the high security unit of a modern prison, in one of the most advanced countries in Europe. This section had numerous cells for dangerous prisoners, sentenced for very serious crimes . . . We went to one with a multiple murderer. He was a dark-skinned giant with a bald head: a pigtail of hair descended from his nape to his waist. Perhaps it was this unusual appearance that had earned him the nickname 'Apache'. As soon as he saw us, he asked us to come into the cell and close the door . . . By gestures he indicated that we should keep quiet and listen. We could now hear a constant hiss, produced by the air-conditioner; after a while the noise became less intense . . . Apart from the hiss, there was absolutely no other noise. The cell was roomy, with a radio and a television and a small toilet annex. The window, a very large one, had no bars because it was made of shatter-proof glass and could not be opened. All one could see was a very tall wall opposite. The murderer was kept in total acoustic isolation. Apart from the low hiss, one might have been buried in a tomb . . . We asked him if he ever spoke to anyone. He saw the guard twice a day; the latter passed him his food through a slit in the wall . . . they sometimes exchanged a few words . . . He had not yet passed over from the animal to the vegetable kingdom but we got an idea of his future condition on entering another cell, where the prisoner, who had horribly murdered several people, had been kept for seven years. He lay on his bed, as pale as a ghost, moaning incomprehensible words.

Antonio Cassese, first chairman of the European Committee for the Prevention of Torture[1]

In the prison in Siberia where Dostoevsky's hero in *The House of the Dead*, Aleksandr Petrovich Goryanchikov, spent ten years, there was for a time a particularly brutal camp commander, a major. The prisoners could do nothing but endure his cruel rigidity and his vicious punishments. Then one day the news spread around the camp, an inspector was coming, a general from St Petersburg. If the prisoners complained to him, surely the vile major would be removed and conditions would improve. There was great excitement amongst the prisoners and the officers. For some days before the inspector arrived, feverish preparations were made.

> ... everything in the prison had been scrubbed, polished, cleaned. The prisoners were freshly shaven. Their clothes were white and clean ... A whole hour was spent in drilling the convicts to answer properly if the great man should greet them. There were rehearsals. The major bustled about like one possessed.[2]

Then the general and his entourage arrived. Aleksandr Petrovich continues with his description of the visit.

> The general walked through the prison-ward in silence, he glanced into the kitchen; I believe he tried the soup. I was pointed out to him, they told my story, and that I was of the educated class.
> 'Ah!' answered the general. 'And how is he behaving himself now?'
> 'So far, satisfactorily, your excellency,' they answered him. The general nodded and two minutes later he went out of the prison. The convicts were, of course, dazzled and bewildered, but yet they remained in some perplexity. Complaints against the major were, of course, out of the question. And the major was perfectly certain of that beforehand.[3]

Breyten Breytenbach tells how the South African prisons inspectorate visited once a year. All the prisoners agreed that this time they were really going to tell the inspectors what terrible treatment they were getting in the prison. The moment came when the chief inspector asked the prisoners, all gathered together in the dining hall, if there were any complaints.

> A dull and sullen silence would go humming through the hall. The few misguided sods who did stand out would be marked people forever afterwards ... and long after the visit they would find themselves punished without understanding what caused the sudden harsh treatment.[4]

The suffragette Lady Constance Lytton was imprisoned in Walton Gaol in Liverpool in 1910 for inciting a crowd to march to the house of the governor of Liverpool Prison and demand the release of the suffragettes imprisoned there. Along with the other imprisoned suffragettes she went on hunger strike as a protest and was appalled by the callous behaviour of the doctor who, after he had force fed her, slapped her on the face.[5] One day soon afterwards the door of her cell was suddenly thrown open and the government inspector appeared.

> I asked, had he come from London? 'Yes.' He inquired in a hurried way, as if he had a train to catch, had I any complaint? 'Yes,' I replied. 'First of all about being fed by force.' He said, in a hurried and insolent manner, all in one breath, so that it was scarcely intelligible, 'Are you refusing to take your food – If so the remedy is in your hands, you have no reason to complain – Any further complaints?' . . . I answered, 'No, I suppose not,' upon which he abruptly left me.[6]

The South African A N C member and writer Albie Sachs, who became a member of the South African Constitutional Court in the new democratic South Africa, spent 168 days in solitary confinement in Cape Town in 1963. He had a complaint about blankets to put to the magistrate who visited to hear complaints.

> 'I'm being bitten to pieces by fleas. I can't sleep at night and my clothes are all bloody. I'd like some clean blankets from outside . . .'
>
> 'Blankets are not my department. My responsibility is merely to see that you are not being assaulted, that there are no Gestapo methods.'
>
> 'This is worse than the Gestapo . . .'
>
> 'There's nothing I can do,' he says brusquely, obviously impatient to get away. 'Ask the Security Branch men . . .'
>
> 'But they told me to ask you.'
>
> 'If you have any complaints which I consider to be reasonable I will make a note of them and see that they are properly investigated. It is not my function to deal with requests. Asking for blankets is not a complaint. If that's all, then I'll go.'[7]

Complaints mechanisms for prisoners and inspection mechanisms for prisons go back a long way. Are they all as ineffective as those in Siberia in the last century, England in 1910 or South Africa in the 60s and 70s? Is it actually possible to protect prisoners from abuse and allow them real opportunities to make complaints, or will the inspectors or supervisors always be on the side of the authorities? Will the prison staff make it clear that those who complain will pay dearly for it when the inspectors have gone? Who ensures that all the rules described in the last chapter are followed and that behind the high and secret walls unimaginable torments are not inflicted on those incarcerated? Who checks the more mundane matters: the food, the size of the cells, the cleanliness of the bedding? Who makes sure that prisoners get their rights, letters to lawyers are not read or stopped, freedom to practise religion is really available? How can one decide whether prisoners are to be believed when they complain? They could be making it all up to get their own back on the prison officers.

It is, in fact, universally accepted that this ultimate exercise of power by the state on its citizens has to be supervised and kept in check by external structures. So there are many complaint and inspection mechanisms, elaborate and complex, stretching from small local groups of lay citizens who have the task of ensuring propriety in their local prison, to committees of the United Nations that consider complaints of ill-treatment that are brought to them for judgement. Also there are prison inspectors, both national and international. In some countries, such as the United States, prisoners can go to court if they feel aggrieved by what has happened to them. Nearly every country in the world has some system or other, at least in principle. The effectiveness of the systems varies but they are an indispensable part of the prison world. Outside the official mechanisms are the unofficial organizations, the groups of ex-prisoners and human rights supporters who fight to protect those whom society often prefers to forget.

There are two key series of questions to be considered in assessing the role and relevance of all these agencies that should be controlling the arbitrary exercise of power so that prisons do not become concentration camps and ensuring that prisoners are free to make complaints without victimization. The first is, for whom are they working? To whom are they accountable? Who sees their reports? The second is, does anything happen as a result of their upholding a prisoner's complaint or issuing a critical report? Does anyone listen? Have they the power to bring about change?

The first level of oversight is of the individual prison. Do people from outside, who are not part of the administration, go into each prison on a regular basis to hear prisoners' complaints and satisfy themselves that nothing corrupt or inhumane is going on? In many countries there are such systems of outside oversight of individual prisons. However, the reputation of those given this function is frequently not high. Certainly prisoners rarely have confidence in them and too often they become part of the legitimizing machinery of imprisonment, making it seem acceptable and respectable when in fact it is not.

There are three main approaches to this function. In the UK and countries following the British tradition, Visiting Committees are the main mechanism overseeing individual prisons. In countries that follow the continental Roman system of law, some supervisory functions are performed by judges. In Eastern countries the prosecutor or procurator has the prison-oversight role.

The Visiting Committees system is highly developed in England and Wales.[8] Each prison has a Board, made up of people of standing in the local community, appointed by the Home Secretary, to carry out various statutory functions. Boards of Visitors are lay people, who were originally called visiting magistrates. The system has its origins way back in history. Until 1877 the majority of prisons in England and Wales were managed by local magistrates. When central government took over the control of prisons in 1877, local magistrates lost the control but retained the power to visit the prisons. A Visiting Magistrates Committee was appointed to each prison. Eventually the Visiting Committees became the Boards of Visitors. The Home Secretary appoints them to the individual prison and each Board has between ten and twenty members. Ideally they should represent a cross-section of society but, predictably enough, they are mostly drawn from groups of people who can afford to take on a substantial commitment to do unpaid work during the day.

Prison Rule 94 sets out their primary duty: 'The board of visitors for a prison shall satisfy themselves as to the state of the prison premises, the administration of the prison and the treatment of the prisoners.'

Members have the right to visit any part of the prison without exception and to interview members of staff and prisoners in confidence. For many years Boards of Visitors were required to carry out two very different functions. First they were required to conduct disciplinary hearings against prisoners for the more serious offences and order prisoners to be punished. Second they had the function of hearing and responding to prisoners' complaints. This combination of functions was widely criticized by many commentators.[9] It was felt that people could not be deciding prisoners were guilty of an offence and punishing them by, say, taking away so many days of their remission on one occasion and listening sympathetically to their complaints about allegedly brutal prison officers the next. Many years after penal reformers began to campaign against this combination of tasks, the disciplinary functions were removed.

Boards of Visitors have been widely condemned as rubber stamps for the actions of the prison authorities and unthinking adjuncts of the power of the governor and staff. Their independence was doubted as they are appointed by the Home Office minister with responsibility for prisons. The Boards could have been packed with political supporters and cronies of the government of the day. However, this was not the way the Boards developed. In 1984 a very damning report on the way they carried out their role, commissioned by the Home Office, was published.[10] In all their functions they were found wanting and confidence in them by prisoners and prison staff was low. This report seemed to energize them and in the mid 1980s they gradually became prison oversight bodies that often acted independently. They frequently opposed the government. At their Annual Meeting in 1987, the Association of the more militant board members, called AMBOV, passed a resolution calling on the government to set a target date for ending the practice of placing prisoners in police cells because of prison overcrowding.[11]

To ensure they are accountable to the public they publish annual reports. These reports are often very critical of the prison authorities and reveal the reality of life in prison and the problems the prison staff and the prisoners are facing. For example, in their report for 1995 the Board of Visitors of Chelmsford Prison noted that attempts to increase education provision for prisoners were 'thwarted' and teachers' morale suffered. There were fears for the effect on the prison of the £800,000 cut projected for 1996.[12] In the same year the Board of Dartmoor complained that the government's budget cuts had brought the refurbishment to a complete stop and left two wings without integral sanitation. They warned that 'draconian cuts' scheduled for the following three years would seriously undermine security and could hasten 'a return to the 1990 riots'. The Board at Pentonville also criticized the budget cuts which were undermining the quality of life for prisoners and would do nothing to enhance their chances of a crime-free life on release.[13] The Board at Swaleside on the Isle of Sheppey criticized the government policy of putting the provision of prison education out to tender. It has been, they said in their 1995 report, 'a failure'. Far too many prisoners, they said, are in solitary confinement 'for far too long'.[14] The Board at Wandsworth has a long tradition of criticizing government prison policy. In their 1987 report, they described how prisoners had to 'paddle through other men's urine towards the end of the slopping-out' sessions.[15] In 1995 they were strong in their attack on the government's budget cuts. At a time when the prison population is rising, imposing cuts in the prison budget 'is to court the sort of disaster that the Prison Service suffered at Strangeways'.[16]

In many countries the function of coming from outside and providing a point of independent judgement on what happens in prison is carried out by a judge. In France the *juges de l'application des peines* hear prisoners' requests for parole or conditional release and are expected to report on the situation in the prison, although this function is regarded as rather toothless.[17] In France each prison also has a control committee on which the local mayor has a place, but these are regarded as even more toothless.[18] In Spain the supervisory judge is expected to ensure that prisoners' fundamental rights are respected and has the power to authorize use of force against prisoners and transfers to other institutions such as hospitals. However, there is evidence that the exercise of this function in Spain is not always done very conscientiously.[19]

Antonio Cassese met many such judges during his inspection visits to European countries. He describes his experience of them:

> they have a great deal of power and should keep an eye on how prisoners are treated and how the penitentiary is administered. To judge from interviews I had with many of them, those magistrates tend to maintain a very bureaucratic approach to inmates and jails: they check the files and, at most, they may pay scrupulous attention

to a single case, talking to individual prisoners in the room set aside for such parleys: they may even work hard to obtain a reduction of specific prisoners' sentences, or get permission for them to see relatives, or merely give advice. However, they never, or hardly ever, set foot in the prisoners' cells.

He concluded that they were 'rather grey characters' who regarded 'their job as a sort of covert punishment'.[20]

In the Netherlands every prison has a supervisory committee, appointed by the Minister of Justice but independent of the prison management. This supervisory committee selects from its members a complaints committee which is normally presided over by a judge. The complaints committee hears the prisoners' grievances and has the power to take action to right the wrong. Prisoners whose complaints are upheld may be given compensation, either a small amount of money or some other benefit. Free legal aid is available to the prisoners if they need it to present their case. If they are not happy with the decision of the complaints committee they can appeal to a higher committee. In 1993, 5 per cent of prisoners in Dutch prisons made a complaint about something.[21]

In East and Central Europe the function is carried out by the public prosecutors, although in many countries not conspicuously successfully. In China the hearing of prisoners' complaints is a function of the procuracy, that is the public prosecution. During a discussion in 1994 with the two members of the procuracy in the juvenile reformatory in Guangzhou, they indicated that they were in the institution every day. One of the complaints made to them recently had been that a recently graduated officer had slapped a prisoner's face. The procuracy made a thorough investigation, they said, and found the case against the officer proved. The young guard was then severely criticized by the prison director. Complaints reach the procurators orally – they go round the prison listening to prisoners – and in writing – there is a locked box where complaints can be posted to which only the procuracy has the key.[22]

TAKING COMPLAINTS TO COURT

In many countries it is the courts that fulfil the watchdog function. The United States is the most prominent amongst these. The main mechanism for regulating the vast machine of US incarceration is resource to the courts. Prisoners or their representatives go to court about a range of problems – overcrowding, bad conditions and ill-treatment – and the courts respond, if they find the case proven, by issuing a court order requiring certain conditions to be met.

Court actions apply to every level of the system. For example, in January 1996, thirty-six states and the District of Columbia, Puerto Rico and the Virgin Islands were under a court order, or what is called 'a consent decree', to limit the population and/or to improve conditions. Thirty-one of these states and other jurisdictions have some of their prisons in this process and in eight the whole system is under court order or consent decree. Only three of all the states in the US – Minnesota, New Jersey and North Dakota – have never been in court about the situation in their prisons. Court intervention affects the jail system too. Of the local jails about 320 are operating under a court order or a consent decree and this includes more than a quarter of the largest jails, for example those in New York City, Los Angeles and New Orleans.[23]

Taking cases to court has been the main weapon for prisoners in the US wanting some redress for the way they have been treated in prison. We have seen that in Folsom Prison in California in May 1993 there were about 1300 cases being brought to court by prisoners there. The leading body working in this way is the National Prison Project of the American Civil Liberties Union (ACLU). In 1991, according to the ACLU, nearly 40,000 law suits affecting the treatment of individual prisoners and 456 'class actions' – cases affecting a group of prisoners – were outstanding.[24]

An example of work done by the National Prison Project is the transformation through court orders of the prison system of Tennessee. In the early 70s the prison system in Tennessee was riddled with brutality. According to one of the leading attorneys in the case,

In the west Tennessee bottomlands along the Mississippi, black prisoners chopped cotton under the shotguns of mounted guards and were crowded together in stifling, violence-ridden dormitories by night.

The strap was an everyday facet of prison life. The records of African-American prisoners were still marked with a large capital 'B' and work assignments were made by race. Medical treatment was provided by unlicensed, untrained prisoner 'medics'. Each prison was a little fiefdom where convict kingpins and 'good old boy' wardens collaborated to maintain order through what the courts would come to describe as a 'reign of terror' based on violence and intimidation.[25]

Early in 1976 the National Prison Project and several local lawyers took up the cases of prisoners who had complained to the court about the conditions in the Tennessee prisons. After six years of unsuccessful litigation a district judge ruled that the Tennessee system was unconstitutional. As is the practice, a 'Special Master' was then appointed to implement the court decision to improve the system. No progress was made for the next three years, during which the system got worse. In 1985 there were prisoner riots across Tennessee. Following the riots, a judge ruled that no more prisoners were to be admitted to the prisons until minimum standards of safety could be guaranteed. Finally the politicians realized that change had to come and 'after a century of brutality and a decade of stonewalling, reform proceeded at a breathtaking pace'.[26]

The Special Master moved between the judges and the state officials, mediating, explaining, educating and organizing technical assistance. Violence was reduced. Prisoners stopped making complaints about the threat to their lives and physical safety. Instead they began to make complaints about family visits and their eligibility for parole.

Another jurisdiction where the National Prison Project of the ACLU became involved is the state of Indiana. The Project's lawyers alleged that the Indiana Department of Corrections had reneged on a settlement originally agreed in court about conditions in the state's largest prison, the Westville Correctional Center. The settlement reached in 1989 required the Department of Corrections in Indiana to hire four full-time doctors and an adequate number of nurses for the 2800 prisoners and two psychologists for a unit that served the whole state prison system with 13,000 prisoners.

The lawyers of the National Prison Project argued that prisoners were being denied proper medical treatment. They claimed that the prison had only two doctors and a third who worked only twelve hours a week. The court required a licensed health care provider to be available to prisoners at least four days a week but the lawyers claimed that this standard was not being met. Also there was only one psychiatrist at the psychiatric unit. Prisoners were required to pay for over-the-counter medications or do without them. Most seriously mentally ill prisoners were not getting supervision and treatment. Instead they were being restrained and secluded. The lawyers said that 'acts of self-mutilation and violent assaults continue almost unabated as patients remain dangerous and unpredictable'.

The lawyers therefore asked a federal court judge to hold the department in contempt of court. The sting in the tail of the litigation activity in the US is the level of fines that the courts can impose. In 1982 Texas was threatened by a federal judge with a fine of $800,000 per day if it did not reduce overcrowding in Texas prisons.[27]

The involvement of the courts in reforming US prisons has been remarkable. How did it happen that court action to improve prisoner treatment became so widespread, affecting almost every state and influencing the thinking and work of every prison administrator? This development is indissolubly linked with the name of Al Bronstein. In 1982 Al Bronstein and other lawyers launched the National Prison Project. For nearly twenty-five years he travelled tirelessly around the United States trying to bring his country's penal institutions into a civilized framework. He filed lawsuits in nearly fifty states and monitored the implementation until real change had been achieved. His style of operation was so successful because of his skill in carrying with him and earning the respect of those officials whose daily work he was characterizing as beyond the pale of decent human behaviour. In the Tennessee case, in court in Nashville in 1978, he said, 'This is not about state officials who are bad, but about a cruelly unconstitutional prison system which mocks their efforts.'

One of the first cases was against the state prison system in Alabama. There, according to Al Bronstein,

> The prisons were so crowded, prisoners were sleeping on top of urinal troughs. Some were dying from inadequate medical care. There was the infamous 'dog-house', a windowless building where seven men shared a tiny cell where no more than three could lie down at a time.

The Alabama case was highly significant. The court laid down 'minimum constitutional standards' for prisons.[28]

Al Bronstein has appeared in the list of the hundred most influential lawyers in the US every year since the list started in 1985.

OMBUDSMEN FOR PRISONERS

The battle in England to establish the post of prisons ombudsman was even longer than the one to remove the function of hearing disciplinary cases against prisoners from Boards of Visitors. The final decision to appoint an ombudsman emerged, as did many other reforms, from the destruction and violence of the Strangeways riot. Lord Woolf, in his report, was unequivocal in his support for an ombudsman.

> The case for some form of independent person or body to consider grievances is incontrovertible . . . A system without an independent element is not a system which accords with proper standards of justice.[29]

Finally, in 1994, a prisons ombudsman was appointed. He was Sir Peter Woodhead, a retired admiral. He started off very energetically but after a short burst of independent and outspoken operations he was reined in. He was told he could not review ministerial decisions about individual prisoners and he agreed to send the results of his investigations to the prison service for comment before passing them on to the prisoner who complained.[30]

INTERNATIONAL COMPLAINTS MECHANISMS

At the pinnacle of prisoners' complaints machinery in Europe are the European Commission for Human Rights and the European Court of Human Rights in Strasbourg. Prisoners have been 'taking cases to Strasbourg' since the seventies and decisions made there have been very influential in changing the way prisoners are treated in the UK. For example, in 1975 a prisoner called Golder was prevented from writing to his solicitor about the way he had been treated in prison. The court ruled that this was a violation of his right to a fair hearing and also a violation of his right to correspond with a solicitor.[31] In 1983 another prisoner, Silver, also succeeded in winning his case after he had been prevented from writing to a solicitor.[32] In 1975 Hamer complained to Strasbourg that because he was in prison he was not allowed to get married. The European Commission for Human Rights, the body that deals with the first stage of the Strasbourg process, found that his case had merit and the British government changed the rules before the case went to the European Court for judgement.[33] Prisoners Campbell and Fell were charged with offences arising out of a prison riot and lost 570 days remission. The European Court ruled in 1984 that it was not right to keep prisoners in prison for 570 days longer than they reasonably expected without allowing them to be legally represented at the disciplinary hearing.[34]

Prisoners do not always win. Members of the Baader-Meinhof group imprisoned in Germany complained in 1973 about being kept in solitary confinement but the Commission decided their conditions of detention were justified.[35] A Swiss prisoner complained in 1975 that he was not allowed to carry on his conjugal relations with his wife whilst in prison and this was a breach of his right to family life. The Commission did not agree and the application was rejected.[36]

Prisoners can also take their complaints to the United Nations. There are two United Nations organs that people can complain to, the Human Rights Committee and the Commission on Human Rights.

The Committee can receive and consider what are called in UN jargon 'communications' from people who claim that their human rights have been violated by a country that has agreed to the Coven-ant.[37] Since the Committee was set up in 1976 it has had more than 500 communications, and many of them have been about the mistreatment of prisoners and inadequate conditions of detention. Although the Committee's decisions are not legally binding, coun-tries have normally accepted its decisions and taken action to change laws when they have been found to be incompatible with provisions of the Covenant. They have also released people from detention when asked to do so and have paid compensation to victims.

The Commission on Human Rights is a separate body. It has established a number of expert working groups to investigate alleged human rights abuses in certain parts of the world. In 1991, it established a Working Group on Arbitrary Detention, with the task of investigating cases where people have been sent to prison without going through the proper processes. This Working Group also receives communications about arbitrary detention, and these can be submitted by the individuals concerned, by members of their families, by governments or by other organizations. The Working Group has also established an 'urgent action' procedure. This comes into play when it seems that someone has been locked up in contra-vention of all the rules and seems to be seriously ill or in other physical danger. In such cases, the Working Group can authorize its chairman to complain by cable immediately to the minister for foreign affairs of the country concerned.[38]

INSPECTION

There are also inspectors. Their function is different from those of the Boards of Visitors and the supervisory judges. It is also very different from taking cases of prisoners' treatment to court. Nor-mally inspectors are interested in the state of prisons, how they are run, how prisoners in general are being treated and how well the prison laws are being followed. Their role is often to judge how far the rules of the prisons are being met rather than to subject the rules to any critical scrutiny. The Prisons Inspectorate of England and Wales is a highly developed model. It was established in 1980. When prisons were run by local magistrates, the way central government kept a grip on the prison system was through its inspectors, who reported on how the prisons were managed. Under an Act of 1835 the inspectors were required to visit every place of detention in Great Britain every year and make a report on it to parliament. When the prisons were centralized by an Act of 1877 the inspectors lost their teeth. They worked within the prison service and their function was basically to check that the staff were doing what they were supposed to do and money was being spent properly. They had no accountability to the public and their activities and conclusions were not in the public domain.[39] In 1979 a report on prisons, the May Report, argued that there should be an independent prisons inspectorate.[40] This idea had provoked an outcry from the Home Office, who strongly resisted it.[41] However, the Home Office mandarins were out-argued and an independent inspectorate was set up. Since then reports have been published containing details of actual day-to-day life in prisons in England and Wales that give an unparalleled insight into the physical and managerial state of the prisons and the way prisoners are treated within them.

The Chief Inspector of Prisons from 1987 to 1995 was Judge, now Sir, Stephen Tumim. An ebullient art-lover with great media skills and an unfailing bow-tie, he put the cause of prison reform into the public consciousness by continually hammering home three basic messages. Prisons should be decent, humane places. Prisoners should be doing something useful whilst they are inside. Treating prisoners properly as fellow citizens is the right thing to do. On average, forty reports were published about particular prisons each year and an annual report was presented to parliament. These reports contained unrestrained criticism of what was bad about prisons in England and Wales in the late 1980s and 1990s. At Risley prison in 1988, conditions were 'totally unacceptable'.[42] Liverpool in 1988 was 'a seedy Victorian prison'[43] with 'mice and cockroaches'.[44] The regime at Preston Prison in 1991 was 'deplorable'.[45] Wormwood Scrubs in 1991 'presented a depressing picture'.[46]

In 1992 Judge Tumim's contract was extended for another three years and in 1995 when his time was up he thought it might be extended again as he had done so well. But the then Home Secretary,

Michael Howard, who tried to court political popularity by taking an anti-penal-reform position, refused to extend his term of office. Instead he looked for someone from a different background and eventually appointed a retired general, Sir David Ramsbotham. With his background as Adjutant General of the British Army, Aide-de-Camp General to the Queen and Inspector General of the Territorial Army, Sir David might have seemed a more reactionary choice. But after his appointment in 1995 he continued and developed the Tumim tradition. One of his first inspections was of the women's prison in North London, Holloway Prison. A few days after the inspection had begun Sir David withdrew his inspection team. The conditions were so bad, he said, that they were not prepared to continue with the inspection until some improvements were made. In 1996 he was taken to task by the Home Secretary for holding a press conference to announce the findings of an inspection before the report had been submitted to the Home Secretary. The Home Office also complained bitterly about the way he made statements suggesting better ways in which they could organize themselves.[47]

Also in 1996 he published a discussion paper supporting a move long advocated by penal reformers. The separate and Home Office controlled prison medical service should be brought to an end. Instead the National Health Service should take responsibility for ensuring the provision of health care in prisons.[48]

The inspectorate is publicly accountable, has shown that it can be independent and, in England and Wales at least, has cast a spotlight into the darkest corners of the most closed institutions. But the inspectorate has no executive power. It only recommends, publicizes, argues and persuades.

Another form of inspectorate, which affects England and Wales and also most countries in Europe, is the Committee for the Prevention of Torture and Inhuman or Degrading Treatment or Punishment, or CPT for short. This committee with its cumbersome name is a remarkable development. It is the outcome of many years of lobbying by a Swiss banker, Jean-Jacques Gautier.[49] After his death the lobbying was continued by an organization he founded, now called the Association for the Prevention of Torture.

The existence of the CPT comes from a European Convention, the Convention for the Prevention of Torture and Inhuman or Degrading Treatment or Punishment, which was signed in 1987 and came into force in January 1989. It is the first body in the world to have been given the power to enter the territory of sovereign states, when it decides to do so, and inspect places of detention, police stations, prisons, secure mental hospitals and immigration detention centres without let or hindrance. The countries that have signed the Convention accept the right of the Committee to come and inspect, ask for access to any place 'where persons are deprived of their liberty by a public authority'[50] at any time of the day or night and require to see relevant documents.

The members of the Committee are nominated by the countries who are parties to the Convention – each country may nominate one[51] – and they range from psychiatrists to government officials and lawyers.[52] Once nominated they are supposed to act in a completely independent way.[53] Members of the Committee and the experts that help the Committee never take part in visits to their own country.[54] The country to be visited is notified in the preceding year that a visit is to take place. Two weeks before the visit, the country is told the dates, length of the visit and other details. A few days before, the details of the places to be visited are given, although this plan may be changed midstream.[55] A typical visit to a country begins with meetings with the national authorities and with the non-governmental organizations and pressure groups that work for prisoners' rights. Then the Committee sets off on its visits to places of detention, sometimes going to places where it has pre-announced its visit and at other times just turning up. At the end of the visit the Committee members meet the national authorities again to sum up impressions and give an idea what the report might say.[56] Sometimes the Committee makes *ad hoc* visits in response to information it has received about flagrant human rights abuses.[57]

First reactions to the existence of this Committee with its remit on torture are often sceptical. Is it really necessary to inspect the places of detention of countries like Holland and Denmark in case the prisoners there are being tortured? Surely everyone knows that prisoners there are treated very well. Prison governors have joked about the visit of the 'torture committee' and how the CPT visited and failed to find the torture chamber in the basement.

Indeed, the Committee has not found examples of torture in Holland or Denmark, but its remit is prevention. It aims to find out whether in places of detention 'there are general or specific conditions or circumstances that are likely to degenerate into torture or inhuman or degrading treatment or punishment, or are at any rate conducive to some inadmissible acts or practices'.[58] In both Holland and Denmark, as in others with a good image as regards their prison conditions, the Committee has found matters that gave it cause for concern and could have become ill-treatment if they had been allowed to continue.[59]

Although the reports written by the Committee are confidential, a decision taken at the beginning of its work by the first countries to be inspected to publish the reports and their replies set a precedent. Reports have generally been published except for the ones on Turkey. Here the Committee has overcome the wish of the Turkish government to hide from the world the tortures carried out by its police by using a procedure which allows the Committee to issue a public statement when it seems that no notice is being taken of its recommendations by a member state.[60]

The published reports give an unparalleled picture of what is going on in Europe's places of detention. The Committee visited the UK in August 1990 and found such overcrowding and bad physical conditions and lack of activities for prisoners in Brixton, Wandsworth and Leeds prisons that they held the UK to be guilty of submitting prisoners to inhuman or degrading treatment and punishment.[61] This was the first such finding by the Committee in any published report. In 1993 the Committee found another case of inhuman and degrading treatment in Luxembourg, where a prisoner had given birth to a baby in hospital and a few minutes after the birth the baby had been taken from the mother by prison staff and given to foster parents.[62] In France, visited in 1991, the Committee described as 'a flagrant example of inhuman and degrading treatment' the practice of chaining women prisoners in civilian hospitals to their beds during labour and after giving birth.[63] In Curaçao in the Netherlands Antilles, part of the kingdom of the Netherlands, the Committee found inhuman and degrading treatment in the prison because of the overcrowding, lack of activities and lack of cleanliness.[64]

Sweden was told in 1992 that the conditions for many of the prisoners in Stockholm Remand Prison were 'wholly unacceptable'.[65] The outdoor exercise area consisted of small cages on the prison roof.[66] Many prisoners were in solitary confinement for long periods.[67] Switzerland was rebuked because on its visit to the regional prison in Berne the Committee found two naked prisoners in dark and squalid cells in a severely disturbed mental state.[68] Prisoners were in their cells with nothing to do all day[69] and the conditions for prison visits were quite unsatisfactory.[70] The Netherlands was severely criticized by the Committee for the conditions it found during its visit in 1992 to the special detention units. In the unit 4A in Demersluis prison in particular the attitude of staff towards the prisoners was antagonistic, uncooperative and sometimes openly contemptuous. They ignored the prisoners' requests for access to doctors, lawyers or social workers.[71] During a visit to Germany in 1991 the Committee heard allegations that prisoners in a special unit for drug traffickers were only allowed three books a month and were not allowed to take part in religious activities,[72] that prisoners had been placed in a specially designed cell in a basement and sprayed with cold water,[73] and that in August 1990 in Straubing prison, 400 police officers had been brought in when 117 prisoners refused to return to their cells after exercise and that the prisoners were subsequently beaten by the police and prison staff.[74] They asked for further information on these allegations. In Greece the Committee noted that HIV-positive prisoners were held in isolation.[75] In Iceland prisoners were required to pay for some forms of medical treatment.[76] Overcrowding was so bad in Italy in 1992 that the Committee described it as inhuman and degrading treatment,[77] with San Vittore prison in Milan, built for 1295, holding 2000.[78] In Liechtenstein in 1993 prisoners spent most of the day locked in a communal room with nothing to do.[79] In Mountjoy and Limerick prisons in Ireland in 1993 the Committee heard allegations of ill-treatment of prisoners by prison staff.[80] In Hungary the Committee found that disturbed prisoners were being locked in padded cells measuring less than two square metres. They recommended that these cells be taken out of service.[81]

The Committee also visited Peterhead Prison in Scotland. There they found four prisoners living in G Hall, a small area which had previously been the punishment block.[82] Each cell in G Hall contained a metal bed bolted to the floor, a cardboard table and chair and a slopping-out bucket. Natural light was limited and one of the cells was smeared with excrement. When dealing with one of the prisoners in G Hall, staff wore full riot gear.[83] The delegation saw the prisoner being served his lunch by three prison staff in full riot gear including protective helmets with face visors.[84]

The Committee concluded that

> prisoners in G Hall were held in what amounted to solitary confine-
> ment for very long periods of time, under miserable material con-
> ditions of detention and with no purposeful activities. Such a situation
> could in itself be described as inhuman. Moreover their relations
> with staff could hardly have been worse . . . it is quite unacceptable
> for riot gear to be worn by prison staff in their day-to-day contacts
> with prisoners.[85]

Much travelling is done and many reports are written. Does anything change? Is the process effective? The Dutch academic lawyer Gerard de Jonge said of the work of the CPT that 'even for a state like Holland . . . an external check on its good intentions is vital'.[86]

When the French prison administration discovered that women prisoners in hospital were chained to the beds, the practice was stopped.[87] Antonio Cassese assessed its effectiveness during the time he was chairman and noted some successes. When the Swiss authorities heard about the two naked prisoners they transferred them to other institutions and improved the cells in which they had been held.[88] Also, the three prisons in the UK described as inhuman and degrading have been improved considerably since 1991. In Northern Ireland the Committee were critical of the segregation of a prisoner who was HIV-positive. After the visit the prisoner was taken out of segregation.[89]

On the other hand some countries resist the Committee's

recommendations. Many criticisms of Sweden's treatment of its remand prisoners made in 1992 were repeated on the follow-up visit in 1994. The changes that the Committee had advocated had not been wholly accepted.[90]

No other region has a mechanism quite like the European Committee but in Africa the equivalent body to the Council of Europe, that is the African Commission on Human and People's Rights, appointed in 1996 a Special Rapporteur on prisons in Africa to study prison conditions there and press for improvements.[91]

The European Committee for the Prevention of Torture owes its existence to the determined work of Jean-Jacques Gautier and the organization he set up to take further the idea of international inspection of places of detention, the Association for the Prevention of Torture (APT). The APT now has a wider vision. For some years they have been lobbying the United Nations to set up such a system across the whole world. They have aided the drafting of an Optional Protocol to the UN Convention Against Torture which, if accepted, would establish a committee similar to the European Committee with a worldwide remit.[92]

Another body with certain prison-visiting rights is the International Committee of the Red Cross, the ICRC. Known mainly for its visits to political prisoners and prisoners of war, the ICRC is based in Geneva, Switzerland, and should not be confused with the Red Cross. It has a quasi-official function in monitoring the Geneva Conventions and is staffed by people called 'delegates' who are normally required to be Swiss. Its work is confidential.[93] When Nelson Mandela was in prison the only outside organization to visit was the ICRC. He describes a visit from the man from the ICRC, Mr Senn, a former Swedish director of prisons who had emigrated to Rhodesia. The meeting was held in private and Mr Senn went away with a list of the prisoners' complaints. Shortly afterwards the prisoners' clothing improved and they were given long trousers to wear instead of the demeaning shorts that were routinely given to African prisoners. The ICRC also provided money so that wives and families would be able to make the trip to visit their menfolk on Robben Island.[94]

For Breyten Breytenbach, also imprisoned in South Africa in the apartheid era, the visits of the ICRC were a highlight of the year.

> ... what a joy it was once a year to meet a group of people who did not attempt to manipulate you, who took and treated you as a normal human being . . . They would measure your exercise yard, test your light bulbs, listen to your heartbeat, taste your food, talk to your medic and go with you down their check-list of questions and observations – and the year after there would be the follow-up, when they'd inform you about their requests and the results achieved . . . They were thorough; they knew what they were doing . . . they never wavered in their commitment to justice.[95]

Finally, prisons are watched over by non-governmental organizations (NGOs), which are voluntary or private organizations. NGOs are an indispensable part of the prison-watching business. When Albie Sachs was in prison he heard that some prominent British parliamentarians and lawyers had sent him birthday greetings by cable. He wondered whether they got tired of protesting against injustices and appealing for redress for a wronged person.

> If only I could tell them how important their petitions are . . . they do give us courage. Our captors wish to obliterate us, if not physically, then spiritually, as personalities. When we hear our names being called out by people in far-off lands we are revived. A prisoner is so helpless in so many ways that he needs people outside to speak and act for him.[96]

NGOs play a large part in the process of implementation of human rights instruments. The United Nations Human Rights Centre states that 'NGOs have often been the first to bring human rights problems to the attention of the United Nations and the international community at large.' NGOs have supported UN efforts by contributing 'information and experience . . . based on their own activities in defence of human rights'. Their unique contribution is that they are 'close to the groups in society which most stand in need of information and education on human rights and are well-placed to reach large numbers of people of diverse backgrounds and interests'. More than one hundred NGOs contribute to the work of the United Nations Commission on Human Rights every year.[97]

There are local NGOs, working in a small area and going into perhaps one or two prisons to help prisoners with their drug or alcohol problems. They are not officially or obviously watchdogs. They have no official oversight functions. But by their role and status they perform an invaluable function. They are completely independent of any authority or agency and their reason for being in the prison is unambiguously to help the prisoners. Prisoners are more likely to trust them and tell them what is really going on. By their presence they are likely to act as a brake on ill-treatment or corrupt practices because if they know about it, it will be harder to conceal.

There are also global NGOs. The most famous is probably Amnesty International, which has more than one million members and supporters around the world. It works to free political prisoners who have not engaged in violence. Its main method of work is for its members to write letters to presidents and prime ministers, asking them to release a named person who is imprisoned for his or her beliefs and not for committing any crime. Amnesty International also campaigns against torture, the ill-treatment of prisoners and the death penalty worldwide.[98]

There is also an organization called 'International Prison Watch' which has its headquarters in Lyon, France. This organization aims to protect the rights of people in prison by investigating abuses and publicizing them widely.[99]

Penal Reform International (PRI) also operates globally.[100] The Special Rapporteur on Prisons in Africa, mentioned above, arose from lobbying by NGOs instigated by PRI and taken up by large numbers of the NGOs working on human rights and prison matters in Africa.

The Prison Project of the US-based Human Rights Watch investigates prisons in various countries and produces reports which are well-publicized and draw the attention of the world to abuses.

So, there are all these rules and all these inspections, local, national and international. NGOs monitor and publicize. Many bodies fight for penal reform. Is there somewhere the good prison – the ideal prison – the model for the rest of the world? In the next chapter we consider this question.

12. *Penal Reform*

> If you endeavour to take out of [a prisoner] that manly confidence which ought to be cherished in every civilised human being, you then begin the work of demoralisation; and it will end in the very Dreggs of debasement & an insensibility to every species of integrity and decency, and eradicate every right feeling in the human breast. You make him regardless of himself, and fearless as to the consequences of doing wrong to others . . . There is a certain pitch to which you can work upon man to bring him to fear . . . but exceed that and you make him reckless . . . Begin to treat him as beneath [your] care and notice, and they then think that you put God, his laws, his omniscience, his providence, as though they were mere nominal attributes and not virtual and real.
>
> Laurence Frayne, a prisoner, from his memoirs of Norfolk Island[1]

So is there such a thing as a 'good' prison? Is there a place where penal reformers can go and find their model prison, the utopia of prisons, the place where all those who had lost their freedom would go if they had the choice? Do some prisons preserve 'that manly confidence which ought to be cherished in every civilised human being'?

No, there is no such thing as a 'good' prison. Wherever and however, a prison is still a deformed society. But there are certainly vast differences between prisons and enormous amounts of effort go into making bad prisons better and reasonable prisons better still. Prison reform is a cause which has touched the imaginations of many through the centuries and continues to do so. The name of John Howard, the eighteenth-century reformer whom John Wesley described as 'I think one of the greatest men in Europe',[2] has been carried on by societies bearing his name in both the UK and Canada. The UK-based Howard League for Penal Reform was founded in 1866. Its recent activity in bringing to public attention the violence and cruelty of young people's prisons and the desperate misery of the inadequate young people sent to them is a worthy continuation of the spirit of John Howard.[3] Elizabeth Fry, who in 1816 began to visit the women imprisoned in Newgate Prison in London and set up an association to improve their circumstances and those of their imprisoned children,[4] has inspired many organizations, including the Elizabeth Fry Societies in Canada. If she had lived today, she would probably have been right behind the campaigning work of the societies bearing her name that exposed to public view the treatment of the women prisoners in Kingston Prison segregation block in 1994 who were stripped naked by a male emergency-response team (see Chapter 7). During the nineteenth century societies sprang up for the relief and succour of many different groups of the poor, and prisoners were not forgotten. The numerous societies for the aid of discharged prisoners came together in 1886 in the National Association of Discharged Prisoners Aid Societies, which in 1966 was transformed into NACRO (the National Association for the Care and Resettlement of Offenders).[5] The early work with discharged prisoners is perhaps crystallized in what happened to ex-prisoner Arthur Harding (see Chapter 8) when he left Wormwood Scrubs in 1903. He was given a gratuity of ten shillings and his clothes were returned to him.

> At the gate there was a lady who gave me a tract and a ticket for a free breakfast. 'God bless you,' she said (the text, in red letters, was 'I say unto Ye, that he that is without sin, let him cast the first stone'.)[6]

It is worth asking how it comes about that ideas of penal reform have proved so abiding and strongly motivating over so many centuries. What were the principles behind the work of these generations of reformers? What drove them in the past and still drives people to take on such an unglamorous, sometimes dangerous, always unpopular cause as prison reform, courting the comments of those around them like 'Can't you find someone to help who hasn't murdered, robbed and damaged other people? Aren't there any law-abiding people to help? What about the victims?'

Clearly Christian ethical principles are one strong motivator. The eighteenth-century reformer John Howard was an active and committed Christian. Through his prison work he hoped to save both the bodies and the souls of prisoners 'for he believed that only the grace of God had made him less depraved than they'.[7]

Elizabeth Fry was a Quaker and many penal reformers have been Quakers. Quaker money has been a strong support for many penal reform groups.

What motivates the modern penal reformer? Obviously, a variety of reasons drive people to work for the cause. For those motivated by religion, the arguments from Christian ethics for treating prisoners well and working to reclaim them are evident. In his gospel, Matthew tells that Jesus said, 'I was in prison and you visited me'.[8] At the last judgement, those who had visited prisons would be counted amongst the righteous.

Others are concerned with the justice of their society. For them the treatment of prisoners, the people at the bottom, the undeserving, the unattractive, the hated, is the supreme test of their society's commitment to justice and human rights. Ordinary citizens who get involved in prisons knowing nothing often become converts to the cause of penal reform, perhaps because they are struck by the waste of human beings, the undeveloped potential of many of those in prison, the enormous resources and the energy, all being expended negatively on making a situation worse, rather than on developing the good.

Christopher Morgan is an English farmer who decided to join a scheme run by the Prison Reform Trust to become a prisoner's penfriend. He ended up writing to Tom Shannon, a fifty-five-year-old life-sentence prisoner. Their exchange of letters was published as the *Invisible Crying Tree*. Christopher Morgan wrote about his children, his new false teeth, cattle prices, digging ponds, poetry. Tom Shannon wrote about the gangsters he lives amongst, the hunger strike he undertook because when he was moved to Blundeston Prison he was given a cell 'covered in excrement, toothpaste, goodness knows what else',[9] the drug addicts in prison stealing from other prisoners' cells. The proceeds of the book were used by Christopher Morgan and Tom Shannon to set up the Shannon Trust, a new body to help life-sentence prisoners on their release. Christopher Morgan perhaps exemplifies the process that many people coming into contact with prisons for the first time go through.

Having discovered for himself, through his correspondence with Tom Shannon, what goes on in prisons, institutions that are after all part of his society and his world, he felt the need to tell others how wrong their preconceptions are, and how much reform remains to be done.

LOOKING FOR THE 'GOOD PRISON'

One objective of penal reformers is reformed prisons. What do the 'reformed prisons' look like? How would lay people unschooled in the carceral world know? How does one tell whether the prison one is entering is really a decent humane place, or is one being presented with a cover-up of a hell-hole of brutality and misery? This is not an easy question to answer. Brutality is easy to hide. It will not necessarily be at all obvious to casual visitors what is really going on. They might not interpret the signs that an informal and violent prisoner power structure rules the roost, that staff brutality is routine or that corruption is endemic. We have heard (see Chapter 11) about the clean-ups and whitewashing that go on in many prisons when visitors are expected. Wonderful nutritious food suddenly appears. A television set is placed in the middle of the dormitory and it is asserted that the prisoners watch it all day. But the observant visitor will notice that there are no electric points in the dormitory to plug it in. When the visit is over it will doubtless be carted back to the director's office and locked away. Some of the windows are missing and it is very cold in the dormitory. 'We take the windows out in the day time to let the prisoners have some fresh air, but we put them back at night.' A pile of freshly baked white loaves stands untouched on a tray. 'They eat very well here.' 'The prisoners are very shy but we found one prepared to talk to you.' A cell full of underfed, pasty-faced teenagers is ruled by a prisoner in his thirties. His job is to keep order. 'He is like a father to them.'

Covering-up is easy but there are some pointers and indications that can give the visitor some clues in interpreting what is being shown. We should imagine a prison visit. It starts at the gate, the entrance, the place where the visitor first appears and asks for admittance. It is not a good sign if you are greeted by a member of staff who reels off, 'I am required to say that if you are taken hostage no negotiations will be entered into for your release.' Neither is a sullen doorkeeper, who ignores you for a long time as you stand there waiting to be noticed. Neither does it bode well when the prison director keeps you talking in his office for twenty minutes whilst five members of the National Guard are summoned as an escort for the visiting party.

Once into the prison it is important to listen. Noise is reassuring. Dead silence is not. Behind the cell doors are perhaps several hundred, perhaps over a thousand, living, breathing human beings. If there is not a sound coming from anywhere, no voices, no music from radios, no sound of activity, what are they doing? Why can they not be heard?

If the doors of occupied cells are thrown open and visitors are ushered in without pre-warning or asking the occupants, an idea is given of the view taken of the prisoners by the prison staff. There is perhaps no respect for their privacy or anonymity. If the visitors enter a dormitory full of prisoners and they all stand up when the visitors enter and look uneasily at one prisoner and wait for that prisoner to decide what is going to be said, it may be that this dormitory is under the control of a cell-boss with henchmen to enforce control. You might see an exercise yard with a hundred or so young prisoners playing football. Three large prisoners are standing on the sidelines, not participating, just watching. This might be an ominous sign.

You could be shown prisoners' living quarters in a poor country, an empty room with rows of bedding laid out on the floor. Most of the prisoners have one blanket and a tiny pile of belongings. On one or two of the places there are three or four blankets, pillows and a lot of possessions. Why are some of the prisoners doing so much better than the others?

You might be told, 'We won't bother to visit the punishment cells. There is no one in them today.' Maybe, maybe not. Staff who show you with pride their latest acquisition, a room equipped with listening devices so they can listen to all the conversations in the prisoners' visiting room without the prisoners' knowledge might have a different view of the rights of prisoners than that set out in the United Nations rules. Bleak visiting cubicles with glass between the visitor and the prisoner, five of them for a prison of 2000 and none in use at the time you are there, might lead you to the conclusion that family contact was not a priority in that prison. The well-equipped education block with no one in it mid morning on a weekday prompts some questions. A strip cell with padded walls, no natural light, no furniture but a concrete slab, and no record of how often it is used might do so too.

One touchstone of the system that casts some light on the underlying philosophy of those in charge is whether one of the punishments they can impose on prisoners is to restrict or take away their family visits. Another measure is do prison staff ever get charged and taken before a court for assaulting prisoners, that is, does the rule of law apply equally in prisons?

What are the good signs that give not a certainty but an indication that the prison might be a humane and decent place? It is probably encouraging to see when you arrive at the entrance that other people at the gate are waiting to get in: for example, outside visitors, groups, teachers, counsellors, volunteers. If you see prisoners and staff talking to each other with some mutual recognition that they are both human beings you could be somewhat reassured. If the punishment block is included in the visit plan without being asked for, this is a good sign. If the offer is made 'Please talk to the prisoners if you like' and the staff showing you round move away out of earshot, this may be an indication that there are no shameful secrets.

If there are some flowers and a few pictures in the visiting room, it suggests that a person in charge has given some thought to the feelings of the visitors, coming on a long journey to see a family member in a distressing environment. Prisoners' art on the walls, noticeboards with up-to-date information about what is going on in the prison and services of help to prisoners in prison and on release, noise, drama and music, a prisoners' newspaper or magazine are all signs of an environment trying to draw out potential and keep prisoners' talents alive.

PENAL REFORM REPORTS

Trying to reform prisons has been going on for a long time. The preliminary to prison reform is usually a report. The preliminary to a prison-reform report is usually a disturbance or serious incident of some sort. There are many prison reform reports on the bookshelves of the world's reformers. Many countries have had at least one report. Some countries have had several. Normally, these reports say more or less the same thing and normally they are not implemented. In Jamaica, for instance, there was published in 1989 *The Report of the Task Force on the Correctional Services*. The report began by looking at previous reports. It endorsed the statement made in the 1954 penal reform report about the fate of three earlier reports on prison reform, of 1926, 1937 and 1948, lamenting the fact that so few of the recommendations made had been implemented. If they had been, the Jamaican government would not still be appointing committees to look at the problems of the prisons and make yet more recommendations with no certainty that those would be implemented either.[10]

In Pakistan there was a prison-reform report in 1955. In 1983 a high-powered cabinet committee was appointed to make more reform proposals. It presented its report to the president in 1986. Its recommendations were not heeded. Yet another reform committee was set up in 1989, by politicians who had themselves been in prison. The report's initial deliberations 'reflected a degree of concern for the prison population the political leaders had acquired in the course of their own incarceration at the hands of the preceding authoritarian regime'. It failed to report because of political disruption and after the 1993 election another committee was set up. The Human Rights Commission of Pakistan concludes, 'Pakistan's efforts to improve the jail system are spread over four decades, but it has been a barren endeavour.'[11]

Most penal reform reports, whatever their starting point, begin by questioning the efficacy of the institution of prison itself. The 1980 report of the Committee on Penal Reform in Barbados began by calling for methods to be found to avoid sending people to prison. Prison is often described as rehabilitative but, in fact, 'people are sent to prison to suffer society's outrage rather than to learn new ways or to develop and polish their personality and character'.

Also, people who are sent to prison develop a bitterness towards society. Time in prison is usually ill-spent.[12] Families become dependent on the state.[13] Prisoners become dependent on prison and cannot survive outside. They learn new ways of committing crime, become unemployable, and prison is very expensive.[14]

The committee set up in New Zealand in 1987 under a retired High Court Judge, Sir Clinton Roper, to look at the prison system and its place in the criminal justice system reached similar conclusions. Imprisonment achieves retribution but that is not constructive for the prisoner nor beneficial to society. The deterrent effect of imprisonment is minimal. Imprisonment takes criminals out of circulation but imprisonment rates are not related in any simple way to crime rates. Appearing in court is as effective as prison in achieving the effect of expressing society's disapproval of the criminal act. For some people both are equally ineffective. There is scant evidence that rehabilitation is effective.[15] It concluded that 'existing prisons are of limited use to society and for the future we must plan for a continuing reduction in prison numbers by other more effective ways of responding to crime'.[16]

These very same sentiments underlie the February 1990 White Paper produced by the Thatcher government, where prison was described as 'an expensive way of making bad people worse'.[17] A similar conclusion was reached in the most recent of the great prison reform reports, that is the report by the English judge, Lord Woolf: 'It is therefore important, as is generally recognised, to reduce the prison population to an unavoidable minimum.'[18]

The report by the Lord Justice Woolf (as he then was – he became a Law Lord in 1992) is the most outstanding in the depth of its analysis of the basic principles that should underlie the practice of imprisonment. The report followed a particularly serious prison riot, at Strangeways Prison in Manchester in 1990. It was published in 1991 and gave an impetus and direction to a reform process that was already under way albeit in a piecemeal fashion. But the radical direction it inspired was soon slowed with the arrival of the ambitious anti-reformer Michael Howard at the Home Office, some well-publicized escapes from top-security prisons and a political competition to appear unforgiving to criminals.

The Woolf Report was outstanding because it set out a philosophy for imprisonment in the 1990s where philosophy had been lacking. It asserted that in running prisons there had to be a balance between three elements: security, control and justice. Obviously there had to be security, so that prisoners did not escape. And there had to be control so that prisoners did not riot. But without justice, security would become an abuse of human rights and without justice, control would become a losing battle. If prisoners are not treated justly, they will react against their circumstances and both security and control will be threatened.[19] Lord Woolf is a highly distinguished lawyer and the Woolf idea of the basis of imprisonment owed a great deal to the maxim laid down by Lord Wilberforce in 1982: 'Under English law a convicted prisoner, in spite of his imprisonment, retains all civil rights which are not taken away expressly or by necessary implication.'[20]

The prisoner remains a citizen. In a modern democracy the idea of the prison is a place where people go whilst retaining their citizenship and their membership of society. They are subjected to temporary exclusion. They are not to be permanent outcasts. Therefore, the same principles of justice as apply in the outside world should apply to prisoners. They should, according to the Woolf report, be consulted whenever possible, involved, treated as people who will eventually be out in society and will have to make decisions and live a responsible life.[21] The Woolf ideas assume that the prisoner is a person who has the capacity to be responsible and to participate in society in a legal fashion. That idea of the prisoner should define the way the prisoners are treated and the prison is run. Such a way of treating prisoners as if they could respond to notions of being responsible citizens is part of the meaning of modern imprisonment. Such treatment becomes a real rehabilitation, a genuine opportunity for the prisoner to re-enter citizenship.

PENAL REFORM FROM INSIDE THE SYSTEM

Such ideas have been the basis of many attempts at penal reform. They are not new. One of the more remarkable efforts was that made by Alexander Maconochie in the last century to reform the vicious penal regime on Norfolk Island. Robert Hughes in *The Fatal Shore* tells of the penal situation that awaited the convicts when they reached Australia after the long journey across the world. For those transported convicts who committed further crimes in Australia and were sentenced to life imprisonment, the authorities prepared a 'place of ultimate terror',[22] a penal colony on Norfolk Island, a thousand miles from Sydney, where the minimum sentence was ten years. In 1829 Lieutenant-Colonel Morriset arrived to take up the command of the island.[23] The regime was cruel. Prisoners wore double or triple leg irons. They worked in a quarry hewing stone.[24] Those being punished were required to work in a quarry under water. Each group of six men shared one knife, fork, spoon and dish, so most of them had to eat like animals. Informers infiltrated every part of the system. Prisoners made up stories about their fellows to curry favour.[25] Punishments were merciless. After the first fifty lashes the prisoner's back was left to partly heal and then the next fifty were delivered on the scabbed skin. When the number of lashes was limited to one hundred by the colonial secretary in Sydney, a new punishment of placing the prisoner in a 'totally dark, soundless stone isolation chamber'[26] was devised. The situation was so desperate that some prisoners found a way out: one of them was to be murdered by the others. Then, the prisoners reasoned, those who had committed the deed would be sent to Sydney for trial and possibly execution. They would at least get off the island. There was a faint chance they might escape. They drew lots to decide who was to be the murder victim and the deed was done.[27] The authorities then changed the system and sent judges to Norfolk Island to try the cases there, so that escape route was closed.[28] Finally the prisoners mutinied. The mutiny was crushed and fourteen prisoners were hanged.[29]

The commandant who followed Morriset was no better. The punishment for singing a song was a hundred lashes.[30] A man with dysentery was accused of being a malingerer and sentenced to two hundred lashes, but he only survived for the first fifty.[31]

This was the penal regime that naval officer Alexander Maconochie found when he was sent to take over Norfolk Island in 1840. Quite soon after his arrival he declared a public holiday for the queen's birthday. He opened the gates of the prison compound and allowed the convicts to have the day off and wander all over the island, as long as they went back when the bugle sounded.[32] They had special food and Maconochie walked around talking to them. After the meal there was an entertainment. No punishments for singing a song this time, but warm applause.[33] In the evening there were fireworks.[34] He ordered books and musical instruments for the prisoners.[35] He dismantled the gallows. He cast away the special double whips used by the floggers.[36] The prisoners were divided into groups of six and were given responsibility for the behaviour of the group as a whole. He set up a system of marks that the prisoner groups could accumulate through working and conforming. The marks were added together and a certain number of marks bought the group its freedom.[37] He built two churches and established a makeshift synagogue. He gave each prisoner a piece of land to cultivate and set up horticulture classes. The prisoners were allowed to grow tobacco and sell the produce from their plots to the staff.[38] He even managed to bring back to humanity a brain-damaged man who had spent two years chained to a rock in Sydney harbour. The man sheltered in a cave hewn out of the rock, and his food was put on the rock and then pushed at him with a pole. The townspeople of Sydney used to, as an amusement, row out to the rock and throw food at him. He eventually ended up on Norfolk Island. Under Maconochie's treatment he became able to work and live with the other prisoners.[39]

But Maconochie had many enemies. They prevailed and in 1843 he was sacked by the Colonial Office in London.[40]

This is not surprising. As another famous reformer, Thomas Murton, said, 'Whenever a true reformer comes in he's going to be opposed to those who have a stake in the old order. Eventually he'll push too hard and they'll get rid of him.'[41]

Thomas Murton was the man from Arkansas whose work as

warden of Tucker Prison Farm provided the basis for the film *Brubaker*. He was appointed to the prison in February 1967. His first actions were to abolish corporal punishment and sack the most sadistic guards. He then set about organizing the prisoners to elect a council. This elected body was divided into two. One of the councils, composed of three prisoners and Murton himself, decided work assignments and levels of custody. Because one of the jobs to be allocated was guarding, this council had to decide which prisoners were going to carry guns and have the job of guarding the other prisoners. The other council, also three prisoners and Murton, met weekly to conduct disciplinary hearings and to hear complaints from prisoners and staff.[42]

The experiment seemed very successful but it did not last long. He was sacked in March 1968.[43] His philosophy was:

> A major purpose of the prison is to train offenders for successful integration into the free world; yet the prison model is antithetical to this endeavor. The reintegration process would be enhanced by the creation of a prison environment similar to that of the free world. This environment should include shared decision-making among administrators, staff and inmates.[44]

A decade later another reformer in another continent faced a similar situation. As he reflected on the offer that had been made to him to take up a reform job of enormous difficulty, Tony Vinson, a professor of social work in Australia, remembered what had happened to Thomas Murton, sacked after a year. As he agreed to accept the chairmanship of the Corrective Services Commission set up to reform the prison system of New South Wales, he wondered if he would last any longer than Thomas Murton had managed to do.[45] In the tradition of prison reform, when Tony Vinson was invited to take over there had just been a report about the New South Wales prisons, this time a Royal Commission headed by a judge, Mr Justice Nagle. The Nagle Report investigated riots in New South Wales prisons in the early 70s. In October 1970 prisoners at Bathurst Prison, where little had changed for eighty years, staged a sit-in to protest about inedible food, rancid meat and weevils in the cereal, and damage to personal belongings during cell searches.[46]

The sit-in ended when the prisoners were assured there would be no reprisals. The following morning the superintendent and his staff beat up the prisoners.

> Heads were cut open. Some [prisoners] were left lying unconscious or semi-conscious on the prison floor ... Another lay naked on the floor surrounded by seven or eight prison officers who beat him with batons.[47]

The Royal Commission found this 'shameful' and 'indefensible' and discovered that the staff thought they were carrying out official policy and the prison department did not deny they might have reached this conclusion. No one was disciplined for what had happened.[48] In 1974 prisoners burnt the prison down, prison staff shot at the prisoners and wounded some twenty or so of them. Another thirty were injured in beatings by staff. One prisoner was permanently paralysed by the beatings.[49]

The Royal Commission concluded that the disease in the New South Wales prison system was deepseated. 'The Department as a whole is inefficient, disorganized and badly administrated ... It must be revitalized.'[50]

The report reached the same conclusions as had been reached by other reports and would be reached by later ones. Prison should be used only as a last resort. The loss of liberty is the punishment. Prisoners should keep all those rights that are not taken away because of the need for security and retain the 'rights and responsibilities of a parent, spouse, citizen or litigant'.[51]

Rehabilitation is unrealistic and the prison should aim to prevent prisoners from deteriorating. It should provide work, education and training opportunities. Prison officers should be properly trained. Prisoners must be able to express their grievances. Daily management should be based on incentives for prisoners rather than coercion.[52]

Justice Nagle recommended that a reform body of five people be set up to sort out the problems. It was this body that Tony Vinson was asked to chair. He lasted for two and a half years but eventually disagreements within the Commission, a threatened strike by prison officers, opposition from the media and political opportunism brought about his resignation.[53] During the time he was in charge he managed in spite of continuing opposition to bring about major change. The visits system was reformed so that prisoners did not have to talk to their visitors through screens. Prisoners were allowed legal visits in private. They were allowed to write an unlimited number of letters on plain, not prison, notepaper. Supervised phone calls to family and friends were introduced. A system of covering costs of visits by families suffering financial difficulties was introduced. Prisoner Needs Committees were set up at every prison to raise with the administration everyday matters of prison life, such as being allowed to wear sports clothing more often, being able to tell relatives where they were as soon as they arrived and discussing possible changes. Workers with the Aboriginal Legal Service were able to visit prisoners. Prisoner-run shops were introduced. Craft objects made by prisoners were put on sale to the public. Education was laid on for the 30 per cent of prisoners who were illiterate. Prisoners tutored other prisoners. Prison libraries were improved. A handbook, 'The Daily Survivor', on how to manage in the outside world, was produced to be given to prisoners on leaving. Health services were improved at the women's prison. Mothers no longer had to hand over their babies as soon as they reached one year old. Nearly one hundred voluntary welfare workers were recruited to go into prisons. Disciplinary hearings were improved, held in more appropriate premises and prisoners were allowed representation. Prison officer amenities were improved and basic salaries raised. Guard towers were refurbished and air-conditioned. Regulations were drawn up on the use of firearms by prison staff. Prison rules on the use of force were revised. More work was provided for prisoners.[54]

Much more remained to be done. But Tony Vinson was cheered by a comment he heard at one of his farewell parties, at one prison where the staff were particularly militant and resistant to change. They were discussing a notably recalcitrant prisoner, and the view of the staff was '. . . the bastard has the same right as any other man to receive a fair deal. We need a certain amount of discipline but no harm has come from treating a man as a man.'[55]

But the problems were not over in New South Wales. New rules restricting the amount of property prisoners could keep in their cells were brought in in 1990. Prisoners were allowed to keep only three magazines each. Disturbances broke out throughout New South Wales and tear-gas was used at one prison to regain control.[56]

REFORM FROM THE OUTSIDE

Reformers working in the system would find their mission lonely and difficult without the support of the non-governmental organizations that are dedicated to helping prisoners, protecting prisoners' rights and publicizing abuses. In most countries of the world at least one prison reform NGO can be found. Some are large and well-connected and have links to the international reform movement. Others are small and struggling, maybe made up of ex-prisoners or prisoners' relatives.

Until the break-up of the Soviet empire there were no genuine NGOs in East and Central Europe. Since 1989 their development has been rapid. Establishing organizations of concerned citizens that are independent of the government has been seen as a way of building a truly democratic society. Democracy is more than voting for a government every five years. It also implies the existence of 'civil society'. Citizens get involved in causes and campaigns, organizations and self-help groups. The Moscow Center for Prison Reform was set up, by former political prisoner Valery Abramkin and others, in 1990. From the beginning it saw the importance of publicizing, showing the world what goes on in Russian prisons so that international opinion was alerted, and lobbying the newly elected members of parliament about law reform.[57] In November 1992 the Center organized the first ever penal reform conference in Russia, which was attended by over 200 people from twenty-four countries.[58] Ex-prisoner Harry Wu addressed the conference. Prison service employees and activists had their first taste of something entirely new: an electric public confrontation about what was going on in prisons, where the activists made their criticisms and expected to be heard and the state employees had to listen and justify what they were doing.

The Moscow Center for Prison Reform made some video films of life in hard labour camps for women shoplifters and petty thieves and went round Western countries showing them. They produced information on the desperate overcrowding and human rights abuses in Russia's prisons and labour colonies. They have regular radio programmes on regional and national stations aimed at prisoners, their families and officials working in the penal system. The programmes contain information about the legal system and prisoners' rights as well as contributions from prisoners and answers to some of the 500 letters the Center receives every month.[59]

In the UK the relationships between NGOs and officials are somewhat different. The electric confrontations between the officials and the activists took place in the 1960s and 70s. Since then a different type of relationship has developed. The prison administration has realized how useful and necessary non-governmental organizations can be. The Prison Reform Trust was set up in 1981. Since then it has worked tirelessly to keep the state of the prisons in the eyes of the public and has used every opportunity to promote debate and spread information about imprisonment. It criticizes what is going on in the prisons whenever there are grounds for criticism. But relationships with the prison administration are close. The Prison Service collaborates in the preparation of the Prison Reform Trust information handbook for prisoners because of its high quality and because it is widely agreed that information from a neutral source is more likely to be trusted by prisoners. It buys large numbers of copies for distribution to prisoners.[60] The Prison Service also has close relationships with a number of other NGOs that work for the welfare of prisoners as well as those arguing for prison reform.

Such a close relationship does not prevail in Japan. The Japanese Centre for Prisoners' Rights was set up in 1995 by some lawyers, academics, citizens' groups and journalists. It is struggling in a very unsympathetic climate to take up the cases of individual prisoners suffering abuses and to support prison staff who have problems with the ethos of their organization. They took up the case of a man who had been held in solitary confinement for thirteen years but, after pressure, was relocated to the normal prison environment. They also support prisoners' families and campaign against the death penalty.[61]

Some organizations not specializing in penal matters realize that the people they exist to care for can be found in prison too. In the UK the Samaritans, an organization that helps people in distress or contemplating suicide, works in prison to help the prison staff prevent suicides. They train selected prisoners as 'listeners'.[62] These prisoners are then available to listen to others' problems in confidence and help if they can. The Port Bell Women's Resettlement Project is run by the National Association of Women's Organizations of Uganda. It was officially launched in June 1995. Women soon to be released from prison were trained to earn their living independently. They were trained as bakers and basket-makers in order to help them keep themselves and their children. They were also trained in basic small business skills and given some knowledge of their basic legal rights. The women began projects towards the end of their training, such as running a child-care day centre, managing a kiosk, growing maize, baking, weaving mats, table mats and baskets, making samosas and other eatables to deliver to schools and shops, and mushroom growing.[63]

Access to law is one way of protecting prisoners' rights. In Pécs, southern Hungary, in 1996 students from the law faculty of the local university were going into the local prison to give legal advice to prisoners. In one prison in South America students doing the same thing were able to reduce the numbers in one pre-trial prison by 30 per cent. They discovered that many of the prisoners were being held illegally. The Lithuanian Prisoners Aid Association finds lawyers to represent poor people consigned to pre-trial prison and with no funds to pay a lawyer.

The relationship between these outside organizations and the prison administrations can be an awkward one for both parties. In the more repressive and closed systems the idea that people from NGOs should have access to prisons and prisoners is regarded as ludicrous. The staff of the prison ask why on earth they should allow such a group of trouble-makers to come in and stir up the prisoners to protest and demand their rights. Surely these NGO people would not understand about security. Prisoners would take advantage of their goodheartedness and persuade them to smuggle forbidden items in or out. They could easily be taken hostage by prisoners. So many of these NGO people are young women and the problems that can pose are easy to imagine. Sometimes these young women are manipulated by very sophisticated prisoners and no end of trouble is the result.

An illustration of the divide is the question of prisoners' names. Outside organizations going into prisons will expect to treat prisoners as they treat everyone else, with respect. They will call them by their name and title, for example Mr Smith, and will expect to shake hands with them. Staff in a system characterized by rigid and inhuman discipline and no relationships with prisoners will find this very threatening and see it as a danger to security and an invitation to riot.

The NGOs have a different perspective. They do not usually understand the way prison officers protect themselves from a relationship they cannot handle by denying prisoners their names or their respectful titles. They are not steeped in the constraints and problems of prisons. They do not live with the daily fear that an escape or a dangerous incident might happen. They might not appreciate that in the end it is the prison personnel who are responsible and they who will lose their jobs if something goes seriously wrong.

They are concerned more about the day-to-day difficulties. Why should they have to wait so long to get in? Should they put up with the remarks made about them *sotto voce* but easy to hear by the prison staff in the gatehouse? If they are women, is there any point in challenging offensive remarks made about their appearance when they are trying to enter the prison? Why is every other prison activity more important than the one the NGO people are doing with the prisoners? Why, when the NGO people and the prisoners are rehearsing a play or taking a class, is the crucial prisoner missing for some other important prison activity? Why, in the middle of some activity that is going really well, does a prison officer fling open the door and bellow a prisoner's name at the top of his voice, at which point the prisoner, although vital for what is going on, has to leave?

Relationships between prisons and the NGOs that work with them are bound to be tense. There is a different agenda and a different perspective. Yet prison administrations striving to run prisons in accordance with international rules can only gain from working with genuine and committed NGOs. They get support in publicizing their problems and the reality of imprisonment. They see pressure put on the politicians. They get backing in campaigns to protect prison budgets and improve prison conditions. They have access to a pool of people dedicated to working with prisoners and not expecting personal enrichment to come from it. Prisons and prison administrators need friends badly. They need friends who are unconstrained by the rules of officialdom and secrecy and have a completely disinterested concern for the well-being of the prisons in their country.

THE PROCESS OF REFORM

So much about prisons needs reform that there is a real question about where to start: crumbling buildings, no work for prisoners, beatings in the punishment block, no treatment for mentally ill prisoners, rotten food, prisoners terrorizing other prisoners. Many reformers maintain that to deal with all that, there is one starting place: the staff. Austin MacCormick was an adviser on prison reform to forty-eight states in the US in the seventies. He said, 'If only I had the right staff, I could run a good prison in an old red barn.'[64]

In Thomas Murton's view, 'A primary consideration in the reform of the prison should be personnel selection, not new construction.'[65]

A prisoner who participated in the riot in Manchester prison in 1990 wrote to the Woolf Inquiry,

> I did agree with the riot at Manchester because something had to be done. Because of the inhuman way they treated every inmate; like animals and not like human beings . . . It is not that the prison service wants extra staff, they want retraining to treat people as human beings.[66]

Throughout the 1980s penal reformers in the UK put much energy into campaigning for an end to the use of buckets and chamber pots, slopping-out and all the other consequences of prisoners not having access to proper lavatories. They were victorious. In 1996 slopping-out finally ended and every prisoner was supposed to have access to a flushing lavatory. But as overcrowding increases many prisoners now find themselves living in a small room with another person and an unscreened flush lavatory. Certainly this is better than the bucket or the pot, because the lavatory flushes, but the contribution to making imprisonment more humane and dignified of the massive effort to install proper plumbing is not enormous. Choosing the right penal reform target is not easy.

The reform process that took place in the Polish prison service from 1990 to 1993 is widely regarded as a worthwhile model. The crux of that process was to focus on the staff. According to Danuta Gajdus, Deputy Director-General at the time, in 1989 the prison service lost control of the prisons. In order to re-establish control without reverting to the violent and repressive methods of the past, it was necessary to adopt a quite different philosophy. The staff would need to accept new principles and a new ethical approach.

Therefore a process was set in motion which involved first of all root-and-branch staff changes. After the new approach was announced and corruption, theft of prison property and drunkenness were stopped, 2500 staff left the prison service immediately, many taking early retirement. Altogether 7000 staff, about 40 per cent, were replaced over two and a half years. The remaining staff needed to be retrained. They all went through a retraining process to emphasize human rights, treatment of prisoners as individuals and rehabilitation as the basis of imprisonment. The system of staff colluding with some powerful prisoners to control the rest and using some prisoners as informers in return for privileges was stopped. Prisons were opened up to the outside world. Some prisoners were allowed temporary release. Outsiders with a genuine reason, such as teachers, students, workers in the mass media, actors and writers, were allowed to visit and many meetings, events, seminars and concerts took place. All prison staff except the guards – i.e. teachers, educators, social workers – were taken out of uniform. Staff were required to wear name badges so that they became more personally responsible for their actions and decisions. Shortage of funds enabled good economic arguments to be made for reform measures such as prisoners wearing their own clothes, receiving more parcels from home, and allowing families to prepare meals for prisoners during visits.[67]

Pavel Moczydlowski, Director-General at the time, has explained the rationale.

> Let me start with an illustration of a specific type of interaction between an inmate and a member of prison staff. Suppose the former is rude and refuses to enter his cell. The officer admonishes him sharply, ordering him to go into the cell. As a rule, inmates tend to obey express orders. If, however, that particular prisoner remembers that particular officer as the one who sold alcohol to inmates or exhorted them to steal tools from the factory they worked at, or could often be seen drunk and idle – the prisoner is unlikely to obey orders.
>
> His reaction can be different, for example, he might tell the officer, 'Shut up, you criminal swine, you ought to share this cell with me and to stay there longer too.' This of course amounts to refusal to obey orders. The officer, being responsible for controlling the situation and maintaining order and discipline in prison, is thus forced to use constraint.
>
> What conclusions can be drawn from this type of social interaction? Having lost the possibility of exercising power (that is, of controlling the situation in prison) by force of moral authority, the officer has to resort to coercion.
>
> The above example also shows that immoral conduct of the staff gives the inmates the courage to revolt and authorize their right to rebellion and disobedience.
>
> What was therefore the basic condition of restoration of control in Polish prisons by lawful means was retrieval of moral authority by the prison administration.[68]

Such a reform process is complex, lengthy and calls for determination and stamina. The very necessary changes in the legal framework are only a start. Profound changes are needed in the culture and concept of penal systems in former totalitarian states.

Getting rid of a critical mass of the staff is one way to bring about a genuine and deep-rooted reform. Demilitarization of staff – that is removing the ranks, pseudo-military uniforms, the saluting and carrying little sticks under arms, getting rid of the whole idea that the activity of incarcerating fellow citizens is related to war and defence – is a fundamental shift. The South African Correctional Service demilitarized in 1996.[69]

Another way of bringing about reform is to try and implement a concept that is quite different from the current basis of the prison system. Such a method requires those running the system to look at everything they do and reform it in the light of a new principle. Such an over-arching principle was the idea of community prisons in the Woolf Report. What is behind the idea of community prisons? Lord Woolf analysed the idea of prison and the purpose of it. Prison, he discovered, was in most ways a negative idea. By being imprisoned, people lost their connections with the outside world. They lost their jobs if they had them. They lost their homes if they had them. Their families often deserted them, if they had them. Their attachments to the outside society, the legal society, were weakened and their attachments to the prison society, the illegal society, were strengthened. So prison was likely to be very ineffective as a method of crime control because it weakened all those forces in people's lives which persuaded them they should keep the law – forces such as the home, family, pressure from loved ones, an economic stake in society, like a job and a house. So he concluded, as we have seen, that there were strong arguments for using prison only as a last resort, for the really serious crimes and the dangerous offenders. He also concluded that the basis of imprisonment should be preparation for return to the community, except for those few prisoners who were going to be in prison for very many years. Prisons should become 'community prisons'.[70] Prison is part of the community, not a place of exile from it.

There are three aspects to community prisons. The first is the decision about which prison a prisoner is placed in. In Britain prisons are divided by security level and function, and once prisoners have been sentenced they may be moved from the prison near their home town to a prison many miles away. Under the principle of community prisons, the objective is to keep prisoners as near their home area as possible. There is much evidence that the most important aspect of life for prisoners and the most likely influence for good is the connection with the family. Keeping prisoners as near their home as possible means that the family can visit frequently. It is also much easier to make arrangements for prisoners to be reintegrated into a community when they are released if the prison is in the home area.

So the first aspect of community prisons is placing the prisoner near to home. The second is the relationship between the prison and all the social organizations in the community outside the prison. Prisons have high walls to keep the prisoners in. Sometimes it seems as if the high walls are actually to keep society out. So a community prison is one where there is a constant flow of visitors, groups, state agencies and NGOs working in the prison and with the prisoners to help the task of reintegration. Brixton Prison in London established a relationship with the National Theatre, which is near to the prison. The people from the education department of the National Theatre agreed to come into the prison for six weeks to run a drama workshop ending with a production. In discussion with the prisoners who had volunteered for the workshop they chose to perform Shakespeare's *Hamlet*. After six weeks of hard work and great problems the production was ready. It was performed in the prison church with the permission of the religious ministers. People connected with the prison were allowed to buy tickets for the performance. One afternoon performance was arranged for the families of the prisoners who were acting. The media were informed and the event was reported on the BBC and by NBC in the United States and on Japanese TV.

Such projects can have considerable significance in the reintegration of prisoners. They enable the prisoners to be successful at something that is valued by society. They train them in learning, concentration, thinking, working in a team, being sensitive to other people. They allow prisoners to see the satisfaction and status that can come from non-criminal activities. They show them that society is prepared to value them and reaccept them.

The third element of community prisons is the contribution that the prison and the prisoners make to the community. It cannot be a one-way traffic. Prisoners need to make a contribution to the community and the prison needs to give something to the outside society. In Malawi, the sixth poorest country in the world, there was in 1995 in the central prison in Zomba a workshop where the prisoners made wheelchairs and other aids for disabled children out of recycled materials. The NGO concerned, Malawi Against Polio,[71] got the measurements from the disabled children of the devices that they needed and then visited the prison once a week to collect the finished items and give the prisoners the next batch of orders. Such projects have a triple benefit. They produce something that is greatly needed by disadvantaged people. By their work, prisoners are making a form of recompense to the community for the harm they have done. And through the work, they have the possibility of feeling once again reconnected to society and part of a caring community.

In Britain an NGO, the Inside Out Trust, has been established specifically to organize prisoners to carry out work for charities. The Trust collects good reusable equipment from people who no longer have any need for it. The prisoners who will repair and refurbish it are taught the skills they need. The Trust liaises with ministries in developing countries and charities working in overseas development to find where the equipment is needed and it is then shipped to its destination. In Parkhurst Prison on the Isle of Wight and in Feltham Young Offenders Institution manual sewing machines are being refurbished for use in villages in Africa. In other prisons books are being repaired and rebound for Book Aid International to send overseas and children's clothes are being made from donated fabric and sent to Africa.

THE ESSENTIALS OF PRISON REFORM

The essence of the work of reformers is perhaps summed up in the words of Pavel Moczydlowski. Prisons are 'anti-social'.[72] They take in people who do not fit into a responsible community and make them even less fit to do so. They must become 'pro-social'. The way they are structured and run must be aimed to minimize conflict, prevent riots, reduce violence and decrease public risk not by repression but by breaking down the barrier that separates prison from society. One way of running prisons is on the confrontation model. The prison administration is on one side and the prisoners on the other. The prison administration satisfies 'the social need for hostility towards offenders'. Such systems are always dangerous. There are riots. Staff have to control the riots. Staff feel very discontented at doing a dangerous and low-status job and the prisons become a long-running political problem.

The other method, the 'pro-social' method, is one which keeps trying to break down the barrier between the prison and society. Such systems go as far as they can in breaking down the separation and isolation of the prison. The check on them is the response of the wider society. Using this approach, 'the actual boundaries of prison are incessantly marked out by social indignation. "Oh, no, this is no longer a prison. That's enough." '

So the process has reached its limits for the time being. But the prisoners know that the limits have been set not by the prison administration but by public opinion. 'In this model, penitentiary administration represents the interests of the prisoners (and, in fact, the best interests of society) and defends them against social aggression.'[73]

The basic task of the prison reformer is to change the relationships, between the staff and the prisoners, the prison and the outside community, and the prison in society. Reforms of the physical environment and the structure of opportunities for prisoners and the provision of fair and just treatment to prisoners can be built on the basis of respectful and understanding relationships.

There are many tools to be used in the struggle to achieve this. Opening up prisons to the outside world, whilst at the same time protecting prisoners from the more prurient interests of the media, is essential. When the staff know there can be no cover-ups, abuses are less likely. It is helpful to mobilize campaigners, writers and socially concerned organizations. Giving staff the opportunity to be seen in a positive light is also important. Wherever possible an emphasis of prison reform should be on developing the reparative elements of prison. Prisoners who can go out during the day and do charitable work for the benefit of others should do so. Those who cannot should be given the opportunity to carry out such work inside.

The work of penal reformers has brought many prisons out of the Dark Ages; they are indefatigable – but they face an uphill task. The political mood is not with them. Many current developments threaten the progress they have made and throw into question the basic premises of their work, that prisoners are members of society and should be treated as such when they are in prison so that when they come out they can make a contribution, and that loss of liberty is a serious punishment. It is part of democracy that it should be used only sparingly. The next chapter looks at these new and frightening trends.

PART FOUR

The Future of Imprisonment

Punishment is a tragic, destructive undertaking, necessary to a degree as a response to serious crime, but not to anything like the degree it is currently used. It should be minimised to the smallest extent possible, and it should be viewed as a moral undertaking rather than an instrument for producing useful effects. If we want to promote disciplined conduct and social control – and these are important goals for any kind of society and not just for right-wing ideologues – we should concentrate not on punishing offenders but on more mainstream activities such as moralising markets, promoting solidarity, and integrating young people as citizens – all of which are matters of social justice and moral education rather than penal policy. The things that punishment does do well – such as scapegoating, and venting frustration, and hardening social division, and offering popular, repressive responses to complex social problems – are, in the long term, destructive of the social fabric.

David Garland, University of Edinburgh, 1995[1]

13. *Prison Expansion and the Private Sector*

The idea of just deserts makes it possible to streamline the system, and particularly to disregard all other values than the question of the gravity of the act. The ideal of matching the gravity of a crime with a portion of pain has the consequence that all other basic values that courts traditionally have to weigh are forced out of the proceedings. What was a system of justice is converted into a system of crime control. The classical distinction between the judiciary, the executive and the legislature has to a large extent dissolved. The courts become tools in the hands of politicians or, in the most extreme cases, the judges – as well as the prosecutors – become politicians themselves. Yet this is above criticism. It has none of the grave illegality about it that marked the Holocaust or the gulags. Now it is democratic crime control by the voting majority. To this there are no natural limits, as long as the actions do not hurt the majority.

Nils Christie in *Crime Control as Industry*[1]

Current trends in the development of imprisonment give penal reformers great cause to fear for the future. The richest and most powerful country in the world is moving in a very dangerous direction. The startling growth of imprisonment in the United States seems to have set in motion a process from which it will be very difficult to pull back. We have seen that in 1980 there were half a million people in US prisons.[2] By mid-1996 there were 1.6 million.[3] Between 1985 and 1995 the prison population grew by 8 per cent a year,[4] although the rate slowed between mid-1995 and mid-1996 to 4.4 per cent.[5] In California the state prison population is now more than six times bigger than it was at the end of the 1970s.[6] In Texas the state prison population increased from 51,700 in 1991 to 132,400 in 1996.[7] The imprisonment rate in Texas at mid-1996 was 659 per 100,000 and this figure does not include those locked up in local jails.[8] At the end of 1985 one in every 320 US residents was locked up. By the middle of 1996 the figure was one in every 163.[9]

The process seems unstoppable and it is assumed in the United States that there is more to come. Estimates suggest an increase in the state and federal prison population of one-quarter over 1995 levels by the year 2000.[10] 'Three strikes and you're out' legislation means that more convicted offenders will be serving life. There is no ceiling or concept of an optimum. Prison sentences are getting longer. Specialist prisons fitted out like old people's homes will be needed for the incarcerated over-eighties. Federal government grants for prisons are available to states. The condition for receiving half the funding is that prisoners in those states must actually serve 85 per cent of the sentence passed without parole or conditional release.

The growth has affected both men and women and spreads across the ethnic groups, though the impact on some is much greater than on others. The rate of growth in imprisonment rates since 1980 for white Americans has been 169 per cent, for black Americans 222 per cent and for Hispanics 449 per cent.[11] More young people are being locked up and a higher proportion of these is going to adult prisons rather than to specialist places for juveniles.[12] More women than ever before are in prison and jail – almost 120,000 at the end of 1995.[13]

Nowhere else in the world is there a comparable situation. Although the imprisonment rate is higher in Russia, this is due to a creaking legal system, technical problems of a shortage of resources and paralysed legislative reform. It does not stem from a belief that this is how a good society should be run, a conviction that a society that cares for its people and wants safety for them achieves this by spending enormous sums on imprisonment. On the contrary, the new criminal code introduced in January 1997 contains a legislative framework for alternatives to prison.

The country to the north of the US, Canada, stubbornly resists the trend. Its imprisonment rate is high by European standards – 119 per 100,000 in 1994 – but much more in the European tradition. The Canadian government works hard to resist the messages coming up from the south urging mass imprisonment as the solution to crime problems.

The direction taken by the United States represents a profound change in the attitude of Western democracies towards imprisonment. Since 1945, Western penal policy has been based on the assumption that incarceration is detrimental to society, a necessary evil. To have some people in prison is unavoidable. When it is unavoidable, it should be humane and constructive, but ideally criminal policy would aim to reduce prison use and replace it with other solutions. Many public policy initiatives have been directed to reducing prison populations, creating alternatives, diverting people from the criminal justice process, always assuming that the use of prison would continue at a residual level and the energy and effort would be put into finding other ways.

The US view that having large numbers of people in prison is not only inevitable but actually desirable has not yet infected Europe in the same way, though there are signs of the contagion spreading. Certainly, the growth in prison levels in some West European countries has been remarkable. The Netherlands is one example. In the Netherlands in 1975 the number of prison cells was 2356 and the rate of imprisonment was 17 per 100,000, one of the lowest in the world.[14] The low imprisonment rate in the Netherlands was a source of wonder and admiration for penal and social reformers around the world. It was much studied and analysed. How did they do it? Why was it? Was it because so many of them remembered the Second World War, the occupation by Germany and the incarceration of many Dutch people? Did this give them all an understanding of the precious nature of liberty and the seriousness of taking it away from anyone, even a law-breaker?[15] If it did, the Second World War is now long past and they have forgotten. In 1994 prison capacity was 8305 and the rate of imprisonment was 55 per 100,000.[16] By the end of 1996 there were 12,000 prisoners and an imprisonment rate of nearly 80 per 100,000.[17]

In the rest of Western Europe the growth is less spectacular, but also large. In Spain in 1988 there were fewer than 30,000 people in prison. By 1994 the figure had risen to over 41,000, an increase of 40 per cent. In Italy over the same six-year period the increase was 48 per cent. In Greece it was 60 per cent and in Portugal 46 per cent. There was an increase in Austria of 16 per cent and even in the traditionally low-imprisonment countries in Scandinavia there were increases of 32 per cent in Norway and 23 per cent in Sweden.[18] In

France the 'Programme 13,000' brought twenty-five new prisons containing 12,850 places into use between 1989 and 1992.[19]

The UK is the country in Europe where the US influence has been strongest. In England and Wales in the 1990s prison numbers grew rapidly. At the end of January 1993 the number in prison was 41,500.[20] On 30 September 1997 it had risen to over 62,600 and another crisis of prison capacity was in full swing.[21] After a substantial prison expansion – 12,500 new places were provided between 1981 and 1996, an increase of one-third – the search was on again for residential institutions that could be turned into prisons. A large boat was purchased from the US for £4 million and turned into a low security prison.

Michael Howard, the right-wing Home Secretary in Britain from 1993 to 1997, made the claim at the Conservative Party Conference in 1993 that 'prison works'.[22] This was a radical departure. Until then Conservative Home Secretaries had been more or less in agreement with the official cross-party received wisdom, that prison was the right destination for an irreducible minimum of cases but was used much too much and should be used less. Ministers in charge of finance were usually leading supporters of Home Secretaries in taking this view. Prisons were clearly expensive capital items, hard to build on the cheap. Once they were up and running the revenue costs were high. And all this expense to lock up people who did not pay their fines, small thieves, receivers of stolen property and young incompetent burglars, seemed quite unjustified.

Michael Howard had a completely different starting point. Prison was not a measure to be avoided whenever possible, but a measure to be imposed whenever it seemed likely that a law-breaker might carry on with crime. So he proposed new legislation to impose much more imprisonment under the US-inspired title of a 'Crime (Sentences) Bill'. The Bill contained measures for an automatic life sentence on a second conviction for a serious violent or sexual offence (two strikes and you're out). A new system of minimum sentences meant that after two or more convictions burglars convicted again would get three years and drug dealers would get seven. Departures from these mandatory sentences were only to be permitted in 'exceptional circumstances'.[23] These very radical proposals were opposed vehemently by the senior judges. Their argument was that under the proposals the required sentence in these cases would be predetermined. There would be very little room for the judge to have any input. Judges would lose their discretion to consider the many factors surrounding the offence and then decide on the sentence. This was not justice, they maintained.[24]

Michael Howard claimed that he had a duty to bring in such measures because he had the task of protecting people against crime and this was the way to do it. The effect of his policies would be that 'More pensioners sleep safely in their beds because more criminals sleep safely behind bars.'[25]

This thinking is inspired by United States conservatives such as James Q. Wilson, John Dilulio and Charles Murray, co-author of the controversial book, *The Bell Curve: Intelligence and Class Structure in American Life*. Published in 1994, *The Bell Curve* argues, in the words of penal reformer Jerome Miller, that 'blacks as a group are seriously disadvantaged if not cursed, in modern industrial society because of their low IQs – mostly as a result of fixed genetic endowment'.[26]

These conservatives have argued that locking up millions of people in the United States 'works'. What is the basis of this new direction in social policy? What do these proponents mean when they say 'prison works'?

They certainly do not mean that in spite of all the evidence to the contrary over two centuries they have found a way of treating people in prison that will stop them committing crime when they come out. The 'prison works' supporters are not saying that prison is a good therapy and after a dose of it criminals will come out cured. They are not saying that prison works from a perspective of what happens to the prisoner. The interest is not what happens to the prisoner at all but what happens to those who are not prisoners, the rest of society, the law-abiding, the victims of the prisoners' actions.

Those who maintain that 'prison works' use two arguments. One is the same argument that was used in the time of transportation of convicts to Australia, the 'cleansing' or 'weeding' argument. In the eighteenth century there was a perception that once the criminals and those prone to crime were dispatched to the other side of the world, society would be cleansed of the bad elements. The weeds would have been pulled up and discarded, and the ordered, cultivated state of the world would be restored. With the bad elements identified, isolated and locked away, crime would be reduced and those left behind would live in safety, knowing that those threatening its peace and order had been eliminated. The supporters of 'prison works' come from this school of thought. They argue that the way to deal with crime and make society safer is to get rid of the people who commit crime, not by sending them to another country but by taking them out of society, putting them away and removing them from citizenship. It might be objected that it is hard to know who is going to be a career criminal, a bad element. People can change and life circumstances can alter. This is not a difficulty for the supporters of this policy. It is well known that those who start off committing crimes continue to commit crime, so locking them up early on in their criminal lives, even if their crimes are not the most serious, is a reasonably good bet. Locking them up for a long time keeps them from committing the further crimes that it can reasonably be predicted they would commit if they were at liberty.

So prison works by locking up the crime-prone people, so that all their as-yet-uncommitted crimes stay uncommitted. They are out of society, and society is better off without them. The US proponents have a second argument to support their thesis. Prison has an additional effective ingredient. It deters those who have not yet started committing crime from doing so. To do that efficiently, however, going to prison has to be really unpleasant. If criminals are to face five years in a well-heated or air-conditioned building with a comfortable cell, access to education and training, free medical care and good sports facilities, they might find it more agreeable than life in the poverty-stricken inner city. But if prison is spartan and hard, the prospect of a long sentence in such a place will force criminals to think twice before committing an assault on a person or on property. So the 'prison works' theorists are in favour of stopping colour television for prisoners, closing exercise gyms, getting rid of the weight-lifting equipment, and stopping prisoners thinking they can complain to the court whenever there is something they do not like. So they are behind the Prison Litigation Reform Act, which passed through the US Congress in 1996 and is likely, according to Al Bronstein and Jenni Gainsborough of the National Prison Project, to

> limit the federal courts' ability to remedy abuses suffered by prisoners in all cases, including those that seek to enjoin the rape of juvenile and women prisoners by guards, the sadistic beatings of prisoners, and the failure to provide prisoners with minimally adequate medical and mental health care.[27]

In the minds of the legislators who passed the Act, it means no more court cases by prisoners complaining that the coffee is cold.

These arguments are the inspiration for the Council on Crime in America. The Council was set up in 1995. It is composed of well-known conservatives, all in favour of the 'prison works' thesis. They deploy a battery of arguments to prove that not enough people are locked up in the US at the moment and those that are locked up are let out too soon. They maintain that the locking-up strategy is the best, most economical, most effective way to protect non-criminal members of society from crime and that there should be a lot more of it. They maintain that most of the people in prison are a genuine threat, and are violent, dangerous people. They predict a

> coming storm of juvenile crime that will be more violent and more random than anything Americans have experienced to date. Between now and the year 2005, the number of males aged 14–17 will increase by 23 per cent. These juveniles will be more crime-prone than their predecessors; they will commit more crimes with guns; and they will commit more crimes against strangers.[28]

A prominent member of the Council on Crime is John Dilulio, head of the Center for Public Management at the Brookings Institution. The answer to crime-induced inner-city blight, according to Dilulio, is 'imprison criminals'.[29] He has called for the current prison population to be doubled. The National Rifle Association and other groups have also argued that the doubling of the numbers in prison in the 1980s led to a dramatic drop in crime.[30]

The argument of the US conservatives is based on a number of premises. Locking up criminals is simple and effective. Since their numbers are finite and they are identifiable, once they have been caught and put away, of course crime rates will fall. They see criminals as a distinct group of people, almost bearing a distinctive mark on them and different from non-criminals. It is as if there is a reservoir of them, filling up at one end of course with new recruits amongst the young, but so long as the locking up strategy is faster and more thorough than the process of new recruits joining, then with determination the reservoir can be drained, or at least kept at a very low level. It is just a question of catching them. When they are locked up they can only commit crime against prison staff and other prisoners. Everyone else will be safe from them. And these proponents argue that recent falls in crime rates in the United States support their thesis. They have tripled the imprisonment rate and crime has gone down. If they could increase it even more, crime could be further reduced. There must be a magical figure at which point all the anti-social people are locked up and then there will be peace. Why not do it? What can be the argument against it?

Cost, it might be suggested. Surely one argument against it is cost. It must be very expensive. Indeed it is, they say, but not nearly so expensive as letting the crimes actually happen that are prevented because the perpetrators are imprisoned. They work out the notional cost of a crime adding up the cost of police time, court time, prison time, the monetary loss to the victim, and add a figure in dollars for the pain and suffering of the victim. They then estimate how many crimes average criminals commit per year and then go on to show how much of the money spent on each crime is saved because the criminals are in prison and the crimes they would commit do not therefore take place.[31]

But the situation is urgent. Unless there is a lot more locking-up made available now, crime rates will rise as the next generation of juveniles comes of age.

They see nothing wrong with having 1.5 or 2 or 2.5 million Americans in prison. There seems to be no upper figure that would in their view be too high. They are not moved by the argument that this is a threat to democracy. In their view the threat to democracy comes not from mass incarceration but from what will happen if crime is allowed to rise unchecked and violence continues to stalk the streets.

Those who disagree with the 'prison works' lobbyists, those whom John Dilulio calls 'the anti-incarceration elite',[32] find flaws in this whole construction. They fault the analysis about effects on crime, the assertion that in the long run mass incarceration makes society safer and the argument that imprisonment is the cost-effective way of reducing crime. They see in the propositions of the Council on Crime in America a danger to the future of American society.

First of all they argue with the interpretation that the reduced crime figures show that prison works. Since 1973, when crime figures began to be collected through surveys, crime rates have fluctuated. Violent crime fell by 20 per cent between 1981 and 1986, rose by 15 per cent between 1986 and 1991 and levelled off between 1992 and 1994. Property crime declined steadily from 1980.[33]

So those opposed to the 'prison works' theory do not dispute that in recent years the amount of violent crime has gone down in many places. But they maintain that the 'prison works' theorists are over-simplifying and over-claiming. There are always fluctuations in the crime rate. The recent drop is being measured against the late 1980s when the rise was rapid and levels of violence were remarkably high. Over a longer perspective there is no decline in violent crime. Also the decline is uneven, and even in the places where there has been a decline it has only taken violent crime to the level it was before the massive rise in incarceration began. Serious violent crime is at about the same level it was ten years ago, in spite of the massive growth in incarceration. The level of violence in America's inner cities, after this massive investment, they argue, is still higher than in any comparable country. Not a great achievement for the expense and social disruption that has been caused.[34]

It is argued that more people in prison may be the reason for the recent fall. But there could be other reasons. One is demographics. Most kinds of crime are usually committed by young men. Therefore, when there are more young men in the population there will be more crime. The number of young men in the US population has waxed and waned with the crime rate. Between 1960 and 1980 the number of young men in the US nearly doubled (a rise from 11.9

million to 21.4 million). Crime rates also increased. Since 1980 the population of young men has slightly declined, as have crime rates.[35]

Another explanation is that crime is affected by the social and economic policies in different places, the state of the economy, the levels of education, attitudes to drug treatment. Different states in the US have vastly different crime rates. If 'prison works' is to hold as a theory then the low-crime states should have a lot of people in prison and the high-crime states should have low imprisonment rates. This is not the case.[36]

The opponents do not maintain that imprisoning enormous numbers of young men in the crime-prone age groups will have no effect on crime rates. It certainly will. In every society there are people that are dangerous, violent and determined to continue with law-breaking because they know no other way. Taking them out of circulation is bound to stop what they would have done if they had been at liberty.[37] Roger Tarling in England has studied the 'incapacitation' effects of imprisonment, as it is called. He concludes that if the prison population is increased by 25 per cent, there should be a reduction in the crime rate of 1 per cent.[38] Certainly locking up a lot of people from the poorest sections of society will reduce some crime for a short while. But most offenders are not caught.[39] And when they are caught and locked up the crime only stops until the next cohort of poor, alienated young men comes in to fill the gap left by those imprisoned.

In the slightly longer term, the opponents argue, the strategy of mass incarceration will cause more crime. The social disruption caused by imprisoning so many young people causes families to fragment even further and this increases crime. The opponents of 'prison works' argue that it is a puny achievement to lock up another million people and by so doing manage to hold violent crime at the extremely high level that it reached before the mass incarceration programme began. There must be a better way.[40]

They also dispute the argument that mass incarceration is a cheap solution to crime. They comment that the figure for the amount of crime saved by incarcerating many people is notional as is the amount of money that each crime is deemed to cost. In 1987 Edwin

*Table 12   Changes in the US in crime and punishment,
1980–94*

	1980	1994	% change
probation	1,118,097	2,962,166	165
jail	163,994	490,442	199
prison	329,821	1,053,738	219
parole	220,438	690,159	213
total	1,832,350	5,196,505	184
adult population	162.8 million	192.6 million	18
per cent of adults under supervision	1.1%	2.7%	145
reported index crimes	13.4 million	14.0 million	4

Source: 'Why are Crime Rates Declining? An NCCD Briefing Report',
NCCD, San Francisco

Zedlewski of the National Institute of Justice carried out a study
which showed that for each year of incarceration at $25,000 the
savings in reduced crimes were $430,000. Experts who looked at his
work concluded that he had seriously overestimated the number of
crimes committed by each offender. If his figures had been right,
crime in the US would have been eliminated by the mid 1980s. It
was not. Another study by the National Institute of Justice calculated
that the annual cost of crime was $450 billion. But about three-
quarters of this figure was intangibles such as the pain and suffering
of victims and a decline in the quality of life.[41]

Even the short-term effect will be much less than is claimed. And
at what cost? It is very expensive. The General Accounting Office
of the government suggests that annual operating costs of state and
federal prisons (excluding jails) were $17.7 billion in 1994. Between
1980 and 1994 about $163 billion was spent on building and running
state and federal prisons. The capital costs between 1996 and the
year 2000 could reach between $15 and $20 billion.[42] According to
Human Rights Watch the cost of a prison place per year is more
than the cost of tuition, room and board at Harvard.[43] It has been

estimated that the cost of a life sentence for a prisoner in California is $1.5 million.[44] The estimate of $40 billion a year spent on locking people up seems a reasonable one.

Where is the money coming from? In the United States it is coming from other areas of social expenditure. Prisons are being built at the expense of other areas. In its 1996 budget, California planned to spend more on prisons and punishment than on higher education.[45] In the United States between 1987 and 1995 spending on what is called corrections rose by 30 per cent. On elementary and secondary education it fell by 1.2 per cent and on higher education by 18.2 per cent.[46] As criminologist Elliott Currie describes it, money for prisons 'was taken from the parts of the public sector that educate, train, socialize, treat, house and nurture the population, especially the children of the poor'.[47]

The prison has become the social agency that deals with the poor. In prison many poor people get free health care, job training, education and drug counselling.

The investment in imprisonment has been massive, overtaking higher education, disrupting families, decimating communities, inflicting suffering on millions. The prison explosion took place simultaneously, as Elliott Currie argues, with starving 'communities of colour' of resources.

> As our poorest communities were sending an unparalleled flood of young people into the jails and prisons, many communities were simultaneously being turned literally into hollow shells – places without stores or jobs, without health care or mental health care, with crumbling schools and non-existent recreation programmes – with virtually no legitimate things for young people to do.[48]

It is an 'extraordinary social experiment'.[49] If 'prison works', the prison explosion should have led to a safe, relatively peaceful society in the US, like some of those in Europe. It should have given the general public some feeling of confidence that crime was being contained. It has not. Throughout the 1980s the proportion of the US public agreeing that violent crime was the most important problem facing the country was between 2 and 6 per cent. In 1995 it was 25 per cent, a halving of the figure of 52 per cent in 1994,[50] but still five times higher than in 1981, the year the prison population started to soar.[51]

Finally, the opponents argue that as a method of reducing crime mass imprisonment is the least efficient method available. Criminals are being produced faster than they can be locked up. Any other approach that concentrated on reducing the number of recruits to the criminal world by looking at the social causes would be more effective.

So mass incarceration is the least effective way of reducing crime. People do not feel safer. The policy is being pursued at enormous expense. Much of the money is being spent to incarcerate people well beyond their crime-prone years. Furthermore, the availability of all this money for imprisonment has, not surprisingly, led to another disturbing development. Imprisoning so many people provides a considerable amount of work for someone. There are prisons to design and build, equipment to be bought, security devices to be installed and then prisoners to guard, feed, clothe, educate, provide telephones for, and subject to psychological testing and urine sampling. A host of industries can thrive on the needs of a few hundred human beings, locked up and with no possibility of making choices about who provides them with services.

Who is getting all these opportunities? Much of it goes to the growing numbers of prison staff, who are public employees, but there is a sizeable tranche available for the private companies. Imprisonment is becoming big business. In the United States many companies are doing very well out of it, companies like Mark Correctional Systems. They make stainless-steel stacking cells that can be put together to form a prison in just a few days. To get the product right they consulted prisoners. The prisoners showed them how to use a cigarette lighter to melt down plastic forks into a tool that could break any ordinary cell bolt. They told them that urine can eventually wear a hole in a cement cell. So the cells made by Mark Correctional Systems are stainless steel, with tamperproof bolts, nothing that would allow prisoners to 'get hurt, hang themselves and sue'.[52]

Small towns are queuing up to get a prison placed in their neighbourhood. In Appleton, Minnesota, the city coordinator, desperate to bring industry to the dying town, tried to persuade all kinds of manufacturers to set up factories there. Eventually he raised the money to build a 500-bed prison. The town would run the prison and lease the places in it to the counties or to the state. There would be jobs for 160 people, all prepared to work for $14,000 a year, whilst guards in state prisons were paid $23,000 a year.[53]

Hawaii was in trouble with the courts because of prison overcrowding. So the Hawaiian authorities went to Texas. They were met at the airport by a 'broker' who took them round to show them what was on offer. They could buy prison places with outdoor recreation and education for a certain price per day. Without these facilities they would be cheaper. The broker was paid commission on the places he sold. The Hawaiian prisoners were then shipped to Texas, 5000 miles from their homes. Prisoners from Massachusetts and New Mexico had also been placed in Texas.[54]

Prison companies are becoming a new and growing investment opportunity. At the end of 1996 a conference was held in Dallas, Texas, for people wanting to 'capitalize on a new era of opportunities'. The conference, 'Privatizing Correctional Facilities; Private Prisons: Maximize Investment Returns in this Exploding Industry', was directed at investment managers and attended by 130 people. The invitation brochure began:

> Dear Executive
> Can you afford to bypass a tremendous opportunity to invest in stocks showing great performance and high returns? Privatization of correctional facilities is the newest trend in the area of privatizing previously government-run programs that can offer such optimal rewards . . .
>
> While arrests and convictions are steadily on the rise, profits are to be made – profits from crime. Get in on the ground floor of this booming industry now!

The brochure had a heading, 'Understand why the private prison industry is one of the fastest growing markets today'. The answer was clear. 'Just consider the current inmate populations in adult facilities combined with population growth at juvenile detention centers.' Young criminals would become older criminals. The future was bright.

Attenders at the conference (cost $1295; government employees only $995; register three, the fourth comes free) got tours of two correctional facilities run by the biggest firms. One was a 'secure, co-correctional, intermediate sanction facility' with three separate programmes, a 120-bed boot camp, a 140-bed substance-abuse programme and a sixty-bed short-term sanction programme. The residents were all non-violent offenders and probation violators. The violators had committed technical breaches of their probation such as not notifying the authorities of a change of address or a new job, or had committed new minor offences. It was run by Correctional Services Corporation.

The other facility on the visits programme was run by Wackenhut, the second largest private incarceration company. This was a pre-release centre with 520 beds for Texas prisoners within two years of parole eligibility. It concentrated on basic education and pre-employment training.

The conference offered sessions on stock market performance of the prison industry, forecasts about the growth potential, risks and rewards. Investment opportunities in firms providing management of juvenile correctional facilities were discussed. The speakers for this session came from organizations with soothing names like Children's Comprehensive Services, Youth Track Inc., Youth Services International.[55] The chairman of the board of Wackenhut Corrections Corporation left Wackenhut in August 1996 to join Youth Services International.[56]

The Prison Reform Trust reports that one of the speakers advised

> A contract must be tightly written so inmates can't be pulled out easily, leaving a prison without revenue. You want to keep it so that there's not a lot the state can do if there's a riot or unhappiness with the management.

Another advised providers to build prisons even if there was no contract. 'Build and they will come,' he said.[57]

What should one make of this phenomenon? Is there anything wrong with asking people whose business is security to run prisons on behalf of the public, providing they keep to the contract they have signed with the public authority and there are no abuses of

those in their care? Who are the private imprisoners and how far
have their operations reached? Why are so many penal reformers
deeply opposed to this development?

Making money out of locking people up is not a new idea. It has
a long and brutal history in the southern states of the US. Wilbert
Rideau tells how in the 1840s all the prisoners in the state penitentiary
in Baton Rouge, Louisiana, were leased to a private firm to serve as
cheap labour for use in its profit-making enterprises.

To ensure the profit, food and clothing were reduced to subsistence
level. The owners worked the prisoners till they dropped and maintained order with 'brutal force'.[58] The prisoners were freed during
the Civil War but privatization returned in 1869 and for the next
thirty years the prisoners were used as slaves in a range of profit-
making activities.[59]

Death rates amongst leased prisoners were very high. A doctor
in Alabama estimated in 1883 that most prisoners leased out as
workers died within three years. In that year a third of the men
working in one coal mine died. Half the prisoners working on a
railroad died every year.[60] It is estimated that about 3000 men,
women and children prisoners died from their treatment during that
period.[61] In some states of the US the contract system persisted until
1960.[62] In Texas prisoners were leased for a few dollars a month to
farmers and other businessmen. According to prison-works theorist
John Dilulio,

> Most convicts died within seven years of their incarceration . . .
> Conditions were so horrid that some inmates were driven to suicide
> while others maimed themselves to get out of work or as a pathetic
> form of protest.[63]

The late twentieth-century phase of privatizing prisons began in
the mid 1980s and not surprisingly it started in the United States. It
arose from a combination of two forces: the attempt to squeeze
rapidly growing prison populations into too little space, and the
popularity of the idea of the private sector carrying out what were
formerly seen as government functions.[64] The movement started in
1979 with private companies running detention centres for the US
Immigration and Naturalization Service. The centres held illegal

immigrants before they appealed against deportation or were deported.[65] Growth was slow. By 1988 only 1 per cent of the places in US prisons and jails was under private contract.[66] But the movement was given impetus by a commission set up by President Reagan which reported in 1988. The Commission recommended contracting out as an appropriate way of running prisons at all levels in the US system.[67] The private prison business is dominated by two large firms. One is the Corrections Corporation of America and the other is Wackenhut. The largest, Corrections Corporation of America (CCA), was incorporated in 1983. It is based in Nashville, Tennessee, and is financed in part by some of the same investors that had helped launch both the Hospital Corporation of America and Kentucky Fried Chicken.[68] Its prison business started in earnest when at the end of 1985 it won the contract to run the 370-bed jail for Bay County, Florida.[69] Its founder, Tom Beaseley, is reported to have said, 'There are rare times when you get involved in something that is productive and profitable and humanistic. We're on the verge of a brand new industry.'[70]

In 1994 CCA formed an alliance with the French company Sodexho to work towards generating business in Europe.[71] In November 1996 CCA and its subsidiaries had contracts for 38,801 prison places in the US, Puerto Rico, Australia and the UK.[72] CCA also owns Transcor Incorporated, the largest US prisoner transport company.[73]

The second largest company, Wackenhut Corrections Corporation, is a subsidiary of Wackenhut Corporation Inc. The parent corporation was founded in the 1950s by a former FBI agent. It operates in the US, Australia and the UK. It was formed in 1984[74] and started with a small 167-bed detention centre for the US Immigration Service in Colorado in 1986. The centre was up and running five months after the signing of the contract.[75] Then it won a contract from the state of California for a 200-bed prison for probation and parole violators. Two further contracts were awarded by the state of Texas and came on stream in 1989.[76] According to its Director of Corporate Relations, Wackenhut Corporation is an 'entrepreneurial pacesetter in the business of corrections management service'. Further, 'the Corporation is committed to the globalization of its diversified services and the worldwide application of its considerable experience and expertise in corrections management'.[77]

At the end of September 1996, Wackenhut had 24,282 prison places either up and running or in development.[78] In November 1996 the Corrections Corporation had fifty-seven prison facilities, and a design capacity of 38,801 places.[79]

What is known about the operations of the private prisons? England is one of the major experimenters with privatization. It was a rapid development. In 1984 the ultra-free-market think tank, the Adam Smith Institute, produced a pamphlet advocating the privatization of prisons.[80] Much of the response to it suggested that it was seen as an eccentric and unrealizable idea, not to be taken too seriously. In 1986 the Permanent Secretary at the Home Office said there were no plans to privatize prisons.[81] But two backbench Conservative MPs, John Wheeler and Sir Edward Gardner, were very keen on the idea. They were both members of the House of Commons Home Affairs Select Committee and the committee carried out an inquiry into private contract prisons. The committee visited the US and then in May 1987 produced a three-page report, supported by the Conservative members of the committee but opposed by the Labour ones, urging an experiment with a private prison, particularly for remand prisoners.[82] In July 1987 the Home Secretary at the time, Douglas Hurd, made it clear that he thought there was no case for 'auctioning or privatizing the prisons'.[83] But that was the last high-level expression of resistance. Shortly afterwards the notion of a private remand prison was being canvassed by a junior Home Office minister[84] and in 1989 a unit was set up at the Home Office to be in charge of contracts for private prisons. Then in 1991 the law was changed to allow all types of prison to be run by private contractors and the race for privatization was on.[85]

The first private prison in England, called the Wolds and catering for 320 remand prisoners, opened in 1992 in North Humberside.[86] The £30 million contract was won by the security company, Group Four.[87] In 1994 the remit of the Wolds was extended to include sentenced prisoners and in 1996 the contract was renewed and the number of places increased to 400.[88] Group Four also won the

£33 million contract for Buckley Hall, near Rochdale. Buckley Hall had serious problems during its first two years of operation. It experienced 117 security failures, including nineteen assaults, and thirty temporary release failures. Internal investigations and revisions of procedure occurred and twenty-eight staff resigned.[89]

The events at Buckley Hall were not unexpected. Often private prisons seem to start off badly and then gradually sort out their teething troubles and settle down. For example, Blakenhurst in Hereford and Worcester, a 650-place prison for sentenced and remand prisoners run by UK Detention Services, a consortium of companies including the Corrections Corporation of America, had a host of problems in its first two years. In 1993 there was a sit-in by prisoners protesting at the food which, according to an ex-prisoner, 'looked as if it had come from Marks and Spencer'. The director, a former governor of Wormwood Scrubs Prison in London, averted the crisis by ordering the catering staff to produce a fry-up of bacon, chips and beans. A month earlier a photograph of the director unlocking one of the cells had appeared in a local newspaper. The key was visible in the photo and most of the prison then had to have new locks fitted for security reasons. Soon afterwards he was sent to the US for retraining.[90] The contractors were fined for breaking the contract by losing control of the prison in February 1994.[91] In July 1996 one of the three firms in UK Detention Services, the building firm Mowlem,[92] pulled out and in December 1996 the other British partner in the consortium, a company run by Sir Robert McAlpine, also pulled out. This left the prison wholly US-owned.[93]

An even more stormy start affected Doncaster Prison, which is run by Premier Prison Services, a joint venture between Wackenhut and another firm, Serco. Doncaster opened in June 1994 and was soon named 'Doncatraz' by press and prisoners. In the first year the Home Office put in a senior prison governor for two weeks to monitor performance. The company was issued with three default notices, about cleanliness, escorting prisoners around the prison and failure to carry out sufficient roll-call checks. About twenty extra staff and managers had to be drafted in and Wackenhut sent a corporate task force to review the workings of the prison. The police were called in seven times in the first few months. Three months after the prison opened the Prison Reform Trust received a letter from a prisoner in Doncaster which said, '. . . people like me are getting smacked every day and the lads that do it get away with doing it in front of the officers who don't do anything . . . This prison is so poorly run it is unbelievable . . . I have had beatings every single day.'[94]

Between the opening date and November of the following year there were ninety-six attempted suicides at Doncaster, the highest figure for any prison for that period. Seven prisoners had succeeded in committing suicide by May 1996.[95] However, when the Chief Inspector of Prisons carried out an inspection in 1996, much must have improved as he gave Doncaster a very favourable report, calling it 'one of the most progressive prison establishments in the country'.[96]

New private prisons do not hit troubles only in England. Privatization of children's prisons started badly in Louisiana too, where a prison for children and young people under eighteen, run by a private company, Transamerican Development Associates, opened in November 1994 in the town of Tallulah. According to Human Rights Watch, 'The location was chosen for economic development purposes.'

The Louisiana Department of Public Safety and Corrections paid a fee for each child incarcerated at the Tallulah institution.[97] When the institution started taking children in November and December 1994, there were considerable problems. The staff were unable to keep control. Some of the children claimed that they were bused there in the middle of the night from other institutions without being told where they were going or what was happening to them. In December 1994 a federal court declared a state of emergency at the institution and the management of it was passed back to the state authorities.[98]

But in spite of the support for privatization in the US, less than 2 per cent of all prison places there are run by private contractors. The real enthusiast for privatization seems to be Australia. A larger percentage of prisons is privatized in Australia than in any other country.[99] There are two private prisons in Queensland, Borallon and Arthur Gorrie, and one in New South Wales, Junee. They too had their problems at the beginning. Borallon was opened in 1990 and is run by the Corrections Corporation of Australia, a subsidiary of CCA.[100] Wackenhut has a share in the companies running Arthur Gorrie and Junee and there have been problems at both. Arthur Gorrie, which is the main reception centre for all Queensland's prisons, opened in 1992 and the management team had to be changed in the first year. Between November 1992 and October 1994, according to *Prison Privatisation Report International*, published by the Prison Reform Trust, 'there were five deaths in custody, riots, fires, beatings and a pack rape'.[101]

The state of Victoria has the highest proportion of private prisons of any jurisdiction in the world. In 1997 Victoria was set to have 45 per cent of its prisoners in private prisons.[102]

In Canada attempts to privatize have not proceeded with the ease that they have in Australia. In 1993 the government of Alberta considered privatization but strong resistance from public employees led the government to announce in 1996 that privatization would not go ahead.[103] In New Brunswick the provincial government was planning to contract with Wackenhut to build and run a new youth prison but after a campaign against privatization the government announced that the prison would be privately built but the decision on how it would be run would be postponed.[104]

Private prisons provide plenty of material for seekers after prison scandals. For example, according to the Prison Reform Trust, in just one month, August 1996, the Correction Corporation of America faced a range of difficulties. Seven boys escaped from a juvenile prison in South Carolina run by CCA so the manager was transferred, the number of staff increased and security stepped up. In a CCA prison in Houston, Texas, two sex offenders beat up a prison officer and escaped. Prisoners at the Eden Detention Center started a disturbance which lasted twelve hours and in which guards shot the prisoners with buckshot and used pepper gas to quell the outbreak. Fourteen prisoners were hurt and one staff member suffered a broken jaw.[105] But the public prison sector has scandals aplenty too. Private prisons are not scandal-free, but prisons are made for scandals and they all have them. It cannot be an argument against them. Nor can the quality of what they provide. It seems that they are no more cruel and uncaring than state institutions. Also, their greatest selling point is that they are supposed to be cheaper than state institutions. Is this really the case?

So far, the evidence is inconclusive. The private prison providers say they are. Wackenhut claims savings. Douglas McDonald, who works for a research company in Cambridge, Massachusetts, and has written extensively on privatization concludes, 'the claims of the private sector's superior cost-effectiveness . . . are less robust than they might first appear'.[106]

A study done for the British Home Office by accountants Coopers and Lybrand in 1996 shows that private prisons are between 13 and 22 per cent cheaper than public sector prisons but suggests that the cost gap has narrowed slightly since 1993/4.[107] However, concerns about the study have been expressed by the Prison Reform Trust, which has a special unit studying all aspects of privatization as it develops. Apparently the definitions of the cost are not entirely satisfactory and the results of the study may be flawed.[108] A further study published in October 1996 which looked at the British data for 1995–6 shows that the cost gap between public and private prisons had narrowed because private prisons had become more expensive and public prisons had become cheaper. Private prisons provided more hours of purposeful activity for prisoners but had higher rates of prisoner assaults. However, the Director-General of the Prison Service, Richard Tilt, said in September 1996, '. . . the great majority of the cost reduction comes from the payment of much lower wages and poorer conditions of service for staff working in the private sector'.[109]

In New South Wales, the Minister of Corrective Services decided not to privatize another prison because the experience with the prison at Junee suggested that private prisons were no cheaper.[110] The General Accounting Office of the US federal government produced a report in 1996 based on an analysis of five studies that compared the cost and quality of private and public prisons. The report advised that no firm conclusions could be drawn from the studies done so far. Because of defects in the research it could not be deduced from currently available information that private prisons were cheaper or better than public prisons. The most soundly based of the studies, carried out in Tennessee, found that there was little difference in average cost per prisoner per day between public and private prisons.[111]

If private prisons are not necessarily cheaper what other reasons are there for privatization? Politicians have argued that a little bit of privatization is a good thing because it will frighten the prison staff in the public sector and their unions into greater co-operation by instilling in them fear of losing their jobs to private competitors. According to this argument, obstruction by prison staff has caused many problems in the past, and has delayed many penal reforms that would benefit prisoners. Staff feeling the cold wind of private competition blowing down their necks are more likely to accept changes in working practices and the need for efficiency savings. Indeed it is argued that privatization in England has had that effect.

Supporters argue that intrinsically anyone can run a prison and it is the duty of the government simply to look for the best deal. As the Adam Smith Institute said in its seminal pamphlet in 1984, 'Both security firms and hotel operations are commonplace in the private sector: it may be an over-simplification but a prison . . . involves little more than a combination of these two talents.'[112]

So governments should opt for the cheapest and most efficient, just as would be done with garbage collection and school meals provision. George C. Zoley, President of the Wackenhut Corrections Corporation, explained how simple it was in an article in the *Prison Service Journal*, the magazine of the prison service staff in England and Wales.

> A free enterprise system provides certain goods and services based upon the demand in the market place. As demand increases, so does competition. This tends to increase quality and lower cost as companies vie for market share. Government is a customer . . .[113]

So it sounds very simple. What arguments are deployed against it? Practical questions abound. This is private enterprise without competition. There is no choice. No one says to the judge in the courtroom, you can send the prisoner to Wackenhut for £400 a week or Premier Prisons for £350, so that competition forces the prices down and saves the state a lot of money. Competition is present at the time of the placing of the contract but after that the state is at the mercy of the contractor.

If the firm goes bankrupt, or is providing a very unacceptable service, what then? Can the state simply take over? What will the terms be? What will happen to the hundreds of prisoners being held in a prison by a company teetering on the verge of collapse?

Problems of justice and accountability feature prominently in the debate. The eminent criminologist Sir Leon Radzinowicz said in 1988, when privatization was first being discussed in Britain,

> . . . in a democracy grounded on the rule of law and public account-ability the enforcement of penal legislation, which includes prisoners deprived of their liberty while awaiting trial, should be the undiluted responsibility of the state. It is one thing for private companies to provide services for the prison system but it is an altogether different matter for bodies whose motivation is primarily commercial to have coercive powers over prisoners.[114]

The *Toronto Star*, when discussing the plans for privatizing the prisons in New Brunswick in Canada, noted that 'prisons always should be in the business of putting themselves out of business. How many profit-seeking firms want to do that?'[115]

Certainly there will be a range of decisions private prison staff have to take where a conflict of interest is inevitable. Anyone working for an organization which has the objective of making a profit has to make decisions in the light of that imperative. If the profit comes from having a peaceful prison, or a full prison, decisions taken will reflect that imperative. If it is better for the director's bonus at the end of the year to have had fewer incidents, then the difficult prisoners will be transferred and the docile ones will be kept, regardless of other considerations. It could well be in the interests of private prison contractors to have their prisons full and keep their prisoners as long as possible. So, even if they do not have the formal power to recommend parole or to take the decisions on prisoner punishments and any consequent additional days in prison, their access and control give them all the informal power they need to affect these decisions.

Is it right to give private companies such control over their fellow citizens? In the state of Victoria in Australia, the Metropolitan Women's Prison run by CCA has employed an 'intelligence' officer. According to the Prison Reform Trust, the intelligence officer will 'collect information on prisoners, staff, visitors, and other persons of interest to the prison system'. The officer will have the power to monitor prison phone calls, put together intelligence checks on visitors to the prison and will be given access to criminal records held in the Justice Department.[116]

Surprisingly, the Conservative thinker and supporter of mass incarceration John Dilulio opposes private prisons. He argues that private prisons are wrong because only governments can administer sanctions.

> . . . to continue to be legitimate and morally significant, the authority to govern those behind bars, to deprive citizens of their liberty, to coerce (and even kill) them, must remain in the hands of government authorities . . . The administration of prisons and jails involves the legally sanctioned coercion of some citizens by others. The coercion is exercised in the name of the offended public. The badge of the arresting police officer, the robes of the judge, and the state patch of the corrections officer are symbols of the inherently public nature of crime and punishment.[117]

These arguments are important ones. But there is a greater cause for concern than whether private prison contractors will go bankrupt or whether it is symbolically acceptable. The involvement of such a large sector of US business in incarceration creates what some people there have called a prison–industrial complex. The analogy is with the military–industrial complex, an unholy triangle between the government contractors who manage the Defense Department and place the orders, the private companies that get the business, and the politicians. Between them they create a policy pressure for more, not just in the US but all around the world where the salespersons are operating. In the time of the Cold War it was more tanks and missiles, ships and guns. In the age of the prison–industrial complex it is more barbed wire, prefabricated cells and electronic door-locking equipment. A few minutes with an issue of the magazine of the American Correctional Association, *Corrections Today*, shows the extent of the business opportunities.

There is Ameritech Speaker ID, the electronic monitoring system that offers significant advantages over bracelets and anklets because it monitors the person instead of the equipment and 'can identify an offender with a cold or even detect a twin'.[118] Modular Detention Facilities can give you a prison up and running in 120 days. There is a plumbing control system that 'helps establish order when inmates seek to wreak havoc with the plumbing'.[119] Airteq electric locks are the quietest locks and 'a quieter prison means better control'.[120] The violent-prisoner chair is illustrated by a photograph of a man strapped with his hands behind his back into a small folding chair.[121] Humane Restraint makes 'leather and nylon restraints that have stood the test of time'.[122] The CRSS company advertises its building service with the proud boast that it won the contract to install electrified fences round prisons in the whole of California.[123] Motor Coach Industries (MCI) produces the 'prison on wheels', the inmate security transportation vehicle with interior cells, windows that withstand over 1500 pounds of force, bulletproof side walls and windows and a special rear door for security officers to make a quick escape if need be.[124] The leading maker of x-ray products makes a body-search machine illustrated by a picture of a fully clothed prisoner standing with his back to the machine and an officer looking at him naked on a screen.[125] Protective helmets are available for prison staff 'to resist the risk of head injury' and 'to assist with behavioral problems'.[126] There is an 'impenetrable steel security wall' which is made of such small mesh that no knife or gun can pass through it and fingers cannot get a grip.[127] A photograph of an ugly and threatening face crowned by a woollen hat peering through a wire fence advertises 'intelli-flex', the alarm system that can tell the difference between rain and snow storms, a sudden gust of wind and a prisoner trying to escape.[128] Jefferson Pipe and Supply Co produces 'Quick Bite', a 'Contraband/Anti-Communication Prison trap' that prevents voice communication from cell to cell and stops prisoners retrieving hidden contraband from the sewer system.[129] Mace Security International 'offers a complete line of tear gas grenades, projectiles and impact cartridges. From riot control to one-on-one confrontations with hostile inmates, we have you covered.' This firm also offers 'ceilingmountable tear gas dispensers that can be electronically triggered from a remote location . . . essential to safely controlling inmate uprisings'.[130]

The striking feature of these advertisements is the ethos they convey, an ethos carried over from the Cold War. The prison world is a battleground. The prisoners are the enemy and they will try anything to outwit their jailers. The job of the system is to thwart every attempt of this enemy to fight back against its surroundings. A whole sector of US industry is now devoted to the war against US citizens. This is not a society incarcerating some of its dangerous citizens and trying to keep them secure whilst working with them to sort out their problems and eventually return them to society. This is a war and the prisoners are prisoners of war, people of another country or another race. The prisoners keep thinking of new ways to break cell fittings, secrete contraband, attack staff. The manufacturers produce a better or another product designed to prevent the prisoners succeeding. It is another arms race. They make a better nuclear missile. So the other side makes an even better nuclear missile.

The danger is that the politicians and the business people will both be perfectly content to lock up a large and growing proportion of the citizenry. It suits them both: it helps the business people to make money and the politicians to get elected. The question has to be asked: why should there be any limit? These processes need never stop. More and more people can go to prison. The logic of three strikes and you're out could equally apply to two strikes and you're out. What is the argument then against one strike and you're out? The logic that follows from that is that if you come from a one-strike-and-you're-out family, you are likely to follow in your father's footsteps, so let us take you out now, before the first crime is committed. You come from a neighbourhood where 50 per cent of the African-American men in their twenties are in prison. Since you have grown up with them and are at risk of becoming a criminal why not put you in prison now and prevent the crimes you are bound to commit at some time in the future?

What is wrong after all with locking up 1 per cent or 3 per cent or 5 per cent of the population if the other 99 or 97 or 95 per cent approve of it? If it were to stop now, what would happen to all the businesses making money out of security and incarceration?

If the present rate of growth of continues, 4.5 million black men will be in prison in the US by the year 2020.[131] This will be very good for the prison business. But very bad for the future of their communities in particular and democracy in general. What will society be like when a majority of the young men from the inner cities have had their education in prison, have been inculcated with prison values?

Jerome Miller suggests what it will be like when the 'rules of survival in a maximum security correctional institution' become 'the ethics of the street'.[132] Breaking ranks with the prisoners, siding with the authorities, informing on other prisoners are all heinous offences in the prison world. Returning violence for violence and not being pushed around by others are rewarded with respect. As Miller says,

> We have socialized particularly inner-city young men to the mores of the prison so that you now have on the streets the warped philosophy of violence that holds correctional settings together. The kinds of behaviours that seem meaningless or senseless to the average observer, like drive-by shootings, killing someone over their sneakers or their athletic jacket, those are not senseless at all to anyone who knows prison life. Those are precisely the things that are done day in and day out in a prison. It has to do with status, it has to do with respect in front of your peers. You learn not to open your mouth and say anything unless you are willing to deliver in violence . . . you don't have a reputation in many large cities unless you've been to prison. You certainly can't be a gang leader unless you've done time.[133]

Naturally the rest of the public will want these young people locked up. And there will be more and more of them. So there will be pressure to do the locking-up more cheaply. The prisoners will be more desperate, prison-hardened, they will have nothing to lose. So there will be pressure for ever more secure prisons without more expense.

Nils Christie has argued in *Crime Control as Industry* that the massive prison expansion in the US is a response to one of the problems faced by modern societies. The problem is the emergence of a large group of unemployed young men whom society has no need of.[134] Indeed it has been argued that the US unemployment rate is kept lower than those of Western Europe by incarcerating 2 per cent of its male workforce. They react with anger and destructiveness to not being needed. The anger and destructiveness have to be controlled. But he argues that the method chosen to deal with this, putting them under penal control, is unprecedented in a democracy and very dangerous.

> It is a blessed situation for industry, it's a blessed situation for people who want to have minority groups under control, and it is a fatal situation for democratic ideals and for basic values within our social systems . . . do we really want to live in societies where a majority of the minority are in prisons and where concentration camps are the major cultural invention in the years to come?[135]

Industry has a natural inclination to grow. If society has no notion of a ceiling on the numbers in prison, no idea of whether it wants to stop and if so at what point, growth will simply continue.

Jerome Miller makes the gloomy forecast of a prison population of between 3 to 5 million people in the United States. It will have become 'a gulag society with the majority of young American men of color in prison or camps'.[136] If this happens, the criminal justice system will have been replaced by a different system – internment.

In a justice system each case is considered and weighed, mitigating and aggravating circumstances are considered. Judges bring to bear human experience and understanding. They start from the premise that society should be strengthened in some way by what happens in the particular case, whether it is denunciation, or mercy or reformation. They look for a solution as well as for retribution.

Internment is introduced in a war, when there are people who might be dangerous, but since it is not possible to know which ones might be dangerous, all of those with certain characteristics are locked up. This is what happened at the beginning of the Second World War to anyone who had come to Britain from Germany, even refugees from Nazism eager to fight against Hitler. To lock up those who by committing a crime, albeit minor, show that they could be career criminals in the future is to move to the internment principle.

The world's leading theorist on punishment, David Garland, describes punishment as serving many functions other than just dealing with crime. Punishment is also 'a forceful display of state power and a means of upholding the rule of law'. It is 'a statement of collective morality and a vehicle for emotional expression'.[137] Extreme punitiveness, he argues, 'may pose as a symbol of strength, but it is actually a symptom of weak authority and inadequate social controls. An increasingly punitive society is generally a society that is in moral decline.'[138]

Indeed a look at the countries that have had very high rates of imprisonment at some time in their history supports this thesis. The Soviet Union at the height of the totalitarian repression used imprisonment like internment to rid society of political and class enemies, as they were called. South Africa did the same under the apartheid system. Is it inevitable that the Western democracies will take this path as they enter the twenty-first century? Or is there a better way? The next chapter aims to answer these questions.

14. *A Better Way?*

Anyone trying to deal with the reality of crime, as opposed to the fantasies peddled to win elections, needs to understand the complex suffering of survivors of traumatic crimes and the suffering and turmoil of their families. I have impressive physical scars . . . a broad purple line from my breastbone to the top of my pubic bone, an X-shaped cut into my side where the chest tube entered . . . But the disruption of my psyche is more noticeable. For weeks I awoke each night agitated, drenched in perspiration. For two months I was unable to write . . . Though to all appearances normal, I feel at a long arm's remove from all the familiar sources of pleasure, comfort and anger that shaped my daily life . . . What psychologists call post-traumatic stress disorder is, among other things, a profoundly political state in which the world has gone wrong, in which you feel isolated from the broader community by the inarticulable extremity of experience . . . As a crime victim and a citizen, I want the reality of a safe community – not a politician's fantasy land of restitution and revenge.

Bruce Shapiro, who was seriously wounded in a stabbing in Connecticut in 1994[1]

The last chapter showed that more and more of the commodity we call prison is being produced. New prison buildings are being put up. Facilities no longer needed for other purposes, such as military bases, even former holiday camps, are being adapted. Creativity is being applied to think of even more ways of depriving human beings of their liberty – putting them on disused passenger boats, for instance. Energy, effort and money on an unprecedented scale are being used in the search for more and better ways of subjecting larger numbers of people to the prison experience. As the last chapter showed, this is an experience with a very limited protection effect, that is unarguably and universally damaging and negative wherever it takes place and however decent are those administering it.

The contradictions and dysfunctionalities at the heart of prison have been well documented since it came into use as the main punishment for crime. In the well-known words of a British White

Paper produced in 1990, when Margaret Thatcher was the Conservative Prime Minister, prison 'can be an expensive way of making bad people worse'.[2] Or, as the same sentiments were put by Dostoevsky in *The House of the Dead*, '. . . if [prisoners] had not been depraved beforehand, they became so in prison'.[3]

Prince Peter Kropotkin commented that prisons are institutions 'based on a false principle'.[4] They fail almost completely in their job of turning people from crime. Prisoners keep going back. In the French Central Prisons, where he served his time, prisoners who had a good prison job before they were released 'used to ask that the post they occupied be kept open for them until their next return'.[5] The information on French recidivism rates for 1882 is not available but prisoners leaving the former abbey that became Clairvaux prison, where Kropotkin was locked up, are probably just as likely to return to crime now as they were then.

Certainly much worthy work is done in prison to knock a few points off the recidivism index for a few prisoners. There is no doubt that some efforts to help prisoners whilst they are in prison to change their way of life will be successful. But they will be successful only when the prison is turned into an ante-room to the outside world, when whatever is done in prison aims to solve the problems that brought them there in the first place and will reoccur when the prisoner leaves the prison and sets off back into the world. Such successes are achieved only by limiting and mitigating prison's effects, linking it up to opportunities for work, self-respect and stability. They take place in spite of prison, not because of it.

The contradictions at the heart of imprisonment were well expressed by Alexander Paterson, who became Prison Commissioner in 1922: '. . . it is impossible to train men for freedom in conditions of captivity'.[6]

We have seen that most of the people in prison are poor. Their crimes are not serious or dangerous. Yet locking them up is the option society chooses. Why have we ended up with this solution to the problem?

The main character in Tolstoy's *Resurrection*, Nekhlyudov, ponders this conundrum as he sits in court watching the trial of a lad who had been sacked from his job, so went out and got drunk, then broke into a shed and stole some old mats.

> It's quite obvious that this lad is no extraordinary villain, but just an ordinary person . . . he became what he is simply because he found himself in circumstances which create such people . . . But what do we do? . . . By chance we get hold of just one such unfortunate lad, knowing quite well that a thousand others remain at liberty, and shut him up in prison, in conditions of complete idleness or work of the most unhealthy, senseless kind, in company with fellow beings like himself, debilitated and confused by life, and then deport him at public expense to Irkutsk in company with the most depraved characters from Moscow and surrounding places . . . We rear not one, but millions of such people, and then arrest one and imagine that we have done something, protected ourselves, and that nothing more can be required of us, now that we have transported him from Moscow to Irkutsk.[7]

Václav Havel, former prisoner and then president, wrote to his wife, Olga, from prison about how sorry he felt 'for the other prisoners, and altogether, for the fact that prisons must exist and that they are as they are, and mankind has not so far invented a better way of coming to terms with certain things'.[8]

Earlier chapters have shown how problematic the institution of prison is. It is a deformed world, where the ills of society are distorted and exacerbated. It is a world of danger, where riots may break out, hostages may be taken, the weak may be terrorized and killed. It is a world where people are given unprecedented power over their fellow men and women and vast apparatuses of supervisory mechanisms and procedures have had to be created to ensure this power is not abused. It is an institution that creaks in every direction – problems adhere to it, like limpets. They cannot be shaken off. When one is solved, another is created.

No one should enter the twenty-first century with any illusions about it nor any hope that it will be magically transformed into something better. It is flawed beyond repair, a necessary evil, a bad use of resources, always to be avoided if something better can be found. And indeed this is the received wisdom about imprisonment when its use has been analysed and its contribution to crime control assessed. In 1990 the Canadian government issued a paper setting out some basic principles. It noted

> Restraint should be used in employing the criminal law because the basic nature of criminal sanctions is punitive and coercive, and since freedom and humanity are so highly valued, the use of other, non-coercive, less formal and more positive approaches is to be preferred wherever possible and appropriate.[9]

The Criminal Justice Act of 1991, as amended in 1993, for England and Wales, requires that the court shall not send a convicted person to prison unless

> the offence, or the combination of the offence and one or more offences associated with it, was so serious that only such a sentence can be justified for the offence: or

> where the sentence is for a violent or sexual offence, that only such a sentence would be adequate to protect the public from serious harm from him.[10]

The Council of Europe recommendation on community sanctions points out that

> the implementation of penal sanctions within the community itself rather than through a process of isolation from it may well offer in the long term better protection for society including, of course, the safeguarding of the interests of the victim.[11]

Looked at rationally the limitations of prison are so obvious, the arguments so long-standing and well rehearsed, that by now one would have thought there would be widespread disenchantment with it as the main response to crime. One would expect prison use to have been reduced to the minimum necessary to contain the uncontrollably violent criminals and the organized criminal gangs whilst resources are poured into projects designed to work out something better.

But is not like that at all. In fact, it is claimed that the public is clamouring for more prison. At least, when politicians offer more prison it seems to make them popular, whilst the non-prison solutions struggle for recognition, acceptance and funds. To suggest that we might do better than pour money into an ineffective solution that creates more social problems than it solves is apparently to court political oblivion. So what do people actually think? Are they clamouring? What are the better things and could they replace prison for a large percentage of the people now locked up? Do we have to carry on this way? Are we ready to move on from the nineteenth-century solution? This chapter deals with these questions.

What do people actually think? First, all the studies from Western industrialized societies indicate that punishment, even the cruel and degrading punishments outlawed by the international conventions signed by most countries in the world, is popular. People are in favour of a lot of imprisonment and many would go further. A majority seems to support the death penalty and corporal punishment. Retribution, inflicting suffering on those who have made others suffer, is what people say they want.

A superficial look at the research gives this impression. But views are not static. Certainly the response varies somewhat over time. In 1938 a Gallup poll in Britain showed that flogging was favoured by 50 per cent and capital punishment by 55 per cent.[12] By the 1980s the proportion in favour of the death penalty was over 70 per cent.[13] In 1996 an opinion poll showed that 70 per cent were in favour of corporal punishment as a penalty of the court.[14] Opinion on the death penalty is surveyed in the United States every year. In 1995 77 per cent were in favour of the death penalty. Yet in 1966 only a minority of those questioned – 42 per cent – were in favour. The figures of those in favour and opposed were very similar until 1972, when the number of death-penalty supporters started to increase.[15]

Levels of enthusiasm for harsh punishments differ from country to country. In the Netherlands the proportion in favour of the death penalty in 1985 was 40 per cent.[16] But everywhere there is a basic level of support for physical punishments. Some figures published in 1988 show that in Canada just over half of the sample questioned was in favour of the death penalty and another 30 per cent, though generally opposed to it, considered that there are some cases where 'it may be appropriate'. This left a mere 16 per cent opposed to it in all circumstances.[17] In Australia, meanwhile, 29 per cent favoured the death penalty for murder and 18 per cent for heroin trafficking.[18] And a poll carried out in New Zealand in 1994 showed that 24 per cent of people were in favour of physically disabling offenders to stop them committing more crimes. (The same question in 1985 showed only 5 per cent in favour.)[19]

The research also showed that people want longer sentences passed on criminals. Most of them think the sentences passed by the courts are too lenient. This is the finding from studies in a number of countries. For instance, surveys carried out in Canada over three decades showed that in the 1960s 43 per cent of those questioned thought sentences were not severe enough but by 1987 the figure was up to 78 per cent.[20] Similar findings come from the UK and the United States. In the United States more than 80 per cent of those sampled have felt that sentences are not harsh enough.[21]

So it seems simple. People know what they want and they have made it clear many times. A majority want harsh, retributive sentences. They want violence to be met with violence and for at least the most heinous murders they want the death penalty. Politicians are only responding to the strongly expressed will of the people when they say they have no leeway in penal policy and that responding to crime by mass incarceration expresses the wishes of the people.

But it is not so simple. More sophisticated surveys of public attitudes to crime show a much more complex picture with much more ambiguity about what the public would see as the best policy. The first area of complexity is knowledge. The surveys show that the public attitudes expressed about crime and punishment are based on profound ignorance. A high proportion of those questioned overstate by a great deal the proportion of crime that is violent. In Canada in 1983, only 4 per cent of people correctly identified the level of crime that was violent as between zero and 9 per cent of the total. Another 15 per cent of respondents were fairly close, guessing 10 to 29 per cent, but the vast majority of Canadians – three-quarters of the sample – were convinced that the level was anything between 30 and 100 per cent.[22]

Also, people claim that the sentences currently given by the courts are too lenient. But, in fact, they have no idea of the actual level of the sentences passed by the courts and when saying that sentencing is too lenient they are responding to their inaccurate view of the sentences passed. They usually base their ideas about leniency on what they read in the newspapers. All the research in the UK, Canada and Australia shows that people consistently underestimate the current severity of sentencing. A study done in the UK in 1995 by Mike Hough, formerly with the Home Office and at the time a professor at South Bank University, was based on in-depth discussions with eleven focus groups, about 100 people all told. Their views bore out earlier survey results. Sentences were much too lenient and judges and magistrates were totally and hopelessly out of touch. Yet when the participants in the groups were asked what proportion of offenders convicted of certain crimes they thought were sent to prison at the moment in Britain, many of them got it completely wrong. Half of them were sure that only one in two of those convicted of rape was sent to prison. In fact, the figure is 91 per cent. Three-quarters of them thought that four out of ten or fewer of those convicted of causing death by dangerous driving went to prison. The actual figure in England and Wales is over 70 per cent.[23]

But it is even more complex than that. Many of the studies showing heavily punitive findings are based on crude and loaded questions. Mike Hough gives the example of a question asked in 1982: 'What are your views about corporal punishment, that is birching and flogging? Should we continue to do without the cat, or should we bring it back?' The response was that 60 per cent wanted the cat back, 62 per cent were in favour of birching and 69 per cent, caning.[24] Similar loaded questions were asked in a survey carried out by ICM and reported in the *Daily Mail* in 1996 in the week of the launch of a government White Paper proposing much more severe sentences: 'At present the average jail sentence for a house burglar with three or more convictions is nineteen months. Do you consider this too lenient?'[25]

It is rather different when an approach is used which discusses crime and punishment in more depth. Giving a choice can elicit a different response. In 1994 in a US survey the question was asked: 'Are you in favour of the death penalty for a person convicted of murder?' Eighty per cent were in favour. A further question was asked: 'In your view, what should be the penalty for murder – the death penalty or life imprisonment with absolutely no possibility of parole?' The proportion supporting the death penalty fell to 50 per cent with 32 per cent supporting life imprisonment without parole.[26]

Being specific also produces a more sophisticated response. The latest of international comparative surveys of attitudes shows that when asked what is the right sentence for a twenty-one-year-old burglar who has burgled before, the proportion of those sampled suggesting imprisonment ranged from 56.2 per cent in the US through 49 per cent in England and Wales, and 48.4 per cent in Scotland to 9.4 per cent in Switzerland. The favoured punishment in Europe as a whole was a community service order.[27]

Table 13   Attitudes to imprisonment – percentage favouring imprisonment as the sentence for a repeat burglar aged 21

State	Date of survey	%
USA	1996	56.2
England and Wales	1996	49.0
N. Ireland	1996	48.7
Scotland	1996	48.4
Canada	1996	43.3
Australia	1992	34.0
Netherlands	1996	31.2
New Zealand	1992	25.6
Italy	1992	22.4
Sweden	1996	22.1
Belgium	1992	18.7
Finland	1996	17.5
Norway	1996	13.8
France	1996	10.7
Austria	1996	9.8
Switzerland	1996	9.4

Source: International Crime Victimisation Survey 1996

The research also shows that the more knowledge people are given and the more choices are presented to them, the more varied and thoughtful become their responses. As we have seen they usually say that in general the sentences passed by the courts are too soft. But when they are given the same information that the court was given when deciding on a particular sentence they are quite likely to accept the court's sentence as the right one. A novel sentencing exercise was carried out in 1991 in Delaware in the US by the Public Agenda Foundation. A representative group of 432 was chosen for the exercise. They were given twenty-three hypothetical cases to deal with, ranging from petty theft to rape and armed robbery. In the first part of the exercise they were asked to decide on a sentence and were given the choice of prison or probation involving a visit to a probation office once a month. They decided to send seventeen of the twenty-three to prison and gave probation to the other six. A majority of them also said that they believed the crime rate was rising, judges were too soft, most prison sentences should be longer and the state government should use capital punishment more often.

After the first sentencing exercise the group watched a video outlining the problem of prison overcrowding and describing five alternative sentences: intensive probation, restitution, community service, house arrest and boot camp. They then met in small groups for about ninety minutes to discuss the issues under the leadership of a neutral moderator. Finally they did the sentencing exercise again using a broader range of options. In the second exercise they wanted to send only five of the twenty-three offenders to prison, the five being the four violent offenders and a drug dealer on his fifth conviction. The group sentenced the other eighteen to the alternative sentences.[28]

It is not just in Delaware that this is the case. A study in Oregon in 1995 based on six focus groups and a telephone survey of 439 adults showed that, after being shown that alternative punishments would involve people being in the community rather than in prison, 92 per cent of people said they were in favour of sentences for non-violent offenders that did not involve prison. In Houston, a 1994 survey suggested that although three-quarters of residents saw crime as the city's greatest problem, only 38 per cent thought that spending more money on locking people up for long periods of time was the solution, compared with over half who favoured spending the money on reducing poverty and keeping young people in school.

A nationwide survey of 1003 Americans entitled 'Americans Look at the Drug Problem', which was carried out in February 1995, showed that over half felt that drug use was a public health rather than a criminal justice problem and would be best handled through prevention and treatment rather than incarceration.[29] In 1996 a sample of people in Ohio were asked about giving life sentences for the third offence. Eighty-eight per cent supported life sentences for specific crimes in the abstract. When they were given the case histories and asked to choose an appropriate sentence, only 17 per cent chose a life sentence. Most went for prison sentences of between five and fifteen years.[30]

Another intriguing complexity is that victims of crime are not generally more punitive than those who have not been victims. Three surveys carried out in the Netherlands showed that people who had been victims of crime were more in favour of preventive measures and were not enthusiastic about tough punishment. A study carried out in England of more than 300 burglary victims in 1982 found that fewer than 30 per cent wanted their burglar to go to prison.[31]

Other questions often asked in the surveys are about the purpose of punishments and the best ways of dealing with crime. Public opinion about what is achieved by sentencing is also more complex than it at first appears. Although on the face of it a majority is in favour of severe sentencing there is actually not much faith in criminal justice as a good way of dealing with crime. When people are asked what actually works in dealing with crime they tend to propose social measures. In the Delaware study, those sampled put illegal drug use and social problems, poverty, lack of education and availability of handguns highest up the list of the causes of crime.[32] The Canadian Sentencing Commission, which reported in 1987, asked a sample of the Canadian public whether any additional money made available would best be spent on more prisons or on alternatives to prison. Nearly three-quarters chose alternatives.[33] In 1986 Canadians were asked to name the most effective way to control crime. Twenty-seven per cent advocated making sentences harsher. Forty-one per cent advocated a reduction in unemployment.[34] In a survey carried out in Alberta in 1994 people were asked where additional money should be spent to achieve greatest impact on crime. Ninety per cent chose education and job training rather than imprisonment. Over two-thirds preferred compensation to be paid rather than a four-month prison sentence for someone who had burgled their house and taken $1100 worth of property.[35]

Of New Zealanders questioned in 1987, fully 85 per cent felt that reducing unemployment would lead to less crime, two-thirds thought 'rehabilitating offenders' would do the same, whereas longer sentences found favour with over half and increasing police numbers with 68 per cent. Eighty-five per cent favoured encouraging non-violence in school and 72 per cent wanted to reduce violence on TV and in films.[36] Even in the United States, where attitudes are at the harsh end of the spectrum, when asked whether crime was best reduced by spending on police, prisons and judges or on social and economic problems, nearly two-thirds wanted money spent on social and economic problems compared with 30 per cent on more law enforcement.[37]

What do people think is the purpose of prison? A survey in 1994 carried out in New Zealand showed over a third of people regarding the main purpose of prison as 're-educating the offender' (though this was down from 46 per cent in 1985), with a quarter citing punishing a wrongdoer as the main purpose, and 30 per cent (up from 18 per cent in 1985) seeing prison primarily as a means of protecting society. Only 3 per cent thought prison was chiefly a deterrent.[38] Over half favoured victim–offender meetings to 'put things right', and 83 per cent wanted periodical detention of offenders to do community work of a public or charitable nature.[39]

So what can the prison reformer looking for a better way glean from this information on what the public thinks? Is the divide between the majority and the reformers unbridgeable? Clearly there is a hunger for punishment, even for the cruel and degrading punishments outlawed in international law. This hunger runs very deep in the collective psyche, and seems to affect a majority, though there is always a minority which sees things very differently. How far this theoretical hunger would translate into practice is hard to say. It is worth imagining what would happen if, for example, corporal punishment became available again to the courts as a punishment. Eventually, the time comes for a convicted person to be beaten. In the build-up to carrying out the punishment the media give the full information on the desperately abusive home background the one to be beaten came from. His mother comes on the television to talk about how he had always tried to shield her from his violent and drunken father. After some hours of this coverage and column inches in the newspapers the response to the idea of actually beating him might in many countries be quite different.

It is also clear that many attitudes, certainly in the UK, the US and Canada, are based on quite inadequate information about the system as it currently works, its perceived leniency and the amount of crime dealt with by the courts that is serious and violent.

An understanding by a majority of the public of the underlying causes of crime, its relationships with social conditions such as unemployment, poverty and family background, and the greater effectiveness of prevention over law enforcement are all evident in the surveys. There is support for approaches to crime that try and provide solutions rather than just lock away problems.

The surveys show that whilst there is a bedrock of support for both ends of the spectrum on punishment there is a group in the middle that changes over time. The level of support for various ways of dealing with crime can be altered by circumstances and political climate. In many people, attitudes to these difficult matters are not fixed, inborn, fundamental or deeply rooted in their view of the world. A substantial proportion can respond and react to debate, facts, discussions and campaigns. They can listen to arguments and change their minds.

An overriding conclusion from a consideration of the information about public attitudes in Western Europe and North America suggests two outstanding features. One is a dire lack of information and explanation about how crimes are dealt with in the criminal justice process – the objectives, limitations and the philosophy behind it. The other is a deep dissatisfaction with a system that seems to be beyond and above most people, grinding on like a rickety machine. It does what it has always done, because it has always done it. It responds to ill-formulated but genuine public concerns with a little tightening up of procedure here, an erosion of rights there, a new bit of law, another activity made unlawful, another offence made imprisonable, more prosecutions for this or that offence, a bit more consideration for victims, with no overarching idea of what is to be achieved by it all.

Never discussed is the fact that most people convicted of a criminal offence in most Western countries do not go to prison. A dramatic exception is the US, where 70 per cent of all offenders convicted of a felony in state courts (about 900,000 in 1992) are sentenced to incarceration: 44 per cent to prison and 26 per cent to jail. In 1992, 81 per cent of those convicted of violent offences, two-thirds of those convicted of property felonies, three-quarters of those found guilty of drug trafficking and 62 per cent of those convicted of drug possession were incarcerated.[40] However, in other Western countries this is not the situation, and most of those convicted are given non-prison sentences. In England and Wales in 1995, 302,000 people were sentenced for indictable (the more serious) offences, and one-fifth of them were sent to prison. Thirty per cent were fined and 28 per cent were given another non-custodial penalty.[41] In Switzerland 17 per cent of those convicted are sent to prison.[42]

Yet another finding from the attitude surveys in Britain and elsewhere is the low visibility and credibility of the penalties other than prison. Any court punishment that is not a prison sentence is characterized as 'walking free' even though, looked at objectively, the other sanctions available to the courts seem to have many advantages. Community service, which was first introduced as a court sanction in England and Wales and has been exported to many other countries, combines making people do something they do not want to do (punishment), carrying out a task that is of benefit to the community (reparation), possibly showing the convicted person how needy people in the community live and what their problems are (social education), and opening up possibilities for becoming involved with the community in the longer term (social reintegration).

Being 'put on probation' is also regarded as walking free. Yet that too is a sensible and constructive approach to many of those who are convicted and have a range of problems that are the cause of them committing crime – drug addiction, drink, nowhere to live, mental illness, damaging home situations, no education and no chance of getting a job. In England and Wales there is even available a 'combination order' which enables the court to make the convicted person do community service and have the supervision of a probation officer as well.

People can also be asked to pay fines to the state, pay compensation to those they have harmed, live in special hostels, take courses or undergo treatment for various conditions. There are day centres where people are required to go for courses.

Looked at rationally this range of options seems remarkably impressive. A serious attempt is made to fit the person to the right sanction so that there is a useful outcome. All these options contain the possibility to do some good. Community service and compensation mean that something is paid back either to society in general or to the victim in particular. Probation and all the forms of treatment attempt to solve problems so that the person stops doing the criminal acts that have caused pain and damage. These measures try and hold the elements of society together rather than tear them apart, solve and rebuild rather than lock away for a while and cause more damage. In most West European countries and in Canada and Australia they are well established and stable, reasonably well organized and staffed by dedicated and well-trained people. In England and Wales three-quarters of community-service orders are carried out as the court requires and the person is not convicted of another crime during the order.[43] In most places the people that are subjected to them commit no more crimes afterwards than people who have been to prison and in some cases the results are even better.[44]

Why then are they politically and emotionally unattractive? Why do we not hear politicians boasting about their achievements in creating thousands more places for community service or for drug treatment? Why are they not more credible, publicly visible, talked about, at the centre of discussion? What explains their status as a poor second-best to the only 'real' punishment, which is prison? Why have they failed to catch the imagination and begun to be seen as the normal punishment for crime, just as prison began to replace physical punishments and transportation and be seen as the normal punishment for crime in the eighteenth and nineteenth centuries?

The path of non-prison penalties is the rational path for most criminals found guilty of most crimes in order to achieve protection, recompense for the harm done and a solution that might reduce crime in the future. But it must be clear by now that looking at crime and punishment rationally is desirable but difficult to achieve. Crime evokes complex emotions which override rational analysis. The hunger for punishment is not rational, but is undeniably a strong reaction in many. Clearly the non-prison penalties lack two elements which make prison so attractive to the public as a punishment. They do not take place behind the high walls of buildings that carry considerable symbolism, the symbolism of excluding the evil, so as to purge society of it, and allow all those not in prison to feel a bit more virtuous. Nor do they satisfy the more rational desire to have anti-social people taken out of circulation so that no more depredations can be carried out on the long-suffering populace.

But they do carry other messages which should have emotional resonance. Restitution and reparation are also long-standing elements of ways of responding to crime, with as rich a history as retribution. And the rational and common sense side of people would certainly be attracted by the possibility of actually solving the problem so that someone on the first steps of a criminal career changes tack and becomes a useful citizen instead.

But little seems to have been done to think through the meaning of non-prison penalties and ensure that they are provided in a way that meets the needs of the public to see that the harm that has been done is understood and there is a wish to make amends. Too often, the image is of the insouciant young man, laughing and showing off to his mates that he escaped prison this time and can get away with anything. This cannot compete with the picture of the uniformed prison guard taking the prisoner down to the cells and then bundling him, often handcuffed, into a van divided into tiny cages for the journey to his prison cell.

The penalties are often organized by professional trained social workers encumbered and insulated by the jargon and ethos of their profession. These professionalized criminal justice workers have a set of objectives to meet that determine if they are doing their job properly or not. How many criminals do they see per week for supervision? How many of their activities are satisfactorily completed? How many high-profile failures have there been? Were all the reports done on time? The choice of social work as the discipline from which the workers come carries the symbolism that the criminal is a sad case who needs help (often doubtless true) and the damage that has been caused is but an unfortunate incident, not the central fact. But to the offended person and the family and neighbours round about them it will be the central fact. To the general public there seems to be no logical connection between breaking into an old couple's house and stealing their dearest possessions and a consequence which might be to have help from a social worker to sort out deep-seated problems, necessary and desirable though that is. The connection is not made, to the elderly couple, their community or the person who did the burglary. And if it were made, would it be accepted? Lots of people have problems. Why did this one choose to burgle a house – their house – and seem to get away with it?

Also, the penalties are conceived within the same framework as prison. Those trying to market them say that they are really tough punishments. There is no soft option here. We have serious supervision, surveillance even, lots of control. Nobody gets away with anything on my scheme, in my probation service, when they are cleaning up graveyards under my supervision. The public is protected very well. So the next stage is logical. Why not really try and replicate prison? Let us make convicted persons' homes into a prison. Let us put little radio transmitters on their ankles so we can plot their every move, and that will control them. Thus is born another idea of the communications age: electronic monitoring of people so that they can be checked at any hour of the day or night. Are they in? Are they free of alcohol and drugs (apparently the technology can now smell as well as just check if they are there)? If they are not in or neither alcohol- nor drug-free, let us log a violation and if there are too many of those, let us send them off to prison where they really belong.

From all these perspectives, alternative penalties are bound to be the criminal justice poor relation. They do not replicate prison. They do not give the same amount of short-term control and protection. Their operators would not look credible in uniforms, rattling keys. They cannot deliver the imagery of exclusion and exile, the symbolism of casting out from civilized beings and serving time, doing penance, in the wilderness.

But they could offer a real alternative, an alternative approach to crime control, offering the symbolism of penitence, moral education, restitution and forgiveness. John Braithwaite is an Australian criminologist who has developed the notion of 'shaming'. Shaming evokes images of the stocks, the pillory, public humiliation, walking round with a sandwichboard saying 'I am a sex offender', community-service workers being dressed in striped convict uniforms, female chain gangs on the public highway in Arizona. This sort of shaming is not at all what John Braithwaite has in mind. His shaming he calls 'reintegrative shaming'.[45] It is not designed to humiliate people and drive them outside the community. It is not the shaming of the outcast and the exile. On the contrary it is a form of shaming that 'reintegrates' because it makes the convicted person actually feel ashamed and want to be readmitted to the society that has been harmed. The shaming process does not involve the hatred of the community but its sorrow and wish to repair the relationships that have been damaged.

The argument is complex but it is based on a simple premise. Many people would not dream of breaking into someone's house, ransacking it in the search for money and jewellery and running off with their spoils to find a buyer for them. Why not? Perhaps because they can imagine what it would feel like to be the houseowner when returning to see the despoilage. Their consciences tell them that to do such a thing to another human being is wrong. And what would people think of them if they did such a thing as burgle a house? Someone who was respected and trusted by a large group of people would become a pariah, a different sort of person, and would cease to be admired and accepted by family, friends, colleagues. Such a person would be made to feel 'shame'.

Braithwaite's theory assumes an 'active conception of the

criminal'. He does not see the criminal as someone so in the grip of influences from the family, the surroundings, the early childhood experiences, that free choice is prevented. The person who commits an act that breaks the criminal law is making a choice 'against a background of societal pressures'.[46]

But there are two sorts of shaming. There is the shaming of the stocks and the pillory, the degradation of prison and the subsequent mark of the prison record for ever, preventing reacceptance into society, the casting out of the criminal. This does not make the shamed person want to make different and non-criminal choices. On the contrary it pushes the person into the deviant group, where there will be acceptance and respect. Once in this group, shame comes from not following its illegal norms, not being daring enough to carry out the more serious crimes, not being the one prepared to use the knife or the gun.

'Reintegrative shaming' on the other hand is a prelude to reintegration. After a period of disapproval there has to be forgiveness and reacceptance. It requires a separation of the criminal act from the person. It is no good describing people as burglars, joyriders, car-stealers, thieves, and letting those labels hang around their necks for ever. The 'burglar' is a person who has burgled, but after the process of dealing with the burglary, righting the wrong to everyone's satisfaction, the burglar must discard the label and become again an accepted citizen. Shaming and punishment of the growing child take place in the family and then there is forgiveness and reacceptance. Approval is withdrawn and then returns. In families where there is no approval to withdraw and then restore, socialization is likely to be less successful.

According to Braithwaite, sanctions imposed by people who are personally relevant to the wrongdoer have more effect than those imposed by 'a remote legal authority'.[47] What your family, friends, neighbours, colleagues think of you matters more than what a strange judge in fancy dress or a concerned probation officer thinks of you. Fear is certainly a deterrent; not fear of the courts and the prison but fear of what people will say, what people will think, how they will look at you and mutter about you behind your back if you are convicted of a crime.

Shaming is 'conscience-building'.[48] Shaming as a response to crime, he argues, will work because it affects the way people see the world and their place in it. They will want to behave differently after being 'shamed'.

Why, Braithwaite goes on to ask, are some people immune to these processes? Why do they work much better in some societies than others, and for some people rather than others? 'Individuals are,' he says, '. . . more susceptible to shaming when they are enmeshed in multiple relationships of interdependency; societies shame more effectively when they are communitarian.'[49]

He concludes,

> Crime is best controlled when members of the community are the primary controllers through active participation in shaming offenders, and, having shamed them, through concerted participation in ways of reintegrating the offender back into the community of law-abiding citizens. Low-crime societies are societies where people do not mind their own business, where tolerance of deviance has definite limits, where communities prefer to handle their own crime problems rather than hand them over to professionals. In this I am not suggesting the replacement of the 'rule of law' with the 'rule of man'. However, I am saying that the rule of law will amount to a meaningless set of formal sanctioning proceedings which will be perceived as arbitrary unless there is community involvement in moralizing about and helping with the crime problem.[50]

Most people would agree with this analysis. It accords with common sense, with what happens in the family, what obviously happens in schools. It goes wrong when children are excluded from school.

Some will argue against it. It could be said that it is too late. The bonds that bind individuals into groups and communities have become too weak to carry the weight that shaming requires. It might also be argued that it can only work if there is agreement about the moral acceptability of the criminal law. If a third of the population does not accept that smoking cannabis is something to be ashamed of then shaming will not make people stop doing it. There is a real danger that community disapproval can lead to mob rule and lynch law, and violence against people the community does not approve of. Those convicted of sexual offences against children are not welcomed back and reintegrated once they have been through the shaming process. Once their backgrounds are revealed they flee their homes in fear of their lives.

But these difficulties are not insuperable. There is much to be said for basing criminal justice more on these principles. Whilst the community can be very intolerant and bigoted, it is not necessarily so. Shaming has worked very successfully in some countries in stopping smoking in many situations. Drinking and driving is now something to be ashamed of in many countries.

A number of groups are working to find ways of putting such ideas into a form where they can be part of a wholesale reform of the criminal justice process. An American Mennonite, Howard Zehr, is one of the leading exponents of a new approach often called restorative justice. This has much in common with reintegrative shaming. Howard Zehr says that victims are so left out because 'they are not a fundamental part of the definition. An offense is against the state. It's the state versus an offender.'[51]

Through most of Western history, he says, we understood crime as a violation that creates obligations: when you violate somebody you create an obligation. Yet the system we now have minimizes or eliminates that obligation. What happens to people who are caught and convicted? They are put through a process that teaches them to think only about what is happening to them. They might be guilty, but it is up to the state to prove it. If there is any chance of being found not guilty they will plead not guilty. All these processes come between the criminal and admitting an obligation to another human being who has been wronged.

A restorative justice yardstick

1. *Do victims experience justice?*

- *Do victims have sufficient opportunities to tell their truth to relevant listeners?*
- *Do victims receive needed compensation or restitution?*

- *Is the injustice adequately acknowledged?*
- *Are victims sufficiently protected against further violation?*
- *Does the outcome adequately reflect the severity of the offense?*
- *Do victims receive adequate information about the crime, the offender and the legal process?*
- *Do victims have a voice in the legal process?*
- *Is the experience of justice adequately public?*
- *Do victims receive adequate support from others?*
- *Do victims' families receive adequate assistance and support?*
- *Are other needs – material, psychological and spiritual – being addressed?*

2. *Do offenders experience justice?*

- *Are offenders encouraged to understand and take responsibility for what they have done?*
- *Are misattributions challenged?*
- *Are offenders given encouragement and opportunities to make things right?*
- *Are offenders given opportunities to participate in the process?*
- *Are offenders encouraged to change their behavior?*
- *Is there a mechanism for monitoring or verifying changes?*
- *Are offenders' needs being addressed?*
- *Do offenders' families receive support and assistance?*

3. *Is the victim–offender relationship addressed?*

- *Is there an opportunity for victims and offenders to meet, if appropriate?*
- *Is there an opportunity for victims and offenders to exchange information about the event and about one another?*

4. *Are community concerns being taken into account?*

- *Is the process and the outcome sufficiently public?*
- *Is community protection being addressed?*
- *Is there a need for restitution or a symbolic action for the community?*
- *Is the community represented in some way in the legal process?*

5. Is the future addressed?

- *Is there provision for solving the problems that led to this event?*
- *Is there provision for solving problems caused by this event?*
- *Have future intentions been addressed?*
- *Are there provisions for monitoring and verifying outcomes and for problem solving?*

From Howard Zehr, Changing Lenses, *Herald Press, Scottdale, Pennsylvania, 1990*

These ideas are being put into practice in a small way in various parts of the world. In New Zealand young people between the ages of fourteen and seventeen are dealt with in the youth court. In some ways the youth court follows the traditional adversarial model. If the young person who is charged denies the offence there is a trial with prosecution and defence and finally a judgement, of guilty or not guilty. Once guilt has been established, the dramatically different model comes into play. The decision on what sentence should be given to the young person emerges from a completely new method called Family Group Conferencing.

The Family Group Conference is brought together by a state official, an employee of the Social Welfare Department, who takes the chair at the conference. It is attended by a large group of interested parties. First, of course, the young person who has committed the crime and members of his or her family have to be there. The young person can ask for a 'youth advocate' to be there too and the family can ask for the presence of anyone else they feel would be helpful, such as someone who works in a drug-addiction agency. Also present is the victim, often accompanied by some supporters, and a police officer usually from the specialist section of the police that deals with youth. Sometimes a social worker attends but judges are never present. Usually between six and twelve people attend the conference but numbers can rise to twenty.

The object of the conference is to reach unanimous agreement on what the sentence on the young person should be. A solution has to be found that commands the support of the wrongdoer, the victim of the wrongdoing and the representative of law and order, the police officer. If the conference cannot reach a unanimous decision the matter is referred back to the judge in the court. The conference sometimes recommends the case back to the court so that a court sanction can be imposed. Usually, however, it draws up a plan involving an apology, restitution to the victim – whether money to be paid or work to be done, doing work of benefit to the wider community – an agreement to perhaps stay indoors at certain times, go to school regularly or not associate with certain friends deemed to be bad influences. The plan is put to the court and the court then adjourns the case for a few months whilst the plan is put into action. If it is successfully completed, the proceedings are dropped.

The conferencing system has wider possibilities, however. If a young person admits an offence the police can refer it straight to the conference and if everyone at the conference agrees that it can be handled out of court, then the conference goes ahead. More than four out of five cases have been handled this way.[52]

An experienced Youth Justice Coordinator who has chaired several hundred conferences described how she feels:

> The crux of the Youth Justice system is *direct* involvement of the offender and the 'offended against', eyeball-to-eyeball ... When victims and families farewell each other with smiles, handshakes and embraces, I know that justice has been served![53]

District Court Judge Fred McElrea from Auckland has written extensively on the new model. In his view, the traditional model of justice

> has largely removed the element of shame ... For a lot of families their young people's offending is a matter of shame, and if that shame is experienced by family members with the youngster at the conference, he cannot just shrug it off. I remember reading of one young man explaining that it was easy to be 'staunch' or 'cool' in court (and indeed to take some pride in being there) but at a family group conference, he explained, '*You're just a flea, man – you're nothing!*'[54]

Family Group Conferencing: an example

A former probation officer called Matt Hakiaha, a Maori, who then became a Youth Justice Coordinator described one of his cases to David Hayley of CBC. Four boys had broken into a school, done some drinking and then accidentally set fire to it, doing extensive damage.

The whole Family Group Conference in this case took about three days. The first day was mainly focused around feelings, feelings of animosity, where teachers, where parents were saying, 'Look, you burned our school down, and our kids have to be catered for now, and they can't be, so they've had to build temporary classrooms.' I've got quite a clear picture in my mind of these four offenders. They were sitting there, so unmoved, so unemotional. And then this young girl walked up with the scrapbook that she had kept in her classroom, and it was half-charred. About one-half was just burned to a crisp, and the other half was charred. And she came and sat in front of these four boys, these four offenders, and she said, 'This is all I've got as a remembrance of my brother, because this scrapbook is photos of my family and a photo of my brother, and he died not so long ago, about a year ago, and that's all I've got now.' And then you saw the tears trickling down these four boys. The impact that was made by the victim was amazing. And I wonder whether a court would do that. I wonder whether a court process would allow this emotion to come out.

From Prison and Its Alternatives, *transcript by CBC, 1996, p. 64*

In Vermont in the United States, experiments have also been going on with new ways of dispensing justice. Vermont is a small state with a population of 579,000 and with a projected prison population of less than 1400 in 1996. In 1993 the Vermont Department of Corrections decided to change radically the purposes and methods of their system for dealing with convicted offenders. They carried out a public opinion survey which showed that people in Vermont believed crime in general was increasing and violent crime was increasing (neither of these beliefs was borne out by the evidence). They wanted life imprisonment without parole for repeat violent offenders and rehabilitation for young, non-violent and first offenders. About one-third of the respondents gave probation a positive rating. Three-quarters believed the whole criminal justice system needed to be overhauled and 92 per cent supported reparation by property offenders to their victims and community work instead of prison for drunk drivers, drug users, shoplifters, 'bad check writers' and young offenders in general.[55]

The Vermont authorities went on to abandon their traditional Corrections Department which had some staff working in prisons and others providing probation. Instead they developed a new two-track system. Track one is aimed at risk management and deals with those who commit violent and more serious crime and are a risk to the community. The emphasis in track one, whether the offender is sent to prison or not, is on dealing with the problems that led to the crime in the first place. So track one contains an intensive probation programme, a day treatment programme or treatment in prison and the work is all done by the professionals employed by the Vermont Corrections Department.

Track two is for those convicted of less serious crimes and the emphasis is on reparation, with a straight reparation sentence, a supervised community sentence or a work camp. The very innovative aspect of the Vermont system is that track two is managed by the community, through new bodies called Community Reparation Boards. The public opinion survey showed that once the idea of Community Reparation Boards was explained more than half of those questioned would support community sentences for small drug dealing, repeat drunk driving, a second-time unarmed burglary, someone passing a dud cheque for the fifth time, someone shoplifting for the third time or a young car thief.[56]

The offender is sentenced to the reparative probation programme by the judge. Then information is put together and a meeting is arranged with the Community Reparative Board consisting of five or six people from the area where the crime was committed. The offender and the board discuss the offence and its impact. The board then devises a plan of specific activities that will be done and the offender and the board sign an agreement. The activities should include reparation to the victim, reparation to the community, learning about the impact of crime on victims and the community and learning ways to avoid crime in the future. The offender is not then supervised by anyone from the department but has to take charge him or herself of completing the programme and provide evidence that what should be done has been done. The board monitors progress. Once agreement has been reached the offender has three months to carry it out. If it is all done satisfactorily the board may recommend to the court that the probation order be discharged. If the offender does not comply the court will take further action. The professional staff of the Corrections Department administer the programmes and provide training for the board members.[57]

In Québec, the general North American trend towards stiffer sentences is being reversed as provincial government launches a programme of non-custodial sentences. 'Adopting a less repressive approach toward crime is not something easy to fulfil. In this regard Québec is going against the conservative trend sweeping across North America. Québec has decided to turn its back on the repressive model,' says a report by the Ministry of Public Security. The incarceration rate in Québec is 104 per 100,000, somewhat lower than the Canadian figure of 116 per 100,000.

The Québec programme aims to move from 'repression and incarceration' to a system based on 'prevention, resolution of conflict and the use of incarceration only for individuals who pose a threat to the population's security'. Six prisons are to be closed.[58]

Shaming has relevance not just to the developed world. Shaming should be of some significance in Africa, where community ties are so close and relationships so important. Amos Wako, Attorney-General of Kenya, said in Nairobi, in 1995,

> In traditional Africa, a criminal who is taken to prison or who is excommunicated from the society, is one who is actually beyond repair through societal means, or who has committed a major crime. What is recorded in our legal books as petty crimes by African standards were completely dealt with by the society itself. For example, if one stole a goat, the elders made sure another goat was

paid and that was the end of the matter. The person who stole was so ashamed that he would not do it again.[59]

Prison was brought to Africa by the colonizers. Before then ways of responding to crime were mainly on the reparative model. Professor Akele describes the process:

> About two centuries after the appearance of the carceral phenomenon the prison still stands, majestic, at the centre of our cities . . . reassuring to honest and law-abiding people and terrifying to potential delinquents, promising retribution to violators of public order and constraining seclusion for criminals. This will not prevent the prison evolving into a state of permanent and endemic crisis. One must understand that the sanction that would most affect the individual who broke the rules and precepts of the society would not, in the traditional African context, be one that deprived of liberty but one that broke or weakened the bonds of solidarity between the person and the group. It is this solidarity that is the basis of penal sanctions in African penal systems. One can see very real and substantial possibilities for innovation and development of a modern penal system based on the penological values of historic law.[60]

At a seminar in Africa held in 1995, Albie Sachs, former prisoner and by then a judge at the Constitutional Court of the Republic of South Africa, maintained that traditional African law was a rich treasury awaiting discovery. There can be no simple attempt to restore pre-colonial traditions. But the values and processes of traditional African law, a respect for human beings, reparation of damage, and personalizing the relationship between the offender and the victim and the involvement of the community in finding justice are all principles worth resurrecting.[61]

Recent developments may be reviving that model in a modern guise. Prison systems in Africa face severe problems and pressures. Zimbabwe's was one of those. In 1992, in response to a rapidly rising prison population with 60 per cent of the convicted prisoners serving sentences of three months or less, the National Committee on Community Service was set up, chaired by a High Court Judge. Legislation to make community service orders part of the law was enacted and a scheme of community service was set up. From the beginning of the scheme up to August 1997 over 16,000 orders had been made on offenders likely to get prison sentences of up to one year.

Instead of the prison sentence, offenders were given an opportunity to do community service work in a social welfare organization, doing practical work of benefit to the community. The results were impressive. Only 6 per cent of those undergoing community service failed to comply with the court's requirements. The economic benefits were substantial. The cost per month of prison in Zimbabwe was roughly $56. The cost of a month of community service was between $10 and $20. The prison population, which had been rising, had stabilized in spite of rising levels of unemployment and crime. High levels of satisfaction about the scheme had been registered amongst magistrates, supervising agencies and participants. There was no backlash against the scheme from the public. In 1996 four more African states – Uganda, Kenya, Malawi and Zambia – started preparing similar schemes.[62]

The Zimbabwean model is perhaps particularly successful and relevant to developing countries because it is low cost. It does not attempt to emulate the structures of the West, where alternatives to prison are supervised and administered by a separate publicly funded social work service. The model is judicially driven and administered through the courts, so it avoids the usual trap of such schemes not being used as alternatives to prison but as alternatives to non-intervention or to a lesser intervention. It establishes a penal model based on productive work and fruitful relationships between offender and community, rather than unproductive time and ruptured relationships. It appeals to African policy-makers and opinion-formers because it bypasses the type of penal system imposed by the colonizers and reverts to a system more in keeping with African penal traditions.

The success of these developments should give food for thought to those Western experts and donors who unthinkingly strive to import the Western system of criminal justice under the cover of technical assistance to poorer countries. They may be poorer economically but they are not necessarily poorer in terms of their criminal justice traditions.

The distinguished BBC journalist Mark Tully writes in *No Full*

Stops in India of the elderly man in the Indian village who told him,

> . . . the worst thing that has happened is that the police started coming into the village. In the old days the police never came – we used to sort out our quarrels ourselves or with the *panchayat* (village council). But nowadays people keep running to the court or the police station. They waste a lot of money and achieve nothing. The police are not just. They always side with the richer person, so no matter how much you offer them you can't beat someone with more money.[63]

Is there anything to learn from Africa with its rich traditions of restitution, shaming and reintegration, or from the New Zealand Family Group Conferencing, which owes so much to earlier Maori tradition? Is the dissatisfaction with the Western system now so great that we should embark on a total rethinking of the way we are responding to persons accused and convicted of criminal acts?

A NEW APPROACH

If a way is to be found out of the punishment spiral perhaps a rethink is needed of the basic principles that underlie the way we respond to those charged with and found guilty of criminal acts. A new approach should start by asking what it is we are trying to achieve when we deal with those proceeded against and convicted of crime. What are worthwhile outcomes? Whose needs are we trying to satisfy? Can the answer to these questions be the same for every criminal act and every circumstance?

For some people the desired outcome is that someone should be punished. This is satisfying enough in itself. The fact that punishment has been inflicted on the wrongdoer makes the victim or victim's family feel better and thus justice is achieved and equilibrium in society is restored. The feeling runs deep that justice is done only when the perpetrator has suffered. The very desirable and necessary development of a movement to campaign for better treatment of the victims of crime has unintentionally given support to an idea that it is in the interests of victims that offenders should undergo more suffering in their punishment.

In this line of thought, justice is being seen as a commodity that the state offers to its citizens, like health and education. What 'justice' comes to mean in this context is a lot of severe punishment for the offender that is represented by a long time in prison and a hard time whilst there. When prisoners are discovered by the media to be working out of prison, on some scheme, for example, to help disadvantaged people, the victims are asked whether they think this is right or not and they often say that it is not right at all. By the offender engaging in activities that help society and might help eventual resettlement in the community, the suffering that the victims endured because of the crime seems to them to be devalued.

Another objective that the whole process of criminal justice, police, sentencing, prisons, parole and probation is expected to deliver is protection. The public thinks it is entitled to be protected by the authorities from serious violence and crimes of a sexual nature. It seems evident to many that people who commit such a crime once are very likely to commit another. People feel therefore that it is not easy to understand why current sentencing practice does not simply take account of this and provide such protection. Whatever else a government does and does not do, it should keep law-abiding people from assault and battery.

These two fundamental and deeply reasonable requirements, first a recognition of the harm suffered by the victim and secondly protection from violence and abuse, might form the basis for a new set of purposes for dealing with criminal acts.

The first purpose and top priority in any system should be the protection of people from murder, severe physical violence and sexual assault, and the assertion of society's strong condemnation of such acts. This is where prison is still the only solution both for removing from society dangerously violent people and for its symbolism. Banishing behind high walls for many years the tiny number of people who have murdered, tortured or violently and cruelly abused makes it clear that such actions are way beyond the limits of human behaviour.

However, if the perpetrators are caught, sentenced and imprisoned, the objective in dealing with them should be an effort to contain and reduce their violent reactions, not, as so many prison regimes do, increase them. Many more resources should be put into dealing with such people and supervising them once it has been deemed safe to release them.

This may protect society from their future acts but it does little to heal the wounds of the victims and the families of those who have been murdered or gravely harmed. A range of services should be available to these victims and their families, based on the experience and knowledge of those who have helped victims of torture and sufferers of other profoundly traumatic experiences to go through the long process of coming to terms with what has happened to them and taking up normal life again. The assumption that this healing process can be made to happen by the knowledge that the perpetrator has been caught and is locked away in prison seems to be quite mistaken. For many people much more attention should be given to their need to come to terms with what has happened and ensure that it does not poison the rest of their lives with hatred and unresolved grief. Victims of serious crime should be eligible for a range of free services which would help them to recover and to carry on with their lives as soon as possible.

There is another group from whom society needs protection. The organized crime gangs, the mafias, who threaten society's stability and the rule of law, must be detected and prevented. Societies where the criminals wield great power are dangerous and unjust societies. When small traders have to pay protection money to stay in business and anyone can be bought off because the criminals have the most money, democratic values are in danger. Normally such people do not end up in prison because their money buys them impunity and their resources are greater than those of the police who are trying to catch them and the prosecutors who are trying to convict them. Once they are caught and put in prison it is a difficult job to keep them there. The resources they can deploy to escape far outstrip those of the prison authorities to keep them in. High security is needed, at least until they cease to count in the criminal business world and their position is taken by someone from the next generation.

Serious violence and organized crime require the application of the traditional criminal justice machinery. But they constitute a minute proportion of the crime processed through these systems in all countries of the world. If everyone were released from the prisons of the world except prisoners in these two categories the prison population would drop to a fraction of its current level. The bulk of the crimes that drive people into prison are not the murders, rapes, serious violent and abusive acts, nor the fraudulent dealings that happen inside the computers of the big banks. They happen in the streets and poor housing areas. They are made up of burgling of poor people's homes to steal a second-hand video recorder, gang fights between the young men from different and competing housing areas, robbing the takings in the small neighbourhood shop and small-scale drug dealing. They also happen in the home, the place where many violent and sexual assaults occur.

For all this type of crime we need a completely different emphasis. At the centre should be the victim and the damage the act has done to the victim's sense of safety and confidence in the benignity of the world. The aim should be to find a solution that makes it less likely that such acts will happen again. Perpetrators need to be moved in understanding to see the effects of actions on others, to comprehend that the victims could have been members of their own families.

Prison can protect from violent and abusive people. Prison can contain people dedicated to organized crime. But it cannot heal or repair the victim's damaged faith in fellow human beings. With prison the victim is not healed. The victim is forgotten. The community breach is not healed – but widened – and society has become more dangerous. After a spell in prison the young man involved in petty crime has become a person who rejects society's values as society has rejected him. And no solution to his problems has been found. On the contrary, prison put the original problems in cold storage and will create more problems. If we need a system that spreads understanding that the act was wrong, someone was hurt and that this matters, we do not need so much prison. For prison is a society which spreads another message entirely. It provides a camaraderie of minimizing the harm and diminishing the responsibility, of blaming someone else. It provides an environment which reinforces the view that

Everyone is doing it. We were just unlucky to get caught. We are only the little criminals. The big criminals are still out there. I was just not cunning enough. Everyone else is getting away with it. Next time I steal or rob I shall not make the mistakes that got me in here. They have rejected us so we will reject them. What they outside think of me no longer matters. What my cell-mates think of me is more important.

The research surveys have shown that people have no idea what is being done in their name, but once they have the information and confront all the dilemmas, many of them want to be constructive. A new system has to involve the public in ways that allow the necessary processes to take place, the acceptance of wrong done, the understanding, the apology and the commitment to carry out some activities that make recompense for the harm.

For many minor offences the lengthy and time-consuming para-phernalia of criminal justice creates an unacceptable distance between the perpetrator and the victim, the act and its resolution. Systems need to be developed that can bring the procedure nearer to the place and people amongst whom it happened and shorten the time between the act and the response to the act.

Such changes will bring problems. The safeguards that are in place when guilt or innocence is being established have to be sacro-sanct. The new approach must apply to those admitting guilt or found guilty in a properly constituted court with all the safeguards. Equal treatment of similar offenders for similar acts is not achieved in the current system. A new system that took justice for minor offences nearer to the community might also not lead to very equal outcomes. Some communities might want much more of their offenders than others by way of recompense. National systems should ensure that the framework prevents enormous differences.

The criminal justice system is about people who have been charged with and convicted of criminal acts. It is not about crime. It is important to put criminal justice within the context of a better way of dealing with crime altogether. First of all, what should be considered as crime. The Dutch criminologist Louk Hulsman does not speak of crime, but only of 'criminalizable events',[64] in order to make the point that a choice is made to deal with a human act as a crime. Crime could be almost infinite. An enormous number of human acts could be so described: taking things that belong to someone else, raising a hand against someone else in anger, consuming mind-altering substances. Sometimes chemicals that were regarded as medicines are reclassified as illegal drugs and it becomes a crime to consume them. Sometimes, as in California, the process works the other way about and a substance, in this case cannabis, becomes legal if prescribed by a doctor in certain circumstances.[65] In many communities differences between people are settled informally. As communities become larger and more anonymous these matters are deemed to require the intervention of authorities and the criminal law but they could as well be resolved to the satisfaction of all parties through a process of mediation.

The modern tendency is to criminalize more acts, to introduce the criminal law into many areas of life. Since the criminal justice system is such a blunt and unsatisfying instrument, to turn more and more human acts into crimes is not likely to make people feel more content with the arrangements made to resolve social conflicts and create social peace.

The modern tendency also is to criminalize more people, and to do so at a younger age. Since the criminal law is so defective at problem solving there is much to be said for reducing its reach down into the younger stages of childhood, the sick and the mentally ill.

Then there is still much to do to make society safer. Violence prevention should be a priority. All the research shows that children growing up in violent circumstances are likely to become violent themselves. An American study shows that more than three-quarters of children exposed to ill-treatment, violence between their parents and a general family atmosphere of hostility went on to be violent in their behaviour.[66]

American studies also show the relative effectiveness of various approaches. Research from the Rand Foundation shows that $1 million spent on providing cash and other incentives for disadvantaged young people to graduate from high school would result in a reduction of 258 crimes per year. If $1 million were spent on training for parents and family therapy for families with difficult children, 160 crimes a year would be prevented. The study estimates that if the $1 million were spent on prison, sixty crimes a year would be prevented.[67]

CONCLUSION

So there is a substantial penal-reform agenda. All over the world penal reformers face a range of tasks crying out for action. The effort will be different in different places although the core remains the same. In Africa, where nearly all countries have accepted that their prisons are monstrosities, places where human rights are abused and poverty and disease exacerbated, there is a genuine search underway for a new and better approach to dealing with people who are convicted of crime. African penal reformers can move forward from that realization, resisting the blandishments of the technical assistance officers and advisers to have a prison system modelled on the one in Denmark, a probation service just like England's, a court system like the one in the United States, all housed in new and costly buildings with the latest technology provided under some aid programme but too expensive to maintain. The way forward in developing countries is to find a system that is just and fair, relevant to the economic circumstances and expectations of the people and that does not consume all the available resources so that there is nothing left for the real job of preventing crime.

In the East, penal reformers are active. In Japan human rights activists are energetically pursuing their objectives. In both India and Pakistan human rights commissions are working on penal-reform programmes.

The desperate penal crisis in Russia and the former Soviet republics calls for a completely new approach. Since the break-up of the Soviet Union, a host of well-meaning efforts and offers of help have been thrust upon the Ministries of the Interior in these countries. Most have been based on an imperfect understanding of the history and background and a failure to move beyond words to action. Some have been more interested to ensure that the influence of the country from which they come prevails in any new system rather than that the outcome should be in the best interests of the country being helped. The changes required are immense. Perhaps the only solution now is to break down the monolithic control of the central ministries and give substantial autonomy to regional and local bureaucrats, within the law, to do what they can to make the system work, by growing food, making products that will sell, using the skills of the prisoners and staff to maintain the buildings, working with local lawyers and NGOs to get released from prison all those pre-trial prisoners kept inside for minor charges because they cannot afford a lawyer.

In the meantime those outsiders with an interest in reforming the legal and penal system of Russia and the republics would do well to consider whether their efforts are genuinely helpful or whether piecemeal, contradictory and competitive interventions are but a hindrance to the recipients. Interventions might rather concentrate on building the confidence of the recipients rather than humiliating them by pointing out their shortcomings.

In South America prison population sizes are modest by American standards. The death penalty is not an issue. Prison regimes are based on humane ideas. It is in the implementation of imprisonment that the gross human rights abuses, inequalities and corruption occur. Massive reform is needed. Many prisoners in South America are imprisoned for the most minor crimes. Most are still unconvicted. The greatest reform would be to remove from prison all those prisoners who pose no danger whatsoever to the public and are locked up, perhaps for years, for no good reason.

The greatest challenge is the United States, with Europe following in its wake, not sure whether to hang on to the European values of minimal use of prison and the prisoner as temporarily excluded from society but still a citizen or to follow the American example. Many dedicated people are making it their life's work to point out the dangers of the US path and the crisis it will bring to their democracy. They are forging alliances between the commentators outside and those who work in the system, the police officers, administrators of jails and prisons, prison staff themselves. It is a great strength of the reform movement that the people in the system know that what is going on is wrong. They say so through the associations to which they belong. They need to be reinforced in their conviction that whilst they are contracted to carry out their instructions and follow their rule-book, they have a higher loyalty to a set of values and principles. It will not be an excuse for the perpetrator of a clear human rights abuse to say, 'I was just obeying orders.' Prison staff need to be given the confidence and courage to keep on pointing out what is wrong. Perhaps they should require that the international norms and instruments governing the treatment of prisoners should be written not just into prisoners' rights, but into their rights too, as staff. There are rules governing how prisoners should be treated. So also should there be equivalent rules governing what prison staff can be asked to do, and making it clear what they cannot be asked to do.

These are difficult times for penal reformers. But the potential for moving forward is there and some of the signs are encouraging. A great deal of interest has been aroused in the imaginative initiatives of those working to develop a new form of justice based on the principles of repairing the harm through realization, restitution, apology and reacceptance.

Most people understand that crime is not prevented by prison. Many would support a movement that made it a source of pride for a community to gradually shift its resources out of imprisonment and into violence prevention, helping disturbed families, providing more educational opportunities, supporting the children who will without such help become the next generation of prisoners, creating new alternatives where members of the public are involved and can use the skills present in so many people of mediating and resolving conflicts.

All this needs to be done. The next generation is entitled to inherit a society where safety is not just for those who can afford private security and is based on deeply authoritarian treatment of the rest of the population. They should be able to live in a society that is both safe and democratic. That is the choice we face.

Notes

PART ONE Imprisonment Around the World
1. Nelson Mandela, *Long Walk to Freedom*, Little, Brown, London, 1994, p. 187.

1. *A Prison is a Prison*
   1. From *Prison and Its Alternatives*, a radio series by David Cayley, transcript by CBC, Ottawa, 1996, p. 47. The series was the basis for his book, *The Expanding Prison: Why Penal Systems Fail and What Can Be Done About Them*, House of Anansi Press, Toronto, 1997.
   2. Based on notes of a visit by the present author in October 1994.
   3. Based on notes of a visit by the present author in August 1993.
   4. Based on notes of a visit by the present author in March 1995.
   5. Based on notes of a visit by the present author in December 1996.
   6. See Americas Watch, *Punishment before Trial: Prison Conditions in Venezuela*, Human Rights Watch, New York, 1997, p. 30.
   7. *Guardian*, 16 November 1994.
   8. Penal Reform International, *PRI Newsletter*, 3, July 1990, p. 2.
   9. Americas Watch, *Brazil: Prison Massacre in São Paulo*, Human Rights Watch, New York, 1992, p. 10.
   10. Penal Reform International, *PRI Newsletter*, 3, July 1990, p. 2.
   11. See Helen Womack, 'Five Killed in Labour Camp Riot in Russia', *Independent*, 9 July 1993.
   12. Raymond Colitt, 'Where Life on the Inside is Deathly', *Financial Times*, 25 January 1997.
   13. See Americas Watch, *Punishment before Trial: Prison Conditions in Venezuela*, p. 1.

2. *The Western Tradition of Imprisonment*
   1. Charles Dickens, *American Notes for General Circulation*, first published 1842, Penguin Books, Harmondsworth, 1985, pp. 146–7.
   2. Information obtained by the present author when visiting in 1989 to carry out a study of Caribbean prisons.

3. See Council of Europe, *Report to the Authorities of the Kingdom of the Netherlands on the Visit to Aruba Carried Out by the European Committee for the Prevention of Torture and Inhuman or Degrading Treatment or Punishment (CPT) from 30 June to 2 July 1994 and Responses of the Government of Aruba*, Strasbourg, 1996, p. 27.

4. See Robert Hughes, *The Fatal Shore*, Collins Harvill, London, 1987, p. 35.

5. Hughes, *Fatal Shore*, p. 71.

6. Quoted in Seán McConville, *A History of English Prison Administration*, Routledge and Kegan Paul, London, 1981, p. 187.

7. Quoted in McConville, *History of English Prison Administration*, p. 189.

8. Quoted in Michael Ignatieff, *A Just Measure of Pain*, Columbia University Press, New York, 1978, p. 46.

9. Quoted in McConville, *History of English Prison Administration*, p. 51.

10. Dickens, *American Notes*, p. 148.

11. Fyodor Dostoevsky, *The House of the Dead*, trs. Constance Garnett, Heinemann, London, 1979 edn, pp. 13–14.

12. Quoted in Christopher Harding, Bill Hines, Richard Ireland and Philip Rawlings, *Imprisonment in England and Wales*, Croom Helm, London, 1985, p. 148.

13. See Ignatieff, *Just Measure of Pain*, p. 177.

14. See McConville, *History of English Prison Administration*, pp. 208–9.

15. See Ignatieff, *Just Measure of Pain*, pp. 199–200.

16. Arnold Bennett, *These Twain*, Penguin Books, Harmondsworth, 1976 edn, pp. 248–9.

17. Peter Kropotkin, *In Russian and French Prisons*, Schocken Books, New York, 1971, p. 329.

18. See Andrew Rutherford, *Growing out of Crime*, Penguin Books, Harmondsworth, 1986, p. 43.

19. Quoted in S. K. Ruck, *Paterson on Prisons*, Frederick Muller, London, 1951, p. 55.

20. See HM Prison Service, 'Corporate Plan', Home Office, London, 1996, p. 6.

21. HM Prison Service, 'Corporate Plan', p. 25.

22. See Direction de l'administration pénitentiaire, 'Les chiffres clés de l'administration pénitentiaire', Ministère de la Justice, Paris, 1996, p. 3.

23. See Elliott Currie, 'Is America Really Winning the War on Crime and Should Britain Follow its Example?', NACRO, 1996, p. 15 for this

estimate. According to the US General Accounting Office, operating costs for federal and state prisons for 1994 were $17.7 billion. To be added to this are the costs of jails, the capital costs of new building (estimated at over $100,000 per new cell, see Steven R. Donziger (ed.), *The Real War On Crime*, HarperPerennial, New York, 1996, p. 49) and the costs of the juvenile prison institutions.

24. Notes made during a visit by the present author in 1984.
25. Gerard de Jonge, Claviger Observandus, 'On the Impact of the CPT on the Dutch Penitentiary System and the Need for Such Committees on a National Level', unpublished paper presented to a PRI conference, Marly-le-Roi, France, 1996, p. 2.
26. Notes of a visit made by the present author in 1984.
27. Notes of a visit made by the present author in 1992.
28. See Ministry of Justice of Denmark, 'Prison System of Denmark', Copenhagen, 1990.
29. See Ministry of Justice of the Netherlands, 'The Prison System', The Hague, 1993, p. 9.
30. According to Section 13 of the German Prison Act. See 'Enforcement of Prison Sentences and Youth Custody in the Federal Republic of Germany', unpublished paper from the German Federal Ministry of Justice, Bonn, May 1997, p. 9.
31. Notes of a visit made by the present author in 1989.
32. See Asia Watch, *Prison Conditions in India*, Human Rights Watch, New York, April 1991, p. 17.
33. See Sankar Sen, 'Prison Reforms – A Convict is No Non-Person', *Statesman*, Delhi, 12 January 1996.
34. Notes of a visit made by the present author in 1995.
35. See 'The State of Cambodian Prisons', a report by the United Nations Centre for Human Rights Cambodia Office, PO Box 108, Phnom Penh, 1995 and Physicians for Human Rights, 'Health Conditions in Cambodia's Prisons', Boston, 1995.
36. See Human Rights Watch, *Global Report on Prisons*, New York, 1993, p. xxxi.
37. See Home Office, *Prison Statistics England and Wales 1996*, HMSO, 1997, Tables 3.8, 4.5, 5.5.
38. See Home Office, *Prison Statistics England and Wales 1996*, Table 1.7.
39. In fact, 32 per cent were in prison convicted of homicide, wounding with intent to harm, rape and robbery with violence, 30 per cent for other forms of theft and 15 per cent for drugs offences. Information provided by Jos Verhagen of the Dutch Prison Administration.

40. In fact, 32.3 per cent were imprisoned for offences involving violence, 26 per cent for theft and 39.4 per cent for 'other cases'. See Council of Europe, *Penological Information Bulletin*, nos 19 and 20, December 1994–1995, Strasbourg, p. 82.

41. See NSW Bureau of Crime Statistics and Research, 'Crime and Justice Facts 1994', Attorney General's Department, Sydney, 1994, p. 35.

42. Information from the report of the Consultative Council on Human Rights of Morocco reported in Penal Reform International, *PRI Newsletter*, 19, December 1994, p. 5.

43. Government of Japan, *Summary of the White Paper on Crime 1994*, Research and Training Institute, Ministry of Justice, Tokyo, 1994, p. 11.

44. See Kathleen Maguire and Ann L. Pastore (eds.), *Sourcebook of Criminal Justice Statistics 1995*, US Department of Justice, Bureau of Justice Statistics, Washington, DC, 1996, p. 567.

45. Government of Japan, *Summary of the White Paper on Crime 1994*, p. 11.

46. See, for example, the comments in Home Office Research and Statistics Department, *Digest 3 – Information on the Criminal Justice System in England and Wales*, London, 1995, p. 53.

47. Amnesty International, *Report 1996*, London, 1996, p. 179.

48. Amnesty International, *Report 1996*, p. 319.

49. Amnesty International, *Report 1996*, p. 99.

50. Home Office Research and Statistics Department, *Digest 3 – Information on the Criminal Justice System in England and Wales*, p. 54.

3. *The Great Incarcerator: The United States*

1. Quoted in Thomas O. Murton, 'Prison Management, the Past, the Present and the Possible Future', in Marvin E. Wolfgang (ed.), *Prisons: Present and Possible*, Lexington Books, Lexington, 1979, p. 9.

2. See Bureau of Justice Statistics, *Prison and Jail Inmates at Midyear 1996*, US Department of Justice, Washington, DC, 1997, p. 2.

3. See Bureau of Justice Statistics, *Lifetime Likelihood of Going to State or Federal Prison*, US Department of Justice, http://www.ojp.usdoj.gov, Washington, DC, 1997, p. 6.

4. See Kathleen Maguire and Ann L. Pastore (eds.), *Sourcebook of Criminal Justice Statistics 1995*, US Department of Justice, Bureau of Justice Statistics, Washington, DC, 1996, p. 548.

5. See Elliott Currie, 'Is America Really Winning the War on Crime and Should Britain Follow its Example?', NACRO, 1996, p. 15 for this

estimate. See chapter 2, note 23 for details of the breakdown of the figure.

6. See Wilbert Rideau, 'The Legend of Leadbelly' in Wilbert Rideau and Ron Wikberg, *Life Sentences: Rage and Survival Behind Bars*, Times Books, New York, 1992, pp. 24–32.

7. See *Soledad Brother, the Prison Letters of George Jackson*, Penguin Books, Harmondsworth, 1971.

8. See Tom Wicker, *A Time to Die: The Attica Prison Revolt*, Penguin Books, Harmondsworth, 1978.

9. Amnesty International, 'United States of America – Reintroduction of Chain Gangs – Cruel and Degrading', London, November 1995, p. 2.

10. *Financial Times*, 22 June 1996.

11. Adam Nossiter, 'Judge Rules Against Alabama's Prison "Hitching Posts" ', *The New York Times*, 31 January 1997.

12. See Robert Chalmers, 'Meet Sheriff Joe Arpaio of Arizona, Toughest Lawman in the West', *Night and Day*, 24 November 1996; Brendan Bourne, 'Women in Chains', *Sunday Express*, 15 September 1996; and John Hiscock, 'Women Line up to Join the Chain Gang', *Daily Telegraph*, 20 September 1996; *Corrections Journal*, 9 September 1996, Pace Publications, p. 7.

13. Rounded-up figure from Bureau of Justice Statistics, *Prison and Jail Inmates at Midyear 1996*, p. 4.

14. Rounded-up figure from Bureau of Justice Statistics, *Prison and Jail Inmates, 1996*, US Department of Justice, Washington, DC, 1996, p. 1.

15. Bureau of Justice Statistics, *Prison and Jail Inmates, 1996*, p. 1.

16. Joel A. Thompson and G. Larry Mays (eds.), *American Jails: Public Policy Issues*, Nelson Hall, Chicago, 1991, p. ix.

17. Human Rights Watch, *Prison Conditions in the United States*, New York, 1991, p. 19.

18. See Human Rights Watch, *Prison Conditions in the United States*, p. 20.

19. See Human Rights Watch, *Prison Conditions in the United States*, p. 20.

20. See Human Rights Watch, *Prison Conditions in the United States*, pp. 23–4.

21. Danny Obioha, in *Pipeline, the Brixton Prison Magazine*, Spring 1996, p. 30.

22. Kate Muir, 'Who's Playing Hangman?' *Sunday Times*, 23 October 1993, pp. 24–8.

23. See *Criminal Justice Newsletter*, vol. 24, no. 16, 15 September 1993, pp. 6–7.

24. See *Corrections Journal*, 22 July 1996, p. 1.

25. See Human Rights Watch, *Prison Conditions in the United States*, p. 26.

26. See Human Rights Watch, *Prison Conditions in the United States*, p. 29.

27. Prison Reform Trust, *Prison Report*, no. 29, Winter 1994, p. 19.

28. See *Corrections Journal*, 9 September 1996, p. 1.

29. See David Lainich, Paul Embert and Jeffrey Senese, 'Mental Health Services for Jail Inmates: Imprecise Standards, Traditional Philosophies and the Need for Change', in Thompson and Mays, *American Jails*, pp. 79–99.

30. See Bureau of Justice Statistics, *Prisoners in 1996*, US Department of Justice, http://www.ojp.usdoj.gov/pub/bjs/ascii/p96txt, Washington, DC, 1996, p. 5.

31. Human Rights Watch, *Prison Conditions in the United States*, p. 36.

32. See Human Rights Watch, *Prison Conditions in the United States*, p. 39.

33. Norval Morris, 'The Contemporary Prison', in Norval Morris and David J. Rothman (eds.), *The Oxford History of the Prison*, Oxford University Press, New York, 1995, p. 236.

34. Human Rights Watch, *Prison Conditions in the United States*, p. 40.

35. See Federal Bureau of Prisons, *Facilities 1992*, US Department of Justice, Washington, DC, 1993, p. 7.

36. See Human Rights Watch, *Prison Conditions in the United States*, p. 80.

37. See Human Rights Watch, *Prison Conditions in the United States*, p. 87.

38. See 'User Fees in Federal Prisons', *National Prison Project Journal*, vol. 8, no. 1, Winter 1993.

39. Federal Bureau of Prisons, *State of the Bureau 1993*, US Department of Justice, Washington, DC, 1994, p. 19.

40. See National Institute of Justice, *Boot Camps for Adult and Juvenile Offenders: Overview and Update*, US Department of Justice, Washington, DC, October 1994, p. 11.

41. See National Institute of Justice, *Boot Camps for Adult and Juvenile Offenders*, p. 33.

42. See National Institute of Justice, *Boot Camps for Adult and Juvenile Offenders*, p. 311.

43. See Doris Layton MacKenzie Ph.D., James W. Shaw and Voncile B. Gowdy, 'An Evaluation of Shock Incarceration in Louisiana', *The Key*, 28, Summer 1994, p. 9.

44. Federal Bureau of Prisons, *State of the Bureau 1992*, US Department of Justice, Washington, DC, 1993, p. 23.

45. See National Institute of Justice, *Boot Camps for Adult and Juvenile Offenders: Multisite Evaluation of Shock Incarceration*, US Department of Justice, Washington, DC, November 1994 and *Boot Camps for Juvenile Offenders: An Implementation Evaluation of Three Demonstration Programs*, National Criminal Justice Reference Service, Rockville, MD, 1996.

46. Michael Tonry, 'Racial Disproportion in US Prisons', in Roy D. King and Mike Maguire (eds.), *Prisons in Context*, Clarendon Press, Oxford, 1994, p. 113.

47. See Steven R. Donziger (ed.), *The Real War On Crime*, HarperPerennial, New York, 1996, p. 102.

48. See *Criminal Justice Newsletter*, vol. 25, no. 11, 1 June 1994, p. 6.

49. See Marc Mauer and Tracy Huling, 'Young Black Americans and the Criminal Justice System: Five Years Later', The Sentencing Project, Washington, DC, 1995, p. 1.

50. See Donziger, *The Real War On Crime*, p. 102.

51. See Bureau of Justice Statistics, *Lifetime Likelihood of Going to State or Federal Prison*, 1997.

52. See Marc Mauer, 'Americans Behind Bars: The International Use of Incarceration, 1992–3', Sentencing Project, Washington, DC, 1994, p. 18.

53. Morris, 'The Contemporary Prison', in Morris and Rothman, *Oxford History of the Prison*, p. 228.

54. Human Rights Watch, *Prison Conditions in the United States*, p. 10.

55. Stephen Donaldson, 'The Rape Crisis Behind Bars', *The New York Times*, 29 December 1993.

56. Press release from Stop Prisoner Rape, 11 January 1994.

57. See the *Guardian*, 21 July 1994.

58. See *Criminal Justice Newsletter*, vol. 26, no. 7, 3 April 1995, p. 4.

59. See D. Ward and A. Breed, 'Report on the US Penitentiary, Marion', presented to the Committee on the Judiciary of the US House of Representatives, US Government Printing Office, Washington, DC, 1995.

60. Human Rights Watch, *Prison Conditions in the United States*, p. 3.

61. Russell Miller, 'The Toughest Jail in the World', *Sunday Times*, 23 May 1993.
62. See 'No Contamination of Federal Prisoners', leaflet from the Committee to End the Marion Shutdown, Chicago, undated.
63. *USA Today*, 17 November 1994, as quoted in Penal Reform International, *PRI Newsletter*, 20 March 1995, p. 5.
64. Jan Elvin, 'Isolation, Excessive Force Under Attack at California's Supermax', *National Prison Project Journal*, vol. 7, no. 4, Fall 1992, p. 5.
65. See *Criminal Justice Newsletter*, vol. 24, no. 17, 1 September 1993, p. 3.
66. See *Criminal Justice Newsletter*, vol. 24, no. 17, 1 September 1993, p. 3.
67. Christopher Reed, 'Horror Stories from Prison That Shames US', *Observer*, 29 January 1995.
68. See Human Rights Watch, *Prison Conditions in the United States*, p. 4.
69. See Bureau of Justice Statistics, *Prison and Jail Inmates at Midyear 1996*, p. 2.
70. See Bureau of Justice Statistics, *Prison and Jail Inmates 1995*, US Department of Justice, Washington, DC, 1996, p. 2.
71. See Bureau of Justice Statistics, *Prison and Jail Inmates at Midyear 1996*, p. 2.
72. Elliott Currie, *Reckoning: Drugs, the Cities and the American Future*, Hill and Wang, New York, 1993, p. 3.
73. See *Criminal Justice Newsletter*, vol. 24, no. 15, 2 August 1993, p. 5.
74. 'FammGram', issue no. 12 July/August 1993, p. 9.
75. See Maguire and Pastore, *Sourcebook of Criminal Justice Statistics 1995*, p. 567.
76. See the *Guardian*, 30 January 1997.
77. See Marc Mauer, 'Three Strikes Policy is Just a Quick Fix Solution', *Corrections Today*, July 1996, p. 23.
78. See Christopher Parkes, 'Judges Take Swing at "Three-Strikes"', *Financial Times*, 22–3 June 1996.

4. *The New Gulag: Russia*

1. Quoted in Moscow Center for Prison Reform, *In Search of a Solution, Crime, Criminal Policy and Prison Facilities in the Former Soviet Union*, Human Rights Publishers, Moscow, 1996, p. xv.
2. See Moscow Center for Prison Reform, *In Search of a Solution*, p. xv.
3. Figure obtained by the present author in May 1997 from Ministry of Interior officials.

4. See Leo Tolstoy, *Resurrection*, trs. Rosemary Edmonds, Penguin Books, Harmondsworth, 1966, pp. 421–69.

5. Fyodor Dostoevsky, *The House of the Dead*, trs. Constance Garnett, Heinemann, London, 1979, p. 163.

6. Dostoevsky, *The House of the Dead*, p. 164.

7. See Aleksandr Solzhenitsyn, *One Day in the Life of Ivan Denisovich*, trs. Ralph Parker, (first published by Victor Gollancz) Penguin Books, Harmondsworth, 1963, p. 45.

8. Valery Abramkin, 'A look into our prison camps', in *Gulag Today, Collection of Articles 1989–1991*, Moscow Prison Center, Moscow, 1992, p. 21.

9. See Ryszard Kapuściński, *Imperium*, trs. Klara Glowczewska, Granta Books, London, 1994, p. 159.

10. Kapuściński, *Imperium*, p. 208.

11. From the collection *Gulag Tango*, by Gennady Molchanov, recorded for Mezhdunarodnaya Kniga, 1992.

12. Valery Abramkin, 'Living in Hell on Earth', *Moscow Times*, 30 August 1994.

13. Abramkin, 'In Search of a Human Approach', in *Gulag Today*, p. 6.

14. Pavel Moczydlowski, 'Prison: From Communist System to Democracy, Transformation of the Polish Penitentiary System', unpublished paper, October 1993, p. 4.

15. Zdeněk Karabec, 'The Problems of a Prison System During a Period of Transition Towards Democracy', *Prison Service Journal*, 98, March 1995, p. 18.

16. Moczydlowski, 'Prison: From Communist System to Democracy', p. 2.

17. Moczydlowski, 'Prison: From Communist System to Democracy', p. 6.

18. Moczydlowski, 'Prison: From Communist System to Democracy', p. 8.

19. Quoted by Kapuściński in *Imperium*, pp. 203–4.

20. Economic and Social Council, 'Report of the Special Rapporteur on his visit to the Russian Federation', United Nations, November 1994, para. 71, p. 19.

21. See Avraham Shifrin, *The First Guidebook to Prisons and Concentration Camps of the Soviet Union*, Bantam Books, New York, 1982, p. 43.

22. See Roy D. King, 'Russian Prisons After Perestroika', in *Prisons in Context*, Clarendon Press, Oxford, 1994, p. 70, for information on Butyrka prison.

23. Notes made by the present author in November 1992.

24. Moscow Center for Prison Reform, *Some Materials Related to the MCPR Recent Activities*, Summer 1994, p. 3.

25. Moscow Center for Prison Reform, *Some Materials Related to the MCPR Recent Activities*, p. 4.

26. See Fred Hiatt, 'Gulag no Longer, but Still the Lower Depths', *Washington Post*, 23 August 1993.

27. See Aleksandr Solzhenitsyn, *The Gulag Archipelago*, trs. Thomas P. Whitney, Collins, London, 1974, p. 125.

28. See Solzhenitsyn, *Gulag Archipelago*, p. 598.

29. See Moscow Center for Prison Reform, *In Search of a Solution*, p. 70.

30. Jack Chisholm, 'Inside the Gulag', *Sunday Times*, 10 June 1990.

31. Notes made by the present author in May 1993.

32. Roman Rollnick, 'Trapped in the Battery of Horrors', *European*, 15–18 July 1993.

33. Notes of a visit by a Penal Reform International delegation, October 1994.

34. See King, 'Russian Prisons After Perestroika', in *Prisons in Context*, p. 76.

35. See Yuri Ivanovich Kalinin, 'The Prison System in the Russian Federation', in *Prison Service Journal*, 97, January 1995, pp. 55–6.

36. Kalinin, 'The Prison System in the Russian Federation', p. 57.

37. See Shifrin, *The First Guidebook*, pp. 146–52.

38. Amnesty International, 'Kazakhstan – Ill-treatment and the Death Penalty: a Summary of Concerns', London, July 1996, p. 1.

39. See Amnesty International, 'Kazakhstan – Ill-treatment and the Death Penalty', p. 2.

40. See Amnesty International, 'Kazakhstan – Ill-treatment and the Death Penalty', p. 4.

41. See Amnesty International, 'Kazakhstan – Ill-treatment and the Death Penalty', p. 3.

42. See Amnesty International, 'Kazakhstan – Ill-treatment and the Death Penalty', p. 2.

43. See Amnesty International, 'Kazakhstan – Ill-treatment and the Death Penalty', p. 5.

44. See Amnesty International, 'Kazakhstan – Ill-treatment and the Death Penalty', p. 9.

45. See Amnesty International, 'Kazakhstan – Ill-treatment and the Death Penalty', p. 10.

46. See Amnesty International, 'Kazakhstan – Ill-treatment and the Death Penalty', p. 2.

47. See Moscow Center for Prison Reform, *In Search of a Solution*, p. 10.

48. Amnesty International, 'Turkmenistan: "Measures of Persuasion". Recent Concerns about Possible Prisoners of Conscience and Ill-treatment of Political Opponents', London, March 1996, p. 17.

49. Amnesty International, 'Turkmenistan: "Measures of Persuasion". Recent Concerns', p. 17.

50. Information supplied to a UK Foreign Office delegation by the Mongolian Director of Prisons.

51. See Penal Reform International, *PRI Newsletter*, 21, June 1995, p. 4.

52. See Moscow Center for Prison Reform, *In Search of a Solution*, p. 24.

53. Quoted in Moscow Center for Prison Reform, *In Search of a Solution*, p. 25.

54. Information supplied by the Belarus League for Human Rights, 1994.

55. 'Zones of Deadly Horror: Human Rights Activists Tell about Tortures in Russian Prisons', in *Some Materials Related to the MCPR Recent Activities*, Moscow Center for Prison Reform, Moscow, Summer 1994, p. 9.

5. *Mind Reform? China and Japan*

1. Quoted in Kate Saunders, *Eighteen Layers of Hell*, Cassell, London, 1996, pp. 3–4.

2. See Saunders, *Eighteen Layers of Hell*, p. xi.

3. Information Office of the State Council of the People's Republic of China, *Criminal Reform in China*, August 1992, p. 1.

4. Zhang Xianliang, *Grass Soup*, Secker and Warburg, London, 1994, p. 54.

5. Xianliang, *Grass Soup*, pp. 55–6.

6. Xianliang, *Grass Soup*, p. 58.

7. Xianliang, *Grass Soup*, p. 236.

8. Xianliang, *Grass Soup*, p. 238.

9. Zhang Xianliang, *Getting Used to Dying*, trs. Martha Avery, Flamingo, London, 1991, p. 253.

10. Xianliang, *Getting Used to Dying*, p. 255.

11. Xianliang, *Getting Used to Dying*, p. 259.

12. Bao Ruo-Wang (Jean Pasqualini) and Rudolph Chelminski, *Prisoner of Mao*, Penguin Books, Harmondsworth, 1976, p. 130.

13. Ruo-Wang and Chelminski, *Prisoner of Mao*, p. 131.

14. Ruo-Wang and Chelminski, *Prisoner of Mao*, p. 132.

15. Ruo-Wang and Chelminski, *Prisoner of Mao*, p. 133.

16. Harry Wu, *Bitter Winds*, John Wiley and Sons, New York, 1994, p. 81.

17. International League for Human Rights, press release, February 1995, p. 1.

18. Nick Rufford, 'Chinese Prisoners Forced to Mine for British Companies', *Sunday Times*, 1 January 1995.

19. See Hongda Harry Wu, *Laogai: The Chinese Gulag*, Westview Press, Boulder, Colorado, 1992, p. 8.

20. *Visit to China by the Delegation Led by Lord Howe of Aberavon, Report*, HMSO, London, 1993, para. 9.3, p. 36.

21. Notes made by the present author in December 1994.

22. Harry Wu, *Troublemaker*, Chatto and Windus, London, 1996, p. 5.

23. *Visit to China by the Delegation Led by Lord Howe of Aberavon, Report*, para. 10.13, p. 44.

24. See Wu, *Laogai: The Chinese Gulag*, p. 17.

25. See Wu, *Laogai: The Chinese Gulag*, p. 18.

26. See Wu, *Laogai: The Chinese Gulag*, p. 19.

27. Committee Against Torture, 'Consideration of Reports Submitted by States Parties under Article 19 of the Convention, Initial Reports of States Parties Due in 1989, Addendum, China', United Nations, 8 October 1992, para. 112.

28. James Pringle, 'Jail Where China Dissident Was Held Boasts Key Reforms', *The Times*, 28 January 1995.

29. Information supplied by the Japanese Ministry of Justice to the present author in March 1996.

30. Notes made by the present author in March 1996.

31. Notes made by the present author in March 1996.

32. Japan Federation of Bar Associations, *Prisons in Japan*, Tokyo, 1992, p. 2.

33. See Japan Federation of Bar Associations, *Prisons in Japan*, p. 2.

34. See Japan Federation of Bar Associations, *Prisons in Japan*, pp. 8, 10, 14 and 16.

35. Japan Federation of Bar Associations, *Prisons in Japan*, p. 16.

36. See Japan Federation of Bar Associations, *Prisons in Japan*, p. 16.

37. Japan Federation of Bar Associations, *Prisons in Japan*, p. 20.

38. See Japan Federation of Bar Associations, *Prisons in Japan*, p. 22.

39. See Japan Federation of Bar Associations, *Prisons in Japan*, p. 6.

40. See Human Rights Watch/Asia, *Prison Conditions in Japan*, Human Rights Watch, New York, 1995, p. 20.

41. See Human Rights Watch/Asia, *Prison Conditions in Japan*, p. 21.

42. See Human Rights Watch/Asia, *Prison Conditions in Japan*, p. 13.

43. See Human Rights Watch/Asia, *Prison Conditions in Japan*, p. 14.

44. See Human Rights Watch/Asia, *Prison Conditions in Japan*, p. 15.
45. See Human Rights Watch/Asia, *Prison Conditions in Japan*, p. 17.
46. See Human Rights Watch/Asia, *Prison Conditions in Japan*, p. 24.
47. Human Rights Watch/Asia, *Prison Conditions in Japan*, p. xiv.
48. See Mari Yamaguchi, 'American Sues Government for Alleged Prison Abuse', press statement, 2 July 1996.
49. Japan Federation of Bar Associations, *Prisons in Japan*, p. 28.

PART TWO A Deformed Society: The Prison World
1. Judith Ward, *Ambushed*, Vermilion, London, 1993, p. 177.

6. *People and Imprisonment*
1. Victor Serge, *Memoirs of a Revolutionary*, Writers and Readers, London, 1984, p. 45.
2. Václav Havel, *Letters to Olga*, Faber and Faber, London, 1990, p. 81.
3. Havel, *Letters to Olga*, p. 79.
4. Nelson Mandela, *Long Walk to Freedom*, Little, Brown, London, 1994, p. 375.
5. Mandela, *Long Walk to Freedom*, p. 237.
6. Mandela, *Long Walk to Freedom*, p. 321.
7. Mandela, *Long Walk to Freedom*, p. 334.
8. Mandela, *Long Walk to Freedom*, pp. 240–41.
9. Havel, *Letters to Olga*, p. 130.
10. Breyten Breytenbach, *The True Confessions of an Albino Terrorist*, Faber and Faber, London, 1984, pp. 123–4.
11. Anselm Chidi Odinkalu and Osaze Lanre Ehonwa, *Behind the Wall*, Civil Liberties Organisation, Lagos, 1991, p. 4.
12. Chidi Odinkalu and Lanre Ehonwa, *Behind the Wall*, pp. 4–5.
13. See Chidi Odinkalu and Lanre Ehonwa, *Behind the Wall*, pp. 5–6.
14. Wilbert Rideau, 'The Sexual Jungle' in Wilbert Rideau and Ron Wikberg, *Life Sentences: Rage and Survival Behind Bars*, Times Books, New York, 1992, p. 77.
15. See Rideau and Wikberg, *Life Sentences*, p. 78.
16. See Rideau and Wikberg, *Life Sentences*, p. 80.
17. See Rideau and Wikberg, *Life Sentences*, p. 81.
18. See Rideau and Wikberg, *Life Sentences*, p. 107.
19. Report by visiting delegate from Penal Reform International in 1995.
20. Asia Watch, *Prison Conditions in India*, Human Rights Watch, New York, 1991, pp. 18–19.
21. Information from Indian government report on the administration of

jails in Tamil Nadu, quoted in Asia Watch, *Prison Conditions in India*, p. 19.

22. 'How to Survive in a Soviet Prison', The Vostok (East) Agency, Krasnoyarsk, 1992, pp. 10–11.

23. 'How to Survive in a Soviet Prison', p. 13.

24. 'How to Survive in a Soviet Prison', p. 14.

25. 'How to Survive in a Soviet Prison', p. 15.

26. 'How to Survive in a Soviet Prison', p. 16.

27. Tony Parker, *The Twisting Lane*, Panther Modern Society, London, 1969, pp. 47–8.

28. See Tricia Dodd and Paul Hunter, *The National Prison Survey 1991, A Report to the Home Office of a Study of Prisoners in England and Wales Carried Out by the Social Survey Division of OPCS*, HMSO, 1992, p. 6.

29. See Dodd and Hunter, *The National Prison Survey 1991*, p. 7.

30. See Dodd and Hunter, *The National Prison Survey 1991*, p. 18.

31. See Dodd and Hunter, *The National Prison Survey 1991*, p. 11.

32. See Dodd and Hunter, *The National Prison Survey 1991*, p. 22.

33. See Dodd and Hunter, *The National Prison Survey 1991*, p. 21.

34. See Dodd and Hunter, *The National Prison Survey 1991*, p. 16.

35. See Dodd and Hunter, *The National Prison Survey 1991*, p. 19.

36. See Dodd and Hunter, *The National Prison Survey 1991*, p. 83.

37. See *Profile of Inmates in the United States and in England and Wales, 1991*, US Department of Justice, Washington, DC, October 1994, p. 16.

38. See *Profile of Inmates in the United States and in England and Wales, 1991*, p. 14.

39. See *Profile of Inmates in the United States and in England and Wales, 1991*, p. 6.

40. See Rhéal Séguin, 'Quebec Launches Prison Reforms', *Toronto Globe and Mail*, 3 April 1996.

41. Information received from Brazilian Federal Ministry of Justice in 1994.

42. Opening Remarks for John Edwards, Commissioner of the Correctional Service of Canada at the Parliamentary Committee on Justice and Solicitor General on Main Estimates, Tuesday, 26 April 1994, p. 2.

43. See Roger Hood, *Race and Sentencing*, Clarendon Press, Oxford, 1992, p. 179.

44. See Marc Mauer, 'Intended and Unintended Consequences: State Racial Disparities in Imprisonment', Sentencing Project, Washington, DC, 1997, p. 3.

45. Coramae Richey Mann, *Unequal Justice*, Indiana University Press, Bloomington, 1993, p. 221.

46. See Mann, *Unequal Justice*, p. 222.

47. See Commission on Human Rights, 'Fifty-Second Session, Implementation of the Programme of Action for the Third Decade to Combat Racism and Racial Discrimination', written statement submitted by Human Rights Watch, United Nations Economic and Social Council, 28 March 1996, p. 3.

48. See Mauer, 'Intended and Unintended Consequences', p. 10.

49. Marc Mauer, in *Prison and Its Alternatives*, a radio series by David Cayley, transcript by CBC, Ottawa, 1996, p. 4.

50. See Commission on Human Rights, 'Implementation of the Programme of Action', p. 3.

51. See *Race and the Criminal Justice System 1995*, Home Office, London, 1996, pp. 21, 25–8. The categories used to record ethnic origin are Black (African, Caribbean, Other), South Asian (Bangladeshi, Indian, Pakistani), Chinese and Other (Chinese, Other Asian, Other). See also Penal Affairs Consortium, *Race and Criminal Justice*, London, 1996.

52. See Barb Lash, *Census of Prison Inmates 1995*, Ministry of Justice, Wellington, 1996.

53. See Roderic Broadhurst, 'Aboriginal Imprisonment in Australia', in *Overcrowded Times*, vol. 7, no. 3, Castine Research Corporation, June 1996, p. 5.

54. See *Report of the Commission on Systemic Racism in the Ontario Criminal Justice System*, Queen's Printer for Ontario, Toronto, 1995.

55. See Katarina Tomaševski, *Foreigners in Prison*, European Institute for Crime Prevention and Control, Helsinki, 1994, p. 20.

56. Figures, which are for 1988, provided by the State Secretary for Justice in Rio de Janeiro.

57. Figures provided by the Hungarian Ministry of Justice.

58. See Tomaševski, *Foreigners in Prison*, p. 9.

59. See Tomaševski, *Foreigners in Prison*, p. 10.

60. Massimo Pavarini, 'The New Penology and Politics in Crisis: The Italian Case', in Roy D. King and Mike Maguire (eds.), *Prisons in Context*, Clarendon Press, Oxford, 1994, p. 59.

61. See Council of Europe, *Report to the Norwegian Government on the Visit to Norway Carried Out by the European Committee for the Prevention of Torture and Inhuman or Degrading Treatment or Punishment (CPT) from 27 June to 6 July 1993*, Strasbourg, September 1994, p. 39.

62. Lill Scherdin, 'AIDS in Prisons in Norway', in Philip A. Thomas and Martin Moerings (eds.), *AIDS in Prison*, Dartmouth, Aldershot, 1994, p. 16.

63. Scherdin, 'AIDS in Prisons in Norway', in Thomas and Moerings, *AIDS in Prison*, p. 17.

64. See NACRO, *Women Prisoners: Toward a New Millennium*, London, 1996, p. 11.

65. See Ralf Jürgens, 'AIDS in Prisons in Canada', in Thomas and Moerings, *AIDS in Prison*, pp. 114–15.

66. See Jürgens, 'AIDS in Prisons in Canada', in Thomas and Moerings, *AIDS in Prison*, p. 119.

67. Office of National Drug Control Policy (ONDCP), *Drugs and Crime Facts, 1994*, US Department of Justice, Rockville, MD, 1995, p. 23.

68. ONDCP, *Drugs and Crime Facts, 1994*, p. 24.

69. Jan Gustavsson and Lars Krantz, *The Misuse of Drugs in Prison – An Attempt to Assess the Extent of Drug Misuse in Prison Utilising Urine Tests*, Swedish Prison and Probation Administration, Norrköping, 1994, p. 17.

70. ONDCP, *Drugs and Crime Facts, 1994*, p. 24.

71. Home Office figures quoted in NACRO, *Criminal Justice Digest*, 94, October 1997, London, p. 10.

72. The requirement is to test a minimum 10 per cent of the prisoners each month. In a prison of approximately 500, about thirteen of such monthly tests would prove positive. These positive tests need to be subjected to forensic analysis at a cost of around £150 a time. In addition approximately three staff would need to be employed on drug testing alone at a cost of £26,000 per staff member.

73. See Penal Affairs Consortium, *Drugs on the Inside*, November 1996, p. 7.

74. See NACRO, *Criminal Justice Digest*, 89, p. 4.

75. Johannes Feest and Heino Stöver, 'AIDS in Prisons in Germany', in Thomas and Moerings, *AIDS in Prison*, p. 23.

76. Home Office figures quoted in NACRO, *Criminal Justice Digest*, 89, p. 8.

77. See Bureau of Justice Statistics, *HIV in Prisons and Jails, 1995*, US Department of Justice, http://www.ojp.usdoj.gov/pub/bjs/ascii/hivpj95txt, Washington, DC, 1997, p. 1.

78. See Bureau of Justice Statistics, *HIV in Prisons and Jails, 1995*, p. 2.

79. Bureau of Justice Statistics, *HIV in Prisons and Jails, 1995*, p. 1.

80. See Jerome G. Miller, *Search and Destroy: African-American Males in*

the Criminal Justice System, Cambridge University Press, Cambridge, 1996, pp. 223–4.

81. See Feest and Stöver, 'AIDS in Prisons in Germany', in Thomas and Moerings, *AIDS in Prison*, p. 25.

82. Monika Platek, 'AIDS in Prisons in Poland', in Thomas and Moerings, *AIDS in Prison*, p. 37.

83. Theodore M. Hammett, Lynne Harrold, Andrea Newlyn and Saira Moini, 'AIDS in Prisons in the USA', in Thomas and Moerings, *AIDS in Prison*, p. 145.

84. See Scherdin, 'AIDS in Prisons in Norway', in Thomas and Moerings, *AIDS in Prison*, p. 15.

85. See Feest and Stöver, 'AIDS in Prisons in Germany', in Thomas and Moerings, *AIDS in Prison*, p. 27.

86. Information supplied by the office of the Secretary of State for Justice in Rio de Janeiro in 1994.

87. See Christopher Thomas, 'Gay Prisoners Refused Condoms', *The Times*, 24 August 1994.

88. Andrew Coyle, 'Mentally Disordered Offenders', unpublished paper presented at a seminar in Poland, October 1994, pp. 2–3.

89. *Inspection of Prisons in the Caribbean Dependent Territories by HM Chief Inspector of Prisons*, London, 1989, para. 3.15.

90. Wilbert Rideau, 'Dying in Prison', in Rideau and Wikberg, *Life Sentences*, p. 171.

91. See Alison Liebling, *Suicides in Prison*, Routledge, London, 1992, p. 25.

92. See *Prison Death Toll Grows*, Howard League for Penal Reform, February 1996.

93. Antonio Cassese, *Inhuman States, Imprisonment, Detention and Torture in Europe Today*, trs. Jennifer Greensleaves, Polity Press, Cambridge, 1996, p. 113.

94. Osaze Lanre Ehonwa, *Prisoners in the Shadows*, Civil Liberties Organisation, Lagos, 1993, p. 137.

95. Aleksandr Solzhenitsyn, *One Day in the Life of Ivan Denisovich*, trs. Ralph Parker, (first published by Victor Gollancz) Penguin Books, Harmondsworth, 1963, p. 23.

96. Notes made by the present author during a visit in 1995.

97. See W. Rentzmann, 'Recruitment, Training and Use of Staff', unpublished paper, undated.

98. The exact figure on 30 September 1995 was 26.6 per cent. See Federal Bureau of Prisons, *State of the Bureau*, US Department of Justice, Washington, DC, 1995, p. 39.

99. See Philippe Brossard, 'Clairvaux, La Morte', and Anne Chemin, 'Près de trois-quarts des établissements pénitentiaires bloqués par les surveillants', *Le Monde*, 15 September 1992; Alice Rawsthorn, 'French Jail Crisis Deepens', *Financial Times*, 19 September 1992; and Jennifer Monahan, 'French Prison Disputes', unpublished paper, 1992.

100. A study by Richard Tilt shows a ratio of 2.33 prisoners to every member of staff in France, compared with 1.42 in England and Wales and 1.07 in the Netherlands. See 'Prison Staffing Issues in Europe', in Jack Reynolds and Ursula Smartt (eds.), *Prison Policy and Practice*, Prison Service Journal, 1996, p. 347.

101. Recorded during a visit by the author in 1988.

102. Notes made by a PRI delegate in 1995.

103. See Elói Pietá, *Prisons in Brazil*, September 1995, p. 9.

104. Constance Lytton, *Prisons and Prisoners*, Virago, London, 1988, p. 178.

105. Information provided to the author by the office of the Secretary of State for Justice in Rio de Janeiro in 1996.

106. Breytenbach, *True Confessions of an Albino Terrorist*, p. 227.

107. Breytenbach, *True Confessions of an Albino Terrorist*, p. 230.

108. Notes of a visit made by the present author in March 1996.

109. *The Times*, 6 August 1994.

7. *Women in Prison*

1. Constance Lytton, *Prisons and Prisoners*, Virago, London, 1988, p. 62.

2. Notes of a visit made by the present author in 1989.

3. Notes of a visit made by the present author in 1995.

4. Information from China Rights Forum, Fall 1995, reported in Penal Reform International, *PRI Newsletter*, 23, December 1995, p. 8.

5. Figure for 1 September 1994. See Council of Europe, *Penological Information Bulletin*, nos 19 and 20, December 1994–1995, Strasbourg, p. 79.

6. Figure for midyear 1996 was 6.3 per cent. See Bureau of Justice Statistics, *Prison and Jail Inmates at Midyear 1996*, US Department of Justice, Washington, DC, 1997, p. 4.

7. Figure for 1 September 1994. See Council of Europe, *Penological Information Bulletin*, nos 19 and 20, December 1994–1995, p. 79.

8. See Council of Europe, *Penological Information Bulletin*, nos 19 and 20, December 1994–1995, p. 79.

9. Information from the report of the Consultative Council on Human Rights of Morocco reported in Penal Reform International, *PRI Newsletter*, 19, December 1994, p. 5.

10. See Bureau of Justice Statistics, *Women in Prison, Survey of State Prison Inmates 1991*, US Department of Justice, Washington, DC, p. 2.

11. See Bureau of Justice Statistics, *Women in Prison, Survey of State Prison Inmates 1991*, p. 5.

12. See Bureau of Justice Statistics, *Women in Prison, Survey of State Prison Inmates 1991*, p. 6.

13. See Bureau of Justice Statistics, *Women in Prison, Survey of State Prison Inmates 1991*, p. 9.

14. See Bureau of Justice Statistics, *Women in Prison, Survey of State Prison Inmates 1991*, p. 3.

15. See *Forum on Correctional Research*, January 1994, vol. 6, no. 1, Correctional Service of Canada, Ottawa, p. 17.

16. Silvia Casale, *Women Inside*, Civil Liberties Trust, London, 1989, p. 66.

17. Una Padel and Prue Stevenson, *Insiders: Women's Experience of Prison*, Virago, London, 1988, p. 13.

18. Padel and Stevenson, *Insiders: Women's Experience of Prison*, p. 27.

19. See Padel and Stevenson, *Insiders: Women's Experience of Prison*, p. 49.

20. See Padel and Stevenson, *Insiders: Women's Experience of Prison*, p. 72.

21. See Padel and Stevenson, *Insiders: Women's Experience of Prison*, p. 87.

22. See Padel and Stevenson, *Insiders: Women's Experience of Prison*, p. 125.

23. See Padel and Stevenson, *Insiders: Women's Experience of Prison*, p. 138.

24. See Padel and Stevenson, *Insiders: Women's Experience of Prison*, p. 155.

25. Report by visiting delegate from Penal Reform International in 1995.

26. See Osaze Lanre Ehonwa, *Prisoners in the Shadows*, Civil Liberties Organisation, Lagos, 1993, p. 40.

27. See Home Office, *Prison Statistics, England and Wales, 1996*, HMSO, London, 1997, Table 2.6.

28. Nawal el Sa'adawi, *Memoirs from the Women's Prison*, The Women's Press, London, 1991, p. 73.

29. See Penal Affairs Consortium, *The Imprisonment of Women: Some Facts and Figures*, London, March 1996, p. 2.

30. See Home Office, *Prison Statistics, England and Wales, 1996*, Table 7.2.
31. Notes made by the present author during a visit in 1995.
32. Lis Somander, *Women Prisoners*, Swedish Prison and Probation Administration, Norrköping, 1994.
33. See National Prison Administration, *Annual Report 1995*, Ministry of Justice of the Republic of Slovenia, Ljubljana, June 1996.
34. See Helsinki Watch, *Prison Conditions in Spain*, Human Rights Watch, New York, April 1992, p. 27.
35. See Lanre Ehonwa, *Prisoners in the Shadows*, p. 19.
36. See report on Portugal in International Prison Watch, *Report 1994*, Observatoire International des Prisons, Lyon, 1994, p. 97.
37. See Penal Reform International and the Institute for Law and Economics, *Human Rights in Prisons*, London, 1997, p. 105.
38. See Valery Abramkin, 'Dangerous Old Women', in *Gulag Today*, Moscow Prison Center, Moscow, 1989–1991, pp. 12–17.
39. Quoted in Lytton, *Prisons and Prisoners*, p. vii.
40. Council of Europe, *Rapport au gouvernement de la République française relatif à la visite effectuée par le Comité européen pour la prévention de la torture et des peines ou traitements inhumains ou dégradants (CPT) en France du 27 octobre au 8 novembre 1991 et réponse du gouvernement de la République française*, Strasbourg, January 1993, p. 38.
41. See Nigel Bunyan, 'Prisoner Had to Give Birth in Handcuffs', *Daily Telegraph*, 28 April 1994.
42. See NACRO, *Women Prisoners: Towards a New Millennium*, London, 1996, p. 7.
43. See Lanre Ehonwa, *Prisoners in the Shadows*, p. 51.
44. See Roy Walmsley, *Prison Systems in Central and Eastern Europe*, HEUNI, Helsinki, 1996, p. 206.
45. See Penal Reform International, *PRI Newsletter*, 5, February 1991, p. 2.
46. See Walmsley, *Prison Systems in Central and Eastern Europe*, p. 307.
47. See Penal Reform International, *PRI Newsletter*, 5, February 1991, p. 2.
48. See Helsinki Watch, *Prison Conditions in Spain*, p. 27.
49. See Marc George, 'Rapport sur les conditions de détention au Portugal', Association for the Prevention of Torture, Geneva, 1994, p. 7.
50. See Walmsley, *Prison Systems in Central and Eastern Europe*, p. 206.
51. See Council of Europe, *Rapport au gouvernement de l'Italie relatif à*

la visite effectuée par le Comité européen pour la prévention de la torture et des peines ou traitements inhumains ou dégradants (CPT) en Italie du 15 au 27 mars 1992, Strasbourg, 1995, pp. 38–9.

52. See Tricia Dodd and Paul Hunter, *The National Prison Survey 1991: A Report to the Home Office of a Study of Prisoners in England and Wales Carried Out by the Social Survey Division of OPCS*, HMSO, London, 1992, p. 13.

53. See Human Rights Watch, *Prison Conditions in the United States*, New York, 1991, p. 61.

54. See Human Rights Watch, *Prison Conditions in the United States*, pp. 61–2.

55. See Russell P. Dobash, E. Emerson Dobash and Sue Gutteridge, *The Imprisonment of Women*, Basil Blackwell, Oxford, 1986, p. 63.

56. See The Honourable Louise Arbour, *Commission of Inquiry into Certain Events at the Prison for Women in Kingston*, Public Works and Government Services Canada, Ottawa, 1996, pp. 245–6.

57. *R* v. *Daniels* (1990) 4 C.N.L.R. 51. See Arbour, *Commission of Inquiry*, p. 246 for details of the case.

58. Ward, *Ambushed*, p. 2.

59. Ward, *Ambushed*, p. 3.

60. Ward, *Ambushed*, p. 4.

61. Ward, *Ambushed*, p. 1.

62. See Robert Hughes, *The Fatal Shore*, Collins Harvill, London, 1987, pp. 79 and 244–81.

63. See Seán McConville, *A History of English Prison Administration*, Routledge and Kegan Paul, London, 1981, p. 231.

64. See Lanre Ehonwa, *Prisoners in the Shadows*, p. 5 and note to p. 5.

65. Human Rights Watch Women's Rights Project, *All Too Familiar: Sexual Abuse of Women in US State Prisons*, Human Rights Watch, New York, 1996, p. 1.

66. See Human Rights Watch Women's Rights Project, *All Too Familiar*, p. 2.

67. See Human Rights Watch Women's Rights Project, *All Too Familiar*, p. 63.

68. See Human Rights Watch Women's Rights Project, *All Too Familiar*, p. 82.

69. See Human Rights Watch Women's Rights Project, *All Too Familiar*, p. 244.

70. See Human Rights Watch Women's Rights Project, *All Too Familiar*, p. 245.

71. See Human Rights Watch Women's Rights Project, *All Too Familiar*, p. 247.

72. See Human Rights Watch Women's Rights Project, *All Too Familiar*, pp. 248–9.

73. See (1993) 2 S C R *Weatherall* v. *Canada* (Attorney General). The court ruled that 'equality does not necessarily connote equal treatment . . . the reality of the relationship between the sexes is such that the historical trend of violence perpetrated by men against women is not matched by a comparable trend pursuant to which men are the victims and women the aggressors . . . the effect of cross-gender searching is different and more threatening for women than for men.'

74. See *Toronto Globe and Mail*, 2 April 1996 and communication from the Correctional Service of Canada.

75. See Correctional Service of Canada, *Board of Investigation – Major Disturbance and Other Related Incidents – Prison for Women from Friday April 22 to Tuesday April 26, 1994*, Protected Document Released Under the Provisions of the Privacy/Access to Information Acts, pp. 23–5.

76. See Correctional Service of Canada, *Board of Investigation*, pp. 30–31.

77. See Correctional Service of Canada, *Board of Investigation*, p. 31.

78. See Correctional Service of Canada, *Board of Investigation*, p. 32.

79. See Correctional Service of Canada, *Board of Investigation*, p. 33.

80. See Correctional Service of Canada, *Board of Investigation*, p. 35.

81. See R. L. Stewart, Correctional Investigator, *Special Report of the Correctional Investigator Concerning the Treatment of Inmates and Subsequent Inquiry Following Certain Incidents at the Prison for Women in April 1994 and Thereafter*, Minister of Supply and Services, Ottawa, 1995, p. 5.

82. See Stewart, *Special Report of the Correctional Investigator*, p. 6.

83. See Stewart, *Special Report of the Correctional Investigator*, p. 7.

84. See Stewart, *Special Report of the Correctional Investigator*, p. 8.

85. See Arbour, *Commission of Inquiry*, p. 33.

86. See Arbour, *Commission of Inquiry*, pp. 34–5.

87. See Arbour, *Commission of Inquiry*, p. 36.

88. See Arbour, *Commission of Inquiry*, pp. 43–9, 54.

89. Arbour, *Commission of Inquiry*, p. 83.

90. Arbour, *Commission of Inquiry*, p. 141.

91. The number of sentenced women in state and federal prisons was 12,331 in 1980 and 74,730 in 1996. See Kathleen Maguire and Ann L. Pastore (eds.), *Sourcebook of Criminal Justice Statistics 1995*, p. 556

and Bureau of Justice Statistics, *Prisoners in 1996*, US Department of Justice, http://www.ojp.usdoj.gov, Washington, DC, 1997, p. 9.

92. See Penal Affairs Consortium, *The Imprisonment of Women: Some Facts and Figures*, p. 2.

93. Information supplied by Prison Service of England and Wales in June 1997.

94. See Home Office, *Prison Disturbances April 1990, Report of an Inquiry by the Rt. Hon. Lord Justice Woolf (Parts I and II) and His Honour Judge Stephen Tumim (Part II)*, HMSO, London, 1991.

8. *The Young*

1. Quoted in Phyllida Parsloe, *Juvenile Justice in Britain and the United States*, Routledge and Kegan Paul, London, 1978, p. 132.

2. Kim Fletcher, ' "Lovely Lad" Ended Hanging in a Cell', *Sunday Telegraph*, 11 November 1990.

3. See Fletcher, ' "Lovely Lad" Ended Hanging in a Cell'.

4. The Committee notes that an incident of hanging occurred on the first night of their visit and the person, a seventeen-year-old, had died from his injuries six days later. See Council of Europe, *Report to the United Kingdom Government on the Visit to the United Kingdom Carried Out by the European Committee for the Prevention of Torture and Inhuman or Degrading Treatment or Punishment (CPT) from 29 July to 10 August 1990*, Strasbourg, 1991, p. 27.

5. See Council of Europe, *Report to the United Kingdom Government*, p. 67.

6. Howard League for Penal Reform, *Suicides in Feltham*, London, 1993, p. 9.

7. Howard League, *Suicides in Feltham*, p. 10.

8. Howard League, *Suicides in Feltham*, p. 11.

9. Information supplied by the Prison Service to MPs and reported in NACRO, *Criminal Justice Digest*, 91, February 1997, p. 9.

10. Notes made by the present author during a visit in 1995.

11. Notes made by the present author during a visit in 1996.

12. See Children's Rights Project, *Children in Confinement in Louisiana*, Human Rights Watch, New York, 1995, p. 2.

13. Children's Rights Project, *Children in Confinement in Louisiana*, p. 31.

14. Children's Rights Project, *Children in Confinement in Louisiana*, p. 19.

15. See Children's Rights Project, *Children in Confinement in Louisiana*, p. 16.

16. See Children's Rights Project, *Children in Confinement in Louisiana*, p. 17.

17. Children's Rights Project, *Children in Confinement in Louisiana*, p. 21.
18. See Children's Rights Project, *Children in Confinement in Louisiana*, p. 24.
19. See Children's Rights Project, *Children in Confinement in Louisiana*, p. 22.
20. Children's Rights Project, *Children in Confinement in Louisiana*, p. 4.
21. See *Experiment of the Cross*, June 1996, Gala-TV Productions, UK.
22. Notes made by the present author during a visit in 1994.
23. The film was shown at a festival of prison films organized in Budapest, Hungary, in June 1992 by the Finkey Ferenc (Hungarian) Society for Penal Reform in conjunction with Penal Reform International.
24. HM Prison Service, 'Bullying in Prison: A Strategy to Beat It', 1993, p. 1.
25. See Ian O'Donnell and Kimmett Edgar, 'Victimisation in Prisons', *Research Findings 37*, Home Office Research and Statistics Directorate, London, August 1996, p. 2.
26. Howard League for Penal Reform, *Banged up, Beaten up, Cutting up: Report of the Howard League Commission of Inquiry into Violence in Penal Institutions for Teenagers Under 18*, London, 1995, p. 33.
27. Howard League, *Banged up, Beaten up, Cutting up*, p. 37.
28. Howard League, *Banged up, Beaten up, Cutting up*, p. 49.
29. Howard League, *Banged up, Beaten up, Cutting up*, p. 38.
30. See Parsloe, *Juvenile Justice in Britain and the United States*, p. 109.
31. See Seán McConville, *A History of English Prison Administration*, Routledge and Kegan Paul, London, 1981, p. 204.
32. See Robert Hughes, *The Fatal Shore*, Collins Harvill, London, 1987, p. 72.
33. Hughes, *Fatal Shore*, p. 91.
34. See Andrew Rutherford, *Growing Out of Crime*, Penguin Books, Harmondsworth, 1986, p. 27.
35. Quoted in McConville, *History of English Prison Administration*, p. 334.
36. Quoted in Parsloe, *Juvenile Justice in Britain and the United States*, p. 43.
37. Quoted in Parsloe, *Juvenile Justice in Britain and the United States*, p. 120.
38. Charles Dickens, *American Notes for General Circulation*, first published 1842, Penguin Books, Harmondsworth, 1985, p. 99.
39. See McConville, *History of English Prison Administration*, p. 204.
40. Quoted in McConville, *History of English Prison Administration*, p. 205.

41. See McConville, *History of English Prison Administration*, p. 337.
42. See Parsloe, *Juvenile Justice in Britain and the United States*, p. 119.
43. See McConville, *History of English Prison Administration*, p. 337.
44. See Parsloe, *Juvenile Justice in Britain and the United States*, pp. 53–6.
45. See Parsloe, *Juvenile Justice in Britain and the United States*, p. 131.
46. See Raphael Samuel, *East End Underworld: Chapters in the Life of Arthur Harding*, Routledge and Kegan Paul, London, 1981, p. 21.
47. See Samuel, *East End Underworld*, pp. 71–2.
48. Samuel, *East End Underworld*, p. 74.
49. See Rutherford, *Growing Out of Crime*, p. 45.
50. Quoted in Rutherford, *Growing Out of Crime*, p. 51.
51. See his address to Conservative Party Conference, October 1979.
52. See *Tougher Regimes in Detention Centres*, HMSO, London, 1984 for a description of this research.
53. See Vivien Stern, *Bricks of Shame*, Penguin Books, Harmondsworth, 2nd edn, 1993, pp. 51–3 for an account of the experiment.
54. Quoted in NACRO, *Criminal Justice Digest*, 91, February 1997, p. 4.
55. See Prison Reform Trust, *Prison Report no. 37*, Winter 1996, p. 28.
56. National Criminal Justice Reference Service, *Boot Camps for Juvenile Offenders: An Implementation Evaluation of Three Demonstration Programs*, reported in Penal Reform International, *PRI Newsletter*, 25, June 1996, p. 6.
57. See Penal Reform International, *PRI Newsletter*, 22, September 1995, p. 5.
58. See *Criminal Justice Newsletter*, vol. 28, no. 3, February 1997, p. 2.
59. *Daily Express*, 5 January 1996.

9. *If Not Death, Then Life*
1. Marie Mulvey Roberts (compiler and editor), *Out of the Night: Writings from Death Row*, New Clarion Press, Cheltenham, 1994, p. 174.
2. See Gwyneth Boswell, *The Prevalence of Abuse and Loss in the Lives of Section 53 Offenders*, Prince's Trust, London, 1995.
3. See Breyten Breytenbach, *The True Confessions of an Albino Terrorist*, Faber and Faber, London, 1984, p. 140.
4. See Dennis Davis, 'Capital Punishment and the Politics of the Doctrine of Common Purpose', in Desirée Hansson and Dirk van Zyl Smit (eds.), *Towards Justice? Crime and State Control in South Africa*, Oxford University Press, Oxford, 1990, pp. 137–8.
5. Breytenbach, *True Confessions of an Albino Terrorist*, p. 135.
6. See Breytenbach, *True Confessions of an Albino Terrorist*, p. 147.

7. See Vivien Stern, *Deprived of their Liberty: A Report for Caribbean Rights*, Barbados, February 1990, pp. 79–80.

8. Notes made by the present author on a visit in 1994.

9. Notes made by the present author of a visit in 1994.

10. See Penal Reform International, *PRI Newsletter*, 3, July 1990, p. 4.

11. See Penal Reform International, *PRI Newsletter*, 15, December 1993, p. 5.

12. See *Caribbean Insight*, vol. 19, no. 12, December 1996, p. 2.

13. See Amnesty International, *Report 1996*, London, 1996, pp. 190–91.

14. See Amnesty International, *Report 1992*, London, 1992, p. 155.

15. See Jan Arriens (compiler and editor), *Welcome to Hell*, Ian Faulkner Publishing, Cambridge, 1991, pp. 245–6.

16. See US Department of Justice press release, *Sixteen States Executed 56 Offenders Last Year*, Washington, DC, 4 December 1996.

17. On 30 April 1996, 1493 people on death row were white and 1272 were black. See Kathleen Maguire and Ann L. Pastore (eds.), *Sourcebook of Criminal Justice Statistics 1995*, US Department of Justice, Bureau of Justice Statistics, Washington, DC, 1996, p. 604.

18. See Foreword by Clive Stafford Smith to Merrilyn Thomas, *Life on Death Row*, Paladin, London, 1991, pp. 1–9 and Arriens, *Welcome to Hell*, pp. 30–33.

19. Sonja Barisic, 'Slayer of Shopkeeper Executed in Va.', *Washington Post*, 11 December 1996.

20. Tod Robberson, 'Murderer Executed in Va. Prison', *Washington Post*, 13 December 1996.

21. Roberts, *Out of the Night*, p. 21.

22. Arriens, *Welcome to Hell*, p. 103.

23. Arriens, *Welcome to Hell*, p. 145.

24. Arriens, *Welcome to Hell*, pp. 177–8.

25. Rod Williams, 'A Gruesome Kind of Mourning', *Sunday Telegraph*, 8 September 1996.

26. Report by PRI delegation.

27. See Amnesty International, *Report 1997*, London, 1997, pp. 258–9.

28. Ger Pieter van den Berg, 'Russia and Other CIS States', in Peter Hodgkinson and Andrew Rutherford (eds.), *Capital Punishment: Global Issues and Prospects*, Waterside Press, Winchester, 1996, p. 84.

29. See Amnesty International, *Report 1995*, London, 1995, p. 177.

30. See Amnesty International, *Report 1997*, p. 118.

31. See Michael Sheridan, 'Chinese Executions Chill Hong Kong', *Sunday Times*, 21 July 1996.

32. See *Report of the House of Lords Committee on Murder and Life Imprisonment*, HMSO, London, 1989 and *Report of the Committee on the Penalty for Homicide*, Prison Reform Trust, London, 1993 for details of these arguments.

33. Information supplied by the Prison Service to MPs and reported in NACRO, *Criminal Justice Digest*, 89, July 1996, p. 8.

34. Quoted in Stephen Livingstone and Tim Owen, *Prison Law*, Clarendon Press, Oxford, 1993, p. 268.

35. See Penal Affairs Consortium, *The Mandatory Life Sentence, Submission by the Penal Affairs Consortium to the House of Commons Home Affairs Committee in December 1994 and January 1995*, London, February 1996, p. 4.

36. See NACRO briefing, *Life-Sentence Prisoners*, London, January 1995, p. 2.

37. See NACRO, *Life-Sentence Prisoners*, p. 3.

38. See Penal Affairs Consortium, *The Mandatory Life Sentence*, p. 5.

39. HM Prison Service, *The Weekly Bulletin*, vol. 2, no. 16, January 1997, p. 1.

40. Václav Havel, *Letters to Olga*, Faber and Faber, London, 1990, p. 278.

41. Tony Parker, *Life After Life*, HarperCollins, London, 1990, pp. 163–4.

42. Parker, *Life After Life*, p. 167.

43. John McGrath, 'Time' in *Scottish Child*, June/July 1992, p. 17.

44. Parker, *Life After Life*, p. 210.

45. Parker, *Life After Life*, p. 211.

46. See Jean-Paul Jean, 'Les Détenus dangereux', unpublished paper for a conference organized by Penal Reform International in Marly-le-Roi, France, from 25 to 27 October 1996, p. 19.

47. The Instruction to Governors from HM Prison Service lays down that 'The standard limit for all prisoners is that property held in possession will be limited to that which fits into 2 of the new volumetric control boxes. The volumetric control box measures 0.7m × 0.55m × 0.25m and has a volume of 0.09625 cubic metres.' In addition one outsize item and one birdcage are permitted. See HM Prison Service, 'Instruction to Governors IG 104/1995'.

48. Information supplied by the Governor of Vucht prison in 1994.

PART THREE Making Prisons Better

1. Wilbert Rideau and Ron Wikberg, *Life Sentences: Rage and Survival Behind Bars*, Times Books, New York, 1992, pp. 4–5.

10. *The Rules*

1. Zygmunt Bauman, *Modernity and the Holocaust*, Polity Press, Cambridge, 1989, pp. 149–50.
2. See Bauman, *Modernity and the Holocaust*, p. 21.
3. See Bauman, *Modernity and the Holocaust*, pp. 152–8 and Kate Millett, *The Politics of Cruelty*, Penguin Books, Harmondsworth, 1994, p. 304.
4. Bauman, *Modernity and the Holocaust*, p. 159.
5. The Prisons Act, Rules (under Section 93). The Prison Rules 1947, Rule 244.
6. See Nigel Rodley, *The Treatment of Prisoners Under International Law*, Clarendon Press, Oxford, 1987, chapter 9, for a discussion of the legal standing of the instruments on the treatment of prisoners and Penal Reform International, *Making Standards Work: An International Handbook on Good Prison Practice*, London, 1995, for a practical commentary.
7. Directorate of Human Rights, *The Council of Europe and the Protection of Human Rights*, Council of Europe, Strasbourg, 1991, p. 5.
8. Quoted in S. K. Ruck (ed.), *Paterson on Prisons*, Frederick Muller, London, 1951, p. 23.
9. Home Office, *Prison Disturbances April 1990, Report of an Inquiry by the Rt. Hon. Lord Justice Woolf (Parts I and II) and his Honour Judge Stephen Tumim (Part II)*, HMSO, London, 1991, para. 14.19, p. 373.
10. The Honourable Louise Arbour, *Commission of Inquiry into Certain Events at the Prison for Women in Kingston*, Public Works and Government Services Canada, Ottawa, 1996, p. 179.
11. Council of Europe, *Report to the Portuguese Government on the Visit to Portugal Carried Out by the European Committee for the Prevention of Torture and Inhuman or Degrading Treatment or Punishment (CPT) from 19 to 27 January 1992*, Strasbourg, July 1994, p. 32.
12. Resolution 1990/20 of the Economic and Social Council, United Nations.
13. Home Office, *Prison Disturbances April 1990*, para. 14.345, p. 419.
14. See Home Office, *Prison Disturbances April 1990*, paras 3.114 to 3.138, pp. 57–9.

11. *Keeping the Rules: The Supervisors and the Inspectors*

1. Antonio Cassese, *Inhuman States, Imprisonment, Detention and Torture in Europe Today*, trs. Jennifer Greensleaves, Polity Press, Cambridge, 1996, pp. 55–6.

2. Fyodor Dostoevsky, *The House of the Dead*, trs. Constance Garnett, Heinemann, London, 1979, pp. 219–20.

3. Dostoevsky, *The House of the Dead*, p. 220.

4. Breyten Breytenbach, *The True Confessions of an Albino Terrorist*, Faber and Faber, London, 1984, p. 199.

5. See Constance Lytton, *Prisons and Prisoners*, Virago, London, 1988, p. 269.

6. Lytton, *Prisons and Prisoners*, p. 290.

7. Albie Sachs, *The Jail Diary of Albie Sachs*, Paladin, London, 1990, pp. 86–7.

8. See Home Office, *Report of the Review of the Role of Boards of Visitors*, London, 1995, for a short history and review of present functions.

9. See *Report of the Committee on the Prison Disciplinary System*, HMSO, London, 1985, p. 23, for a summary of the arguments.

10. See Mike Maguire and Jon Vagg, *The 'Watchdog' Role of Boards of Visitors*, Home Office, London, 1984.

11. See NACRO, *NACRO News Digest*, 48, January 1988, pp. 6–7.

12. See NACRO, *Criminal Justice Digest*, 88, April 1996, pp. 5–6.

13. See NACRO, *Criminal Justice Digest*, 88, April 1996, p. 6.

14. See NACRO, *Criminal Justice Digest*, 89, July 1996, p. 6.

15. Quoted in Vivien Stern, *Bricks of Shame*, Penguin Books, Harmondsworth, 2nd edn, 1993, p. 82.

16. See NACRO, *Criminal Justice Digest*, 89, July 1996, p. 6.

17. See Claude Faugeron, 'France: Prisons in France: Stalemate or Evolution?' in Dirk van Zyl Smit and Frieder Dünkel (eds.), *Imprisonment Today and Tomorrow*, Kluwer, Deventer, 1991, pp. 257–8.

18. See Faugeron, 'France: Prisons in France', in van Zyl Smit and Dünkel, *Imprisonment Today and Tomorrow*, p. 257.

19. See Council of Europe, *Report to the Spanish Government on the Visits to Spain Carried Out by the European Committee for the Prevention of Torture and Inhuman or Degrading Treatment or Punishment (CPT) from 1 to 12 April 1991, 10 to 22 April 1994 and 10 to 14 June 1994*, Strasbourg, March 1996, p. 66.

20. Cassese, *Inhuman States*, pp. 115–16.

21. See Gerard de Jonge, 'Claviger Observandus, On the Impact of the CPT on the Dutch Penitentiary System and the Need for Such Committees on a National Level', unpublished paper presented to a PRI conference, Marly-le-Roi, France, 1996, p. 2.

22. Notes made by the present author during a visit in 1994.

23. Information supplied to the present author by the National Prison Project, Washington, DC.

24. Nigel Newcomen, 'Standards and Accreditation, Lessons from the USA?', *Prison Service Journal*, 93, May 1994, p. 3.

25. Gordon Bonnyman, 'Reform Advances in Tennessee after Decades of Brutality', in *National Prison Project Journal*, vol. 8, no. 4, October 1993, p. 2.

26. Bonnyman, 'Reform Advances in Tennessee', p. 3.

27. See *Criminal Justice Newsletter*, vol. 25, no. 14, 15 July 1994, p. 5.

28. Julia Cass, 'Hard Time', *Philadelphia Inquirer*, 2 March 1995.

29. Home Office, *Prison Disturbances April 1990, Report of an Inquiry by the Rt. Hon. Lord Justice Woolf (Parts I and II) and his Honour Judge Stephen Tumim (Part II)*, HMSO, London, 1991, para 14.345, p. 419.

30. See NACRO, *Criminal Justice Digest*, 88, April 1996, p. 3.

31. *Golder* v. *United Kingdom* (1975) 1 EHRR 524, Series A no. 18. See Stephen Livingstone and Tim Owen, *Prison Law: Text and Materials*, Clarendon Press, Oxford, 1993, pp. 144–57, for a discussion of these cases.

32. *Silver* v. *United Kingdom* (1983) 5 EHRR 347, Series A no. 61 (Commission Decision Available at (1980) 3 EHRR 475).

33. *Hamer* v. *United Kingdom* (1979) 4 EHRR 139. See Livingstone and Owen, *Prison Law*, p. 161.

34. *Campbell and Fell* v. *United Kingdom* (1984) 7 EHRR 165, Series A no. 80. See Livingstone and Owen, *Prison Law*, pp. 182–3.

35. See Livingstone and Owen, *Prison Law*, p. 234.

36. See Livingstone and Owen, *Prison Law*, p. 160.

37. See United Nations, *Human Rights Machinery*, Fact Sheet No. 1, Geneva, 1987.

38. See Henry J. Steiner and Philip Alston, *International Human Rights in Context*, Clarendon Press, Oxford, 1996, pp. 374–455 for an evaluation of these procedures.

39. See Rod Morgan, 'Her Majesty's Inspectorate of Prisons', in Mike Maguire, Jon Vagg and Rod Morgan (eds.), *Accountability and Prisons: Opening Up a Closed World*, Tavistock Publications, London, 1985, p. 106.

40. See Home Office, *Report of the Committee of Inquiry into the United Kingdom Prison Services*, HMSO, London, 1979, paras 5.50 to 5.62, pp. 92–6.

41. See 'Paper 15, Inspection', discussion paper by the Home Office, in

Inquiry into the United Kingdom Prison Services, Volume II, pp. 237–42.

42. Report by HM Chief Inspector of Prisons, *HM Remand Centre, Risley*, Home Office, London, 1988, para 5.03, p. 68.

43. Report by HM Chief Inspector of Prisons, *HM Prison Liverpool*, Home Office, London, 1988, para. 7.01, p. 74.

44. Report by HM Chief Inspector of Prisons, *HM Prison Liverpool*, para 4.26, p. 36.

45. Report of a Short Inspection by HM Inspectorate of Prisons, *H.M. Prison Preston*, Home Office, London, 1991, p. 1.

46. Report by HM Chief Inspector of Prisons, *HM Prison Wormwood Scrubs*, Home Office, London, 1991, p. 1.

47. See Richard Ford, 'Howard Rebuffs Prison Inspector Over Wider Role', *The Times*, 30 September 1996.

48. Her Majesty's Inspectorate of Prisons for England and Wales, *Patient or Prisoner? A New Strategy for Health Care in Prisons*, discussion paper, Home Office, London, 1996.

49. See Antonio Cassese, 'A New Approach to Human Rights: The European Convention for the Prevention of Torture', *American Journal of International Law*, vol. 83, no. 1, January 1989, p. 130.

50. Council of Europe, Article 2, European Convention for the Prevention of Torture and Inhuman or Degrading Treatment or Punishment – *Text of the Convention and Explanatory Report*, Strasbourg, 1991, p. 5.

51. See Article 4 (1) of the Convention.

52. See Malcolm Evans and Rod Morgan, 'The European Convention for the Prevention of Torture: Operational Practice', *The International and Comparative Law Quarterly*, 41, July 1992, note 29, p. 596, for a list of the professional backgrounds of all the members in 1991.

53. See Article 4 (4) of the Convention.

54. See European Committee for the Prevention of Torture and Inhuman or Degrading Treatment or Punishment, *1st General Report on the CPT's Activities Covering the Period November 1989 to December 1990*, Council of Europe, Strasbourg, 20 February 1991, p. 10, and Evans and Morgan, 'The European Convention for the Prevention of Torture', p. 604.

55. See Evans and Morgan, 'The European Convention for the Prevention of Torture', p. 601.

56. See European Committee for the Prevention of Torture, *1st General Report on the CPT's Activities*, p. 20.

57. See Evans and Morgan, 'The European Convention for the Prevention

of Torture', pp. 599–600, for reference to *ad hoc* visits in 1990 and 1991, both to Turkey, and European Committee for the Prevention of Torture and Inhuman or Degrading Treatment or Punishment, *5th General Report on the CPT's Activities Covering the Period 1 January to 31 December 1994*, Council of Europe, Strasbourg, 3 July 1995, p. 4, for details of five *ad hoc* visits carried out in 1994.

58. See European Committee for the Prevention of Torture, *1st General Report on the CPT's Activities*, p. 16.

59. See Council of Europe, *Report to the Dutch Government on the Visit to the Netherlands Carried Out by the European Committee for the Prevention of Torture and Inhuman or Degrading Treatment or Punishment (CPT) from 30 August to 8 September 1992*, Strasbourg, 15 July 1993, and Council of Europe, *Report to the Danish Government on the Visit to Denmark Carried Out by the European Committee for the Prevention of Torture and Inhuman or Degrading Treatment or Punishment (CPT) from 2 to 8 December 1990*, Strasbourg, 6 September 1991.

60. See, for example, *Public Statement on Turkey*, 15 December 1992, CPT/-Inf(93)1.

61. See Council of Europe, *Report to the United Kingdom Government on the Visit to the United Kingdom Carried Out by the European Committee for the Prevention of Torture and Inhuman or Degrading Treatment or Punishment (CPT) from 29 July to 10 August 1990*, Strasbourg, 26 November 1991, p. 25.

62. See Council of Europe, *Rapport au gouvernement du Grand-Duché de Luxembourg relatif à la visite effectuée par le Comité européen pour la prévention de la torture et des peines ou traitements inhumains ou dégradants (CPT) au Luxembourg du 17 au 25 janvier 1993*, Strasbourg, 12 November 1993, p. 22.

63. See Council of Europe, *Rapport au gouvernement de la Republique française relatif à la visite effectuée par le Comité européen pour la prévention de la torture et des peines ou traitements inhumains ou dégradants (CPT) en France du 27 octobre au 8 novembre 1991*, Strasbourg/Paris, 19 January 1993, p. 38.

64. See Council of Europe, *Report to the Authorities of the Kingdom of the Netherlands on the Visit to the Netherlands Antilles Carried Out by the European Committee for the Prevention of Torture and Inhuman or Degrading Treatment or Punishment (CPT) from 26 to 30 June 1994 and Response of the Government of the Netherlands Antilles*, Strasbourg, 18 January 1996, p. 49.

65. Council of Europe, *Report to the Swedish Government on the Visit to Sweden Carried Out by the European Committee for the Prevention of Torture and Inhuman or Degrading Treatment or Punishment (CPT) from 5 to 14 May 1991*, Strasbourg, 12 March 1992, p. 47.

66. See Council of Europe, *Report to the Swedish Government*, p. 19.

67. See Council of Europe, *Report to the Swedish Government*, p. 23.

68. See Council of Europe, *Partie 1, Rapport au Conseil fédéral de la Suisse relatif à la visite du Comité européen pour la prévention de la torture et des peines ou traitements inhumains ou dégradants (CPT), effectuée en Suisse du 21 au 29 juillet 1991*, Strasbourg, 5 March 1992, p. 17.

69. See Council of Europe, *Partie 1, Rapport au Conseil fédéral de la Suisse*, p. 23.

70. See Council of Europe, *Partie 1, Rapport au Conseil fédéral de la Suisse*, p. 27.

71. See Council of Europe, *Report to the Dutch Government*, pp. 32–3.

72. See Council of Europe, *Report to the Government of the Federal Republic of Germany on the Visit to Germany Carried Out by the European Committee for the Prevention of Torture and Inhuman or Degrading Treatment or Punishment (CPT) from 8 to 20 December 1991*, Strasbourg, 19 July 1993, p. 37.

73. See Council of Europe, *Report to the Government of the Federal Republic of Germany*, p. 28.

74. See Council of Europe, *Report to the Government of the Federal Republic of Germany*, p. 27.

75. See Council of Europe, *Report to the Government of Greece on the Visit to Greece Carried Out by the European Committee for the Prevention of Torture and Inhuman or Degrading Treatment or Punishment (CPT) from 14 to 26 March 1993 and Response of the Government of Greece*, Strasbourg, 29 November 1994, p. 57.

76. See Council of Europe, *Report to the Icelandic Government on the Visit to Iceland Carried Out by the European Committee for the Prevention of Torture and Inhuman or Degrading Treatment or Punishment (CPT) from 6 to 13 July 1993*, Strasbourg/Reykjavik, 28 June 1994, p. 37.

77. See Council of Europe, *Rapport au gouvernement de l'Italie relatif à la visite effectuée par le Comité européen pour la prévention de la torture et des peines ou traitements inhumains ou dégradants (CPT) en Italie du 15 au 27 mars 1992*, Strasbourg, 31 January 1995, p. 32.

78. See Council of Europe, *Rapport au gouvernement de l'Italie*, p. 28.

79. See Council of Europe, *Rapport au gouvernement de la Principauté du Liechtenstein relatif à la visite effectuée par le Comité européen pour la prévention de la torture et des peines ou traitements inhumains ou dégradants (CPT) au Liechtenstein du 14 au 16 avril 1993*, Strasbourg, 21 May 1995, p. 20.

80. See Council of Europe, *Report to the Irish Government on the Visit to Ireland Carried Out by the European Committee for the Prevention of Torture and Inhuman or Degrading Treatment or Punishment (CPT) from 26 September to 5 October 1993*, Strasbourg/Dublin, 13 December 1995, p. 28.

81. See Council of Europe, *Report to the Hungarian Government on the Visit to Hungary Carried Out by the European Committee for the Prevention of Torture and Inhuman or Degrading Treatment or Punishment (CPT) from 1 to 14 November 1994 and Comments of the Hungarian Government*, Strasbourg, 1 February 1996, p. 50.

82. See Council of Europe, *Report to the United Kingdom Government on the Visit to the United Kingdom Carried Out by the European Committee for the Prevention of Torture and Inhuman or Degrading Treatment or Punishment (CPT) from 15 to 31 May 1994*, Strasbourg, 5 March 1996, p. 100.

83. See Council of Europe, *Report to the United Kingdom Government on the Visit to the United Kingdom Carried Out by the European Committee for the Prevention of Torture (CPT) from 15 to 31 May 1994*, 5 March 1996, p. 101.

84. See Council of Europe, *Report to the United Kingdom Government*, 5 March 1996, p. 102.

85. See Council of Europe, *Report to the United Kingdom Government*, 5 March 1996, p. 105.

86. Gerard de Jonge, 'Claviger Observandus', p. 9.

87. See Council of Europe, *Rapport de suivi du gouvernement français en réponse au rapport du Comité européen pour la prévention de la torture et des peines ou traitements inhumains ou dégradants (CPT) relatif à sa visite en France du 27 octobre au 8 novembre 1991*, Strasbourg, 1994, p. 29.

88. See Cassese, *Inhuman States*, p. 41.

89. See Council of Europe, *Report to the United Kingdom Government*, pp. 25, 28–9.

90. See Council of Europe, *Report to the Swedish Government on the Visit to Sweden Carried Out by the European Committee for the Prevention of Torture and Inhuman or Degrading Treatment or*

Punishment (CPT) from 23 to 26 August 1994, Strasbourg, 3 April 1995.

91. See Penal Reform International, *PRI Newsletter*, 28, March 1997, p. 2.

92. See APT, *Introducing APT, Activities in 1995, Specific Goals for 1996*, Geneva, 1996, p. 7.

93. See International Committee of the Red Cross, *ICRC: Answers to Your Questions*, ICRC Publications, Geneva, 1995.

94. See Nelson Mandela, *Long Walk to Freedom*, Little, Brown, London, 1994, p. 397.

95. Breytenbach, *True Confessions of an Albino Terrorist*, p. 206.

96. Sachs, *Jail Diary*, p. 272.

97. United Nations, *World Public Information Campaign for Human Rights*, Fact Sheet no. 8, Geneva, July 1989, p. 11.

98. See Amnesty International, *Report 1996*, London, 1996, pp. 27–34.

99. See International Prison Watch, *Report 1994*, Lyon, 1994, p. 11.

100. See Penal Reform International, *Annual Report 1996*, London, 1997.

12. *Penal Reform*

1. Robert Hughes, *The Fatal Shore*, Collins Harvill, London, 1987, p. 482.

2. Quoted in Seán McConville, *A History of English Prison Administration*, Routledge and Kegan Paul, London, 1981, p. 79.

3. See Howard League for Penal Reform, *Suicides in Feltham*, London, 1993, and Howard League for Penal Reform, *Banged up, Beaten up, Cutting up: Report of the Howard League Commission of Inquiry into Violence in Penal Institutions for Teenagers Under 18*, London, 1995.

4. See Russell P. Dobash, E. Emerson Dobash and Sue Gutteridge, *The Imprisonment of Women*, Oxford, Basil Blackwell, 1986, pp. 43–4.

5. See Vivien Stern, 'The Future of the Voluntary Sector and the Pressure Groups', in Elaine Player and Michael Jenkins (eds.), *Prisons after Woolf*, Routledge, London, 1994, p. 243.

6. Raphael Samuel, *East End Underworld: Chapters in the Life of Arthur Harding*, Routledge and Kegan Paul, London, 1981, p. 72.

7. Richard Condon, quoted in McConville, *History of English Prison Administration*, pp. 79–80.

8. Matthew 25:36.

9. Tom Shannon and Christopher Morgan, *Invisible Crying Tree*, Doubleday, London, 1996, p. 121.

10. See *Report of the Task Force on the Correctional Services, Ministry of the Public Service*, Kingston, Jamaica, March 1989, pp. 3–4.

11. Human Rights Commission of Pakistan, *A Penal System Long Overdue*

for Change – a Report by the Human Rights Commission Penal System Reform Project, Lahore, September 1996, p. 8.

12. See *Report of the Committee on Penal Reform*, Barbados, 1980, p. 2.

13. See *Report of the Committee on Penal Reform*, Barbados, p. 3.

14. See *Report of the Committee on Penal Reform*, Barbados, p. 5.

15. See the Crown, *Prison Review, Te Ara Hou: The New Way. Ministerial Committee of Inquiry into the Prisons System 1989*, Wellington, 1989, pp. 21–2.

16. *Prison Review, Te Ara Hou: The New Way*, p. 22.

17. Home Office, *Crime, Justice and Protecting the Public*, HMSO, London, 1990, para. 2.7, p. 6.

18. Home Office, *Prison Disturbances April 1990: Report of an Inquiry by the Rt. Hon. Lord Justice Woolf (Parts I and II) and his Honour Judge Stephen Tumim (Part II)*, HMSO, London, 1991, para. 10.70, p. 248.

19. See Home Office, *Prison Disturbances April 1990*, paras 9.19–9.42, pp. 225–8.

20. See *Raymond* v. *Honey* (1983) 1 A.C.1 at p. 10, *per* Lord Wilberforce.

21. See Home Office, *Prison Disturbances April 1990*, paras 14.275–14.288, pp. 409–11.

22. Hughes, *Fatal Shore*, p. 455.

23. See Hughes, *Fatal Shore*, p. 461.

24. See Hughes, *Fatal Shore*, p. 462.

25. See Hughes, *Fatal Shore*, p. 463.

26. See Hughes, *Fatal Shore*, p. 465.

27. See Hughes, *Fatal Shore*, p. 468.

28. See Hughes, *Fatal Shore*, p. 470.

29. See Hughes, *Fatal Shore*, pp. 470–79.

30. See Hughes, *Fatal Shore*, p. 480.

31. See Hughes, *Fatal Shore*, p. 481.

32. See Hughes, *Fatal Shore*, p. 503.

33. See Hughes, *Fatal Shore*, p. 504.

34. See Hughes, *Fatal Shore*, p. 505.

35. See Hughes, *Fatal Shore*, pp. 506–7.

36. See Hughes, *Fatal Shore*, p. 510.

37. See Hughes, *Fatal Shore*, pp. 499–501.

38. See Hughes, *Fatal Shore*, p. 510.

39. See Hughes, *Fatal Shore*, pp. 511–12.

40. See Hughes, *Fatal Shore*, p. 519.

41. Quoted in Tony Vinson, *Wilful Obstruction*, Methuen Australia, North Ryde, 1982, p. 7.

42. See Thomas O. Murton, 'Prison Management: The Past, the Present, and the Possible Future', in Marvin E. Wolfgang (ed.), *Prisons: Present and Possible*, Lexington Books, Lexington, 1979, p. 31.

43. See Murton, 'Prison Management', in Wolfgang, *Prisons: Present and Possible*, p. 32.

44. See Murton, 'Prison Management', in Wolfgang, *Prisons: Present and Possible*, p. 26.

45. See Vinson, *Wilful Obstruction*, pp. 7–9.

46. See Vinson, *Wilful Obstruction*, p. 10.

47. Quoted in Vinson, *Wilful Obstruction*, p. 11.

48. See Vinson, *Wilful Obstruction*, p. 11.

49. See Vinson, *Wilful Obstruction*, pp. 12–13.

50. Quoted in Vinson, *Wilful Obstruction*, p. 15.

51. Quoted in Vinson, *Wilful Obstruction*, p. 15.

52. See Vinson, *Wilful Obstruction*, pp. 15–16.

53. See Vinson, *Wilful Obstruction*, p. 202.

54. See Vinson, *Wilful Obstruction*, pp. 164–73.

55. Vinson, *Wilful Obstruction*, p. 223.

56. Information from the Penal Reform Council of New South Wales, New South Wales Prison Coalition and the *Independent Monthly*, October 1990, reported in Penal Reform International, *PRI Newsletter*, 4, November 1990, p. 3.

57. See Moscow Center for Prison Reform, 'Projects', Moscow, 1993.

58. See Moscow Center for Prison Reform, *Prison Reform in Former Totalitarian Countries, The Proceedings of the International Conference Held in Petrovo-Dalneye, Moscow Region on November 14–19 1992*, Issue One, Moscow, 1993, p. 3.

59. See Chapter 4, notes 1, 24 and 29.

60. See Prison Reform Trust, *Annual Report 95/96*, pp. 23–4.

61. See Penal Reform International, *PRI Newsletter*, 24, March 1996, p. 2.

62. See HM Prison Service, *Prison Service Annual Report and Accounts April 1993–March 1994*, HMSO, London, 1995, para. 76, p. 18.

63. See Penal Reform International, *PRI Newsletter*, 22, September 1995, p. 2.

64. Quoted in Murton, 'Prison Management', in Wolfgang, *Prisons: Present and Possible*, p. 19.

65. Murton, 'Prison Management', in Wolfgang, *Prisons: Present and Possible*, p. 34.

66. See Home Office, *Prison Disturbances April 1990*, Annex 2E, para. 1.7, p. 475.
67. See NACRO Community Prisons Initiative, 'Changes in the Polish Prison System, Note of a Seminar held on 6 July 1992 at the Basil Street Hotel', NACRO.
68. Pavel Moczydlowski, 'Prison: From Communist System to Democracy, Transformation of the Polish Penitentiary System', unpublished paper, October 1993, p. 22.
69. See Penal Reform International, *PRI Newsletter*, 26, September 1996, p. 5.
70. See Home Office, *Prison Disturbances April 1990*, para. 1.196, pp. 24–5.
71. Notes made by the present author during a visit in 1995.
72. Moczydlowski, 'Prison: From Communist System to Democracy', p. 18.
73. Moczydlowski, 'Prison: From Communist System to Democracy', p. 19.

PART FOUR **The Future of Imprisonment**

1. David Garland, 'Does Punishment Work? Does the Evidence Matter?', in David Garland, *Does Punishment Work? Proceedings of a Conference*, Institute for the Study and Treatment of Delinquency, London, 1996, p. 36.

13. *Prison Expansion and the Private Sector*

1. Nils Christie, *Crime Control as Industry: Towards GULAGS, Western-Style*, Routledge, London, 2nd enlarged edn, 1994, p. 175.
2. See Table 5, p. 61.
3. See Bureau of Justice Statistics, *Prison and Jail Inmates at Midyear 1996*, US Department of Justice, http://www.ojp.usdoj.gov, Washington, DC, 1997, p. 2.
4. See Bureau of Justice Statistics, *Prison and Jail Inmates, 1995*, US Department of Justice, Washington, DC, August 1996, p. 2.
5. See Bureau of Justice Statistics, *Prison and Jail Inmates at Midyear 1996*, p. 2.
6. See Elliott Currie, 'Is America Really Winning the War on Crime and Should Britain Follow its Example?', NACRO, 1996, p. 6.
7. See Bureau of Justice Statistics, *Correctional Populations in the United States, 1992*, US Department of Justice, Washington, DC, January 1995, p. 64, and Bureau of Justice Statistics, *Prisoners in 1996*, http://www.ojp.usdoj.gov/pub/bjs/ascii/p96txt, Washington, DC.
8. See Bureau of Justice Statistics, *Prison and Jail Inmates at Midyear 1996*, p. 3.

9. See Bureau of Justice Statistics, *Lifetime Likelihood of Going to State or Federal Prison*, US Department of Justice, http://www.ojp.usdoj.gov, Washington, DC, 1997, p. 6.

10. See General Accounting Office, *Federal and State Prisons, Inmate Populations, Costs and Projection Models, Report to the Subcommittee on Crime, Committee on the Judiciary, House of Representatives*, Washington, DC, 25 November 1996, p. 3.

11. Information made available by Marc Mauer, Sentencing Project, Washington, DC.

12. See Bureau of Justice Statistics, *Prison and Jail Inmates, 1995*, p. 10.

13. 63,998 in state or federal prisons and 52,136 in local jails. See Bureau of Justice Statistics, *Prison and Jail Inmates, 1995*, pp. 5 and 10.

14. See Gerard de Jonge, unpublished paper.

15. See David Downes, *Contrasts in Tolerance*, Clarendon Press, Oxford, 1988, p. 78.

16. See Council of Europe, *Penological Information Bulletin*, nos 19 and 20, December 1994–1995, Strasbourg, p. 77.

17. See Gerard de Jonge, 'Claviger Osbervandus, On the Impact of the CPT on the Dutch Penitentiary System and the Need for Such Committees on a National Level', unpublished paper presented to a PRI conference, Marly-le-Roi, France, 1996, p. 3.

18. See Council of Europe, *Penological Information Bulletin*, nos 19 and 20, December 1994–1995, p. 78.

19. See 'Direction de l'administration pénitentiaire, Les chiffres clés de l'administration pénitentiaire', Ministère de la Justice, Paris, 1996, p. 3.

20. See Prison Service, 'Occupation of Prisons, Remand Centres, Young Offender Institutions and Police Cells on 31 January 1993', 2 March 1993, unpublished.

21. See Prison Service, 'Occupation of Prisons, Remand Centres, Young Offender Institutions and Police Cells on 30 September 1997', 20 October 1997, unpublished.

22. Michael Howard, speech to Conservative Party Conference, Conservative Central Office, London, 1993.

23. See NACRO, *Criminal Justice Digest*, 92, April 1997, pp. 14–15 for details of the Crime (Sentences) Act 1997.

24. See NACRO, *Criminal Justice Digest*, 89, July 1996, pp. 10–11 and Vivien Stern, 'Howard's Sentencing Proposals Provoke Strong Opposition', *Solicitors Journal*, vol. 140, no. 40, 25 October 1996, p. 1017.

25. Michael Howard, speech to Conservative Party Conference, Conservative Central Office, London, 1996.

26. Jerome G. Miller, *Search and Destroy: African-American Males in the Criminal Justice System*, Cambridge University Press, Cambridge, 1996, p. 178.

27. Alvin J. Bronstein and Jenni Gainsborough, 'Prison Litigation: Past, Present and Future', *Overcrowded Times*, vol. 7, no. 3, June 1996, pp. 15–16.

28. See Council on Crime in America, *The State of Violent Crime in America*, Washington, DC, 5 January 1997.

29. See Naftali Bendavid, 'A Bull in Crime's China Shop', *Legal Times*, vol. 18, no. 39, 12 February 1996, p. 21.

30. See Steven R. Donziger (ed.), *The Real War On Crime*, HarperPerennial, New York, 1996, pp. 81–4 for a description of the National Rifle Association campaign.

31. See Marc Mauer and Malcolm C. Young, 'Truths, Half-Truths, and Lies: Myths and Realities about Crime and Punishment', Sentencing Project, Washington, DC, October 1996, p. 3.

32. See Bendavid, 'A Bull in Crime's China Shop', p. 21.

33. See James Austin and Robyn L. Cohen, *Why are Crime Rates Declining?*, National Council on Crime and Delinquency, San Francisco, 1996, pp. 1–3.

34. See Austin and Cohen, *Why are Crime Rates Declining?*; Mauer and Young, 'Truths, Half-Truths, and Lies', p. 1; and Currie, 'Is America Really Winning the War on Crime and Should Britain Follow its Example?'

35. See Austin and Cohen, *Why are Crime Rates Declining?*, p. 4.

36. See Austin and Cohen, *Why are Crime Rates Declining?*, p. 4.

37. Elliott Currie estimates that 15–20 per cent of the most recent decline in US crime rates may be the result of locking up more people. See 'Is America Really Winning the War on Crime and Should Britain Follow its Example?', p. 11.

38. See Roger Tarling, *Analysing Offending Data, Models and Interpretations*, HMSO, London, 1993, p. 154.

39. It is estimated that in Britain 3 out of every 100 offences committed against individuals and their property lead to a criminal conviction or a caution from the police. See Home Office Research and Statistics Department, *Digest 3 – Information on the Criminal Justice System in England and Wales*, London, 1995, p. 25.

40. See Currie, 'Is America Really Winning the War on Crime and Should Britain Follow its Example?', p. 11.

41. See Mauer and Young, 'Truths, Half-Truths, and Lies', p. 3.

42. See General Accounting Office, *Federal and State Prisons, Inmate Populations, Costs, and Projection Models*, p. 4.

43. See Human Rights Watch, *Prison Conditions in the United States*, New York, 1991, p. 7.

44. See Donziger, *The Real War On Crime*, p. 21.

45. According to the Justice Policy Institute, 9.4 per cent of the General Fund was allocated to corrections and 8.7 per cent to higher education. See Tara-Jen Ambrosio and Vincent Schiraldi, *From Classrooms to Cell Blocks: A National Perspective*, The Justice Policy Institute, Washington, DC, February 1997, p. 14.

46. From National Association of State Budget Officers (NASBO) (April 1996), *1995 State Expenditures Report*, Washington, DC, 16, Table 3 quoted in Ambrosio and Schiraldi, *From Classrooms to Cell Blocks*, p. 6.

47. See Currie, 'Is America Really Winning the War on Crime and Should Britain Follow its Example?', p. 7.

48. Currie, 'Is America Really Winning the War on Crime and Should Britain Follow its Example?,' p. 6.

49. Currie, 'Is America Really Winning the War on Crime and Should Britain Follow its Example?', p. 5.

50. See Kathleen Maguire and Ann L. Pastore (eds.), *Sourcebook of Criminal Justice Statistics 1995*, US Department of Justice, Bureau of Justice Statistics, Washington, DC, 1996, p. 128.

51. See Kathleen Maguire and Ann L. Pastore (eds.), *Sourcebook of Criminal Justice Statistics 1994*, US Department of Justice, Bureau of Justice Statistics, 1995, p. 140.

52. Ian Ball, 'Fast Way of Getting Out of Crowded Jails Crisis', *Daily Telegraph*, 20 June 1990.

53. See Don Terry, 'Town Builds a Prison and Stores its Hopes There', *The New York Times*, 3 January 1993.

54. 'Texas Caters to Demand Around US for Jail Cells', *The New York Times*, 9 February 1996.

55. See leaflet advertising the conference put out by World Research Group, 12 E 49th St, 17th Floor, New York, NY 10017, USA.

56. See Prison Reform Trust, *Prison Privatisation Report International*, 3, August 1996, London, p. 4.

57. Prison Reform Trust, *Prison Privatisation Report International*, 6, January 1997, London, p. 4.

58. See Wilbert Rideau, 'Angola's History', in Wilbert Rideau and Ron Wikberg, *Life Sentences: Rage and Survival Behind Bars*, Times Books, New York, 1992, p. 35.

59. See Rideau and Wikberg, *Life Sentences*, pp. 35–6.

60. See Coramae Richey Mann, *Unequal Justice*, Indiana University Press, Bloomington and Indianapolis, 1993, p. 254.

61. See Rideau and Wikberg, *Life Sentences*, p. 36.

62. See John J. Dilulio, Jr, 'The Duty to Govern: A Critical Perspective on the Private Management of Prisons and Jails', in Douglas C. McDonald (ed.), *Private Prisons and the Public Interest*, Rutgers University Press, New Brunswick, 1990, p. 160.

63. Dilulio, Jr, 'The Duty to Govern', in McDonald, *Private Prisons and the Public Interest*, p. 159.

64. See McDonald, *Private Prisons and the Public Interest*, p. 1.

65. See Aric Press, 'The Good, the Bad and the Ugly: Private Prisons in the 1980s', in McDonald, *Private Prisons and the Public Interest*, p. 26.

66. See Norman R. Cox, Jr, and William E. Osterhoff, 'Managing the Crisis in Local Corrections: A Public–Private Partnership Approach', in McDonald, *Private Prisons and the Public Interest*, p. 234.

67. See *President's Commission on Privatization (1988) Privatization: Toward More Effective Government*, US Government Printing Office, Washington, D C.

68. See Press, 'The Good, the Bad and the Ugly', in McDonald, *Private Prisons and the Public Interest*, p. 28.

69. See Douglas C. McDonald, 'Public Imprisonment by Private Means, The Re-emergence of Private Prisons and Jails in the United States, the United Kingdom and Australia', in Roy D. King and Mike Maguire (eds.), *Prisons in Context*, Clarendon Press, Oxford, 1994, p. 30.

70. Quoted in J. Robert Lilly and Paul Knepper, 'Corrections–Commercial Complex', *Prison Service Journal*, 87, 1992, p. 50.

71. See Prison Reform Trust, *Prison Privatisation Report International*, 1, June 1996, London, p. 2.

72. See Prison Reform Trust, *Prison Privatisation Report International*, 5, November 1996, London, p. 3.

73. See Prison Reform Trust, *Prison Privatisation Report International*, 1, June 1996, p. 4.

74. See Prison Reform Trust, *Prison Privatisation Report International*, 2, July 1996, London, p. 3.

75. See George C. Zoley, 'A Discussion of the Wackenhut Experience Providing Correctional Management Services in the US', *Prison Service Journal*, 87, 1992, p. 38.

76. See Zoley, 'A Discussion of the Wackenhut Experience', *Prison Service Journal*, 87, 1992, p. 39.

77. Patrick F. Cannan, 'Prototypes for Privatized Correctional Services', in *CJ The Americas*, vol. 6, no. 4, August–September 1993, p. 16.

78. See Prison Reform Trust, *Prison Privatisation Report International*, 5, November 1996, pp. 3–4.

79. See Prison Reform Trust, *Prison Privatisation Report International*, 5, November 1996, p. 3.

80. See Adam Smith Institute, *Justice Policy*, Omega Report, London, 1984.

81. See *Twenty-fifth Report from the Committee of Public Accounts, Session 1985–1986, Prison Building Programme*, HMSO, London, 1986, p. 8.

82. See *Fourth Report from the Home Affairs Committee, Contract Provision of Prisons*, HMSO, London, 1987.

83. *Official Report*, House of Commons, 16 July 1987, col 1,299.

84. See Vivien Stern, *Bricks of Shame*, Penguin Books, Harmondsworth, 2nd edn, 1993, p. 272 and Stephen Shaw, 'The Short History of Prison Privatisation', *Prison Policy and Practice*, Prison Service Journal, London, pp. 168–72.

85. See Stern, *Bricks of Shame*, pp. 273–4.

86. See Stern, *Bricks of Shame*, p. 274.

87. See *Sixth Report of the Committee of Public Accounts*, HMSO, London, 1995, para. 2 (iv), where the five-year contract is valued at £29.87 million.

88. See Prison Reform Trust, *Prison Privatisation Report International*, 5, November 1996, p. 2.

89. See Prison Reform Trust, *HM Prison Buckley Hall*, 21 June 1996.

90. See Ian Burrell, 'Riots on the Menu at Private Prison That Left Out Chips', *Sunday Times*, 29 August 1993.

91. See Prison Reform Trust, *Prison Report*, no. 29, Winter 1994, p. 16.

92. See Prison Reform Trust, *Prison Privatisation Report International*, 4, January 1997, p. 3.

93. See Prison Reform Trust, *Prison Privatisation Report International*, 6, January 1997, p. 4.

94. See Prison Reform Trust, *Prison Report*, no. 29, Winter 1994, p. 15.

95. See Prison Reform Trust, *Prison Privatisation Report International*, 1, June 1996, p. 2.

96. Her Majesty's Chief Inspector of Prisons, 'Doncaster Prison', press notice, 31 December 1996, p. 1.

97. Children's Rights Project, *Children in Confinement in Louisiana*, Human Rights Watch, New York, 1995, p. 12.

98. See Children's Rights Project, *Children in Confinement in Louisiana*, pp. 19–20.

99. See Prison Reform Trust, *Prison Privatisation Report International*, 6, January 1997, p. 1.

100. See Kristel Beyens and Sonja Snacken, 'Prison Privatization: An International Perspective', in Roger Matthews and Peter Francis (eds.), *Prisons 2000*, Macmillan, Basingstoke, 1996, p. 242.

101. See Prison Reform Trust, *Prison Privatisation Report International*, 3, August 1996, p. 1.

102. See Prison Reform Trust, *Prison Privatisation Report International*, 6, January 1997, p. 1.

103. See Prison Reform Trust, *Prison Privatisation Report International*, 6, January 1997, p. 3.

104. See Prison Reform Trust, *Prison Privatisation Report International*, 2, July 1996, pp. 2–3.

105. See Prison Reform Trust, *Prison Privatisation Report International*, 4, October 1996, p. 4.

106. Douglas C. McDonald, 'The Costs of Operating Public and Private Correctional Facilities', in McDonald, *Private Prisons and the Public Interest*, p. 103.

107. See *Review of Comparative Costs and Performance of Privately and Publicly Operated Prisons*, quoted in NACRO, *Criminal Justice Digest*, 89, July 1996, p. 3.

108. See Prison Reform Trust, *Prison Report*, no. 36, Autumn 1996, p. 13.

109. See Prison Reform Trust, *Prison Privatisation Report International*, 4, October 1996, p. 3.

110. See Prison Reform Trust, *Prison Privatisation Report International*, 1, June 1996, p. 3.

111. See US General Accounting Office, 'Private or Public Prisons: Comparing Costs and/or Quality of Service', Gaithersburg, MD, 1996.

112. Adam Smith Institute, *Justice Policy*, p. 64.

113. See Zoley, 'A Discussion of the Wackenhut Experience', *Prison Service Journal*, 87, 1992, p. 38.

114. From *The Times*, 22 September 1988, quoted in Shaw, 'The Short

History of Prison Privatisation', in *Prison Policy and Practice*, p. 172.

115. 'Imprisoning Justice to the Bottom Line', *Toronto Star*, 2 August 1995.

116. See Prison Reform Trust, *Prison Privatisation Report International*, 4, October 1996, p. 4.

117. Dilulio, Jr, 'The Duty to Govern', in McDonald, *Private Prisons and the Public Interest*, p. 173.

118. *Corrections Today*, July 1996, p. 2.

119. *Corrections Today*, July 1996, p. 13.

120. *Corrections Today*, July 1996, p. 37.

121. *Corrections Today*, July 1996, p. 49.

122. *Corrections Today*, April 1996, p. 113.

123. *Corrections Today*, July 1996, p. 39.

124. *Corrections Today*, July 1996, p. 47.

125. *Corrections Today*, April 1996, p. 127.

126. *Corrections Today*, July 1996, p. 102.

127. *Corrections Today*, October 1996, p. 10.

128. *Corrections Today*, July 1996, p. 69.

129. *Corrections Today*, April 1996, p. 172.

130. *Corrections Today*, April 1996, p. 15.

131. See Donziger, *The Real War on Crime*, p. 106.

132. Miller, *Search and Destroy*, p. 91.

133. From *Prison and Its Alternatives*, a radio series by David Cayley, transcript by CBC, Ottawa, 1996, p. 7.

134. See Christie, *Crime Control as Industry*, pp. 59–61.

135. From *Prison and Its Alternatives*, transcript by CBC, pp. 4–5.

136. Miller, *Search and Destroy*, p. 234.

137. David Garland, 'Does Punishment Work? Does the Evidence Matter?', in David Garland, *Does Punishment Work? Proceedings of a Conference*, Institute for the Study and Treatment of Delinquency, London, 1996, p. 34.

138. Garland, 'Does Punishment Work? Does the Evidence Matter?', in Garland, *Does Punishment Work?*, p. 36.

14. *A Better Way?*

1. Bruce Shapiro, 'Unkindest Cut', *New Statesman and Society*, 14 April 1995.

2. Home Office, *Crime, Justice and Protecting the Public*, HMSO, London, 1990, para. 2.7, p. 6.

3. Fyodor Dostoevsky, *The House of the Dead*, trs. Constance Garnett, Heinemann, London, 1979 edn, p. 11.

4. Peter Kropotkin, *In Russian and French Prisons*, Schocken Books, New York, 1971, p. 301.

5. Kropotkin, *In Russian and French Prisons*, p. 307.

6. Quoted in Roy D. King and Rod Morgan, *The Future of the Prison System*, Gower, Aldershot, 1980, p. 2.

7. Leo Tolstoy, *Resurrection*, trs. Rosemary Edmonds, Penguin Books, Harmondsworth, 1966, pp. 165–6.

8. Václav Havel, *Letters to Olga*, Faber and Faber, London, 1990, p. 270.

9. Quoted in Josine Junger-Tas, *Alternatives to Prison Sentences: Experiences and Developments*, Kugler Publications, Amsterdam/New York, 1994, p. 6.

10. Section 1 (2) (a) and (b) Criminal Justice Act 1991, as amended by Criminal Justice Act 1993.

11. Council of Europe, *European Rules on Community Sanctions and Measures*, Strasbourg, 1994, p. 7.

12. See Nigel Walker and Mike Hough, *Public Attitudes to Sentencing: Surveys from Five Countries*, Gower, Aldershot, 1988, p. 2.

13. See Walker and Hough, *Public Attitudes to Sentencing*, p. 3.

14. Martin Kettle, 'Parents' Role a Model for Life', *Guardian*, 7 November 1996.

15. See Kathleen Maguire and Ann L. Pastore (eds.), *Sourcebook of Criminal Justice Statistics 1995*, US Department of Justice, Bureau of Justice Statistics, Washington, DC, 1996, p. 183.

16. See Walker and Hough, *Public Attitudes to Sentencing*, p. 77.

17. See Walker and Hough, *Public Attitudes to Sentencing*, p. 93.

18. See Walker and Hough, *Public Attitudes to Sentencing*, p. 151.

19. See 1994 Listener/Heylen Monitor Poll, cited in *Criminal Justice Quarterly*, 1994, Issue 8, Wellington, New Zealand, p. 6.

20. See Walker and Hough, *Public Attitudes to Sentencing*, p. 112.

21. See Maguire and Pastore, *Sourcebook of Criminal Justice Statistics 1995*, pp. 172–3.

22. See Walker and Hough, *Public Attitudes to Sentencing*, p. 114.

23. See Michael Hough, 'People Talking about Punishment: A Report of a Qualitative Study of Public Attitudes to Sentencing', South Bank University, October 1995, unpublished report.

24. See Walker and Hough, *Public Attitudes to Sentencing*, p. 3.

25. See 'Why Britain Feels Betrayed on Crime', *Daily Mail*, 1 April 1996.

26. See Maguire and Pastore, *Sourcebook of Criminal Justice Statistics 1995*, p. 183.

27. See Pat Mayhew and Philip White, *The 1996 International Crime Victimisation Survey*, Research Findings No. 57, Home Office Research and Statistics Directorate, Home Office, London, 1997.

28. John Doble and Stephen Immerwehr, 'Delawareans Favour Alternatives', in Michael Tonry and Kathleen Hatlestad (eds.), *Sentencing Reform in Overcrowded Times*, Oxford University Press, Oxford, 1997, pp. 263–4.

29. See Edna McConnell Clark Foundation, *Seeking Justice, Crime and Punishment in America*, New York, 1995, p. 44.

30. See Marc Mauer, 'Intended and Unintended Consequences: State Racial Disparities in Sentencing', Sentencing Project, Washington, DC, January 1997, p. 23.

31. See Walker and Hough, *Public Attitudes to Sentencing*, p. 76.

32. Doble and Immerwehr, 'Delawareans Favour Alternatives', in Tonry and Hatlestad, *Sentencing Reform in Overcrowded Times*, p. 265.

33. *Sentencing Reform, A Canadian Approach: Report of the Canadian Sentencing Commission*, Ministry of Supply and Services Canada, Ottawa, 1987, p. 53.

34. See Walker and Hough, *Public Attitudes to Sentencing*, p. 123.

35. The Church Council on Justice and Corrections, *Satisfying Justice*, Ottawa, 1996, p. xi.

36. See *Criminal Justice Quarterly*, Issue 8, 1994, Wellington, New Zealand, p. 7.

37. See Maguire and Pastore, *Sourcebook of Criminal Justice Statistics 1995*, p. 166.

38. See *Criminal Justice Quarterly*, Issue 8, 1994, p. 5.

39. See *Criminal Justice Quarterly*, Issue 8, 1994, p. 6.

40. See Maguire and Pastore, *Sourcebook of Criminal Justice Statistics 1995*, p. 499.

41. See NACRO, *Criminal Justice Digest*, 90, October 1996, p. 7.

42. Personal communication from Swiss officials.

43. See 'Probation Statistics', reported in NACRO, *Criminal Justice Digest*, 88, April 1996, p. 11.

44. The complex problems involved in making these comparisons are well set out in Josine Junger-Tas, *Alternatives to Prison Sentences: Experiences and Developments*, RDC Ministry of Justice and Kugler Publications, Amsterdam, 1994, chapter 5, pp. 53–76.

45. John Braithwaite, *Crime, Shame and Reintegration*, Cambridge University Press, Cambridge, 1989, p. 55.

46. Braithwaite, *Crime, Shame and Reintegration*, p. 9.

47. Braithwaite, *Crime, Shame and Reintegration*, p. 69.

48. Braithwaite, *Crime, Shame and Reintegration*, p. 73.

49. Braithwaite, *Crime, Shame and Reintegration*, p. 14.

50. Braithwaite, *Crime, Shame and Reintegration*, p. 8.

51. Howard Zehr, *Changing Lenses*, Herald Press, Scottdale, Pennsylvania, 1990, p. 66.

52. See Jonathan Burnside and Nicola Baker (eds.), *Relational Justice: Repairing the Breach*, Waterside Press, Winchester, 1994, pp. 94−5.

53. See Burnside and Baker, *Relational Justice: Repairing the Breach*, p. 95.

54. See Burnside and Baker, *Relational Justice: Repairing the Breach*, p. 97.

55. See 'Summary Findings − Doble Study "Crime and Corrections: The Views of the People of Vermont" ', unpublished paper.

56. See 'Sentencing Options: Restructuring Corrections for the 21st Century', unpublished paper, Vermont Department of Corrections.

57. Michael Dooley, 'Restorative Justice in Vermont: A Work in Progress', Vermont Department of Corrections, pp. 31−6.

58. Rhéal Séguin, 'Quebec Launches Prison Reforms', *Toronto Globe and Mail*, 3 April 1996.

59. Penal Reform International, *PRI Newsletter*, 24, March 1996, p. 3.

60. Address by Professor A. Akele to the Seminaire pour les chefs des administrations pénitentiaires des pays francophones d'afrique, Institut Henry-Dunant, Geneva, 1990 (translation by the present author).

61. Notes made at the seminar − unpublished.

62. See Penal Reform International, *Annual Report 1994*, *Annual Report 1995*, *Annual Report 1996*, *PRI Newsletter*, 30 September 1997, p. 2, and 'A Sin Against the Future, the *Courier* Speaks to Leading International Penal Reformer Vivien Stern', *Courier*, 156, March−April 1996, Commission of the European Communities, pp. 78−9.

63. Mark Tully, *No Full Stops in India*, Viking, Harmondsworth, 1991, p. 38.

64. See *Prison and Its Alternatives*, a radio series by David Cayley, transcript by CBC, Ottawa, 1996, p. 41.

65. See *Criminal Justice Newsletter*, vol. 28, no. 1, 2 January 1997, p. 1.

66. Terrence P. Thornberry, 'Violent Families and Youth Violence', Fact Sheet 21, US Department of Justice, Office of Juvenile Justice and Delinquency Prevention, Washington, DC, December 1994.

67. See Marc Mauer and Malcolm C. Young, 'Truths, Half-Truths, and Lies: Myths and Realities about Crime and Punishment', Sentencing Project, Washington, DC, October 1996, p. 3.

Index

NOTE: **Bold** page references are to Tables. *Italics* refer to chapter and part openings and main extracts.